Strategic Thinking Skills

Stanley K. Ridgley, Ph.D.

THE
GREAT
COURSES®

PUBLISHED BY:

THE GREAT COURSES
Corporate Headquarters
4840 Westfields Boulevard, Suite 500
Chantilly, Virginia 20151-2299
Phone: 1-800-832-2412
Fax: 703-378-3819
www.thegreatcourses.com

Copyright © The Teaching Company, 2012

Stanley K. Ridgley, Ph.D.

Assistant Professor
Department of Management
Drexel University

Professor Stanley K. Ridgley is Assistant Professor in the Department of Management at Drexel University's LeBow College of Business. He earned a B.A. in Journalism from The University of North Carolina at Chapel Hill, an M.A. in Political Science from Duke University, an M.B.A. in International Business from Temple University, and a Ph.D. in International Relations from Duke University. He has also studied at Lomonosov Moscow State University and the Institut de Gestion Sociale in Paris. Prior to joining the faculty at Drexel, Professor Ridgley was an Assistant Professor of International Business and Strategic Management at the Fox School of Business at Temple University.

Professor Ridgley teaches courses on global business policies, international business fundamentals, competitive intelligence, strategic management and entrepreneurship, and advanced strategic business presentations. He has lectured and presented widely to university students and business professionals in the United States, Russia, India, France, Colombia, and Singapore. While teaching at Temple University, he received the Musser Award for Excellence in Leadership.

As a presentation coach for teams of business students, Professor Ridgley coached the winning team for Target Corporation's annual Business Case Competition at Temple University in 2010 and 2009 and coached an Indian M.B.A. team's winning presentation in the All India Management Association's 2009 National Competition for Young Managers. He also is the voice and face of Pearson Education's online Business Presentation Instruction Module.

i

A former military intelligence officer for the U.S. Army, Professor Ridgley served five years in West Berlin and near the Czech-German border. He received the George S. Patton Award for Leadership from the 7th Army NCO Academy in West Germany. ■

Table of Contents

Table of Contents

Table of Contents

Strategic Thinking Skills

Scope:

S trategic thinking is about unraveling the mysteries of the chaotic world around us and harnessing powerful forces to our own ends. It means utilizing tools of analysis and tactics to take decisive and prudent action that gives us the best possible chance of achieving our objectives—whether those objectives are personal or professional.

In this course, we learn what the finest strategic minds of history can teach us and how their insights can transform us into decisive, capable strategic thinkers. We learn how to overcome both internal and external obstacles that block the way to achieving our goals. Strategic thinking sharpens your awareness of the world around you so that previously inexplicable events become intelligible. You begin to connect the dots in many areas and at different levels. Causes and effects, sometimes far removed from each other, take on clarity as we begin to understand the funnel of causality. Seemingly isolated events are connected to each other in patterns that we can readily recognize.

The framework for strategic thinking is a series of powerful analytical tools that enables us to make sense of a complex world and can transform the way we think, behave, and interact with others. These are the same tools that inform both corporate strategy staffs and military intelligence units in accomplishing scenario development, strategic choice, and tactical execution.

We begin with lectures on the origins of strategy to discover how the concept of strategic thinking emerged in theorizing about ancient warfare and how principles of strategic action began to crystallize in the minds of the great theorist/practitioners. Strategy has its ancient origins in the military, both in Greece and China, so we start there, with the theorist-practitioners Thucydides and Sun Tzu and the ancient battles of Delium and Cannae.

Military strategic thought flourished during the Enlightenment, culminating in the Napoleonic era of advanced strategic and tactical developments. Modern efforts to name and systematize principles of military strategy really began with Napoleon. We consider Napoleon's own ideas and actions, as well as the contrasting lessons drawn from Napoleon by the two leading theorists of 19th-century strategy, Jomini and Clausewitz.

Entering the modern era, we examine how strategic dynamism began to suffuse and revolutionize the thinking in other realms of endeavor and slowly evolved into an indispensable tool in the worlds of the military, business, politics, sports, and even entertainment. The military principles of combat can be understood as principles of competition, offering us a variety of tactical options for use in our own strategic endeavors.

In our middle lectures, we turn to the various tools and intellectual perspectives offered by modern strategic thought. Here, it is important to grasp the difference between strategy and the tools of strategy. Strategy is not a ready-made plan we can pull from a shelf, nor is it a tool we can take from a toolbox.

Regardless of the area of endeavor, the key to any successful strategy is an overall sense of mission, what business strategists Hamel and Prahalad called "strategic intent." Far from an empty exercise, crafting a clear and meaningful mission statement shapes the entire strategic planning process. That process as explicated here consists of mission, objective, situation analysis, strategy formulation, strategy implementation, and control. This simple planning process serves as the structure for our thinking and is a constant loop that leads us back to situation analysis. We constantly evaluate the external and internal environments and modify our strategy according to arising needs.

We learn the fundamental competitive choices available to us, their advantages and disadvantages, and how to position ourselves for the most successful strategic outcomes. We also learn the sources of competitive advantage and one superb technique—the blue ocean strategy—whereby we may achieve it and sustain it.

Where many strategies fall short is in the implementation, the crisp and correct execution of tactics. We review tactics and principles—including the frontal assault, the flank attack, the indirect approach, and rear area battle—

that empower us on the field of conflict of our choice, and we explore the special power of surprise and its force-multiplier effect. We also learn of the incredible utility of the intelligence cycle and scenario planning as engines of predictive capability, predictive of both the specific likely actions of competitors and the likely course of macro-factors that can affect our plans.

Key to the success or failure of much strategic action, regardless of the venue, is the mindset of the strategist. Lectures on cognitive psychology, strategic intuition, game theory, systemic problems, and perspectives on "luck" demonstrate that our own self-perception and the perception of the world around us can have a tremendous impact on the effectiveness of our strategy. Likewise, one of our lectures encompasses the well-known obstacles to great strategy and relates how these obstacles can often be circumvented if acknowledged and properly considered.

The course concludes with a final lecture that sketches the lives of four strategic thinkers, vignettes of powerful and focused idea entrepreneurs who harnessed the power of strategic imagination for their own ventures and achieved tremendous success. In this final lecture, we recapitulate the principles of strategic thinking and illustrate the potential rewards awaiting those who cultivate strategic thinking skills as a way of life, those who do not fear the future but harness its potential for their own benefit.

At the end of our course, you may find that your perspective on the world has undergone profound transformation as you begin to see patterns and routines, to identify categories, and to sense the broader macro-shifts in a particular correlation of forces that affect you in unique ways. You gain clarity and you may see the fog of uncertainty begin to clear, replaced by a certitude of purpose and direction as you begin to master the concept of strategic choice—the selection of the correct tools to apply to your unique situation. By adopting various combinations of techniques and tools of analysis, and by seizing a substantial role in developing your circumstances, you improve your chances of achieving your objectives. And this is the great gift of strategic thinking: clarity and efficacy of action in a forever changing and chaotic world. ∎

The World of Strategic Thinking
Lecture 1

How can you learn to plan more effectively, outsmart your competitors, and avoid unpleasant surprises? The answer is strategy. This course arms you with the essential tools that allow you to think strategically in business and in life. In these lectures, you'll learn a broad array of skills and techniques for problem solving, critical decision making, competitive intelligence, and long-term planning. As we'll see, strategic thinking is a way of peering into the future with confidence that our actions today will yield the best possible outcome tomorrow.

A Quarterback's Strategic Thinking

- Consider the crucial 10 to 15 seconds in a football game between the call of a play in the offensive huddle and the snap of the ball.

- The offense has made a plan to achieve the intermediate objective of moving the ball to make a first down. This plan takes into account the situation on the field, that is, the distance required to make the first down, the number of downs remaining, and the distance needed to score. The defense looks at the same situation on the field and calls a play to resist the offense.

- What happens next is where truly powerful strategy emerges. In that narrow window of time between the break of the huddle and the snap of the ball, the quarterback collects and processes information on his opponent and may change the play as a reaction to the other team's anticipated course of action.

- This ability to change the play—or the plan—is what distinguishes genuine strategy: the dynamic of action and reaction that yields optimum results.

Powerful strategy emerges in the game of football, with both offense and defense adjusting their lines of attack almost instantaneously based on the actions of their opponents.

A Cultivated Skill

- We aren't born with a fully developed ability to think strategically. It is a skill that must be cultivated and practiced. In fact, most people are stuck in the mode of cognitive confinement, or static thinking; they consciously reject thinking about tomorrow.

- Albert Einstein once observed that insanity is the propensity to do the same thing over and over again, expecting different results each time. This is the antithesis of strategic thinking, and it occurs in the workplace more often than we'd like to admit.

- Many of our co-workers or employees don't engage in a methodical process of questioning, evaluating assumptions, gathering information, analyzing and planning, and then taking action. Many people simply function in routines they don't question.

- We all think about the future, of course, but there is a difference between strategic thinking and daydreaming about what might be. Strategic

5

thinking is about setting goals and developing long-range plans to reach those goals, plans based on careful analysis of internal and external environments and on the actions of others.

- Strategic thinking involves thinking logically and deeply about the future. It means embracing the idea that where we want to be five years from now should inform what we do today.

Key Terms, Definitions, and Concepts
- The term "strategic intent" refers to the "big ideas" that strategy aims to advance. It is this intent that compels us to think about the future: the home you'd like to buy, the career you'd like to have.

- The term "strategy" itself refers to more than just a plan. It is a way of perceiving and considering the future with our aims and goals in mind. It is also a way of dealing with a constantly changing environment, both responding to that environment to achieve our goals and attempting, where possible, to change that environment to our benefit.

  o The ancient military strategist Sun Tzu offers us one of the most well-known examples of strategic theory in his opus *The Art of War*. Sun Tzu's brilliance lies in his recognition of the fluid nature of reality and the fact that any practitioner of strategy must constantly adapt to it.

  o In the Western world, the concept of strategy flowered in the 19th century with the work of the French general Antoine de Jomini, most notably his *Summary of the Art of War*. Jomini's contribution to strategic thinking lies in his identification of interior lines of communication and his notion of concentration of force.

  o Carl von Clausewitz, a Prussian military officer, disagreed with Jomini in important respects. He viewed uncertainty, chance, and probability as three-fourths of conflict—what he called "friction"—and to overcome this friction, he offered the notion of coup d'oeil, a French expression for a stroke of intuition and genius. This is the concept of the rapid and accurate decision making.

- One of the most influential strategists of the 20th century was Sir Basil Liddell Hart, whose contribution was the "indirect approach"—a form of misdirection. Hart's idea was that we should never expend our energies with frontal assaults on an entrenched enemy; instead, we should seek interesting alternative routes to achieve our objectives.

Strategy versus Tactics

- We sometimes hear the word "strategy" used in conjunction with "tactics," but there's a difference between the two. We tend to think of strategy as part of some higher realm of planning, while tactics are the execution of strategy.

- If your strategy is to become a doctor or lawyer, the courses you take are part of that strategy, but the ways you choose to study and prepare would be tactics.

- Clausewitz distinguished between strategy and tactics by focusing on levels of conflict. In his words, "Just as tactics is the employment of military forces in battle, so strategy is the employment of battles ... to achieve the object of war."

- Strategy encompasses well-executed tactics and cannot be divorced from tactics. Many a great strategic plan can falter because of a failure to recognize this crucial point.

- Strategic thinking does not end with the crafting and execution of a strategy. Strategic thinking means constant interaction with the environment during the execution of the strategy. Successful strategy is dynamic, adaptive, and opportunistic, and it depends on the swift, bold, and decisive execution of tactics.

Strategic Theory and Thinking

- The realm of business has proven to be a fertile area for the development of strategic theory. Harvard business professor Michael Porter elevated strategic thinking to a new level of respect in the nation's business schools, beginning with his pathbreaking work in the 1980s on competitive advantage, competition, and strategic thinking.

- For Porter, "strategy means choosing a different set of activities to deliver a unique mix of value," in other words, doing things differently. This definition bridges the gap between the military and business and between ancient and modern ideas.

- "Choosing a different set of activities" enabled the ancient general Hannibal to defeat the far more numerous Romans at the Battle of Cannae in 216 B.C. and allowed Apple to play a significant role in the personal computer revolution of the 1980s.

- Strategic thinking is goal-directed, structured, and focused on the future in a precise way. It is analytical and ambitious. It concerns power and trends, as well as uncertainty and the resolution or accommodation of that uncertainty.

- Strategic thinking is also instrumental; we use strategic thinking as an instrument to achieve our goals. It becomes a resource, much like money, or time, or labor. Note, too, that it is useful across a range of activities, from the grand and sweeping to the at-home and everyday.

The Importance of Intelligence
- Intelligence and analysis play a significant role in critical thinking, providing the raw material to build a sound strategic structure. Not only do we want to find out what the other side is doing, but we want to mislead our opponents about our intentions, as the U.S. military did with its feigned invasion of Kuwait from the sea during the first Gulf War in 1991.

- In competitive situations, the "surprise attack" smacks of the not-so-genteel aspects of conflict, but in sports, business, and politics, we can admire a well-crafted surprise. Again, in football, surprise and deception are integral parts of the game and are crucial to gaining competitive advantage. The "draw play," for example, attempts to draw defenders into the wrong parts of the field.

- Surprise and stratagem serve us as useful tools to advance our strategic goals. Deception can turn a bad situation into a good one, and it can turn a good situation into victory. The five basic types of surprises at our disposal are those of intention, time, place, strength, and style.

- In a full sense, strategy equips us with tools that help us meet the future with confidence. Tools of analysis can aid our understanding of the powerful forces that shape that future. As we'll see in a future lecture, the SWOT analysis (strengths, weaknesses, opportunities, and threats) is an analytical tool that helps us look at all aspects of a situation to ensure that our strategic intent matches our resources and capabilities.

A Robust Definition
- Strategy is a method or plan that we craft to bring about a desired future, such as achievement of a goal or solution to a problem. It's a plan that assesses, acquires, and allocates necessary resources to the most effective and efficient use. And it's a plan that anticipates and incorporates competitor responses.

- Peter Drucker, the great 20th-century management thinker, observed that there are two types of thinking: thinking about objects and thinking about people. Static thinking involves planning around objects and is quite easy; the variables are few and relatively unchanging. Strategic thinking, however, is much more difficult, because it involves anticipating the actions and reactions of competitors and preparing accordingly.

- Thinking strategically helps us to make sense out of chaos and enables us to use the forces around us to our advantage, rather than allow those forces to pummel us. We learn to quarterback our own lives, both by planning ahead and by adapting our plan in the moments of decision that matter most.

- Strategic thinking skills are most critical in the moments when an outcome is uncertain and additional strategic action is needed. This is the quarterback in the seconds before the snap, the courtroom attorney in a last-minute maneuver, the closing minutes on a stock-exchange trading floor, or the perfect teaching moment with a child.

- In this course, we will cultivate the benefits of strategic thinking, enabling us to enjoy increased productivity and work satisfaction, greater predictability, less stress, greater efficiency, and a better chance of victory.

Suggested Reading

Dixit and Nalebuff, *Thinking Strategically: The Competitive Edge in Business, Politics, and Everyday Life.*

Harvard Business School Press, *Thinking Strategically.*

Porter, "What Is Strategy?"

Rice, *Three Moves Ahead.*

Sloan, *Learning to Think Strategically.*

Questions to Consider

1. Strategy is one of the most used—and abused—terms in the lexicon of modern business. This is largely because genuine strategy is so difficult to craft, risky to accept, and challenging to implement; as a result, *poseurs*, such as off-the-shelf "efficiency tools," masquerade as strategy. What are some of the programs and processes you know of that position themselves as "strategy" and how do they differ from genuine strategy?

2. Use the game of football as a learning tool. Watch a football game with an eye toward observing specific players on the field; watch their actions and where they look before each play. Do they attempt to deceive their opponents? Watch the quarterback and consider his actions after he breaks the huddle. What does he do? What are his thoughts? How does he react to what he sees?

3. Ensure that you understand the difference between strategy and a mere off-the-shelf efficiency tool or efficiency process. What is the difference and why do you think that efficiency tools so successfully masquerade as strategy?

The World of Strategic Thinking
Lecture 1—Transcript

Every time we lift our heads to consider how our actions affect the future, we begin to think strategically. Every time we consider how other people respond to our actions, we are thinking strategically. Strategic thinking is a way of making sense of the complex world around us; it's a way of peering into the future without fear, but rather with a surety and confidence that our actions today will yield the best possible outcome tomorrow.

Let's take an example from sports, from a game that is dear to the hearts of many Americans and one of the most instructive of games where strategy is concerned—American football. Even if you've never enjoyed or even understood a game of American football, I think you'll find that it is an especially tractable game to strategic analysis. There is an explicitly gladiatorial ethos, it is complex, and the content is perhaps surprisingly cerebral.

Let's focus on a crucial 10–15 seconds in the game. This is the time between the call of a play and the snap of the ball to start the play. During these crucial seconds, much of a strategic nature happens on both sides of the ball.

The offense has called a play—a plan, if you will, to achieve the intermediate objective of moving the ball to achieve a first-down. This plan is according to a particular situation on the field. The distance to achieve a first-down, the number of downs remaining, the distance needed to score.

These are all objective positional aspects that we consider when we decide which play to call. The defense looks at the same situation on the field and calls a plan to resist the offense.

And that's it, then the play is executed, right? Wrong. Circumstances change rapidly, and the great commander—the capable strategic thinker—must be able to respond properly and promptly.

What happens next is where truly powerful strategy emerges. As the quarterback walks to the line of scrimmage, he has but seconds before the play must be launched, the ball snapped. In this 10–15 second window, he surveys the defense. He looks at their formation, he tries to recognize the pass coverage, whether zone or man-to-man coverage. He looks for clues in the posture of the players as to what the defense might do. He surveys his environment right up to the moment of execution of the plan. And if changes in that environment make it necessary, he will change the plan.

The defense, too, is acting; it is disguising its coverage; key players are moving around, feinting and deceiving, giving false signals.

In that narrow window of time between the break of the huddle and the snap of the ball, the quarterback collects information on his opponent, he processes it, and he may change the play as a reaction to the other team's anticipated course of action. And then he executes that play, continuing his adjustments as the play develops.

A premier example of a quarterback with this combination of insight and ability to execute is Hall of Fame quarterback Joe Montana. His former coach, Bill Walsh, also in the Hall of Fame, put it this way:

> The single trait that separates great quarterbacks from good quarterbacks is the ability to make the great, spontaneous decision, especially at a crucial time. The clock is running down and your team is five points behind. The play that was called has broken down and 22 players are moving in almost unpredictable directions all over the field.
>
> This is where the great quarterback uses his experience, vision, mobility, and what we will call spontaneous genius. He makes something good happen.

This ability to change the plan (and "make something good happen") is what distinguishes genuine strategy—it is the dynamic of action and reaction that yields optimum results throughout a game as a team's strategy is executed. The strategic action–response dynamic I just described comes to us not merely from the football hall of fame. It goes back more than 2000 years, to the time of Sun Tzu and ancient Greece.

Imagine sitting at a conference table with the greatest strategic thinkers of all time—Sun Tzu and Hannibal, Machiavelli, Napoleon, and Clausewitz. Add in business strategists like Michael Porter, Gary Hamel, and C. K. Prahalad, and a winning coach, like Vince Lombardi. Add in great political leaders like Winston Churchill, CEOs from top companies, and the most successful entertainers and media figures. What would you ask them? How might their insights transform you into a powerful and capable strategic thinker? Let's find out over the course of 24 lectures.

We aren't born with a fully-developed ability or desire to think strategically. It is a skill that must be cultivated and practiced. Many people simply don't think strategically. If anything, some people do the exact opposite of thinking strategically—they consciously reject thinking about tomorrow. They think only of today.

Philosophically, this might be akin to an "Eat, drink, and be merry" view of life. For example, young people who enjoy a good party, awaken in the morning with awful hangover headaches, and who swear they'll never do it again. And yet they repeat their behavior the following weekend, and the next, either forgetting about the inevitable result, or thinking that the aftereffects somehow might be different this time.

This kind of "thinking" is prevalent in the workplace. I call this cognitive confinement, or static thinking. It happens in sports, too. I recall the old chant from my college days when we had a particularly unimaginative coach. When he found something that wouldn't work, he stuck to it. It led to chants from the bleachers: "Up the middle, up the middle, up the middle, punt!" This, of course, referred to his predictable play-calling that led to predictable on-field results.

The great physicist Albert Einstein observed that insanity is the propensity to do the same thing over and over again, but expecting different results each time. This is the very antithesis of thinking strategically. And this occurs in the workplace more often than we'd like to admit.

Many of our associates don't engage in a methodical process of questioning, evaluation of assumptions, investigation, information-gathering, analysis, planning, and then action. Many people simply function in routines they don't question.

Perhaps they live life day-to-day. Perhaps they face the same problems every day, always losing their keys; always getting caught in traffic in the same place at the same time; always dealing with the same bottlenecks at work; unable to get people around them to work together toward common goals; always working at cross-purposes with other people, teams, or divisions.

We all think about the future on occasion, of course, but there is a tremendous difference between strategic thinking and daydreaming about what might be. Strategic thinking is about setting goals and developing long-range plans to reach those goals, plans based on careful analysis of internal and external environments and on the actions of others.

Strategy is future-oriented. Strategic thinking involves thinking logically and deeply about the future. It means embracing the idea that where we want to be 5 years from now—5 months from now—should inform what we do today.

This notion of strategic thinking is shaped greatly by military influence. This hardly surprises us, since the military arts have developed a vast historical treasure of strategic theory and practice. But strategic thinking is not necessarily military in character, it's simply a way of looking at the world with engagement and with purpose in mind.

My own background, and my approach to strategy in this course, combines approaches from the military, business, sports, and politics. As a fencer in college, I learned what all sportsmen learn with regard to battling with an opponent—the importance of studying the competition, learning as much as you can about his tendencies, his habits, his weaknesses. Later, as a young military intelligence officer during the Cold War in West Germany, I was introduced to the deeper aspects of competitor analysis and the importance of retaining flexibility on the battlefield during the execution of any plan. Now, I teach strategic management at a major university, and the lessons of competition remain robust and equally applicable.

I think the best approach to strategy, as you'll see—is to learn what we can from the long history of military strategy, but also to give equal attention to strategy in business, politics, sports, and other aspects of life.

To prepare us for our journey into the realm of strategic thinking, let's learn some of the key terms, definitions, and concepts that we use throughout the course.

First, *strategic intent*. Strategy aims to advance our own big ideas. Strategic thinking has a term for this—these big ideas. It's what business academics Gary Hamel and C. K. Prahalad called "strategic intent." Strategic intent is essential to any powerful and effective strategy. For Coca-Cola decades ago, this was making it possible to "buy a Coke" anywhere in the entire world. For Tata Motors in the 21st century, this was building and selling the world's cheapest car.

For any strategy to rise above the level of mere technique, it must have a powerful and inspirational strategic intent, whether to animate an individual, or to inspire a corporation, or to fire the imagination of a nation. John F. Kennedy declared, "We choose to go to the moon in this decade."

Strategic intent compels us to think about the future: the home we want, the career we want, the retirement we want. Without a powerful vision, effective strategy is nonexistent. Strategy is one of those rare terms that can be used as a rhetorical garnish on our prose—it provides cachet and *gravitas*.

Instead of mere plans for the weekend, we develop a strategy. This is probably only natural, since generals craft strategy. Smart people craft strategy. We want to craft strategy, too. But what is it, and where did the term originate?

When I put these questions to my students, they respond with answers within a narrow band—strategy is a plan, a grand plan, an ultimate plan. We may think of it as a plan, but that would be too simplistic. It involves much more than simply eyeballing a set of facts and pulling an answer out of the hip pocket. It is a way of perceiving and considering the future with our aims and goals in mind.

Planning is, indeed, part of strategy, but if it were just a plan, nothing would distinguish it from much of the mundane scheduling that virtually all of us do. A strategic plan is a way of dealing with a constantly changing environment, both responding to that environment to achieve our goals and attempting where possible to change that environment to our benefit.

Sun Tzu offers us one of the most well-known examples of strategic theory in his opus *Art of War*, which first appeared in the form that we know today approximately 2300 years ago. Scholars argue over the identity of the author, but his work finally appeared at some point in the 3rd century B.C.

Sun Tzu's brilliance lies not in offering an explicit set of maxims for conduct of war, but in his recognition of the fluid nature of reality and how any practitioner of strategy must constantly and swiftly adapt to that reality.

Our word strategy is derived from the Greek word *strategos*, which originally meant "army leader." It was once the term for a military governor in ancient Greece. The term *strategy* did not appear in the English language for the first time until the early 19th century. Thanks to Napoleon and his wars, the 19th century saw a flowering of the concept of strategy in the western world with a series of publications by Antoine de Jomini, most notably his *Summary of the Art of War* in 1838. Jomini's contribution to strategic thinking lies in, first, his identification of interior lines of communication. For example, a family that lives together has clear interior lines of communication compared to a family where some members live apart.

Second, his notion of concentration of force. Concentration of force in space and time as keys to victory in competition. Jomini's approach to strategy is like the calling of a play during a huddle. In fact, Jomini conceived of strategy as beginning from a kind of geometric precision. On the other hand, we have Clausewitz. Carl von Clausewitz disagreed with Jomini in important respects. He focused more on what the quarterback does after the huddle. A Prussian military officer, who served on the opposite side of Jomini in the Napoleonic wars, Clausewitz viewed uncertainty, chance, and probability as three-fourths of conflict—what he called friction—thus, he called war "the province of chance." It was a constant battle with the unexpected.

To overcome this friction, he offered us this famous and enduring advice on how to grapple successfully in competition—the notion of *coup d' oeil*, the French expression for the stroke of intuition and genius. This is the concept of the rapid and accurate decision that confers competitive advantage on the strategist who exhibits *coup d' oeil*.

Together these two Europeans, Jomini and Clausewitz, offer complementary positions for bringing strategy to bear on conflict. Jomini focused more on defining the best practices of his day. Clausewitz focused instead on how to think about what to do beyond the best practices of the day. Both are necessary, and the same sort of complementary emphasis on best practice versus going beyond best practice can be found in the business world as well.

One of the most influential strategists of the 20th century was Sir Basil Liddell Hart, whose contribution was the concept of the "indirect approach"—a form of misdirection. This was the notion that we should never expend our energies with frontal assaults on an entrenched enemy. His theory was of course influenced by the ghastly trench warfare of World War I and its direct assaults across open ground.

Hart insisted that instead of grinding our strength against enemy strength, we should seek interesting alternative routes to achieve our objectives. We should shroud our moves and intentions in mystery, and we should keep our competitors off-balance and ignorant of our aims. His ideas were not so influential in Britain, but eagerly absorbed in Germany, which developed the Blitzkrieg.

An example in business is the case of Swatch. This popular watchmaker developed a side business providing internal movements to manufacturers of Swiss-made, luxury watches. Eventually, Swatch became dominant in the manufacture of these internal watch movements and Swatch decided to cut off sales of those critical parts and reserve them exclusively for its own high-end watches. That's the indirect approach.

We sometimes hear strategy used in conjunction with tactics. Sometimes the words are used interchangeably. There is a difference. We tend to think of strategy as part of some higher realm of planning. Generals around sand tables, executives in the corporate suite, coaches in the film room, political candidates huddling with their advisors.

The term *tactics*, on the other hand, yields images of squad leaders leading their troops to the objective, linebackers blitzing on third-down, the marketing department rolling out a new ad campaign, candidates giving speeches, and workers collecting signatures.

But strategy and tactics exist on a continuum. And whether we categorize an activity as tactics or as strategy is often simply a matter of where we are located on the hierarchy of action. My strategy may be a part of someone else's grand strategy, and thus, from their perspective, my strategy becomes their tactics.

But the distinction works for you as an individual as well. If your strategy is to become a doctor or lawyer, the courses you take are part of that strategy, but the ways you choose to study and prepare would be tactics.

Similarly, Clausewitz distinguished between strategy and tactics by focusing on levels of conflict. In his words, "Just as tactics is the employment of military forces in battle, so strategy is the employment of battles ... to achieve the object of war."

And so we see that Clausewitz defined tactics as the use of engagements in the execution of the strategy. Each level of organizational activity requires strategic thinking and the tactical execution of that strategy.

Tactics are the execution of strategy, and in the execution of a strategic plan on the battlefield, exigencies arise. The unexpected strikes us. The battle unfolds in ways that surprise us.

These developments require reaction on the battlefield. Improvisation, seizing of critical moments, the good sense to retreat, the strategic intuition to move left instead of right—this ability to react at the moment in the appropriate way is a part of strategic thinking that is as important as crafting a cool and deliberate plan before the fact. In all of these, the thinking remains the same, differing only in the scale of time and space and resources.

Strategy encompasses well-executed tactics and cannot be divorced from it. Many a great strategic plan can falter because of a failure to recognize this crucial point. Moreover, strategic thinking does not end with the crafting and execution of a strategy. Strategic thinking means constant interaction with the environment during the execution of our strategy. For example, always treat with respect anyone you interact with.

Successful strategy is dynamic, it is adaptive, it is opportunistic, and it depends upon the swift, bold, decisive, and crisp execution of tactics. Although many fundamental ideas about strategy were pioneered in thinking about war, strategic thinking has naturally extended itself into business, politics, and sports, where great organizations of all kinds, not just armies, require guidance of the sort that strategic thinking provides.

Business has proven to be a very fertile area for the development of strategic theory. Harvard Business Professor Michael Porter almost single-handedly elevated strategic thinking to a new level of respect in the nation's business schools, beginning with his path-breaking work in the 1980s on competitive advantage, competition, and strategic thinking.

Porter says that "strategy means choosing a different set of activities to deliver a unique mix of value." Doing things differently. For me, Porter's definition is seductive in an incredibly positive manner. Porter's concept of strategy as "choosing a different set of activities" bridges the gap between the military and business, and between ancient and modern as well.

Let's consider the ancient warrior Hannibal, and his victory at the Battle of Cannae. In 216 B.C. at the Battle of Cannae, the great Carthaginian general Hannibal was outnumbered badly by the Romans, so he should have lost. But, armed with fewer resources than his Roman enemies, Hannibal configured his forces differently. He didn't follow the "best practices" of his day and line his soldiers up in the usual way. Instead, he outmaneuvered and outsmarted his Roman enemy with a battle plan that enveloped his numerically superior foe and completely destroyed it. And it was Hannibal's bold way of rejecting the usual forward march of phalanxes that yielded his success in battle.

Similarly, "choosing a different set of activities" was a defining feature of the early Apple Computer and its role in triggering the personal computer revolution. Apple inventions of the early 1980s, especially the Macintosh computer, were a deliberate turn away from the mainframe computers of that time. This willingness to "Think Different" was Apple's strength from the beginning and went on to become a marketing slogan for the company starting in 1997 as Steve Jobs returned to the company and reenergized it.

Strategic thinking is goal-directed, it is structured, and it is focused on the future in a precise way. It is analytical; it's ambitious. It concerns power and trends. It concerns uncertainty and the resolution of that uncertainty or learning to coexist with and accommodate that uncertainty.

It is instrumental. This means that we utilize strategic thinking as an instrument to achieve our goals. It becomes a resource, much like money, or time, or labor. Strategic thinking also becomes a lubricant that makes all of our other resources work better.

Strategic thinking is useful across a range of activities from the grand and sweeping to the at-home and every day. Begin you day doing just five minutes of an activity that contributes to one of your strategic goals. Anywhere we find strategy being used in any capacity, strategic thinking is present.

To demonstrate the versatility and usefulness of strategic thinking principles, in this course we take conceptual cuts at our strategic concepts and see how they play out in examples from the realms of business, sports, politics, and the military. Here are just some of the topics we cover.

The principles of conflict. Over the centuries, soldiers and scholars alike have attempted to develop strategic doctrine, or so-called "principles of war," the idea being that there may be some key to human conduct that remains valid, regardless of the circumstances of time and space. And, over the centuries, these various theories have tended to overlap.

Thomas Jefferson once said of religion that if you would know the truth, then look at what the great religions of the world agree on—there you will find important keys to human conduct. Whether this is true or not for religion, it does seem to be true for military strategic doctrine as embodied in principles of war. The United States' own official principles of war, first published in 1921, resemble the principles of war that can be found in many other countries and times.

When we talk about strategy, we really cannot ignore the role of "intelligence" in our discussions. Intelligence and analysis plays an increasingly important role in critical thinking. It provides the raw material to build a sound strategic structure.

Not only do we want to find out what the other side is doing, we want to mislead him about our own intentions. In the first Gulf War in 1991, the U.S. military used multiple deception techniques to confound Saddam Hussein's forces then occupying Kuwait. One ploy was a faked invasion of Kuwait from the sea, which tied down close to 100,000 Iraqi soldiers.

The 4th and 5th Marine Expeditionary Brigades cruised in circles in the Persian Gulf as if poised for an amphibious assault on mined and well-defended beaches. The ploy distracted attention from the actual ground assault by General Norman Schwarzkopf, who crafted a masterful—and classic—"left hook" around the flank of the defending Iraqi army. In this case, the invasion deception was clearly communicated to the Iraqis, who then adjusted their own defensive actions in accord with what U.S. planners wanted.

In competitive situations, the "surprise attack" smacks of the not-so-genteel aspects of conflict. We think of Pearl Harbor; we think of the ambush. In sports, in business, and in politics, we can admire a well-crafted surprise. Think of American football, where surprise and deception are integral parts of the game and are crucial to gaining competitive advantage. Here are some terms that are used all the time—fake punt, reverse, draw play, play-action pass. On defense, we hear of how a team is "attempting to disguise its coverage." As an example, let's look at the draw play. This play attempts to "draw" defenders into the wrong parts of the field. Specifically, the draw looks like a pass play, which draws the defenders into spreading out downfield to defend against the pass, but it's actually a running play. This puts the defense off-balance and a step slower in reacting.

The opposite is the play-action pass, which is a pass play that is designed to look like a run. Here, the "play-action" might be the quarterback pretending to hand the ball to a running back, before actually making a pass. In both the "draw" and "play-action" stratagems, the idea is to get the defense to commit to the wrong course of action and give our own plan a greater chance for success. It slows the reaction of our opponent.

Surprise and deception serve us as useful tools to advance our strategic goals. Deception can turn a bad situation into good, and it can turn a good situation into victory. The five basic types of surprises at our disposal are surprises of intention, time, place, strength, and style. And in our lecture on surprise, we look at each one.

And strategy in a full sense equips us with tools that help us meet that future with confidence. Tools of analysis can aid our understanding of the powerful forces that shape our future—if not in completely satisfactory manner, then at least in much better fashion than the alternative presented by complete ignorance.

One of the most effective tools my students find empowering is the analysis of strengths, weaknesses, opportunities, and threats. It's an analytical tool that ensures that we look at all aspects of ourselves or our firm—as well as the external environment—to ensure that our strategic intent matches well with our resources and our capabilities. We discuss that tool in Lecture 10.

Let's gather everything we've touched on so far to define strategy itself. That is, our definition should be robust enough to encompass all of the fields of activity where strategy is used, and it should encompass all the strategic thinking skills we'll cover in this course. Let's offer it now.

Strategy is a method or plan that we craft to bring about a desired future—such as achievement of a goal or solution to a problem. It's a plan that assesses, acquires, and allocates necessary resources to the most effectiveand efficient use. And it's a plan or method that anticipates and incorporates competitor responses.

So it's apparent that strategic thinking is much more than just getting your schedule together for the week. It's not just a schedule—even a clever schedule. Peter Drucker, the great 20th century management thinker, observed that there are two types of thinking—thinking about objects and thinking about people. Static thinking involves planning around objects, and is quite easy. The variables are few and relatively unchanging. You prepare a schedule.

Strategic thinking, however, is immensely more difficult, because it involves anticipating the actions and responses of competitors and preparing accordingly. When we learn to think strategically, it helps us to make sense out of chaos. It helps us to impose order onto a reality that remains stubbornly disorderly.

Strategic thinking skills are most critical in the moments when an outcome is uncertain and additional strategic action is needed. Our strategic thinking skills are fully in play. This is the quarterback in the seconds before the snap, the courtroom attorney in a last-minute maneuver, the closing minutes on a stock exchange trading floor, or the perfect teaching moment with a child.

But in those critical moments of sometimes rapid move and countermove, you must bring together a whole set of skills—skills that you can learn. Strategy is a complex, multifaceted subject, deeply rooted in history. When we learn to think strategically, it helps us to make sense out of chaos, and there are many contemporary applications.

We can learn to utilize the forces around us to our advantage, rather than allow those forces to pummel us. We learn to quarterback our own lives, both by planning ahead, and by adapting our plan in the moments of decision that matter most.

In this course, we cultivate the benefits of strategic thinking. As a strategic person, we can enjoy increased productivity, work satisfaction, more predictability, less stress, greater efficiency, a greater chance at victory, all of which enhances our chances of succeeding in life on our own terms. And that is an incredibly exhilarating prospect.

The Origins and Relevance of Ancient Strategy
Lecture 2

Philosophers and generals study the great thinkers of the past, and we would do well to emulate them if we wish to deepen our understanding of strategic thinking in the 21st century. The broader our context, the more elaborate our backdrop, the more useful the tools of strategy become. In this lecture, we'll learn strategic lessons from six of the best military commanders and thinkers in history; as we do, try to come up with ways that these lessons can be relevant in your own life and work.

Thucydides
- **Thucydides** was a 5th-century-B.C. aristocrat who served as a general in the Peloponnesian War, the great conflict between the Greek city-states of Athens and Sparta. Thucydides carried the rank of *strategos*, or general, and his *History of the Peloponnesian War* covers the conflict down to the year 411 B.C.

- Nearly 2500 years after it was written, this ancient treatise serves as the starting point for the field of international relations, the foundation for a school of thought called political realism, and our earliest account of strategic thinking in action.

- The work of Thucydides conveys skepticism about such concepts as justice. For example, in the famous Melian dialogue, the Athenians assert their superior armed might as the only arbiter required to exact cooperation from the inhabitants of the island of Melos. The passage sweeps away notions of fairness, justice, reason, and even intervention by the gods.

- The Melian dialogue presents us with an archetype for power politics or realpolitik. Think of a situation in which power remains paramount in your professional life. Is there a market or competitive field where overwhelming force or vicious competition is not only the most effective strategy but also the only logical one? How can you leverage your organization's advantages to score an overwhelming victory?

Pagondas

- Despite the fact that the generals of Athens were called *strategos*, they didn't use a great deal of actual strategy in the Peloponnesian War. To see strategy at work in this war, we must look at an apparently insignificant battle that featured none of the leading generals from either side.

- On the surface, the Battle of Delium, fought in 424 B.C., looks like just another ancient bloodletting. But at Delium, an obscure Theban general named **Pagondas** exhibited a radically new mode of combat.

- At the start of the battle, the Athenians marched out to the valley near Delium with about 20,000 troops, but they turned back after their supporting troops failed to appear. Rather than allow the Athenians to flee, Pagondas urged the Thebans to pursue and close with them. With this move, he developed the principles of forward defense and preemption—striking an enemy that poses a long-term threat rather than an immediate threat.

- At a crucial moment in the battle, Pagondas ordered fresh companies of Theban cavalry, held in reserve, to attack the Athenians in concert with the infantry. This was the first recorded use of deliberate reserves joining an attack. In response, the Athenians panicked; their ranks shattered; and they fled.

- Among the innovations Pagondas introduced in this battle was his own monitoring of the situation from a distance—rather than positioning himself at the forefront of the fighting—and the modification of troop formation.

- The Battle of Delium counts as the birthplace of a science of Western tactics and gives us our second strategic lesson: Surprise innovations can often turn the tide of an evenly matched struggle. In your life, are you stuck fighting a battle with traditional tactics? If so, can you think of any innovations that will allow you to catch your opponent off guard?

Sun Tzu

- China offers us one of the most well-known examples of strategic theory, *The Art of War*, popularly attributed to **Sun Tzu**, a general who flourished in the 5th century B.C. This work was perhaps expanded by others in subsequent centuries, and it greatly influenced military thinking in Asia and, later, the West.

- Sun Tzu's brilliance lay in his recognition of the fluid nature of reality and the fact that any practitioner of strategy must constantly adapt to that reality. Sun Tzu's principles can be applied to the battlefield, public administration and planning, and diplomacy and international negotiation.

- Key to Sun Tzu's thinking is his realization that all plans are temporary. He knew that a plan can become obsolete as soon as it's crafted. For him, the decision to position one's forces in competition depends on two major factors: (1) objective conditions in the physical environment and (2) the subjective beliefs of competitors in that environment.

- In this, Sun Tzu originates a view shared by elite strategic theorists down to the present: that the most brilliant plans are those that spring into being in the dynamic of action and response. Sun Tzu believed that strategy requires rapid responses to changing conditions based on sound judgment and principles.

- How can you apply Sun Tzu's lessons in your life? Consider situations in which you rely on outdated plans; then think like Sun Tzu: Figure out how and why your plans went awry and how that understanding can help you correct course.

Hannibal Barca

- **Hannibal** was a Carthaginian general who plagued the Roman Republic from the 3rd century into the 2nd century B.C. Outnumbered in the enemy's homeland, he fought the Romans to a great victory in 216 B.C. at the Battle of Cannae, thanks to his revolutionary manipulation of forces.

At the Battle of Cannae in 216 B.C., the Carthaginian general Hannibal outmaneuvered and outsmarted the Romans with a battle plan that turned their own tactics against them.

- In Hannibal's time, standard tactics dictated that formations of soldiers would line up abreast of each other in a phalanx, march forward, collide, and do battle. Numerical superiority was thought to be the key to victory. Armed with fewer resources than his Roman enemies, however, Hannibal configured his forces differently and achieved a stunning success.

- At Cannae, the Romans marched forward in a narrow and deep phalanx that matched the front of Hannibal's smaller force. This narrow front greatly negated the Roman numerical advantage.

- Roman training dictated that soldiers pursue a fleeing opponent. Thus, when Hannibal's leading troops appeared to break and withdraw, the Romans pressed forward, leaving their flanks to Hannibal's infantry.

- The Romans were also taken unawares by a change in cavalry tactics. Once Hannibal's cavalry had driven off the Roman cavalry, his horsemen did not pursue the Romans. Instead, they fell upon the rear of the masses of Roman infantry, which became even more tightly packed. The envelopment of the Romans was complete, and their destruction, inevitable.

- Hannibal achieved this great victory not with superior numbers but superior strategy and extraordinary tactical execution. And that's his lesson to us: When faced with superior competitors, use your knowledge of their habits and weaknesses to outsmart them. How can you invert commonplace thinking and outmaneuver your competitors when they're falsely feeling confident?

Vegetius
- **Vegetius** was a Roman administrator who lived in the late 4th century A.D., during a period of Roman decline. At the request of Emperor Valentinian, Vegetius prepared a treatise called *Epitoma rei militaris*, or *A Summary of Military Matters*, which became the most popular military handbook for more than 1000 years after its publication.

- The *Summary* contains a list of seemingly pedestrian topics—the selection of recruits, their training, and so on. The link to high-concept strategy here is that strategy encompasses three elements: intentions, capabilities, and resources. Vegetius's work addresses how the military may develop its capabilities to achieve the aims of strategy.

- Throughout his work, Vegetius hammers home the need for thorough training, strong discipline, hard work, and sound planning. These elements of preparation form the heart of strategic capability.

- Key among his directives was an emphasis on the need for, and uses of, strategic reserves. As an exercise, write out all the areas where you feel your company has uncommonly strong reserves. Where can you hold off deploying all your resources to lure your competitors into a false sense of confidence? How can you spring these resources on the competitor suddenly and with overwhelming effect?

Machiavelli
- In his famous work *The Prince*, **Niccolò Machiavelli**, one of the most important political theorists in history, advocated a coldly reasoned

line of behavior to maintain a monarch in power: a ruthless pursuit of self-interest. In the lesser-known *Art of War*, Machiavelli extended this amoral reasoning to the battlefield.

- Machiavelli offers us two key concepts: *virtu* and *fortuna*, representing the internal and external elements of strategic thinking.

  o The concept of *virtu* for Machiavelli incorporates numerous qualities: flexibility, foresight, individuality, ability, energy, political acumen, prowess, and vital force. It is a skill that one can develop and sharpen.

  o Conventional thinkers of the time treated Fortuna as a mostly benign goddess. In contrast, Machiavelli conceived fortune as a malevolent and uncompromising source of human misery and disaster. Thus, he counseled generals to "beat and maul" fortune into submission. Today, we would call his advice a bias toward action.

  o *Virtu* provides the ability to respond to fortune at any time and in any way necessary. This joining of the actor with the environment is an early formulation of the concept of emergent strategy. Given that we cannot predict what Fortuna will hand to us, we must develop the internal qualities and capabilities that enable us to meet those uncertainties in the best manner possible.

- As a final challenge for this lecture, ask yourself whether you have developed the flexibility, foresight, and energy to outwit unpredictable fortune. Think back to an unexpected situation that overwhelmed you in the past. Have you learned from it, and if not, how can you?

The Lessons of the Past
- Ancient strategists provide us with modes of thinking and practical guidance that we can use in the present.

- First, any area, no matter how dominated by thoughtless effort, can be transformed by the application of tactics. Try to use special forces at special times and in special ways.

- Second, understand that plans must change. Learn to recognize the fluid nature of reality and be aware that any strategy must constantly adapt to that reality. The most brilliant plans are those that spring into being in the action-response dynamic of the moment.

- Third, preparation is the heart of strategic capability. Whether you're running a household or a billion-dollar business, training, discipline, hard work, and sound planning are the foundations of strategic reserves, which are necessary for many kinds of maneuvers. If you have no reserves, you have no strategy.

- Fourth, know your opponents. You can gain astonishing leverage if you know the preparations and capabilities of your opponents. A combination of surprise and superb tactical execution can allow you to defeat an opponent with twice your strength.

- Fifth, be bold; seize your fortune. The greatest challenge in strategic thinking is getting started.

Names to Know

Hannibal (247 B.C.–183–181 B.C.): Son of a famous general and sworn to eternal hostility against Rome from a young age, Hannibal Barca's name will always be associated with one of the greatest victories in all of history: his defeat of the Romans at Cannae.

Machiavelli, Niccolò (1469–1527): A humanely educated man who is most remembered for his tract on political power, Machiavelli also offered his take on conflict in his treatise *The Art of War*. Literally a Renaissance man, Machiavelli collaborated on military projects with both Leonardo da Vinci and Michelangelo.

Pagondas (fl. 5th century B.C.): This obscure Theban general is credited with inventing the science of battlefield tactics, demonstrating a radical new approach to warfare of the time by his innovations at the Battle of Delium (424 B.C.) during the Peloponnesian War.

Sun Tzu (fl. 5th century B.C.): One of a handful of almost universally known strategists, the impact of Sun Tzu on strategy and the way we think about strategy has suffused thinking not only in present-day military circles but in business and political realms, as well. Descriptions of warfare in *The Art of War*, traditionally credited to Sun Tzu, suggest that the work was composed early in the Warring States period (475–221 B.C.). Famous generals who utilized Sun Tzu's principles were Chinese communist Mao Zedong, Vietnamese general Vo Nguyen Giap, and American generals Norman Schwarzkopf and Colin Powell in the First Gulf War of 1991.

Thucydides (460 B.C. or earlier–after 404 B.C.): This ancient Greek historian is the founding father of the modern political science school of realism, which sees the international system as resulting from configurations of state power. Carrying the rank of *strategos* in the Athenian military, he both fought in the Peloponnesian War and wrote about it.

Vegetius (fl. 4th century A.D.): The avatar of adequate training and preparation of military forces, Vegetius preached the necessity of proper development of superior military capability prior to battle. He wrote his treatise *Epitoma rei militaris* at the request of Emperor Valentinian, divining how the "ancient Romans" organized and utilized their legions so that Rome's military prowess might be resuscitated.

Suggested Reading

Hanson, *Ripples of Battle*.

Jay, *Management and Machiavelli*.

Koliopoulos and Platias, *Thucydides on Strategy*.

Machiavelli, *The Art of War*.

Thucydides, *The Peloponnesian War*.

1. In your own personal or professional life, what is a situation where power remains paramount? Thinking about your own situation, what advice might you give the Athenians or the Melians?

2. Think of a way that you or your associates are stuck using traditional tactics. Recalling how General Pagondas outmaneuvered the Athenians, try to think of a completely new way to behave that might catch a competitor or opponent you face off guard.

3. Considering the action-response dynamic that infuses Sun Tzu's writings, resolve to replace at least one way that you are merely working through an established list or procedure with a more deeply considered response to the circumstances you actually face.

4. Survey competitors or potential competitors in your environment. Do they have quirks or weaknesses that you know about? How might you, like Hannibal, exploit such knowledge to outmaneuver them when they're falsely feeling most confident?

5. Write out all areas where you, your workplace, or another organization you care about has uncommonly strong reserves. Where can you hold off deploying all those resources? How might you spring those resources on a competitor suddenly and with overwhelming effect?

6. Consider your own approach to good and bad fortune. Think back to an unexpected situation that overwhelmed you in the past. What have you learned from it? What personal traits could you cultivate in order to handle similar situations more effectively in the future?

The Origins and Relevance of Ancient Strategy
Lecture 2—Transcript

A good strategy is a process, dynamic and emergent. A bad strategy is a static plan, little more than a thoughtless checklist. Throughout history, we see average thinkers enter the world of strategy-making with a flawed preconception of what constitutes great strategy.

They sometimes search for a "secret strategy," when the real secret is thinking strategically. They search for a secret external to them, when the secret is within them—perhaps. Strategy is no simple schedule; it's no formula in a manual. This perspective on strategy has informed the best military commanders of history and continues to inform the best leaders of today, wherever they compete.

So in this lecture we'll learn strategic lessons from five of the best military commanders and thinkers in history. As we do, try to come up with ways that these lessons can be relevant in your own life and work. These lessons must be adapted to your own situation; remember, the person who merely follows a checklist will always lose to the rival who knows when to abandon the checklist.

The ancient world learned this lesson painfully, again and again, only with the spilling of much blood. But the meaning and importance of strategy eventually became crystal clear—at least to a few—and it is the hard-won clarity of the ancients that we should strive to acquire as thoroughly as possible.

The first steps toward strategic thinking are the most precarious, so you may want to pause the lectures in this course several times to think hard about your own professional or personal challenges. For this lecture in particular, learn from the challenges these thinkers met. Then try to apply the principles you learn in this lecture to improve your own strategic thinking.

So let's examine the origins of strategy in the ancient world, with focus on a handful of the most influential thinkers and practitioners. They aren't the only great strategic figures of ancient times, of course. But each of the figures we consider represents a fundamental turning point in the development of strategic thinking.

Just as important, although military affairs were the crucible for their insights, what they have to offer can inform our own efforts at strategic thinking in many areas of life, whether in business, as parents, or in the community.

Let's begin in ancient Greece in the 5th century B.C. An aristocrat by the name of Thucydides fought in a great war between the Greek city states of Athens and Sparta, which lasted 27 years—from 431 to 404 B.C. Thucydides carried the rank of strategos or general, and he penned a history of the war until the year 411. His masterful *History of the Peloponnesian War* offers insights about causes and effects. It focuses on the behavior and motivations of the two sides and excludes references to the acts of gods and goddesses. It is what might be called "scientific history" and carries much of the character of a modern historical account. Nearly 2500 years later, this ancient treatise serves as the starting point for the field of international relations, the foundation for a school of thought called political realism, in our earliest account of strategic thinking in action.

Thucydides wrote clearly, concisely. In fact, his work exhibits a coolness and detachment. And it conveys skepticism about concepts such as justice—especially in this short and famous passage from a dialogue between the Athenian military and inhabitants on the Aegean island of Melos. In this so-called Melian Dialogue, the Athenians forthrightly asserted their superior armed might as the only arbiter required to exact Melian cooperation.

"You know as well as we do that right, as the world goes, is only in question between equals in power ... while the strong do what they can and the weak suffer what they must."

In this one key passage, notions of fairness, justice, reason, even intervention by the gods, were swept away. Ancient Greece in the time of Thucydides was a squabbling group of city-states that constantly aligned and realigned themselves into different coalitions when they weren't uniting to battle with enemies external to Greece.

In modern terms, these cities sought a balance of power so that no city-state could grow strong enough to dominate its neighbors.

So here is our first lesson. Thucydides wrote about power, and the Melian Dialogue presents us today with an archetype for power politics or realpolitik. In your own professional life, what is a situation where power remains paramount? Is there a market or competitive field where overwhelming force or vicious competition is not only the most effective strategy, but the only logical one? How can you leverage your organization's advantages to score an overwhelming victory?

But here's something surprising: despite the fact that the generals of Athens were called strategos, there wasn't a lot of actual strategy in use. In fact, you might take it as a rule of thumb that the longer a conflict drags on—as the Peloponnesian War actually did—the more likely it is that one or both sides lack an effective strategy.

So when we want to see strategy at work within the Peloponnesian War, we find ourselves looking at an apparently insignificant battle that featured none of the leading generals from either side.

This was the Battle of Delium in 424 B.C., where the Thebans defeated the Athenians. Historian Victor Davis Hanson has said this: "What went on for about an hour or so in that nondescript plain changed the life of ancient Greece and the nature of European civilization itself." The consequences of this battle, according to Hanson, included a transformation of philosophy (Socrates fought in the battle), an artistic renaissance, and the creation in the West of infantry tactics.

On the surface, this astonishingly important battle seems like every other ancient bloodletting. During this time, the engagement of hoplite infantry was a standard and sanguinary affair. Some soldiers wore heavy armor, some not. Multiple hoplite phalanxes totaling thousands of armored soldiers would crash into each other. They would slash with edged weapons until one side or the other would be literally pushed off the field of battle, leaving thousands of dead and dying behind.

In such a melee, generalship was hardly needed. The Greeks prized personal courage, and the leaders of both sides joined their troops in chaotic battle.

But this battle at Delium unfolded very differently. We are not quite certain how or why, but an obscure Theban general by the name of Pagondas exhibited a radically new mode of combat.

Pagondas was the Theban general who led his people to victory over the Athenians. We know almost nothing about Pagondas except that his brilliant moves at Delium meant a tremendous breakthrough in the science of tactics. He not only assembled his resources differently, positioned them differently, and maneuvered them differently, he commanded them differently as well.

The stakes of this battle at Delium are obscure. There was, in fact, no reason at all to have the battle in this particular place, other than the two sides elected to fight it—no key features of the terrain that made this stretch of territory inherently valuable; there was nothing urgent at stake.

The course of the battle was straightforward. The Athenians marched out to the valley near Delium with 20,000 troops, but they turned back after their supporting troops failed to appear. Rather than allow the Athenians to flee, General Pagondas urged the Thebans to pursue and close with them. In this move, Pagondas developed the principles of forward defense, later embraced by Vegetius. And the principle of preemption—striking an enemy that poses a long-term threat rather than an immediate threat.

The battlefield itself was rippled with gentle slopes, able to conceal bodies of troops. A ravine to the left and a ravine to the right marked the boundaries of the field and channeled the forces toward each other. Pagondas and his Thebans defended a vigorous attack on their left while attacking on their right. This was standard, as both sides traditionally posted their finest troops on the far right flank.

The battle raged for an hour, and as the Athenians pressed their attack on the Theban left, they sensed victory. But then a specter appeared, charging the Athenians from over the nearest hill. It must have been a terrifying sight!

Fresh companies of Theban cavalry, held in reserve now attacked in concert with the infantry. They must have been conjured from the air itself!

General Pagondas had ordered them forward at the moment of greatest peril. This was unheard of! This was extreme! This was the first recorded use of deliberate reserves joining an attack. And integrated with horse cavalry, it was psychologically devastating to the Athenians, who panicked. Their ranks shattered, and they fled.

Four incredible things had occurred at once—first, General Pagondas had maintained a reserve force of cavalry and he had maneuvered them out of sight to his extreme left. Second, at the moment of seeming Athenian triumph, he ordered his cavalry forward to surprise, to disrupt, and to cut down the Athenian infantry. Third, unlike his Greek counterpart, General Pagondas was not at the forefront of the fighting. Instead, he monitored the situation and controlled his forces from a distance, much as a modern general might do. And fourth, he had deepened the ranks of his own right wing to give added weight to his flank and ensure superiority at that point.

Pagondas was also responsible for other innovations. He created a unit of shock troops with a select band of 300 called the "charioteers and footsoldiers." This is the first use of what we call today an elite corps or special forces. Delium also saw the first use of a flame thrower, which Theban forces used to scourge the remnants of Athenian troops, who had taken refuge after the battle in the Precinct of Apollo at Delium.

And so, the battle of Delium counts as the birthplace of a science of Western tactics. It is here, at Delium, that the abstract knowledge of how to manipulate forces on the battlefield to overcome enemy numerical superiority, unfavorable terrain, or inadequate training and weaponry began.

The old checklist approach had been replaced. Just crashing and slashing into one another with all one's might had been replaced. The arrival of tactics meant that forces could appear at special times, have special abilities, use special formations, and place the commander in a special location.

So here we come to our second strategic lesson for today: surprise innovations can often turn the tide of an evenly matched struggle. So here's your task—where are you stuck fighting a battle with traditional tactics? Can you think of a completely new way to fight, one that will catch your competitor or opponent off guard, just as General Pagondas outmaneuvered the Athenians through innovation?

Roughly contemporaneous with the internecine Greek wars of the 5th century and halfway around the world, another civilization was spawning another influential contributor to strategic thinking.

China offers us one of the most well-known examples of strategic theory, *The Art of War*, popularly attributed to Sun Tzu. Some scholars have suggested the work might have several authors, or even that Sun Tzu might be wholly mythical, but a majority of scholars now think that the author was an actual historical figure, a military general named Sun Wu who served under King Helu of Wu in and around 512 B.C. This work was perhaps expanded by others in subsequent centuries, and it greatly influenced military thinking in Asia and impacted Western military thought beginning in the 19th century.

Sun Tzu's brilliance lay not in providing a checklist of how to wage war or to compete against one's enemies, but in his recognition of the fluid nature of reality and how any practitioner of strategy must constantly adapt to that reality.

In fact, Sun Tzu enunciated his principles so that they can apply in several arenas from the battlefield, to public administration and planning, to diplomacy and international negotiation.

Key to Sun Tzu's thinking—and the lesson of his work for our own strategic thinking—is his realization that all plans are temporary. Sun Tzu knew that a plan can become obsolete as soon as it's crafted. He said that the decision to position your forces in competition depends on two major factors. The decision must be based first on objective conditions in the physical environment and second, the subjective beliefs of your competitors in that environment.

Here, Sun Tzu originates a view shared by elite strategic theorists all the way to the present—that the most brilliant plans are those that spring into being in the dynamic of action and response. In hindsight, the plan can appear foreordained, however brilliant, but it is really the result of decision and counter-decision in the heat of moment by those trained to think strategically and tactically.

This action–response dynamic infuses Sun Tzu's writings with power and confers on those writings their relevance today. Sun Tzu thought that strategy was not mere planning in the sense of working through an established list. Instead, strategy requires rapid responses to changing conditions based on sound judgment and principles. Sure, planning works in a controlled environment, but in a rapidly changing environment, competing plans collide, and this collision creates unexpected situations. It is our response to those unforeseen situations that mean the difference between victory and defeat.

Sun Tzu's approach to the study of war elevated the activity to the realm of philosophy, digging a deep foundation for what, to some, might appear the work of the artisan, of the craftsman. For Sun Tzu, the activity of war was too pivotal in the lives of men to leave to the whim of mere practitioners. He said this: "Warfare is the greatest affair of state, the basis of life and death, the Way (Tao) to survival or extinction. It must be thoroughly pondered and analyzed."

Again, let's pause and think. How can you apply Sun Tzu's lessons to your own life? Where do you rely on an outdated plan? Think like Sun Tzu—figure how and why your plans went awry, and how that understanding can help you correct course.

Hannibal Barca was a Carthaginian general who plagued the Roman Republic from the 3rd century into the 2nd century B.C. He fought the Romans to a great victory in 216 B.C.—a victory that has forever stood as the archetype for a crushing annihilation of an enemy. Hannibal fought outnumbered in the enemy's homeland, and he still won. He succeeded in this thanks to his different approach to battle.

In 216 B.C. at the Battle of Cannae, Hannibal triumphed over the numerically superior Romans thanks to his revolutionary manipulation of the forces at his disposal. This new approach to battle earned him the title Father of Strategy by one of his biographers Theodore Ayrault Dodge, himself a courageous veteran of the American Civil War.

At the time, the standard tactics dictated that formations of soldiers would line-up abreast of each other in a phalanx, march forward, collide, and do battle with much pushing and shoving. It was thought that numerical superiority was the key to victory. Hannibal was outnumbered badly, so he should have lost.

But, armed with fewer resources than his Roman enemies, Hannibal configured his forces differently. He didn't follow "best practices" of his day and line his soldiers up in the usual way. Instead, he outmaneuvered and outsmarted his Roman enemy with a battle plan that turned the Romans' own tactics and tendencies against them. It was Hannibal's bold way of thinking that yielded his success in battle, not the following of a checklist of the contemporary strategy.

Hannibal's forces were outnumbered: estimates vary, maybe 80,000 Romans versus 40,000 infantry and 10,000 cavalry. In the conventional military thinking of the day, this meant a Roman victory should be inevitable. Especially as we note that Hannibal's forces were a motley collection of mercenaries from Africa, Spain, and Gaul and were more poorly armed than their Roman counterparts. But the Carthaginians had the advantage of superior strategy and tactics under superior generalship.

Here are the ways that Hannibal upended the conventional thinking of his time. Opposing Hannibal was the Roman army under two consuls—Paulus and Varro—and they rotated command of the army each day. Paulus was cautious and Varro was impetuous. This Jekyll and Hyde leadership arrangement meant discontinuity in execution. In fact, Hannibal knew the hotheaded Varro was commanding on the day of the battle, and he counted on Varro's fervor to lead the Roman army to its destruction in a series of blunders.

First, the Romans marched forward in a narrow and deep phalanx that matched the front of Hannibal's smaller force. The Romans could have easily extended their front to either side of the Carthaginians. That maneuver alone might have saved them from eventual destruction. But they did not. The Romans presented a narrow front, and this alone greatly negated the Roman numerical advantage. Of what use are superior numbers if the vast majority of them cannot reach the enemy?

Second, Roman training dictated that they pursue a fleeing opponent. So, when the Gauls and Spaniards to their front appeared to break and withdraw, the Romans pressed forward. This left the African infantry to the Roman flanks, where they were most vulnerable.

Third, the Romans were taken unawares at a change in cavalry tactics. Once Hannibal's cavalry had driven off the Roman cavalry, his horsemen did not pursue the Romans as was customary. Instead, the horsemen fell upon the rear of the masses of Roman infantry, which became more tightly packed by the minute. The envelopment of the Romans was complete, their destruction inevitable.

Hannibal achieved the greatest and most complete victory in the history of warfare by utilizing not superior numbers and strength. But by superior strategy and extraordinary tactical execution to envelope a superior foe and completely destroy it.

Fifty thousand Roman soldiers died that day—not from lack of equipment, not from lack of numbers, not from lack of courage; they perished because of superior strategy and flawless execution. And that is Hannibal's lesson for us—when faced with superior competitors, you can use your knowledge of their habits and weaknesses to outsmart them. Pause now; survey your own competitors. Which ones have quirks or weaknesses that you know about? How can you invert commonplace thinking and outmaneuver them when they're falsely feeling most confident?

The most brilliant of strategic contributions are often those we take most for granted. The world at large has largely forgotten the man called Vegetius. And this is because his brilliance has become our commonplace.

Vegetius was a Roman administrator who lived in the late 4th century A.D., during a period of Roman decline. In fact, the empire disintegrated a century later. At the request of Emperor Valentinian, Vegetius prepared a treatise called *Epitoma Rei Militaris*, or *A Summary of Military Matters*. With the Roman Empire in decline, Emperor Valentinian wanted to know how his own "ancient" Romans had organized their military matters so successfully.

The result was Vegetius's *Summary*, which became the most popular military handbook for more than 1000 years after its publication. It became, in fact, the military bible of Europe until the Napoleonic era. George Washington carried a copy with him, and even made his own notations.

Open a copy and discover a list of seemingly pedestrian topics—the selection of recruits, their training in arms, and the training in battle formations; organizational topics of unit division, promotion and pay, and auxiliary services; legion battle tactics; and the use of fortifications and naval power.

A layman might ask, "How does this detailed and mundane prescription for the organization of a Roman legion link to high concept strategy? Where is the theory? Where are the secrets of battle, the keys to victory?" The key, as we shall see time and again, lies here—in our own minds, in our cerebrations.

The triumvirate of strategy is intentions, capabilities, and resources. The whole of Vegetius's work addresses how the military may develop its capability to achieve the aims of strategy.

The dominant theme running throughout Vegetius's work is built around the development of superior military capability prior to battle. He hammers home the quartet of thorough training, strong discipline, hard work, and sound planning. These are the elements of strategic preparation that form the heart of strategic capability.

Key among his directives was an emphasis on need for strategic reserves, and he was quite specific as to their use.

Vegetius wrote this:

> It is much better to have several bodies of reserves than to extend your front too much. [Reserves] should be posted in rear of the wings and some near the center, to be ready to fly immediately to the assistance of any part of the line which is hard pressed, to prevent its being pierced ... and thereby to keep up the courage of the soldiers and check the impetuosity of the enemy.

Here in Vegetius, we find echoes of General Pagondas centuries earlier at Delium, who first exercised the use of a reserve force to decisive effect. Vegetius codified this notion and many others. The work of Vegetius was too late to resuscitate the failing Roman Empire, but his prescriptions guided military thought and organization for 10 more centuries. Few ideas are that durable.

You probably have strategic reserves in your own business conflicts. Stop and write out all areas where you feel that your own company has uncommonly strong reserves. Where can you hold off deploying all your resources to lure your competitors into a false sense of confidence? How can you spring these resources on the competitor suddenly and with overwhelming effect?

As in so many other areas, the Renaissance saw a flowering of political theory and strategic thought. Niccoló Machiavelli is one of the most important political theorists in history. He is a bridge from the ancient to the modern. The World of Machiavelli—the time of the Renaissance, which began in the Italian city of Florence in the late 1300s. Machiavelli was born in Florence 1469 and received an excellent humanist education. He worked in several government positions as civil servant and diplomat, and he grew increasingly distressed by the inability of Italian city-states to resist the increasingly bold incursions of France, Spain, and the Holy Roman Empire.

In 1512, the government of Florence was overthrown by a Spanish army, and Machiavelli was put in jail, tortured, and exiled to his farm outside of Florence in 1513. It was there he began to reflect and to write.

His most famous work, *The Prince*, has cemented his place in history. But we are equally concerned with Machiavelli's lesser-known work—*The Art of War*, published in 1521.

Prior to Machiavelli, much writing and instruction emphasized moralizing and divine guidance. In *The Prince*, Machiavelli advocated a more coldly reasoned line of behavior to maintain a monarch in power—a ruthless pursuit of self-interest. *The Prince*, in fact, was a manifesto of guidance that Machiavelli prepared for the Italian ruling family of the Medicis. In *The Art of War*, Machiavelli extended this amoral reasoning to the battlefield.

In the welter of political advice that Machiavelli crafts, he offers to us two key concepts worth our consideration—virtù and fortuna. Virtù and fortuna represent the internal and external elements of strategic thinking. Let's look at each, in turn. Virtù is not, as we think of it today, virtue—the notion of living life as a good and pious fellow, someone imbued with moral excellence—far from it.

As with so much of the analytically rich writings of Machiavelli, virtù is a word freighted with substance and nuance. It incorporates many qualities in combination—flexibility, foresight, individuality and ability, energy, political acumen, prowess, vital force. Virtù is a skill you can develop, sharpen just as you might practice the professions of weaver or blacksmith or tailor, each with its own vocational requirements.

Machiavelli says this:

> A ruler must be half lion and half fox, a fox to discern the toils, a lion to drive off the wolves. Merciful, faithful, humane, religious, just, these he may be and above all should seem to be, nor should any word escape his lips to give the lie to his professions. ... He should, if possible, practise goodness, but under necessity should know how to pursue evil.

Coupled with virtù is the notion of fortuna. Conventional thinkers of the time treated Fortuna as a mostly benign goddess, as the source of human goods as well as evils. In contrast, Machiavelli conceived fortune as a malevolent and uncompromising source of human misery, affliction, and disaster.

An unpredictable and destructive force, and Machiavelli therefore counseled that the good general must "beat and maul" Fortune into submission, so as to rule or be ruled. Machiavelli believed that one should meet the external forces of fortuna aggressively. One cultivates virtù to overcome the destructive caprice of Fortuna.

Machiavelli put it this way: "Fortune is still a fickle jade, but at least the half our will is free, and if we are bold we may master her yet."

Machiavelli's metaphors lack our enlightened view of gender, but following his advice is not about being evil. Instead, this is what we today would call a bias toward action. It's a call for boldness, decisiveness. The impetuous and active ruler is rewarded. In *The Art of War*, virtù describes the strategic prowess of the general who adapts to different battlefield conditions as the situation dictates. "In a word, he must realize and face his own position, and the facts of mankind and of the world."

This is what virtù provides: the ability to respond to fortune at any time and in any way that is necessary. This joining of actor with the environment is an early formulation of the concept of emergent strategy. Since we cannot predict what fortuna will hand to us, we must focus and develop the internal qualities and capabilities that enable us to meet those uncertainties in the best manner possible.

So this is your last challenge for today. Ask yourself, "Do I have virtù? Have I developed the flexibility, foresight, and energy to outwit even unpredictable fortune?" This isn't an easy question to answer honestly. Think back to an unexpected situation that overwhelmed you in the past. Have you learned from it? And if not, how can you?

The ancients of strategy provide us not only enjoyable tales of long-ago battles, but of actual modes of thinking and practical guidance that we can use right now.

First, start with tactics. Any area, no matter how dominated by thoughtless effort, can be transformed by the application of tactics. Try to have special forces used at special times in special ways.

Second, plans must change. Learn to recognize the fluid nature of reality and how any strategy must constantly adapt to that reality. The most brilliant plans are those that spring into being in the action–response dynamic of the moment.

Third, prepare, prepare, prepare. Strategic preparation is the heart of strategic capability, and this has been true every since the Roman Empire. Whether you're running a household or a billion-dollar business, training, strong discipline, hard work, and sound planning are the foundation of strategic reserves, which are necessary for many kinds of strategic maneuver. If you have no reserves, you have no strategy.

Fourth, know your opponents. You can gain astonishing leverage if you know the preparations and capabilities of your opponents. A combination of surprise and superb tactical execution can allow you to defeat an opponent with twice your strength.

Fifth, boldness. You can seize your fortune. The greatest challenge in strategic thinking is getting started. The long and hoary tradition of strategic thought has already struggled with issues we face every day—that's why it's a natural gateway to strategic thinking in our own lives. We can learn from ancient strategic ideas, but even more important is to learn from their example—to have strategic ideas of our own.

The Dawn of Modern Strategic Thinking
Lecture 3

The study of early-modern military strategy enables us to discover deep lessons of how strategy emerges, how it comes to terms with the environment, and how it can help us achieve our goals. Napoleon himself urged careful study of the great military strategists as the surest way to become a great captain. Thus, in this lecture, we examine the contributions of Napoleon, Clausewitz, Jomini, and the geopoliticians.

The Enlightenment and Strategic Thinking

- Beginning in the 17th century, the Enlightenment mobilized the power of reason to reform society and advance knowledge across numerous fields—science, politics, medicine, education, and war. Inevitably, the Enlightenment emphasis on reason and its exploration of the fundamentals of social life would prompt new thinking about war.

- The 18th-century works of the French general Maurice de Saxe and Frederick the Great began to outline the battle principles that would lay the groundwork for **Napoleon**. Saxe revived and extended the Roman insights transmitted by Vegetius. Frederick the Great's most important achievement came in the ability to drill large numbers of troops effectively.

- The ascension of Napoleon marks the dawn of the modern era of strategic thinking. All of the elements for a military strategic revolution were present: new thinking, new technologies, and increasing populations.

Napoleon

- Studying Napoleon enables us to discover deep lessons in how strategy has developed from its ancient forms, how it has come to terms with an environment that changes constantly, and how it can confer competitive advantage in the goals we pursue. Napoleon himself urged careful study of generals from the past.

- The Napoleonic era stretched roughly from 1799 to 1815. Napoleon declared himself emperor in 1804, and he became, for a time, the master of continental Europe, achieving military victories over a series of European coalitions. Napoleon exemplifies strategic thinking in that he demonstrates the power of ideas over material resources.

In Napoleon, the elements for a revolution in military strategy came together in a "perfect storm."

- Napoleon's insights into strategic thinking and other topics are distilled in a volume called *The Military Maxims of Napoleon*. These serve even today as a practical guide to how a great strategic mind approaches tactical problems and weaves their solution into a coherent whole.

- Napoleon recognized that some people view strategy as a checklist of techniques. The unspoken assumption here is that if you learn the techniques, then you, too, can be a great general. This is possibly the greatest danger for us as strategic thinkers today: to think of strategy as a formula. On this point, Napoleon said, "Unhappy the general who comes on the field of battle with a system."

- He also understood the paradox that the best strategy can be overturned by its very implementation. He said, "In war, theory is all right so far as general principles are concerned; but in reducing general principles to practice there will always be danger." The key, instead, is to retain flexibility and cultivate the skill of responding to an opponent's actions.

The Strategies of Central Position and Indirect Approach

- Napoleon used the strategies of central position and indirect approach throughout his campaigns in the early 19th century. Which strategy he chose depended on such factors as terrain, weather, troop numbers, and overall capabilities as he judged them.

- When Napoleon was outnumbered, he would use the central position strategy, maneuvering his army to a position between the coalition armies facing him and driving a wedge between them. He would then seek battle with one army while leaving a masking force to hold the second in place.

- This maneuver was the expression of Napoleon's almost maniacal devotion to the principle of concentration in time and space. The idea here is that when you attack, you mount a preponderance of force at the point of attack, even if you are outnumbered overall.

- When Napoleon had strength comparable to his opponents and room to maneuver, he would use the strategy of indirect approach. This involved positioning a small force to the front of the enemy to feign a major attack. Simultaneously, the main force would march to the enemy's flanks or rear, placing Napoleon's troops on the enemy's lines of communication and supply and forcing the enemy to fight at a disadvantage or withdraw.

Antoine Jomini

- Napoleon is tightly bound up with the names of the two most influential military theorists of the 19th century, **Antoine Jomini** and **Carl von Clausewitz**. Both offered powerful interpretations of the Napoleonic Wars, and they influence the making and implementation of strategy even today.

- Jomini was a Swiss citizen and an officer in Napoleon's Grand Armée. He rose to prominence by his writing on military matters, and his *Art of War* is the work often credited with being the first to define strategy, tactics, and logistics as three distinct realms. Of these, defining the overall principles of strategy was his primary concern.

- According to Jomini, the fundamental principle of strategy was concentration, specifically, concentration of forces at the decisive point on the battlefield. This concentration consisted of four interrelated elements.

  o The first element involves bringing the majority of forces to bear on the decisive areas of a theater of war and the enemy's communications, without compromising your own. In modern-day business, this might equate to bringing resources to bear on a single critical part of the competitive market.

  o The second element is maneuvering to engage major forces against only parts of the enemy's forces.

  o The third element is using tactical maneuvers to bring major forces to bear on the decisive area of the battlefield that it is important to overwhelm.

  o Finally, the fourth element is to ensure that these forces at the decisive location are put into action quickly. In other words, it isn't enough to concentrate your resources at a critical place and time; your organizational control must be such that you can deploy those resources to achieve your goal.

- In addition to the principle of concentration, Jomini brought geometric precision to strategy and tactics, developing 12 geometric orders of battle, or specific geometric formations to engage an enemy.

Carl von Clausewitz
- Clausewitz was a Prussian officer whose posthumously published *On War* remains an influential treatise on strategy. He positioned war in a larger context, demonstrating the connections between the military and political spheres.

- Clausewitz viewed conflict as a function of three variables: violence, chance, and political aims. It was the job of the strategist to balance these three to achieve victory.

- Of the three, the variable with the most relevance for us as strategic thinkers is the element of chance—the interplay of the military commander's courage, talent, and skill with the capabilities at his disposal. In the furor of battle, Clausewitz believed that the commander's insight—what he called coup d'oeil ("glance of the eye," lightning insight)—in the face of chance was the key to victory.

- Military establishments today recognize the importance of intuition in battle, and the latest research suggests that intuitive decision making can be taught.

The Influence of Jomini and Clausewitz

- The impact of Jomini was seen in the latter 19th century, while Clausewitz achieved greater prominence in the 20th century.

- In the American Civil War, Jomini's influence inspired the tactics of massed frontal infantry assaults on both sides that led to massive casualties. But the fault is not Jomini's; rather, it is the commanders who thought of strategy in terms of a checklist.

- The Civil War also yielded several practitioners who appeared ahead of their time in their creativity and ability to adapt to fluid and chaotic situations. They recognized the futility of massed infantry assaults against an entrenched enemy armed with long-range rifles and minié balls.

  o The Southern general **Stonewall Jackson** believed in maneuver and surprise as powerful weapons, not just enhancements of the "real business" of making war. His Shenandoah campaign of 1862 was a brilliant demonstration of the power of feint, deception, and speed of maneuver as force multipliers.

  o Nathan Bedford Forrest, another Southern general, summed up his own strategic theory with the aphorism "Get there first with the most." This short phrase encompasses a core of strategic theory that includes surprise, maneuver, objective, speed, capabilities, and mass. Forrest's 1864 victory over a Union force at the Battle of Brice's Crossroads exemplified Jominian principles, particularly that of concentration.

- o Much later, in the Second World War, General **Heinz Guderian** led Hitler's panzers across Belgium and France following the same principle as Forrest: applying overwhelming force at a single point and then pursuing an enemy relentlessly.

- World War I was the most horrific cauldron of war and death the world had known to that point. Military strategists of the time attempted to concentrate their forces as prescribed by Jomini, but they failed to recognize that technology had shifted the advantage to the defense.

- The horrors of World War I led to a rethinking of strategy. The prominent military thinker Basil Liddell Hart concluded that the frontal assault had limited utility; instead, he advocated his own theory of indirect approach that took into account the new weapons introduced in World War I, particularly the armored tank.

- In the 1930s, other strategic theories emerged as responses to changing political and technological conditions. One of the most notorious of these was the field of geopolitics and its insight known as geographical determinism: Geography determines the destinies of states and the fate of men.

- o One of the most famous dictums of geopolitics was formulated by **Sir Halford Mackinder** in 1904, and it is ominous in what it portends: "Who rules Eastern Europe, commands the Heartland. Who rules the Heartland, commands the World Island. Who rules the World Island, commands the World."

- o Geopolitics was adopted by Nazi Germany as a pseudoscientific justification for German expansion, but today, the field has made a comeback.

Takeaway Points from Early Military Strategists

- The two tools worth remembering from these early military strategists are the indirect approach and the strategy of the central position. But we must also learn how and when to use such tools. For instance, the frontal assault is used far too often.

- Strategic thinking requires much more than memorization of principles; it requires you to develop a keen and agile mind that is capable of independent and responsive thought.

Names to Know

Bonaparte, Napoleon (1769–1821): Once master of continental Europe, Napoleon is best remembered for a departure from his normally crisp execution of strategy when he failed to mask his flank and rear at the battle whose name is synonymous with defeat—Waterloo. Yet his legacy also extends to this day in the realms of the civil law tradition, modern civil government bureaucracies, and military theory and practice.

Clausewitz, Carl von (1780–1831): The way we think about war and strategy cannot be divorced from this 19th-century officer and theorist, who revolutionized strategy in the same way that Adam Smith revolutionized economics. He fought in the Napoleonic Wars for both the Prussians and the Russians and participated in the battles of Waterloo and Borodino. He died in 1831, and it was left to his widow, Marie, to prepare his manuscript *On War* for posthumous publication.

Guderian, Heinz (1888–1954): A great theorist and practitioner of the art of swift tank warfare, Guderian's *elan* and mastery of the battlefield were rivaled only by the great Erwin Rommel.

Jackson, Thomas (Stonewall; 1824–1863): Ahead of his time with regard to battlefield tactics, General Jackson's motto during the American Civil War was to "mystify, mislead, and surprise" the enemy.

Jomini, Antoine (1779–1869): Theorist and general, Jomini authored the bible of 19th-century military strategy and influenced the world's militaries of that era more than any other individual theorist. He is distinguished by his effort to apply geometrical concepts to the battlefield.

Mackinder, Sir Halford (1861–1947): A geographer by trade, Mackinder is forever linked to efforts to create a social science of geopolitics by dint of his famous formula for achieving world domination that appeared in a pivotal article in 1904.

Suggested Reading

Buskirk, *Modern Management and Machiavelli*.

Chandler, *The Military Maxims of Napoleon*.

Clausewitz, *On War*.

Gray, *Modern Strategy*.

Jomini, *The Art of War*.

Liddell Hart, *Great Captains Unveiled*.

———, *Strategy*.

Von Ghyczy, Von Oetinger, and Bassbord, *Clausewitz on Strategy*.

Questions to Consider

1. Napoleon's maxims yield surprising insights that transcend the battlefield, and this is doubtless because he was an able administrator and shrewd politician, as well as a superior battlefield general. His preparedness maxim bears consideration and suggests strongly to us that we should assess our strategic position periodically to gauge our readiness to withstand the most likely challenge. Are you prepared for the battlefield?

2. Napoleon's strategy of the central position offers a practical guide to conflict situations in our daily lives that involve two or more allies teaming up against us. The fundamental idea is to concentrate our power in both time and space against only a portion of the opposing strength.

In this way, you can take on opponents who may seem more powerful. Is there a situation in your personal or professional life that is suited to Napoleon's central position strategy?

3. Napoleon's strategy of indirect approach gives us a method to grapple with a foe who is our equal. Rather than attack his or her strength, we approach on an oblique, sometimes feigning a frontal assault with a "demonstration." Companies can do this quite well, just as armies do, approaching opponents from an unlikely direction while leading them to believe that we're approaching exactly where they expect. Identify an oblique approach you might use to challenge one of your competitors.

4. Antoine Jomini attempted to establish "best practices" for the military of his time by demystifying the Napoleonic Wars for his readers. Using best practices is a modern business goal that propels businesses to the frontiers of efficiency. Doing so is not strategy, but it is absolutely essential to success. Do you engage in the best practices of your profession? Are you pursuing best practices in your dealings with others, in the systems that support your daily life?

5. Clausewitz placed great stock in the notion of the general's coup d'oeil, or battlefield intuition. Each of us can develop our judgment and decision-making abilities, but coup d'oeil means going beyond basic analysis and listening to our intuition. Has there been a time in your life when your intuition or a "hunch" provided you with the needed solution to a problem? If so, analyze where that insight came from and cultivate the habit of listening to your intuition rather than suppressing it.

The Dawn of Modern Strategic Thinking
Lecture 3—Transcript

Our thinking about strategy and conflict changed dramatically with the coming of the era of Napoleon in the late 18th century.

The American and French Revolutions of that century dramatically changed the international, political, and social landscapes. These revolutions gave birth to new forms of government rooted in the values of the Anglo-Scottish Enlightenment and in the Continental Enlightenment of the previous hundred years.

The Enlightenment mobilized the power of reason to reform society and advance knowledge across numerous fields—science, politics, medicine, education, and war.

It was inevitable that enlightenment emphasis on reason and exploration of fundamentals of social life would prompt new thinking about war. Intelligent men began to question the way we think. They questioned the way we compete. And, they questioned the way we think about competing.

The 18th century works of the great French general Maurice de Saxe and Frederick the Great began to limn the outlines of battle principles that would lay the groundwork for Napoleon Bonaparte. Maurice de Saxe, in a work published posthumously in 1757 called *Reveries on the Art of War*, revived and extended the Roman insights transmitted by Vegetius. Frederick the Great's most important achievement came in the ability to drill large numbers of troops so effectively that they could, for example, fire their weapons twice as fast as the enemy.

It is with Napoleon, one of the greatest European soldiers ever to stride the stage of history, that we mark the dawn of the modern era of strategic thinking. All of the elements for a military strategic revolution were present: new thinking, new technologies, and increasing populations. All that was needed was the melding of the right man with the moment to assemble them to powerful effect. The ascension of Napoleon to the role of Europe's greatest soldier came as the result of this perfect storm.

We look now at Napoleon's genius and the two great theorists of the 19th century who interpreted his battles for us—Antoine Jomini and Carl von Clausewitz.

We study Napoleon to discover lessons, deep lessons in how strategy has developed from its ancient forms, how it has progressed and come to terms with an environment that changes constantly, and how it can confer competitive advantage in the goals we pursue.

Napoleon himself urged careful study of the greatest generals in his famous Maxim Number 78. "Read, and reread the campaigns of Alexander the Great, Hannibal, Caesar, Gustavus Adolphus, Turenne, Prince Eugene, and of Frederick the Great; model yourself after them; that is the only means of becoming a great captain and of acquiring the secrets of the art of war. Your genius enlightened by this study, you will then reject every maxim contradictory to those of these great men."

The Napoleonic era stretched roughly from 1799 to 1815. This was a 16-year period that saw the military and political rise of Napoleon Bonaparte. His rise paralleled the fall of the French monarchy and success of the French Revolution in 1789.

Napoleon named himself Emperor in 1804, and he became for a time the master of all of continental Europe and sought to spread the ideals of the French Revolution—*liberte, egalite, fraternite*. He reformed the French legal system and introduced the Napoleonic Code, the influence of which can still be seen and felt in the modern civil law constructs of 21st-century Europe.

His greatest fame, however, stems from his many military victories over a series of European coalitions. Napoleon exemplifies strategic thinking in that he demonstrates the power of ideas over material resources. He often fought and won against numerically superior forces, which leaves us with the question: How did he do it?

Thorough preparation and development of superior capabilities, superior strategy based on superior capabilities, and crisp execution of the proper tactics to fulfill that strategy.

The contribution of Napoleon to strategic thinking is manifold. Throughout his career, the great general would record his insights, and they are distilled in a famous volume called *The Military Maxims of Napoleon*. They are useful and they are pithy, and I think they'll delight you as much as they delight me. His own maxims serve even today as a practical guide of how a great strategic mind approaches tactical problems and weaves their solution into a coherent whole. You solve these tactical problems not singly, but in a comprehensive, linked fashion that is designed to achieve greater aims.

Napoleon's thinking was so clear, so purely focused on the battlefield that his axioms speak with immediacy. Like thunderbolts from the past. An army which cannot be re-enforced is already defeated. The moment of greatest peril is the moment of victory. An army ought to be ready every moment to offer all the resistance of which it is capable. There is only one favorable moment in war; talent consists in knowing how to seize it.

A commander in chief ought to ask himself several times a day: If the enemy should appear on my front, on my right, on my left, what would I do? And if the question finds him uncertain, he is not well placed, he is not as he should be, and he should remedy it.

Napoleon recognized that some people view strategy as a checklist of techniques. The unspoken assumption here is if you learn the techniques, then you, too, can be a great general. This is possibly the greatest danger for us as strategic thinkers today, to think of strategy in this one-dimensional manner; to think of strategy as static, or as a formula. On this point, Napoleon said: "Unhappy the general who comes on the field of battle with a system."

Napoleon understood well this paradox. The best plan, the best strategy, can be overturned by its very implementation. Napoleon said, "In war, theory is all right so far as general principles are concerned; but in reducing general principles to practice there will always be danger."

Certainly you have to understand the fundamental principles of conflict— this is essential to any strategic thinker. But we cannot stop there. It is in the execution of our strategy that we discover our mettle—not to blindly follow our own plan, but to adjust what we do to what our competitor does, in a constant process. Napoleon exalted flexibility and the skill of response to an opponent's actions.

Napoleon offered us two great strategies that he employed throughout the Napoleonic wars of the early 19th century. These strategies were certainly available to others had they but employed them in the same way as Napoleon with the same preparation and vigor.

For it was what Napoleon did at the front end and at the back end of the battle that made his strategy work. Napoleon first developed the capabilities necessary to execute them. Second, he executed his strategy with attention to detail and follow-through. He constantly adapted his maneuvers to the changing conditions of the battlefield.

Let's look at Napoleon's two broad strategic maneuvers: the Strategy of the Central Position and the Strategy of Indirect Approach. Time and again, Napoleon employed these maneuvers at the appropriate place and time to achieve victory. The strategy he chose depended on several factors, including terrain, weather, numbers of troops involved, and overall capabilities as he judged them.

When Napoleon fought outnumbered, he would use the Central Position strategy, maneuvering his army to a position between the coalition armies facing him. He would drive a wedge between them. Because of command and control difficulties of the time, the two opposing armies could not coordinate their actions. Napoleon would seek battle with one while leaving a masking force to hold the second army in place. He would destroy the first in detail and then turn on the other.

This maneuver was the expression of Napoleon's almost maniacal devotion to the principle of concentration in time and space. Concentration means that when you attack, you mount a preponderance of force at the point of attack, even if, overall, you are outnumbered.

Napoleon put it this way: The secret of great battles means knowing how to deploy and concentrate at the right time. The art of war means being able, even with an inferior army, to have stronger forces than the enemy at the point of attack or at the point which is attacked.

With this strategy of the central position, Napoleon could achieve the highest concentration of men in the primary battle while limiting the enemy's ability to concentrate his forces. This maneuver served him well for years. And he used it in his last battle.

This was Napoleon's battle plan at the 1815 Battle of Waterloo, located in Belgium. Napoleon began to drive a wedge between the two allied armies on June 16 and he recorded several small victories against the Prussians the next two days. Then he turned to face the British. He sent a masking force to block the Prussians from regrouping or reinforcing, but this force, under Marshall Grouchy, failed to find the Prussians.

The Prussians, under Marshal Blucher, slipped through the screen. They fell upon the French flank at the crucial point of the battle, after Napoleon had already committed his reserve. This was Napoleon's final and greatest defeat, an ignominious rout.

It was not the preparation that failed. It was not the strategy that was flawed. It was in the execution of the strategy that Napoleon's Grand Armée was defeated—the failure to mask his flank and rear from the Prussians.

What of the other strategy? That of the indirect approach? When Napoleon had strength comparable to his opponents and room to maneuver, he would use the Strategy of Indirect Approach. He would position a small force to the front of the enemy. This force would "demonstrate"; it would skirmish, feigning a major attack.

Simultaneously, the French main force would swiftly march to the enemy flanks or to the rear. Presumably, the enemy would be distracted by the "demonstration" skirmishing at the front and be surprised by Napoleon's swift march to the rear.

Napoleon would place himself on the enemy's lines of communication and supply. The enemy would be forced to fight at a disadvantage, or withdraw, losing much in the retreat.

Now, apart from his military maxims, Napoleon left us no great compendium of his strategic perspective or of his personal system of battle. It was left to others to analyze his battles and to tease from them the strategic secrets locked within.

Napoleon is tightly bound up with the names of the two most influential military theorists of the 19th century—Antoine Jomini and Carl von Clausewitz. Both theorists offered powerful interpretations of the Napoleonic wars, and they influence the making and implementation of strategy even today. In fact, the lessons of Napoleon are largely the lessons of Jomini and Clausewitz.

Antoine Jomini was a Swiss citizen and an officer in Napoleon's Grand Armée, a student of the campaigns of Frederick the Great. He first rose to prominence by his writing on military matters, which brought him to the attention of Marshal Ney, an officer whom Napoleon called the "Bravest of the Brave." No mere armchair theorist, Jomini fought with distinction at the battles of Austerlitz and Lutzen. He spent the last decades of his life as a general and advisor for the Russian tsar.

Throughout his professional life, Jomini sought the lodestone of military art to divine the secrets of battle. And in his *Art of War* (1838), he believed he had discovered them. This is the work often credited with being the very first to define strategy, tactics, and logistics as three distinct realms. Of these, defining the overall principles of strategy was his prime concern.

Jomini said: "There have existed in all times fundamental principles, on which depend good results in warfare. ... These principles are unchanging, independent of the kind of weapons, of historical time and of place."

According to Jomini, the fundamental principle of strategy was that of concentration. Concentration of forces at the decisive point on the battlefield. This concentration consisted of four interrelated elements:

First, bringing, by strategic measures, most of your forces to bear upon the decisive areas of a theater of war and upon your enemy's communications, without compromising your own.

If we apply this principle of concentration to modern-day business, one way it can play out is if we bring our resources to bear on a single critical part of the competitive market, whether that be a critical geographical location or a critical demographic of a particular market segment. In this way, we can match or overmatch a larger competitor in a particular slice of the market.

Second, maneuvering to engage your major forces against parts only of those of the enemy.

Third, by tactical maneuvers, to bring major forces to bear on the decisive area of the battlefield or on that part of the enemy's lines that it's important to overwhelm.

Fourth, ensuring that these masses of men brought to bear at the decisive place are put into action fast and together to make a simultaneous effort.

This means that it isn't enough to concentrate your resources at the critical place and time; your organizational control must be such that you can deploy those resources to achieve your goal, whether to destroy an enemy army or to surprise a competitor with a market launch that floods a particular market segment with a new product.

In addition to the principle of concentration, Jomini brought geometric precision to strategy and tactics. I mean this literally.

Jomini believed in the geometry of war. He introduced geometric principles of angles and force to space ratios into analysis. Jomini developed 12 geometric orders of battle. These orders of battle consisted of specific geometric formations, ways to engage an enemy. These basic geometric formations included: parallel, L-shape, reinforced wing(s), reinforced center, oblique line, concave line, concave broken up into an echelon (with successive waves or units of troops), center attack plus one wing attack.

The wise general chooses whichever order of battle is in accord with the appropriate principle. In this, Jomini has been criticized as the ultimate reductionist, reducing strategy to a checklist.

But Jomini was far from this simplistic. Jomini's purpose was to impose order upon chaos and to demystify the Napoleonic Wars for generals and laymen alike. He recognized that the circumstances of time and place mattered a great deal. That the same principles of action would not hold true if a battle was conducted in places as varied as desert, swamp, plain, or mountainous terrain. But the principle was where you started.

Jomini's great contemporary was Carl von Clausewitz. Jomini and Clausewitz did not like each other, but such dislike doubtless sprang more from their natural competitiveness than from their theoretical differences. They were, after all, both men of war, shaped by the battles they fought. And, of course, they fought on opposite sides.

Clausewitz was a Prussian officer whose posthumously published *On War* (1832) remains today the most influential of military treatises on strategy. He positioned war in a larger context. Clausewitzian thought moved us from the battlefield and into the halls of kings and presidents and demonstrated the connections between the political and military spheres.

Clausewitz viewed conflict as a function of three variables—violence, chance, and political aims. It was the job of the strategist to balance these three inputs to achieve victory. Of the three, the variable with the most relevance for us as strategic thinkers is that element of chance—the interplay of the military commander's courage, talent, and skill with the capabilities at his disposal as pitted against an opponent. In this grappling with an opponent in the furor of battle, Clausewitz believed that the commander's insight in the face of chance was the key to victory.

He called this *coup d'oeil*—the Glance of the Eye, or lightning insight. This is one of the greatest contributions of Clausewitz, this notion of swift and intuitive decision making in battle. Only recently has cognitive psychology caught up with Clausewitz. Military establishments today, particularly the United States Marines, recognize the importance of intuition in battle—or *coup d'oeil.* Moreover, the latest research suggests that intuitive decision making can be taught.

This doesn't mean that everyone can become a Napoleon. It does mean that our own decision making can be sharpened if we learn to listen to that amalgam of experience and expertise that percolates in our consciousness just below the surface. Napoleon himself believed in the efficacy of intuitive decision making. Napoleon was partial to the notion that the general's piercing insight in the heat of a battle would yield victory.

Napoleon said this: "The issue of a battle is the result of an instant, of a thought. There is the advance, with its various combinations, the battle is joined, the struggle goes on a certain time, the decisive moment presents itself, a spark of genius discloses it, and the smallest body of reserves accomplish victory."

This insight doesn't come from mere God-given ability. It is not a quality that stands apart from the principles of conflict. Instead, it arises from the thinker's learning and experience and immersion in those principles. It comes from a deep understanding of the strategist's craft and of figuring out what to do when the principles don't apply.

The impact of Jomini was seen in the latter 19th century while Clausewitz achieved greater prominence in the 20th century. Part of Jomini's initial impact may have been a result of his long life, his many writings, and his relentless self-promotion—he survived Clausewitz by almost 40 years and died in 1869.

Jomini's influence can be seen in the American Civil War, in particular, and it inspired the tactics of massed frontal infantry assaults on both sides that led to massive casualties. But the fault is not Jomini's; rather it is the commanders who thought of strategy in terms of a checklist. If technology had outstripped the prescribed strategic and tactical execution of Jominian principles, then profound strategic thinking would have adapted those principles to the changed technological circumstances.

Some did adapt. The Civil War yielded several practitioners who appeared ahead of their time in their creativity and ability to adapt to fluid and chaotic situations. They recognized the futility of massed infantry assaults against an entrenched enemy armed with long-range rifles and the devastating new round—the Minié ball.

Southern General Stonewall Jackson believed in maneuver and surprise as powerful weapons, not just enhancements of the "real business" of making war.

His Shenandoah campaign of 1862 was a brilliant demonstration of the power of feint, deception, and speed of maneuver as force multipliers. Jackson's motto was, "Always mystify, mislead, and surprise the enemy."

Another Southern general's battlefield thinking was so far ahead of its time that it was not until the second world war that his battlefield maneuvers would be fully appreciated and utilized by a new generation of warriors. Nathan Bedford Forrest's most famous aphorism appears deceptively simple, even simplistic: "Get there first with the most." But this short phrase encompasses a core of strategic theory that includes surprise, maneuver, objective, speed, capabilities, and mass.

It's not likely that the self-taught Forrest studied Napoleon or Jomini, but he understood strategy at a visceral level. Perhaps no other general of the Civil War employed the principle of concentration better than Forrest. His 1864 victory over a Union force twice the size of his own at the Battle of Brice's Crossroads exemplified Jominian principles.

This was Forrest's masterpiece and the archetype example of pursuing an enemy until he is all but destroyed. In this Mississippi battle, Forrest engaged and defeated a larger force and then led a 60-hour pursuit of panicked Union forces, halting the chase only after he, himself, was no longer able to physically remain in the saddle from exhaustion.

It was this element of strategy more than any other that turned the Civil War into a protracted conflict. That bloodiest of all American conflicts was fought from 1861 to 1865. Four years. Given the overwhelming preponderance of

Northern objective advantages, the war should have lasted no longer than two years. Strategic thinking and leadership was the difference.

Much later, in the Second World War, General Heinz Guderian led Hitler's panzers across Belgium and France in 1940, following the same principle as Forrest, applying overwhelming force at a single point and then pursuing an enemy relentlessly.

World War I was the most horrific cauldron of war and death the world had known up to that point. For four years, hundreds of thousands of soldiers hurled themselves over open ground against machine guns and resulted in a bloodletting and human slaughter on a titanic scale. Strategy is partly to blame—the strategic culture of militaries of time advocated the offensive *a outrance*, or to "the bitter end."

They were attempting in World War I to concentrate their forces as was prescribed by Jomini, but they had failed to recognize that technology had shifted the advantage to the defense.

World War I saw a collision of obsolete strategy—horse cavalry charges that had worked in 1870, for instance—with the new weapons of war like the machine gun.

The horrors of World War I led to a rethinking of strategy, and one of the most prominent military thinkers of the early 20th century developed a strategic theory that appears quite powerful and is useful outside the purely military affairs.

Basil Liddell Hart's study of the frontal assault in hundreds of battles over two millennia of war led him to conclude that the frontal assault had limited utility. He advocated his own theory of indirect approach that incorporated firsthand experience of World War I with the new weapons introduced in that conflict, particularly the armored tank.

Basil Liddell Hart's deep development of the strategy of the indirect approach appears an amalgam of earlier thought, but it gained a sense of urgency from the horrific casualties suffered in World War I on the Western front.

As we moved from World War I into a new era of warfare in the 1930s, other strategic theories emerged as responses to changing conditions, political as well as technological. One of the most notorious of these was the field of geopolitics, made notorious by its most enthusiastic proponents.

At the heart of every great theory is an insight so blinding and yet so obvious that it inspires thousands. The problem comes when the insight is pushed beyond its natural limits and entire philosophies are built around it, to the exclusion of other, perhaps equally, valid insights.

Geopolitics arose in the early 20th century, and eventually claimed status as a separate social science. It was geographical determinism: Geography determined the destinies of states and the fate of men.

Sir Halford Mackinder believed that particular geography bestowed certain immutable advantages on the holder of particular terrain. Moreover, these advantages, over time, could lead a nation-state under a determined leader to eventually extend influence over the entire world.

One of the most famous dictums of geopolitics was formulated by Sir Halford Mackinder in 1904, and it is ominous in what it portends: Who rules Eastern Europe, commands the Heartland. Who rules the Heartland, commands the World Island. Who rules the World Island, commands the world.

But geopolitics soon suffered as it was adopted by Nazi Germany as a pseudo-scientific justification for German expansion. But today, geopolitics has made a comeback. The term has seeped into the public discourse as a kind of rhetorical incantation to lend *gravitas* to what one says.

Two lectures from now, we devote an entire lecture to the contribution of geography to our understanding of strategy. From the Enlightenment theorists to Napoleon and on into the 20th century, modern military thought about strategy has gained clarity and precision. Here are some key points:

Regardless of how chaotic a situation may be, there are principles that can give shape to your thinking about the situation. Immersion in such principles allows for *coup d'oeil* flashes of insight. The upshot of this 200-year stretch of strategic history is that there are unvarying principles of strategy, but they are akin to techniques. They do not stand alone as a magic formula. They do not transform a soldier into a great general.

No, there is no checklist to guarantee victory. Theorists give us tools: Two tools worth remembering are the indirect approach, and the strategy of the central position. But we must learn how and when to use such tools. For instance, the frontal assault is used far too often. Strategic thinking requires much more than memorization of principles. Strategic thinking requires you to develop a keen and agile mind that is capable of independent and responsive thought.

Strategic thinking requires you to develop yourself as a strategist, and you do this by thorough preparation of your capabilities—a unique set of capabilities—understanding of general principles of conflict, and detailed tactical follow-through.

So keep your own strategic thinking capabilities in mind as we turn next time to a consideration of current-day strategic principles, starting with those of the United States Army.

Modern Principles of Strategic Conflict
Lecture 4

The hallmark of a sound principle is its successful application, across time and circumstances. In situations of competition and conflict, the principles of war that we'll look at in this lecture offer us guiding ideas for executing any strategy against a determined opponent. In the effort to learn how to think strategically, the principles of conflict are a valuable tool.

France, Spring 1940

- In the spring of 1940, the French, safely behind their impregnable Maginot Line, believed they were ready for a German attack. But the line left a small portion of the Belgian border unprotected, especially the area covered by the dense Forest of Ardennes. The French thought the Ardennes would deter the Germans from attacking in that region.

- The Germans, however, had no intention of grinding their army against the French Maginot Line. Instead, they attacked through the Ardennes and, in doing so, achieved that rarity in modern warfare: strategic surprise.

- The Germans combined two strategic principles: (1) the assembly of activities in innovative ways and (2) the indirect approach. They launched what became known as blitzkrieg, or lightning war, combining the use of tanks, aircraft, and infantry, and they swung around the French defenses, invading Belgium and, ultimately, cutting the Maginot Line off from the rest of France.

- In delivering the knockout blow to France, the Germans used an assortment of tactical principles of war to realize their strategic intent: offensive, mass, maneuver, economy of force, and surprise.

- The hallmark of a sound principle is its successful application, across time and in situations in which the technology, place, and combatants may change, but the principle holds true. Let's now turn to a set of principles of war distilled by the British colonel John Frederick Charles Fuller during World War I and adopted (in slightly different form) by the U.S. military.

Principles of War

- Objective: Direct every military operation toward a clearly defined, decisive, and attainable objective.

- Offensive: Seize, retain, and exploit the initiative.

- Mass: Mass the effects of overwhelming combat power at the decisive place and time.

- Economy of force: Employ all combat power available in the most effective way possible; allocate minimum essential combat power to secondary efforts.

- Maneuver: Place the enemy in a position of disadvantage through the flexible application of combat power.

- Unity of command: For every objective, seek unity of command and unity of effort.

- Security: Never permit the enemy to acquire unexpected advantage.

- Surprise: Strike the enemy at a time or place or in a manner for which it is unprepared.

- Simplicity: Prepare clear, uncomplicated plans and concise orders to ensure thorough understanding.

Objective

- The ultimate military purpose of war is the destruction of the enemy's armed forces and will to fight. Of course, the ultimate objectives of operations other than war are considerably less destructive; nevertheless, it's important to have a clear objective or mission.

- This objective must be clear to everyone who has anything to do with the planning and execution of operations. At the personal level, we must be clear in our ultimate objective; it must inform and guide our use of all the principles.

- Too often, we get bogged down in the minutiae of the task, confusing tactics with the goal. History is replete with master tacticians who were unable to connect to the larger strategic picture. Even Robert E. Lee has been faulted as being a master tactician but a mediocre strategist.

- Any operation must have a purpose, and that purpose must be clear from the beginning. Each operation must contribute to the ultimate strategic aim. The attainment of intermediate objectives must directly, quickly, and economically contribute to the operation.

- The army uses an analytical framework of mission, enemy, troops, terrain, and time available (METT-T) to guide it in rapid development of its operations. Commanders designate physical objectives, such as an enemy force, dominating terrain, or other vital areas essential to the mission. These then become the basis for all subordinate plans, and no action is taken that doesn't contribute to achieving the main objective.

- Likewise, in your own strategic planning, the mission or objective must dominate and condition your thinking and actions. To adapt the military framework, think of the "enemy" as a competitor, your "troops" as your employees or your own energy and resources, and the "terrain" as the organizational landscape in which you maneuver.

Offensive
- The second principle of competition tells us that offensive action is the best way to attain an objective. Such action is effective and decisive.

- Offensive action is how we seize and hold the initiative while we maintain our freedom of action. In war, sports, business, and politics, this is fundamentally true across all levels of operations. We "play defense" only as a temporary necessity and only as a respite before we can seize the initiative and continue our offensive actions.

- The reason for this should be clear: The side that retains the initiative through offensive action forces competitors to react rather than allowing them to act.

Mass
- Mass is the synchronization of combat power in concentrated time and space on the enemy. In everyday terms, the idea is to deliver a massive blow to your competitor.

- Applying this principle is not as easy or as intuitive for some people as it may seem. Synchronizing the many moving parts of a large organization is difficult in the best of circumstances. Moreover, in situations other than war, we may seek less of a massive battle and more of an accommodation.

- Nonetheless, when the decision is made to join the battle, this principle suggests that we mass our resources for a decisive engagement. We must also sustain our massed resources and our attack so that the effects have staying power.

Economy of Force
- Because the mass we have is never unlimited, we also need economy of force. We must deploy and distribute our resources so that no part is left without a goal to accomplish.

- In military operations, combat power is finite and must be used judiciously. It is allocated to various tasks in measured degree—limited attacks, defense, delays, deception, or even withdrawal operations. All of these must be carefully measured so that we can achieve mass elsewhere at the decisive point and time on the battlefield.

- In business, we must be likewise judicious and not squander our resources in peripheral ventures.

Maneuver

- The principle of maneuver enables us to go after bigger prizes. In competition, we want to position ourselves for maximum advantage. How this advantage is measured varies according to the enterprise. For instance, you might be maneuvering against other job-seekers, other mid-level executives, or other candidates in a political race.

- Maneuver is the movement of forces in relation to the enemy to gain positional advantage. Effective maneuvering keeps the enemy off balance and is used to exploit successes, to preserve our own freedom of action, and to reduce vulnerability.

- Prudent and vigorous maneuvering continually poses new problems for the enemy. It renders the enemy's actions ineffective and can eventually lead to defeat.

- At all levels of operations, successful application of maneuver requires agility of thought, plans, and organization. It's also necessary for us to apply the previous principles of mass and economy of force.

- Our ability to maneuver is how we can determine where and when to join the fight, by setting the terms of battle, by declining battle, or by acting to seize unexpected tactical advantage.

- By maneuvering with skill, we can make ourselves unpredictable and, thereby, raise uncertainty and hesitation in the minds of our competitors.

Unity of Command

- Responsibility is a totem that many people pay homage to but honor only when absolutely necessary. In fact, diffusion of responsibility and closed-door decision making seem to be characteristic of modern corporate America. But in arenas of conflict, responsibility cannot be abdicated. Unity of command and unity of effort are required if the objective is to be reached.

- In the military, unity of command means that all forces are under one commander who has the authority to direct them in pursuit of a unified purpose. Unity of effort, on the other hand, requires coordination and cooperation among all forces—even though they may not necessarily be part of the same command structure—toward a commonly recognized objective.

- Unity of command is an ideal that shortens response time and leads to rapid decision making and execution, but it is not always attainable; this is why unity of effort becomes paramount.

Security
- Security is a precondition for unity of effort. To protect our position from competitor encroachments, it's necessary to recognize that we can't make plans and execute them without considering our competitors' actions. We have to protect our own resources, market share, goal line, operations, and personnel.

- The security of our plans and capabilities enhances our freedom of action by reducing risk. Active security reduces our vulnerability to hostile acts, influence, or surprise.

- If we know and understand our competitors' strategy, tactics, doctrine, and staff planning, if we can anticipate their likely courses of action, then we can take adequate security measures.

Surprise
- Surprise, if achieved at the strategic level, can bestow such incredible advantage on one side that it settles any outstanding question. In conflict, surprise stands as a force multiplier.

- It follows that you want to surprise your opponents, and you want to do so as often as possible to keep them off balance and interfere with their plans.

- Surprise can be achieved through speed, effective intelligence, deception, application of unexpected force, operations security, and variations in tactics and methods of operation.

Simplicity

- Pulling all these principles together is the principle of simplicity. The simpler the plan, the better the chances of executing it successfully. This is especially true in large organizations or with complex projects.

- In the corporate world, it is the simple and direct strategy with simple execution that best marshals the resources and spirit of the firm. Simple plans and clear, concise orders minimize misunderstanding and confusion.

- Simplicity in plans allows better understanding and leadership at all echelons and permits branches and sequels to be more easily understood and executed.

Summarizing the Principles

- John Fuller, the British officer who first enunciated these nine principles, suggested that they can be remembered by grouping them under three headings: control, pressure, and resistance.

- If we remove these principles from the venue of war and consider them simply as methods for dealing with a pesky adversary or aggressive competitor, their universal applicability becomes more apparent.

- As we'll see in lectures to come, these principles make a valuable contribution to the effort to think strategically—to exert a measure of control over a chaotic and sometimes hostile world.

Suggested Reading

Alger, *The Quest for Victory.*

Buskirk, *Frontal Attack.*

Foch, *Principles of War.*

Ries and Trout, *Marketing Warfare.*

1. Consider how, in 1940, the French erred as a result of military thinking rooted in World War I. Are your own ideas the product of older experiences, perhaps no longer relevant to the modern challenges you face today? Do an "idea inventory" to see if your conception of how the world works measures up to 21st-century dynamics.

2. Before considering the principles of conflict in this lecture, honestly assess the principles that guide your thinking now. Are they successful? Do you find yourself constantly outmaneuvered at work, in sports, in your personal life?

3. Choose any three principles of conflict and consider whether they have been used against you recently. You should be able to recognize maneuvers for what they are and, with a bit of preparation, guard against them with the principle of security.

4. Choose any three principles of conflict and apply them to a situation you face in your daily life. Consider whether the application of these principles might improve your chances of success.

Modern Principles of Strategic Conflict
Lecture 4—Transcript

Let's visit France in the spring of 1940. No, not the cafés and bistros of the Champs-Élysées. Come with me to the frontier between France and Germany, where the two hostile states are faced off against each other. This is the beginning of World War II. The two nations have been at war since the previous autumn, and Germany has already overrun Poland, but it's been a phony war here on the Franco-German border. Almost no fighting between France and Germany. A *Sitzkrieg*, as some folks cleverly called it.

Should the Germans attack? The French are ready—or so they think. The French sit behind their impregnable Maginot line, a series of strongpoints and forts built the entire length of the Franco-German border and manned by 15 percent of the entire French army. Imagine yourself in one of these forts, designed to stop a direct German attack across the border—built of concrete, bristling with weapons, and the largest of them staffed with 1000 soldiers each. Impregnable!

The French had learned the lesson of the previous war: that technology dictated that defense had an almost insurmountable advantage. And so the French acted accordingly.

But the line of forts stopped in the north at the Belgian border. The forts did not reach to the English Channel. And so a small portion of the Belgian border area was relatively unprotected, especially the area covered by a dense forest called the Ardennes. This forest was thought to be impassable to tanks and motorized transport.

The French thought that the Ardennes was a barrier that would deter the Germans from attacking in that sector. This is what the French expected, and it probably made sense to conventional military thinkers. It had a kind of internal logic. But on the German side of the border, the thinking was different.

New and revolutionary doctrines of war had been developed by a new generation of young and brash military officers, such as Erwin Rommel and Heinz Guderian. These theorist-soldiers recognized the new reality of the changing technology of war. They recognized the power of the armored tank and the deadly future of mechanized warfare, the power of mobility and massed firepower.

The Germans had no intention of fulfilling their role in the French battle plan; they had no intention of grinding up their army on the French Maginot Line. And so, the Germans did not attack directly across the border into the teeth of the French defensive line. Instead, the Germans attacked through the Ardennes. Exactly where the French did not expect an attack. And in doing so, the Germans obtained that rarity in modern warfare—Strategic Surprise.

The Germans combined two strategic principles. Both have been used since ancient times. First is the assembly of activities in new and innovative ways. The second is the principle of the indirect approach. Remember the tale of Hannibal at the Battle of Cannae in our first lecture? How Hannibal had taken the conventional arms and armies of the time and assembled their activities in new and effective ways for spectacular results? The same thing occurred here—in France—in May of 1940.

Military technology had advanced since 1918, the end of the First World War in Europe. But military establishments had generally failed to recognize how the new technologies would transform the battlefield of the next war. This was particularly true of mobile warfare involving the tank. Generals are usually accused of fighting the last war, and this occasion was no different.

The Germans launched what became known as Blitzkrieg—or lightning war. This involved using the available technology in new and different ways. In this case, they used it in new and deadly ways. They combined the use of tanks, aircraft, and infantry in what we today call "Combined Arms" warfare. In 1940, it was an innovation.

The second strategic principle the Germans used was the Strategy of Indirect Approach. Rather than hurl themselves against the French defensive wall in a frontal assault, they swung around the French defenses. The Germans invaded Belgium and split the French army. They turned the French left flank and then cut the Maginot Line off from the rest of France.

It was over in six weeks. The Germans had defeated France and the British Expeditionary force, which fled ignominiously at Dunkirk—one of the most complete victories and most humiliating defeats in military history.

In delivering the knockout blow to France, the Germans used an assortment of tactical principles of war to realize their strategic intent—offensive, mass, maneuver, economy of force, and surprise.

Let's talk about those principles of war, the principles of competition. All smart and successful organizations make use of war principles but call them something else. So let's do call them "Principles of Competition" because they can be utilized by anyone involved in any conflict, great or small, they can be used at the organizational level, and they can be used at the personal level.

Many countries and many theorists have devised principles of war over the centuries. This noble and venerable lineage stretches back to the time of Sun Tzu, Vegetius, Caesar, Machiavelli, Clausewitz, Jomini, Foch, and many other notables. But regardless of the time and place and personality, the principles have always retained a sameness. They may change at the periphery, but they maintain a steadfast core character.

The hallmark of a sound principle is its successful application, across time, to situations in which the technology and place and combatants may change, but the principle holds true. Principles serve as a north star to guide us, to keep us—generally—going in the right direction.

For this lecture, let us appropriate for ourselves a set of principles of war distilled by British Colonel John Frederick Charles Fuller during World War I and into the mid-1920s and adopted almost immediately (in a slightly different form), by the United States military. These are principles that had been handed down less formally for centuries.

I think the best way to proceed is first to present a quick overview of the principles as found in the U.S. Army Field Manual, second, to review the basics of each principle in more detail and show how each principle can enhance our chances of success in situations of conflict and competition.

The United States Army's Principles of War are nine in number. They consist of: The Objective: Direct every military operation toward a clearly defined, decisive, and attainable objective. The Offensive: Seize, retain, and exploit the initiative. Mass: Mass the effects of overwhelming combat power at the decisive place and time. Economy of Force: Employ all combat power available in the most effective way possible; allocate minimum essential combat power to secondary efforts. Maneuver: Place the enemy in a position of disadvantage through the flexible application of combat power. Unity of Command: For every objective, seek unity of command and unity of effort. Security: Never permit the enemy to acquire unexpected advantage. Surprise: Strike the enemy at a time or place or in a manner for which he is unprepared. Simplicity: Prepare clear, uncomplicated plans and concise orders to ensure thorough understanding.

Let's look more closely at each of these principles. The objective, the ultimate military purpose of war, is the destruction of the enemy's armed forces and their will to fight. Now, the ultimate objectives of our operations other than war are considerably less destructive and warlike. Nonetheless, we must have a clear objective or mission.

Our strategic intent must be clear to everyone who has anything to do with the planning and execution of our operations. Our strategic plan. At the personal level we must be clear in our ultimate objective. It must inform and guide our use of all of our principles.

Too often, we can bog down in the minutiae of the task. We can begin to confuse tactics with our goal. History is replete with master tacticians who were unable to connect to the larger strategic picture. Some critics have faulted the great Civil War General Robert E. Lee with being a master tactician, but a mediocre strategist for failing to connect his many battlefield victories into a coherent campaign with logic, scope, and a vision for a decisive victory in war.

Any operation must have a purpose and it must be clear from the beginning. Each operation must contribute to the ultimate strategic aim. The attainment of intermediate objectives must directly, quickly, and economically contribute to the operation. The army uses an analytical framework of mission, enemy, troops, terrain, and time available (METT-T) to guide it in rapid development of its operations, and commanders designate physical objectives such as an enemy force, dominating terrain feature, or other vital areas essential to the mission. These become the basis for all subordinate plans, and no action is taken that doesn't contribute to achieving the main objective.

Likewise, in our own strategic planning, the mission or objective must dominate and condition our thinking and our actions. To adapt the military framework, you can think of the enemy as a competitor, or simply the forces that challenge you. Your troops are your employees or else your own energy and resources.

Your terrain is the business-scape or the organizational landscape on which you maneuver. That is, your terrain includes the network hierarchy, the physical layout of your firm, the power structure with which you must deal. And if you plan for your firm, your terrain also includes the market space in which you maneuver against your competitors.

The second most important principle is the offensive. This principle tells us that offensive action is the best way to attain our clearly defined objective. It is effective, and it is decisive. Here we reject the adage that "Good things come to those who wait." Instead, we act. We act boldly, decisively, and with purpose.

Offensive action is how we seize and hold the initiative while we maintain our freedom of action. In war, in sports, in business, and in politics, this is fundamentally true across all levels of our operations. We "play defense" only as a temporary necessity, and only as a respite before we can seize the initiative and continue our offensive actions.

The reason for this should be clear. The side that retains the initiative through offensive action forces competitors to react rather than act. In the case of Blitzkrieg, the Germans seized the initiative in 1940 and retained it all the way to the defeat of France

Military doctrine holds that "An offensive spirit must therefore be inherent in the conduct of all defensive operations." I submit that this is true in all situations where strategy is useful.

OK, so you are on the offense (even when you're on defense). What do you actually do? Let's look at mass. Mass is the synchronization of combat power in concentrated time and space on your enemy. In everyday terms, the idea is to deliver a massive blow to your competitor. Generals like to say that it is akin to hitting the enemy with a closed fist, not a poke in the chest with a couple of fingers. Rain on your enemy with a perfect storm.

Now, this is not as easy or as intuitive for some folks as it may seem. Synchronization of many moving parts of a large organization is difficult in the best of circumstances. Coordination is tough. But lots of things conspire against us to throw sand in the gears. Moreover, in more genteel surroundings, far from the grit and gunfire of military battle, we may seek less of a massive battle and more of an accommodation. Our motives and our goals may be complex.

Nonetheless, when the decision is made to join battle, this principle suggests that we mass our resources for a decisive engagement. We must sustain our massed resources and our attack so that the effects have staying power. "Mass seeks to smash the enemy, not sting him," says army doctrine. Germany, in World War II, massed her Panzer tanks for a decisive breakthrough in 1940 against the weakest part of the French line.

But the mass you have is never unlimited. So you need economy of force. Economy of force is wonderfully intuitively named. We economize the forces and resources at our disposal. Fuller, who named it, thought economy of force was the single principle that best summarized all the principles of war. We deploy and distribute our resources so that no part is left without a goal to accomplish. We want none of our energy to languish— unused, neglected, forgotten. "No part of the force should ever be left without a purpose."

In all of this, we strive to attain a balance. It's very much like a cooking recipe to prepare the perfect dish. All of the ingredients must be allocated in the correct proportions. Likewise, in a conflict situation, when the time comes to act, all parts must move in accord with our plan, and all of those parts will have a role to play.

In military operations, combat power is finite. It must be judiciously employed. Given the stakes, nothing can be wasted. We allocate our combat power to its various tasks in measured degree—limited attacks, defense, delays, deception, or even withdrawal operations. All of this must be carefully measured so that we can achieve mass elsewhere at the decisive point and time on the battlefield.

In business, we must be likewise judicious and not squander our resources in peripheral adventures. Short-term gain can be alluring, and in our short-horizon culture in the United States, the short-term gain usually wins out. But the strength of a hunter can be sapped pursuing rabbits when there's big game that requires more patience and all available resources.

How do we go after the big prizes? By the principle of maneuver. In competition, we want to position ourselves for maximum advantage. How this advantage is measured varies according to our enterprise. Do we maneuver against other job-seekers, against other mid-level executives, against a tennis opponent across the net, against other candidates in a political race?

Maneuver is the movement of our forces in relation to the enemy to gain positional advantage. When we maneuver effectively, it keeps the enemy off-balance. We use maneuver to exploit successes, to preserve our own freedom of action, and to reduce our vulnerability.

When we focus on prudent and vigorous maneuver, it continually poses new problems for the enemy. It renders his actions ineffective, and it can eventually lead to his defeat.

Maneuver is much more than simply moving around, whether in sports or in business or in war. At all levels of operations, successful application of maneuver requires agility of thought, plans, and organization. It's also necessary for us to apply the previous principles we learned: mass and economy of force. Our ability to maneuver is how we can determine where and when to join the fight by setting the terms of battle, by declining battle, or by acting to seize unexpected tactical advantage. By maneuvering with skill, we can make ourselves unpredictable and thereby raise doubt and uncertainty and hesitation in the minds of our competitors. But how can a group of people maneuver with skill? We need unity of command.

Responsibility is a totem that many people pay homage to, but honor only when absolutely necessary. In fact, diffusion of responsibility and closed-door decision making seem to be characteristic of modern corporate America. But in arenas where conflict is prevalent, responsibility cannot be abdicated.

For decisive, directed, and focused action, responsibility cannot be diffused. Unity of command and unity of effort are required if the objective is to be reached.

In the military, unity of command means that all the forces are under one responsible commander. It requires a single commander with the requisite authority to direct all forces in pursuit of a unified purpose. Unity of effort, on the other hand, requires coordination and cooperation among all forces—even though they may not necessarily be part of the same command structure—toward a commonly recognized objective.

Of course, unity of command is not always attainable. It's an ideal that shortens response time, leads to rapid decision making and execution. And this is why unity of effort is the handmaiden to unity of command. Even in the military, unity of command may not be possible because of interagency or combined operations, and this is why unity of effort becomes paramount. Unity of effort—coordination through cooperation and common interests—is an essential complement to unity of command.

What is a precondition for unity of effort? Security. We want to protect our own position from competitor encroachments, don't we? And so it's necessary to recognize that we can't make our plans and execute them outside of consideration of our competitors' actions. We have to protect our own resources, our own market share, our own goal line, our own operations, and our own personnel.

We have to shroud our own intentions in a fog of deception and trails of false scents. The security of our own plans and capabilities enhances our freedom of action by reducing our risk. Active security reduces our vulnerability to hostile acts, influence, or surprise. If we know and understand our competitors' strategy, tactics, doctrine, and staff planning, if we can anticipate their likely courses of action, then we can take adequate security measures.

So we're secure. What can unity of effort achieve? Surprise. Surprise is such an important principle in warfare that some writers consider it the single most important principle of strategy. German General Waldemar Erfurth penned a classic treatise on surprise between the two World Wars, and he exalts surprise as a kind of panacea to fighting while outnumbered. Surprise, if achieved at the strategic level, can bestow such incredible advantage on one side that it can settle the question.

Our earlier example of the French defeat in 1940 is one such example of surprise deciding the outcome. Now, of course, many other things had to go right for the attacking Germans for surprise to have its decisive effect. For instance, the advantage bestowed by surprise must be exploited. But by itself, surprise in conflict stands as a force multiplier.

Generals know that surprise can decisively shift the balance of combat power. By seeking surprise, forces can achieve success well beyond the effort expended. We see examples of surprise in conflict almost every day. In sports such as football, trick plays and deception are designed to surprise the opposing team.

We want to surprise our opponent don't we? And we want to do so as often as possible to keep him off-balance and so to interfere with his own plans. Many factors can contribute to surprise. We can achieve surprise with speed, effective intelligence, deception, application of unexpected force, operations security, and variations in tactics and methods of operation. Surprise can be in when we do something, or how fast, the size of resources deployed, and the direction or location of our main effort. Deception can aid the probability of achieving surprise.

Pulling everything we've been discussing together we have the principle of simplicity. Complexity is the enemy of any good plan. The simpler the plan, the better the chances of executing it successfully. This is especially true with large organizations, or with projects that have lots of moving parts.

The military has a saying that originated in Clausewitz. "Everything in war is very simple, but even the simplest thing is difficult." To the amateur strategist and to the armchair general, military operations are not difficult. Hindsight can make military geniuses of us all. We can replay battle after battle, with great realism in today's simulation. But generals have only one time to get it right, and they must get it right as history unfolds and as the bullets fly. On the cusp of a major conflict, with everything still in doubt and thousands of unknown variables poised to affect the outcome in ways we cannot begin to predict; it is the simple plan that is our salvation.

In the corporate world, it is the simple and direct strategy with simple execution that best marshals the resources and spirit of the firm. Simplicity contributes to successful operations. Simple plans and clear, concise orders minimize misunderstanding and confusion. Here's an example. In the 1992 presidential election, Democrat political operative James Carville crafted a simple strategic message and theme for the ultimately successful Bill Clinton campaign. The message embodies several of the principles of competition as we have reviewed them here—the offensive, mass, and simplicity. The message was: "It's the economy, stupid."

This simple, hard-nosed message maintained focus and discipline in a sometimes faltering campaign. It massed effort on the weak point of the opposition party. It was a simple message for the Clinton campaign to execute. And it was a simple message for the rank and file voter to understand. Several very good reasons lobby for simple plans.

Other factors being equal, the simplest plan is preferable. Simplicity is especially valuable when followers and leaders are tired. Simplicity in plans allows better understanding and leadership at all echelons and permits branches and sequels to be more easily understood and executed.

So these are the principles of war, as well as our principles of competition: Have a clear objective in mind, you must have a mission; seize the initiative and don't let go (think of the Germans in World War II versus the French in 1940); mass your efforts on a critical point (this harkens back to Jomini's principle of concentration of mass and outnumbering your opponent on that critical point); use all available power, but only minimal power to secondary efforts; limit your opponent's room to maneuver and expand your own room to maneuver; unity of effort and (where possible) unity of command; secure yourself against your opponent gaining unexpected advantages; surprise your opponent; KISS: Keep it Simple, Strategist!

And if you want an even simpler way to remember the nine principles, John Fuller, the British officer who first came up with such a list suggested they can be remembered in just three groups: Control, pressure, and resistance.

Now these aren't the only strategic principles one might imagine. British Defense Doctrine, for example, has added maintenance of morale to the list we've been discussing. Indeed, a 1982 book by military scholar John Alger identified no fewer than 100 different principles of war offered by various thinkers throughout history.

Moreover, some of us may have an aversion to talk of war and military conflict. In fact, there are certainly theories that argue against competitive and warlike language of this sort. But we can always relocate these principles from the venue of armed conflict. If we consider them simply as methods or ways to deal with a pesky adversary or aggressive competitor, the universal applicability of the principles becomes more apparent. I believe that the ultimate test of whether these (or any) principles are valuable or not is in their utility.

Do they help you achieve your goals? As we'll see further in lectures to come, if the point is to learn how to think strategically—to exert a measure of control over a chaotic world and sometimes hostile world—then, the principles of conflict are a valuable contribution to that effort.

Geography—Know Your Terrain
Lecture 5

Many of the finest thinkers in history have, at various times, discovered geography's enduring impact on the fate of peoples and nations. If geography is immutable, then can we uncover modes of behavior that take advantage of geographical verities? In this lecture, we delve into the influence of micro-geography on our own decision making to discover how our interactions with our physical space in conflict situations can aid or detract from our chances of victory.

Geopolitics

- Geopolitics is a body of systematized thinking about the effects of geography on human politics and conflict. Its premise is that the unchanging characteristics of the physical world in which we live condition human behavior and interactions. In this view, geography has a decisive impact on the interests and actions of nations and peoples.

- The field is sometimes derided as "geographic determinism," meaning that it seeks a single-factor explanation for complex phenomena. Geopolitics also had an unfortunate association with the Nazi aspirations of Adolf Hitler. Today, the core idea of geopolitics is that geography is an important source of political, military, and economic power.

- Geopolitical notions have leavened our way of thinking for years, and some geopolitical truisms have seeped into our discourse. For instance, the development of the American democracy is sometimes explained as a result of the two ocean barriers that shielded the young nation from the depredations of more entrenched European models.

- Geopolitics has even given us "laws" or "maxims" that purport to instruct us on the fundamental effects imposed on humans by geography. According to the geopolitical theorist **Nicholas Spykman**, "Geography is the most fundamental factor in the foreign policy of states because it is the most permanent. Ministers come and ministers go, even dictators die, but mountain ranges stand unperturbed."

- Geography not only matters in the grand sweep of politics, but it also affects us in phenomena closer to home. Further, minor geographical features that may seem inconsequential in isolation can take on tremendous importance as events unfold. The sunken road of Ohain, for example, proved to be disastrous for Napoleon's cavalry at Waterloo.

Inherent Positional Power

- Geography is not important in and of itself. It takes on importance only as human beings and machines use it to a purpose, and its value is usually temporary.

- In competition, the interaction among opponents and the battlefield takes on the character of a three-way dialectic. Opponents maneuver against each other as they interact with the battlefield. Locations on the battlefield take their significance for the moment with respect to the deployment of forces. This is the process of maneuver, or positioning.

- The geography of every battlefield has inherent positional power, whether that battlefield is the field at Waterloo or the office conference room. This inherent positional power arises from the principles of competition that dictate the terms of engagement on the battlefield.

- Of course, the positional power inherent in a battlefield would vary tremendously based on a different rule structure. Strategy would change, as well. For example, changing the geographical position of the goal in a football game would alter both the strategies of the opposing teams and the positional power on the field.

- The football example gives us two notions of power as it springs from geography: potential positional power and realized positional power. Potential power springs from the investment in the battlefield of the technology and tactics available to both sides. Realized power springs from the actual deployment of forces, their condition, their numerical strength, and the skill and timing of maneuver.

Positioning in Chess and Other Forms of Battle

- The game of chess teaches us about deployment of resources, coordination of attack and defense, the necessity of planning and constant evaluation, and the virtue of foresight. It also teaches us much about the critical factor of geography.

- The chessboard consists of 64 squares in an eight-by-eight arrangement, alternately colored dark and light. Given the rules of chess and the resources we know will be deployed, the board offers us verities about the inherent positional power of certain areas of its geography.

- From the standpoint of pure potential power, the center four squares are the most important on the board, and the strategy of a winning game is based on seizing early control of those four central squares. But during the course of the game, the value of the squares changes with every change in the position of the pieces.

- Consider what happens when we add the pieces. As we've seen, the three-way interplay of the two combatants and their relationship to the field of battle is a complex dynamic. Pieces, of course, have a certain power inherent to their ability to move. The more versatile the movement of a piece, the more powerful it is.

- But a piece's power can be enhanced or limited by its location on the board. The pieces on the board in combat derive power from the configuration of their various locations. Conversely, the locations on the board fulfill their power potential from the overall configuration of the combatants. A type of synergy is in effect.

- The seating arrangement in a conference room is similar. It takes on significance from the purported rank of those sitting at the table. Assorted power configurations arise from different seating configurations. The shape of the table and the types of chairs also affect the configuration of power.

- In negotiation, the micro-geography and position of the venue can confer advantage, and we find some competitors attempting to alter the terms of negotiation through physical alterations. For example, at P'anmunjŏm, the demilitarized zone between North and South Korea, such gamesmanship is the norm.

- A good example of the use of space in battle comes from the sport of boxing. Boxers in the ring maneuver against each other in space and time, using a repertoire of feints, punches, jabs, and so on. The space in the ring is finite and featureless, yet each square foot takes on significance vis-à-vis the interaction of the combatants.

Intelligence Preparation of the Battlefield

- The military has developed a systematic and sophisticated method for learning about and understanding the ground on which it is to fight. Its tool is called Intelligence Preparation of the Battlefield (IPB), and it's a process easily adaptable to our own challenges.

- In military scenarios, we know that the "high ground" confers advantages in principle. Conversely, we know that "taking the hill" is a daunting proposition. Rivers, valleys, and mountain ranges offer barriers to an enemy and to our own advance.

- The IPB process systematically assesses the information relevant to friend and foe on a particular battlefield. An intelligence officer collects and evaluates this information continuously and communicates it to the commander, who uses it to support decision making.

- IPB can be easily adapted for use in the business world and in personal decision making. The military's system formalizes and deepens a process that almost everyone conducts informally already.

- The broad lesson we take from IPB is the importance of geography in our own competitive situations. What potential sources of power are locked in the geography of the likely battlefield? How does geography potentially enhance or degrade strategy? Can you modify your strategy to take advantage of geography or to prevent it from degrading your strategy?

Steps in the IPB Process

- First, define the battlefield environment. Identify characteristics of the battlefield that influence both friendly and competitor operations. Establish the limits of the battlefield and identify elements that are unknown but should be known.

- Second, describe the battlefield's effects on operations. This step always includes an examination of terrain and weather but may also include the characteristics of geography and infrastructure and their effects on friendly and threat operations, as well as such factors as politics, civilian press, local population, and demographics.

- The third step is to evaluate the competitor. If the competitor is known, determine how it normally organizes for combat and conducts operations under similar circumstances. This information can be drawn from historical databases and well-developed threat models. With new or less well-known competitors, intelligence databases and threat courses of action may have to be developed simultaneously.

- Finally, determine the competitor's possible courses of action. The main question to be answered here is: Given what the competitor normally prefers to do and the effects of the specific environment in which it is operating, what are its likely objectives and courses of action?

Defense in Depth

- One of the greatest examples of conducting and acting on IPB occurred during World War II. The major lesson of the example is how to respond if you know when and where you'll be attacked. There are several responses to a scenario like this, but the one chosen in this example was brilliant. We'll call it defense in depth.

- This technique was used by the Russians at the 1943 Battle of Kursk. At the time, the Russians held territory, centered on the town of Kursk, that bulged into the German front over an area 120 miles wide and 90 miles deep. In an attempt to cut off the Russian position, the Germans planned an attack from the north and south in a pincer movement.

- But the Russians knew of the attack well beforehand through their intelligence network. Over several months, they prepared successive defense lines, making use of the geography of the area to channel the German attack in directions to make them vulnerable.

- The Russians planned to slow and wear down the Germans by forcing them to attack through a web of minefields, planned artillery fire zones, and concealed antitank strong points.

- The German attack began to stall almost immediately after it started. The Russian defense was like a meat-grinder that chewed up the entire German strategic tank reserve in a week. The Germans never broke through, and the strategic initiative passed from the Germans to the Russians for the last time.

The Lessons of Geopolitics

- Clearly, the effects of geography play into the outcome of battles both great and small. The effects of geography may not be as decisive as geopoliticians would have us believe, but they may be enough to tip the scales our way, if we plan judiciously.

- Regardless of the stakes, if the battle is worth fighting, then it's worth conducting your own IPB to give yourself the greatest chance for victory.

- Geography—your position on the field of battle—should not be left to chance. Select it beforehand, if possible. Note the inherent strengths of the various options open to you, evaluate the conditions of the conflict to come, and manipulate those conditions to your benefit.

Name to Know

Spykman, Nicholas (1893–1943): Spykman is known in some quarters as the godfather of containment, the strategy that guided the United States in its rivalry with the Soviets for 40 years after World War II. Attacked as America's geopolitician during the war for daring to envision a postwar world based on raw power considerations, Spykman's predictions were substantiated in subsequent years after his early passing.

Suggested Reading

Braden and Shelley, *Engaging Geopolitics*.

Brzezinski, *The Grand Chessboard*.

Earle, ed., *Makers of Modern Strategy*.

Hansen, *Foundations of Chess Strategy*.

Hugo, *Les Misérables*.

Landes, *The Wealth and Poverty of Nations*.

Spykman, *America's Strategy in World Politics*.

Questions to Consider

1. We tend to think of "geography" in grandiose terms but sometimes forget that our own micro-geography can lend us competitive advantage. Taking in the "lay of the land" has always been an activity of the finest generals, and developing a practiced eye for the playing field is essential for successful strategic thought. What are the factors that make for a geographic advantage in your own interactions? Do you consciously structure situations to give yourself the geographic advantage?

2. Do your interactions in daily life have rules, either specified or implied? Unwritten rules or conventions can be as important—even more important—than those that are specified. Make a list of unwritten rules in your interactions and identify their sources, whether from tradition or from power relationships. Compare these rules with what is officially

stated and take note of the gap. Does this gap offer room to maneuver for advantage?

3. Intelligence Preparation of the Battlefield is too important and useful a concept to be restricted to the venue of combat. If you face challenges repeatedly on the same ground, in the same place, in the same metaphorical space, then a thorough preparation of that conflict space might be worthwhile for you. It's even more critical when you move onto uncharted terrain. Develop your own principles for dealing with opponents on territory of your choosing and evaluate the pros and cons of that territory.

4. Although we all like to take the initiative, sometimes it's necessary to play defense, and against a strong opponent, this can be demanding. When defending against a powerful opponent, remember the Russian lesson at Kursk: Once a challenger commits, wear him or her down with constant battle and successive lines of defense on well-prepared terrain. This is especially effective when you can choose the battlefield. Identify the resources you could use in a situation in which you were forced to defend your ground against a strong opponent.

Geography—Know Your Terrain
Lecture 5—Transcript

"Geography is destiny!" This phrase, "geography as destiny," occurs and reoccurs in the popular culture. Its persistence, in fact, lends to it a kind of folk-legitimacy that makes us wonder is there not something to it?

Books, studies, and popular discourse continue to give credence to the notion that geographical forces condition human behavior in predictable ways, and that we should understand this power, so better to manipulate it to our ends.

David Landes's powerful 1998 book, *The Wealth and Poverty of Nations*, is constructed on the premise that geographic location is the key factor in explaining economic results worldwide—why some nations are poor and others rich.

We have an entire body of systematized thinking on the effects of geography on human politics and conflict. It is, in fact, a branch of social science that seeks to explain world events in just such determinate terms. This minor discipline has become one of the buzzwords that has grown in popularity since the 1990s, and it often leavens the heady wine-and-cheese conversations that people conduct over international politics.

That discipline is "geopolitics." Geopolitics has been around for as long as recorded history. Even Aristotle engaged in a bit of geographic and ecological determinism when he formulated his conception of "The Ideal State." The geopolitical premise is that the unchanging characteristics of the physical world in which we live condition human behavior and our interactions.

While other influences may be transitory, the permanence of geographic influences can form the basis for explaining the actions of nations and for predicting the future. Geography has a decisive impact on the interests and actions of nations and peoples. In fact, geopolitics elevates geography to primacy in explaining international political activity.

Remember Sir Halford Mackinder's famous geopolitical dictum about Eastern Europe being the key to the Heartland; and thereby the World Island; and thereby rule of the entire World?

Well, with vague metaphorical concepts like "Heartland" and "World Island," it's perhaps not surprising that geopolitics has had critics. The field is also derided as "geographic determinism," just as Karl Marx's economic theories are criticized as "economic determinism." Determinism seeks single-factor explanations of complex phenomena. And geopolitics had an unfortunate run of association with the Nazi aspirations of Adolf Hitler, which tainted the word for more than four decades after the close of World War II.

Today, by contrast, most folks using geopolitics probably have no idea of its lineage, its theories, or even what it means. The core idea of geopolitics is this: Geography is an important source of political, military, and economic power. And different aspects of geography afford different degrees of power. Geopolitical notions have leavened our way of thinking for years. Some geopolitical truisms have seeped into our discourse.

For instance, traditional Swiss neutrality is explained as a result of the surrounding Alps, a mountainous barrier allowing this small country a political choice unavailable to many other nations. Similarly, American democracy is sometimes explained as a result of the two vast ocean barriers that shielded a young and growing nation from the depredations of more-entrenched European models.

The open plains of Eastern Europe explain the many invasions suffered by the Russians from Western Europe throughout history. After all, it's a fact that the eastern banks of the north-south rivers throughout Eastern Europe are an average of six feet lower than the western banks. For traditional armies, this makes invasion from West to East much easier than in the other direction.

Geopolitics has even given us laws or maxims that purport to instruct us on the fundamental geographic effects imposed on humans by geography. After all, with so much theory and thought that is intangible and abstract, it is reassuring that here is a discipline that seems rooted in specific features of reality—that is rooted, quite literally, in the soil. And whose impact does not change. This was the view of Nicholas Spykman, a prominent second-generation geopolitical theorist who died in 1943. Spykman said this: "Geography is the most fundamental factor in the foreign policy of states because it is the most permanent. Ministers come and ministers go, even dictators die, but mountain ranges stand unperturbed."

This is breathtaking stuff, and it plays out on a tapestry of enormous scale, both in time and space. But geography matters not only in the grand sweep of politics. It also impacts us in phenomena closer to home.

Let's consider the micro-geography of situations that arise in our professional lives, both as individuals and for our firms or our teams. Here we talk of how we interact with the ground, the air, our surroundings, in competitive situations; how we interact with the ground we stand on while we interact simultaneously with our opponents. The minor geographical features that may seem inconsequential in isolation can take on tremendous importance as events unfold. They can sometimes take on history-changing importance.

What geographical features? Take the simple matter of, say, a sunken road. A road that cuts down between banks of earth on each side. It is on just such a nondescript feature that world history hinged on June 18, 1815. It was the Sunken Road of Ohain. It was unseen. And awaited its moment in history. A hollow path no more than 12 feet deep in some places and as wide. It stretched across a battlefield for more than four miles. The battlefield? A place called Waterloo.

The maneuvering of great armies against each other is usually described as the product of generalship, or of numerical superiority, or of technological supremacy or innovation. But geography can sometimes play a decisive role in the outcome of great conflicts. The 1815 Battle of Waterloo is one such conflict that offers up a historical pivot point for our consideration.

One of the most stirring accounts of the Battle of Waterloo appears in Victor Hugo's *Les Miserables*. The battle pitted French Emperor Napoleon Bonaparte's 74,000 troops against the British Duke of Wellington and an assortment of Germans, Dutch, Belgians, and Prussians, approximately

70,000 in all. In June of 1815, the two armies had joined the engagement, and the battle had been raging several hours. Napoleon observed the movements of his army from the crest of a ridge. He could see into the valley below and up to the next ridge where began the plateau of Mont Saint Jean.

Napoleon stared and he calculated. The question before him was: Should he send in his *cuirassiers* against the British—his heavy cavalry. Almost 4000 cavalrymen riding gigantic horses, a terrifying sight led by General Milhaud.

The great general surveyed the ground, his keen eye missing nothing. In the classic work of literature *Les Miserables* the writer Victor Hugo described it this way:

> Before giving the order for this charge of Milhaud's cuirassiers, Napoleon had scrutinized the ground, but had not been able to see that hollow road, which did not even form a wrinkle on the surface of the plateau. The Emperor swept his glass for the last time over all the points of the field of battle. He pondered; he examined the slopes, noted the declivities, scrutinized the clumps of trees; he seemed to be counting each bush. He gazed at the English barricades of the two highways ... he observed the old chapel of Saint Nicholas ... he bent down and spoke in a low voice to the guide Lacoste. Put on the alert by the little white chapel, he had probably put a question as to the possibility of an obstacle, to the guide. The guide made a negative sign with his head. ... The guide ... Lacoste ... had answered No. We might almost affirm that Napoleon's catastrophe originated in that sign of a peasant's head.

And Napoleon acted. He ordered his *cuirassiers* forward (that's the armored cavalry, named for the cuirass or breastplate they wear). He ordered his *cuirassiers* to break the infantry squares of the British and to carry the table-land of Mont-Saint-Jean.

The Sunken road of Ohain awaited them—a road that disappeared into a cut not visible from the French commander's position.

And it was on this sunken road that world history turned for a few hours on June 18, 1815. The *cuirassiers* galloped down the hill and up the opposite ridge in two long columns, left and right. But on the right, disaster struck. Again, Hugo describes it:

> The head of the column of cuirassiers reared up with a frightful clamor. On arriving at the culminating point of the crest, ungovernable, utterly given over to fury and their course of extermination of the squares and cannon, the cuirassiers had just caught sight of a trench—a trench between them and the English. It was the hollow road of Ohain. "It was a terrible moment. The ravine was there, unexpected, yawning, directly under the horses' feet, the second file pushed the first into it, and the third pushed on the second; the horses reared and fell backward, landed on their haunches, slid down, all four feet in the air, crushing and overwhelming the riders; the inexorable ravine could only yield when filled; horses and riders rolled there pell-mell, grinding each other, forming but one mass of flesh in this gulf: when this trench was full of living men, the rest marched over them and passed on. Almost a third of Dubois's brigade fell into that abyss.

> This began the loss of the battle.

There is no doubt that had they not been enfeebled in their first shock by the disaster of the hollow road the cuirassiers would have overwhelmed the centre and decided the victory.

Geography is not important in and of itself. A mountain has no inherent value. A river. A plain. A sunken road. Geography takes on importance only as human beings and machines utilize it to a purpose. And its value is usually temporary.

In competition, this interaction takes on the character of a three-way dialectic. Opponents maneuver against each other as they interact with the battlefield. Locations on the battlefield take their significance for the moment with respect to the actual deployment of the forces engaged. This is the process of maneuver, or positioning.

The geography of every battlefield has inherent positional power, whether that battlefield is the field at Waterloo, the office conference room, a football field, or the ordinary chessboard. This inherent positional power arises from the principles of competition that dictate the terms of engagement on the battlefield. It doesn't take much acumen to recognize that the positional power inherent in a battlefield would vary tremendously based on a different rule structure. And strategy would change accordingly as well.

Let's look at sports for an example. Take American football. We know that each team can score a touchdown by moving the ball along the field to one end zone or the other at either end of the football field for a score of six points. This geographic fact conditions the strategy of the game.

But what if we changed this. What if we paint a large red circle in the middle of the field, and we award points for moving the ball into this large red circle. We quickly can see how the positional power of the game's geography would be changed dramatically. The end zone value goes way down and the center of the field assumes incredible importance.

From the previous example, we can see arising two notions of power as it springs from geography. There is potential positional power and there is realized positional power.

The potential power springs from the investment in the battlefield of the technology and the tactics available to both sides. Realized power springs from the actual deployment of forces, their condition, their numerical strength, and the skill and timing of maneuver.

Let's take another example, this one from the game of chess. As an instrument of instruction, the game of chess is a powerful tool in many respects. It teaches us deployment of resources, coordination of attack and defense, the necessity of planning, the criticality of constant evaluation, and the virtue of foresight.

And chess also teaches us much about the critical factor of geography. The chessboard without its pieces is a deceptively simple affair. It consists of a board with 64 squares in 8-by-8 arrangement, alternately colored dark and light. Given the rules of chess and the resources we know will be deployed, the board offers us verities about the inherent positional power of certain areas of the board's geography. Given those rules and resources, technology and tactics, we can see that certain squares have more potential value than others.

Let's examine the board with that in mind. From the standpoint of pure potential power, the center four squares are the most important on the board, and chess is essentially a struggle for control of these four squares as necessary to victory. The eight surrounding squares rank next in importance. And so the strategy of a winning game is based on seizing early control of those four central squares as essential to eventual victory. But during the course of the game, the value of board squares changes with every change in position of the pieces.

Let's consider what happens when we add the pieces. The three-way interplay of two combatants and their relationship to the field of battle is a complex dynamic. Pieces, of course, have a certain power inherent to their ability to move; the more versatile the movement of a piece, the more powerful. But a piece's power can be enhanced or limited by its location on the board. The pieces on the board in combat derive power from the configuration of their various locations. Conversely, the locations on the board fulfill their power potential from the overall configuration of the combatants. A type of synergy is in effect and this is what is meant by interactivity.

Let's move from the chess board to the office conference room. Consider the seating arrangement at a conference table. The seating arrangement takes on significance from the purported rank of those seated at the table. Assorted power configurations arise—configurations of power based on the seating of those attending. The shape of the table, the types of chairs all impact the configuration of power. In negotiation, the micro-geography and position within a venue can confer advantage, the terms of negotiation can be changed to physically alter the position. Let's take an extreme example of the office conference room and the potential power that configuration and environment can confer if manipulated in appropriate ways.

Panmunjom is a small Korean village situated in the demilitarized zone between North and South Korea. It was the site of the armistice that ended the Korean War in 1953 and it still serves as the site of negotiations between the South and the North. The geography and spatial relationships in the negotiating room take on hyper-significance in this highly focused, highly charged touch point. Gamesmanship and high-stakes maneuvering within the cramped confines of the negotiating room is the norm in Panmunjom. Said one journalist: "In one of the conference rooms the North Koreans once sawed a few inches off chair legs so that their counterparts at the negotiating table would look small and silly."

On another occasion, the North Koreans violated the agreed-upon protocol when they attended a round of negotiations with AK-47 assault rifles hidden under their jackets. It was an obvious intimidation tactic, but the allies struck back with their own ploy. They turned up the heat—literally. The Koreans sweated in their heavy clothes but were unwilling to take off their coats to reveal their weapons.

At Panmunjom, positioning and machismo are part of the show. The soldiers assigned to Panmunjom are chosen for their intimidating appearance. The South Koreans must meet a height requirement almost two inches taller than the national average, and they must have a black belt in martial arts. Americans assigned to Panmunjom are selected for their physical bearing and height. In the venue of the negotiating room, this emphasis on space and height is little more than a micro version of seizing the high ground before a confrontation. We face our own version of it in the ubiquitous office meeting.

Let's change our venue to sports and see how this concept of geographical positioning plays out. A good example of the use of space in battle is the sport of boxing. If you're not philosophically opposed, watch a boxing match. Observe the combatants maneuvering against each other in space and in time. Note the repertoire of punch, feint, counterpunch, jab, and cross. Note the combinations of punches. Note that the boxers do not stand in one place slugging it out against each other, they maneuver around the ring in the space available to them. The ring itself is featureless and finite, but each square foot takes on significance with relationship to the boxers and vis-a-vis their position in the ring itself. But is this true in other sports? Actually, it is.

Let's have a look at American football. In football, too, the field of play yields positional power based on principles. Commentators constantly talk about "good field position" and how well a team does "in the red zone," those last 20 yards before the goal line. As for how to get to those last 20 yards, it is generally best to maintain the ball in the center of the field equidistant from each sideline. This provides a balance of options to right and left, and puts the defense into a position of more uncertainty.

So we can see that geographical positioning can play a major role in either enhancing or decreasing our power in a conflict situation. The military has developed a systematic and sophisticated method for learning about and understanding the ground on which it is to fight. The tool is called "Intelligence Preparation of the Battlefield," or IPB. And it's a lesson or a process easily adaptable to our own challenges in arenas other than that of the military.

In military scenarios, we know that "the high ground" confers advantages in principle. Conversely, we know that "taking the hill" is a daunting proposition. Rivers and valleys and mountain ranges offer barriers to an enemy and to our own advance.

The IPB process systematically assesses the information relevant to friend and foe on a particular battlefield. An intelligence officer collects and evaluates this information and communicates it in the form of intelligence to the commander. The relevant U.S. Military Manual describes intelligence preparation in the following way.

> IPB is a systematic, continuous process of analyzing the threat and environment in a specific geographic area. It supports staff estimates and military decision making. The IPB process helps the commander selectively apply and maximize his combat power at critical points in time and space on the battlefield by determining the threat's likely courses of action and by describing the environment your unit is operating within and the effects of the environment on your unit.

The intelligence officer employs the IPB process continuously, very much like the intelligence cycle we review in another lecture. Continuous feedback in the IPB process, in theory, can enhance the commander's decision making. Intelligence preparation of the battlefield consists of four steps.

First, we define the battlefield environment. This means we identify characteristics of the battlefield that can influence both friendly and competitor operations. We establish the limits of the battlefield and identify what we don't know, but must know.

Second, we describe the battlefield's effects on our operations—on what we intend to do. This step always includes an examination of terrain and weather but may also include discussions of the characteristics of geography and infrastructure and their effects on friendly and threat operations as well as such factors such as politics, civilian press, local population, and demographics.

In the third step, we evaluate our competitor. If it's a known competitor, we determine how the threat normally organizes for combat and conducts operations under similar circumstances. We can rely on historical data bases and well-developed threat models. But if we face a new or less well-known competitor, we may have to develop our intelligence data bases and threat courses of action simultaneously.

In the fourth and final step, we determine our competitor's possible courses of action. The main question that we must answer is: Given what our competitor normally prefers to do, and the effects of the specific environment in which he is operating now, what are his likely objectives and the courses of action available to him?

The intelligence officer performs the IPB process continuously to ensure that intelligence for the commander is always current and useful.

You can see that this IPB process is quite a useful tool. It's the systematic evaluation of the battlefield's environment and an assessment of how it can help or hinder you. Likewise, what it means to your opponent and how it shapes his likely courses of action. And you can see how IPB is easily adapted for use in the business world as well as your personal decision making. IPB is done informally by everyone already; the IPB process simply formalizes it and deepens it so as to gain even more insight.

For us as individuals, the broad lesson here is the importance of geography in our own competitive situations. What potential sources of power are locked in the geography of the likely battlefield? How does geography potentially enhance or degrade strategy? Can you modify your strategy to take advantage of geography, or to prevent it degrading your strategy?

One of the greatest examples of conducting IPB and then acting on it occurred during World War II. The major lesson of the example is how to respond if you know when and where you'll be attacked. Now, there are several responses to a scenario like this, but the one chosen in this example was brilliant. Call it "Defense in Depth." This was the technique used by the Russians at the 1943 Battle of Kursk, the greatest tank battle in history. To call it "Defense in Depth" is an understatement.

At Kursk, the Germans mounted what would turn out to be their last major offensive on the Eastern Front of World War II. It was here that the Russians held territory that bulged into the German front over an area 120 miles wide and 90 miles deep and centered on the town of Kursk. In an attempt to cut off the Russian position and trap hundreds of thousands of prisoners, the Germans attacked from north and south in a pincer movement.

But the Russians knew of the attack well-beforehand through their intelligence network. Over several months, they prepared successive defense lines, making use of the geography of the area to channel the German attack in directions to make them vulnerable. In fact, the Russians altered the terrain significantly and made the battlefield a living hell for the Germans, a tanker's nightmare.

The Russians planned to slow, exhaust, and wear down the Germans by forcing them to attack through a web of minefields, planned artillery fire zones, and concealed anti-tank strong points comprising eight progressively spaced defense lines 150 miles deep. To get an idea of how formidable the defenses were, this defensive belt of 8 successive lines was more than 10 times as deep as the French Maginot Line.

The German attack commenced and began to stall almost immediately. The Russian defense was like a meat-grinder that chewed up the entire German strategic tank reserve in a week, culminating in the Battle of Prokhorovka, the largest armored battle in history. The Germans never broke through, and the strategic initiative passed from the Germans to the Russians for the last time.

So the "Defense in Depth" is one response to an attack you know is coming. Build your defense in-depth so that you withdraw to carefully prepared successive lines. In such a case, encourage your opponent to wear himself out on your metaphorical fortifications. Choose the battlefield carefully, and modify it to suit your defense. Prepare a gauntlet for your competitor to pass through.

It is apparent that the effects of geography play into the outcome of battles both great and small—battles that can affect the course of world history, and battles that may be important to no one but us. The effects of geography may not be as decisive or determinate as geopoliticians would have us believe, but its effects may be enough to tip the scales our way, if we plan judiciously.

Regardless of the stakes, if the battle is worth fighting, then it's worth conducting your own intelligence preparation of the battlefield to give yourself the greatest chance for victory.

Geography—your position on the field of battle—should not be left to chance. Evaluate your position. Select it beforehand, if possible. Note the inherent strengths of the various options open to you, evaluate the conditions of the conflict to come, and manipulate those conditions to your benefit. This is the lesson that geopolitics bequeaths to us. So examine your terrain systematically, and don't forget to look for sunken roads.

Grand Strategists and Strategic Intent
Lecture 6

S trategic intent—what we sometimes call vision, dreams, or big ideas—is essential to any powerful and effective strategy. For such a strategy to rise above the level of mere technique, it must have an inspirational strategic intent at its core, whether to animate an individual, to inspire a corporation, or to fire the imagination of a nation. In this lecture, we'll look at articulations of strategic intent from the realms of legend, sports, politics, and business.

A Definition of Strategic Intent

- In a classic work from 1989, two influential scholars, **Gary Hamel** and **C. K. Prahalad**, coined and defined the term "strategic intent" in the *Harvard Business Review*.

- These two thinkers recognized the great flaw in much of our thinking about strategy up until the 1990s: the pursuit of imitative techniques as a substitute for strategy.

- In contrast to this "strategy of imitation," strategic intent inspires a person or a team with an obsession to win. It articulates a long-term vision or aspiration of the group, reaching beyond current capabilities and forcing group members to develop resources to accomplish the goal. The need to be inventive or resourceful is a result of establishing stretch goals.

- Merely tailoring your ambition to current capabilities is a formula for maintaining the status quo, but establishing stretch goals without strategic intent is a recipe for failure.

  o The concept of stretch goals linked to strategic intent is one of the secrets to the Japanese economic renaissance in the aftermath of World War II.

o It entails envisioning a future that seems nearly impossible, then striving to acquire the capabilities and resources to make that future possible. Numerous Japanese companies adopted versions of this philosophy, including Honda, Matsushita, Sony, and Toyota.

- Strategic intent entails identifying an extreme gap between resources and ambitions and developing a strategy to fulfill those ambitions.

Strategic Intent in Myth and in Football

- Expert mythologist Joseph Campbell identified the "hero's journey" as the archetypal story that has animated all societies throughout history. Every man and woman knows this story and is moved by it. It is the story of Prometheus stealing fire, of Ulysses's return home after the Trojan War, and the quest for the Holy Grail.

- In this adventure, the hero finds the strength within himself or herself to conquer all obstacles, no matter how seemingly impossible. If this sounds grandiose and far removed from your world, it's not. Your life is filled with heroes and villains, conflict and conquest, failure and triumph. In establishing your own strategic intent, it's useful to keep the hero's journey in mind.

- Another clear example of strategic intent comes from the world of sports. Few men embody the idea of strategic intent as much as **Vince Lombardi**, the legendary coach of the NFL's Green Bay Packers. Lombardi's grasp of strategic intent was sure and unambiguous: "Winning isn't everything, it's the only thing."

- As we've said, every strategy requires a powerful strategic intent to animate it. Equally, the intent must be translated into achievable midrange goals. For his players, Lombardi translated the overall goal of winning into a clear statement of strategic intent: "You never win a game unless you beat the guy in front of you...."

- If we consider a football team as a value chain, with victory dependent on each player's individual effort and continuous high performance, it's clear how the notion of strategic intent fits into strategic planning.

- It's also clear that mere technique can never successfully substitute for strategic intent. An offensive lineman is not motivated to perfect his blocking technique merely to achieve "best practice" in the field. A quarterback does not give a record-breaking performance in some vague "search for excellence."

Competition between Nations and between Good and Evil
- Two more famous examples of strategic intent coupled with appropriate tactics come from two contrasting arenas—the first is competition between nations; the second, competition between good and evil.

- In the 1960s, President **John F. Kennedy** was faced with a Soviet threat that appeared as a powerful and plausible alternative to the democracies of the West. Kennedy responded to this challenge with boldness, issuing a brilliant articulation of strategic intent: "We choose to go to the moon in this decade…." As we know, Kennedy's goal was achieved less than 10 years later.

- **Martin Luther King** gives us an example of the melding of a powerful strategic vision with a perfectly executed strategy. He marshaled the forces of an entire nation with a vision of social justice, and he crafted a strategy that every single person could execute as a significant player—the strategy of nonviolent civil disobedience.

  o The spirit of nonviolence inspired King to move a generation of men and women in a quest for social justice. In front of 200,000 listeners, King articulated his powerful vision in his famous "I Have a Dream" speech.

  o Against King stood a phalanx of opposition animated by its own strategic intent. Alabama Governor George Wallace had articulated that intent in his inaugural address: "Segregation now, segregation tomorrow, segregation forever."

  o But King rode a groundswell of slowly increasing popular support as the evils of segregation were revealed. His movement's successful tactics resulted in the Civil Rights Act of 1964, among other successes. Against a corrupt and racist system equipped with every advantage, King brought nothing more than his strategic intent and a powerful strategy.

- Let's consider another example from international politics. For 40 years after the end of World War II, the United States was enmeshed in the Cold War, an ideological struggle between democracy and communism. Our nation pursued a single coherent foreign policy for all of those years, inspired by a core strategic intent.

  o That policy had as its touchstone a strategic intent inspired by American diplomat **George Kennan**. In 1946, Kennan sent his famous classified telegram, presenting the idea that Soviet leadership was impervious to reason but highly sensitive to the logic of force.

  o The reasonable extension of this assumption was that the United States ought to meet Soviet power with American power and to "contain" Soviet expansionist schemes. The strategic intent of containment became the foundation of American foreign policy for the next 40 years.

  o As we know, the United States eventually triumphed; Eastern Europe was liberated from communist oppression in 1989, followed by the collapse of the Soviet Union in 1991.

Strategic Intent in Business
- India's largest multinational conglomerate, Tata Group, led by the visionary businessman Ratan Tata, offers us another example of the power of strategic intent.

- In 2003, Tata established a clear strategic intent for his automotive company. He envisioned the People's Car, a four-passenger vehicle meeting minimum safety and emission standards that would cost about $2000. Although his engineers balked, Tata insisted on both the price and a brutal timetable for production.

- The result was the unveiling of the Tata Nano in early 2008, a tiny, inexpensive, four-passenger automobile designed and built in India.

- The innovative cost-cutting measures used in production of the Nano have since revolutionized the way automobiles are made and sold— in price, size, distribution, and technology. The development of the Nano may have created an entirely new management revolution akin to the Japanese *kanban* system, just-in-time processes, and *kaizen* (continuous improvement).

Absent or Misguided Strategic Intent
- Digital Equipment Corporation (DEC) is an example of a company that refused to make the hard choices necessary for coherent strategy and found itself paralyzed, unable to even articulate a strategic intent.

  o In 1992, faced with the necessity of charting its strategic direction in a chaotic electronics industry, the company issued this statement: "DEC is committed to providing high-quality products and services and being a leader in data processing."

  o The vague language and lack of focus in this statement is an indicator of faltering leadership. It was surely not designed to rally the troops at a time of company crisis. Six years later, DEC was swallowed by Compaq.

- Levi Strauss, the maker of blue jeans, serves as an example of misguided strategic intent. Under CEO Bob Haas, who assumed leadership in 1984, the company adopted a strategic vision that looked inward, ignored the customers, and seemed to have nothing to do with selling jeans. As a result, its market share plummeted from 48 percent to 17 percent between 1990 and 2000.

- Another example on a far greater scale than a single company comes from imperial Japan in the 1930s. At the time, the prime minister of Japan envisioned an Asian economic alliance, free of the Western powers, to be called the Greater East Asia Co-Prosperity Sphere.

- It was purported to be a new international order that sought a euphemistic "co-prosperity" for countries throughout Asia. Of course, it was really a front for Japanese imperialist ambitions and led to the establishment of puppet regimes in every place the Japanese were ascendant.

- As we know now, Japan overreached. It did not have the capabilities to match its ambitions. Although its strategy worked for a time, in the long run, it was not tenable.

Abraham Lincoln

- As a final example of a powerful and successful statement of strategic intent, let's turn to one of America's most revered leaders, Abraham Lincoln.

- Lincoln grappled with the greatest trial of any president in American history: He was forced to wage war against his countrymen. But he did not do so simply and reactively or as a mere technical process. Instead, he waged war with the strategic intent of maintaining the Union as a free country.

Lincoln faced the possibility of the dissolution of the country by bloody civil war; he met the challenge with a strategy aimed at preserving the Union.

- Lincoln's articulation of strategic intent was made in the Gettysburg Address, a eulogy for those who had died in battle in the Civil War: "we here highly resolve that these dead shall not have died in vain— that this nation, under God, shall have a new birth of freedom—and that government of the people, by the people, for the people, shall not perish from the earth."

Charting a Bold Course

- From foreign policy, to social policy, to business, sports, and even myth, strategic intent provides a powerful impetus to drive cogent strategy and motivate people to implement the strategy.

- Strategy without strategic vision is merely soulless technique, a great flurry of activity. There is nothing courageous about making a bold pronouncement in vague language. Lack of strategic intent means a loss of focus and the routinization of process.

- We've seen that articulating a strategic intent requires boldness, grounded in a strategic and accurate assessment of reality. It means charting a course and closing off some options because you have elected consciously to pursue one goal with single-minded fervor.

Names to Know

Hamel, Gary (1954–): *Fortune* magazine has called Hamel "the world's leading expert on business strategy," and *Forbes* has ranked Hamel as one of the world's top 10 most influential theorists on business, competition, management, and strategy.

Kennan, George (1904–2005): Few people can claim to have set the foreign policy course for an entire nation for 40 years, but as a young embassy official in the Soviet Union in the 1940s, Kennan did exactly that when he crafted what would become the U.S. policy of containment with regard to the Soviets.

Kennedy, John F. (1917–1963): Few presidents can claim the kind of strategic vision that Kennedy possessed, founding the Peace Corps, laying the groundwork for the U.S. Special Forces, and charting a course for eventually reaching the moon.

King, Martin Luther, Jr. (1929–1968): America's great civil rights leader carried a passion for justice along with a strategic vision and the proper tactics to see that vision through to completion.

Lombardi, Vince (1913–1970): One of the great motivators and leaders that sports has ever produced, Lombardi's teams won the first two Super Bowls, and his aphorisms on leadership have since entered the lexicon as classics.

Prahalad, C. K. (1941–2010): Prahalad teamed with Gary Hamel in one of the great scholarly collaborations in business history, developing pathbreaking theoretical and practical notions that guide multinational corporate thinking today. Prahalad is most remembered for his last works, focused on market solutions to alleviate poverty at the "bottom of the pyramid."

Suggested Reading

Campbell, *The Hero with a Thousand Faces.*

Hamel and Prahalad, "Strategic Intent."

———, *Strategic Intent.*

Questions to Consider

1. Strategic intent is a powerful core for any strategy. We can sometimes lose sight of this core, wrapped in the minutiae of the day and focused on task accomplishment. In the process, our strategy can lose its focus. Select a major goal in your professional life right now and assess whether your strategy is guided by a strong, focused core of strategic intent. Can you narrate this intent in one or two short sentences?

2. Strategic intent means identifying an extreme gap between resources and ambitions and developing a strategy to fulfill those ambitions. Are your own goals ambitious, or have you intentionally set goals that are easily met? If it's the latter, set a major goal today that seems out of reach and then realistically assess what resources must be acquired and what capabilities developed to achieve that goal.

3. We sometimes shortchange ourselves by not thinking grandly enough. John F. Kennedy and Martin Luther King were grand thinkers and visionaries who were able to articulate strategic intent to achieve almost

impossible goals. Do you have grand goals, or have you unintentionally limited yourself by closing off certain options before they are even considered? Spend a few minutes each day thinking "grandly" about ideas that most people would reject, telling themselves, "You can't do that."

Grand Strategists and Strategic Intent
Lecture 6—Transcript

At the center of any truly great strategy, we find a pure, crystalline core. Business schools call this core strategic intent. But it can go by other names: vision, direction, big idea, dream, North Star, Holy Grail, El Dorado. Without this vibrant core of strategic intent, you have no strategy. You have only aimless technique. Perhaps a catchy slogan, like, "When the going gets tough, the tough get going."

Strategic intent animates any great adventure, whether accompanied by practical strategy or not. Take the legend of King Arthur and his Knights of the Round Table, a quasi myth that began in the 5th or 6th century.

Arthurian legend offers us a fabulous example of the Hero's Quest. The Hero's Quest is a universal story, and it's the framework for virtually every inspirational and successful utterance of strategic intent.

Every great strategy begins with a big idea—a strategic intent. Strategic intent is the articulation of a powerful, achievable, and motivating stretch goal. No strategy can succeed without it. In fact, no plan can be considered a legitimate strategy without a powerful vision or intent. Historical figures as disparate as King Arthur, Napoleon, Vince Lombardi, Bismarck, Woodrow Wilson, and Martin Luther King have articulated powerful strategic visions.

Strategic intent at the core of any plan is a great idea. Without it, you have only a menu of tactical actions. Without strategic intent, strategy is an engine without fuel. Worse, it's a picture of an engine without fuel, which is the unfortunate reality of many so-called strategies. Slogans, procedures, techniques, tactics to give an appearance of strategy. Great sound and fury, but nothing at the core.

This lecture is about the nexus between strategy and strategic vision.

Let's begin with a clear notion of what constitutes strategic intent. This particular formulation comes to us from business. In a classic work from 1989, two influential scholars coined the term and related their concept of strategic intent in the *Harvard Business Review*. Gary Hamel and the late C.K. Prahalad have been two of the most influential business thinkers of the last 50 years. Together, they created the concept of "core competency" in business analysis. In fact, *The Wall Street Journal* called Hamel the world's most influential business thinker, and *Fortune* magazine called him the world's leading expert on business strategy.

As with many modern ideas, this idea of strategic intent has been around for a long time—much longer without a name than with. In fact, the timeless universal story of the Hero's Quest captures the essence of the idea. But Prahalad and Hamel gave new form in their treatment of strategic intent.

These two thinkers recognized the great flaw in much of our thinking about strategy up until the 1990s. This flaw was the pursuit of imitative techniques as a substitute for strategy. In fact, they called it a "strategy of imitation." Instead, strategic intent inspires a company or a person or an army or a team with an obsession with winning at every level of the organization. But it is not simply ambition.

Strategic intent articulates the long-term vision or aspiration of the company. It means reaching for something beyond your current capabilities and developing resources to accomplish the goal. Current capabilities and resources are not sufficient, and so this forces you to become more inventive and resourceful in a world where resources are scarce. This is called establishing stretch goals. An older, more traditional view is to tailor your ambition to current capabilities, but this is in reality a formula for maintaining the status quo.

On the other hand, stretch goals without strategic intent are a recipe for failure. The concept of stretch goals linked to strategic intent is one of the secrets to the Japanese economic renaissance in the aftermath of World War II. It entails envisioning a future that seems near-impossible, and then striving to acquire the capabilities and resources to make that future possible. Numerous Japanese companies adopted versions of this philosophy— Honda, Matsushita, Sony, Toyota.

Strategic intent means identifying an extreme gap between resources and ambitions and developing a strategy to fulfill those ambitions.

Let's look at a variety of examples of strategic intent. Expert mythologist Joseph Campbell identified the Hero's Journey as the archetypal story that has animated all societies throughout history. Every man and woman knows this story and is moved by it. The Hero's Quest is the story of Prometheus stealing fire, of Ulysses' quest for home after the Trojan War, Jason and the Golden Fleece, King Arthur's Knights of the Round Table and the quest for the Holy Grail, of the real-world stories that captivate.

Of modern movie heroes—Luke Skywalker. In this adventure, the hero finds the strength within himself to conquer all obstacles no matter how impossible. It is transformation through triumph. For the establishing of your own strategic intent, it's useful to keep in mind the Hero's Quest.

If this sounds grandiose and far from your world, it's not. Your life is filled with heroes and villains, conflict and conquest, failure and triumph. Your story is what you contrive, and the ease of it is that your story elements are all decided for you—its characters, its impersonal forces, its plot, the villain, the conflict, the climax, and the identity of the hero.

You needn't become a scholar of mythology to put Campbell's discovery to work for you. The Hero's Quest is an epic. When thought out and articulated, it can provide high-toned power and purpose. The Hero's Quest provides you with the framework. The Hero's Quest ends with the ship in home port, the knight saving his princess, the Union preserved, social justice achieved, the journey brought to successful conclusion. Perhaps its biggest advantage is that it resonates with people. The story sounds familiar and comfortable.

If we move from mythology, one of the clearest examples of strategic intent comes from the world of sports. Few men embody the idea of strategic intent as much as the late great football coach Vince Lombardi. Lombardi was the legendary coach of the NFL's Green Bay Packers and won the first two Super Bowls in the mid-1960s. Lombardi's grasp of strategic intent was sure and unambiguous. He used it well. "Winning isn't everything … it's the only thing." The quote may have originated elsewhere, but it has been forever linked to Lombardi. Its corollary is equally powerful and unambiguous. "Show me a good loser … and I'll show you a loser."

Compared to the endlessly qualified rhetoric and ambiguity that permeates modern society, these phrases crash on us as powerful and unsettling. It's their clarity. They lack compromise. They leave no wiggle room, no room for waffling. They leave no escape for excuse mongering. They are unequivocal.

Every strategy requires a powerful strategic intent to animate it. Equally, our intent must also be translated into achievable midrange goals, whether it's our personal strategy or a strategy for an entire organization.

To take our Vince Lombardi example, the famous coach did not stop at articulating a powerful intent that could easily stand alone as a catchphrase or motivational slogan. He did not say, "The game comes down to who wants it more." He made the intent tangible for his players.

Here's how Lombardi translated the overall goal of winning into a clear statement of strategic intent, making it crystal clear for each player. "You never win a game unless you beat the guy in front of you. The score on the board doesn't mean a thing. That's for the fans. You've got to win the war with the man in front of you. You've got to get your man." If we consider a football team as a value chain, with victory dependent on each player's individual effort and continuous high performance, it's clear how the notion of strategic intent fits into strategic planning.

It's also clear that mere technique can never successfully substitute for strategic intent. An offensive lineman is not motivated to perfect his blocking technique merely to achieve "best practice" in the field. A running back does not crash into the line again and again, punishing his body merely in the spirit of total quality management. Does a quarterback give a record-breaking performance under tremendous defensive pressure in some vague "search for excellence?" No. Of course not.Strategic intent imbues an obsession for winning at every level of the organization. Strategic intent, backed up by a clearly articulated plan and tactics, is key to every winning strategy.

Two more very famous examples come from two very contrasting arenas— the first is competition between nations, the second is competition between good and evil. Both are sterling examples of the power of strategic intent coupled with appropriate tactics.

Both examples come from the 1960s and were articulated by two of the most influential leaders in American history. The first comes from John F. Kennedy.

President Kennedy was faced with a Soviet threat that appeared as a powerful and plausible alternative to the democracies of the West. Soviet technology had beaten the U.S. into space with the first satellite in 1957. It had put the first man into orbit in early 1961. America's own early effort was feeble by comparison, a 15-minute suborbital flight in May of that year.

Confronted with this challenge, Kennedy gauged the mood of the nation and he responded with boldness. He didn't call for imitation of the Soviets. He didn't call for "continuous process improvement."

Instead, Kennedy issued a brilliant articulation of strategic intent. His statement of intent was clear, concise, bold, and it fired the imagination of a nation:

> We choose to go to the moon in this decade and do the other things, not because they are easy, but because they are hard, because that goal will serve to organize and measure the best of our energies and skills, because that challenge is one that we are willing to accept, one we are unwilling to postpone, and one we intend to win.

NASA responded brilliantly with the Saturn 5 Booster and Project Apollo and a host of new technological advances throughout the 1960s that achieved Kennedy's goal less than ten years later, on July 20, 1969, when astronaut Neil Armstrong set foot on the moon.

And Kennedy already had a strategy for achieving his strategic vision even before he made the speech. He had already asked his advisors, "How can we beat the Russians in space?" and scientist Werner von Braun had already sent a memo arguing that the Soviets would be difficult to beat in the short term, but that the wealthy U.S. could leap ahead to invest in rocket technology the Soviet Union didn't yet have. Kennedy's strategic intent was grand, but it was grounded in a realistic strategy.

Strategic intent can animate nations to great technological achievements, as we may see again in the space race between China and India. It can also animate people to overturn social injustice, even against overwhelming odds.

Martin Luther King exemplifies the melding of a powerful strategic intent and vision with a perfectly executed strategy. He marshaled the forces of an entire nation with a vision of social justice embodied in his dream, and he crafted a strategy whereby every single person could execute the strategy as a significant player—the strategy of nonviolent civil disobedience.

The spirit of nonviolence inspired King to fire a generation of men and women in a quest for social justice. In front of 200,000 listeners, King articulated his powerful vision in his famous "I Have a Dream Speech" in Washington, D.C., on August 28, 1963, during the March on Washington for Jobs and Freedom.

U.S. Congressional Representative John Lewis, who also spoke that day, said that Martin Luther King

> had the power, the ability, and the capacity to transform those steps on the Lincoln Memorial into a modern-day pulpit that will forever be recognized. By speaking the way he did, he educated, he inspired, he informed not just the people there, but people throughout America and unborn generations.

It was a call for justice, liberation, and equality. Against King stood a phalanx of opposition animated by its own strategic intent. And as we shall see, negative strategic intent can be powerful, too—a powerful force for evil.

Alabama Governor George Wallace had articulated that intent in his inaugural address in January of that same year of 1963: "Segregation now, segregation tomorrow, segregation forever." It was little more than a call for the status quo to keep a portion of the U.S. population in subservient status. This clear articulation of intent was enough to turn many against the segregationists, particularly when their brutal attacks and corrupt legal system were exposed. This was hardly the heady stuff of inspiration.

King rode a groundswell of slowly increasing popular support as the evils of segregation were revealed because of his movement's successful tactics that resulted ultimately in the Civil Rights Act of 1964, among other successes. Dr. King did not hail nonviolence as the implementation of a new management technique. Nor did he articulate a catchy slogan and then sit back, hoping for something good to happen.

He succeeded with clear and powerful strategic intent. Against a corrupt and racist system equipped with every advantage, Dr. King brought nothing more than his strategic intent and a powerful strategy. It exemplifies what we call these days in business "stretch goals" animated by strategic intent.

Let's consider another example from international politics. For 40 years after the end of World War II, the United States engaged in a world-wide competition with its main rival, the Soviet Union. This was called the Cold War, and it began in the period after World War II—an ideological struggle between democracy and communism. In the words of Winston Churchill, an Iron Curtain had descended between East and West. The U.S. pursued a single coherent foreign policy for all of those years, inspired by a core strategic intent.

That policy had as its touchstone a strategic intent inspired by American diplomat George Kennan. In the immediate post-World War II world, the Soviet Union emerged as a threat to the democracies of Western Europe and to the stability of the entire system of states. The Western response was erratic and reactive—incoherent. It wasn't clear what Soviet intent was or how to respond in a way that could avert nuclear disaster, until 1946. It was then that diplomat George Kennan sent his famous classified "X" telegram from the U.S. embassy inside the Soviet Union. It was later published in *Foreign Affairs* magazine. In July of 1947, the telegram was published in *Foreign Affairs* as "The Sources of Soviet Conduct."

The logic behind the analysis was that the Soviet leadership was impervious to reason, but was highly sensitive to the logic of force. The reasonable extension of this assumption was that the U.S. ought to meet Soviet power with American power. Where actual power was not used, the Soviets should face American will and American resolve.

The proper response, then, of the United States was to contain Soviet expansionist schemes by meeting the Soviet challenge wherever it arose worldwide. At the core of this was the strategic intent of containment, and this became the foundation of American foreign policy for the next 40 years.

Containment served as a succinct and clear articulation of U.S. strategic intent. There was no sloganeering to "be number one" in the field. In fact, the United States was a reluctant leader.

But the U.S. eventually triumphed, as first Eastern Europe was liberated from communist oppression in 1989 followed by the collapse of the Soviet Union in 1991.

From the early 21st century, we have a superb textbook example of the power of strategic intent from India's largest multinational conglomerate under the leadership of a visionary Indian businessman—Ratan Tata.

Ratan Tata is chairman of the Tata Group, and he established a clear strategic intent for his automotive company in 2003. He envisioned a four-passenger vehicle meeting minimum safety and emission standards that the average Indian could afford.

But it was to be much more than simply another cheap automobile. Tata articulated a strategic intent that no other person in his company believed possible at the time. He insisted that it was to be the world's cheapest automobile—the People's Car—and it would cost no more than one lakh (at the time, $2000). His engineers balked at this, but Tata would not budge, and he insisted on the price and a brutal timetable. They met both.

The result was the unveiling of the Tata Nano in early 2008, a tiny, inexpensive four-passenger automobile designed and built in India and the end product of an incredible focus and vision of one man—Ratan Tata. "Today, we indeed have a People's Car, which is affordable and yet built to meet safety requirements and emission norms, to be fuel efficient and low on emissions," said Tata at the launch.

But the Nano did much more than provide inexpensive transportation for the poorest Indians. Its innovative cost-cutting measures have revolutionized the way automobiles are made and sold—in price, in size, in distribution, and technology. Cost-cutting engineering secrets include a hollowed out steering-wheel shaft, a trunk with space for a briefcase, and a rear-mounted engine with power akin to a high-end riding mower. Tata uses lighter steel, a smaller engine, and has negotiated longer-term sourcing agreements with parts suppliers.

All told, the development of the Nano may have created an entirely new management revolution akin to Japanese *kanban* cards, just-in-time processes, and *kaizen* (continuous improvement). In honor of the founder of modern India, you might call it "Gandhian engineering," which fuses unconventional ways of thinking with a frugality born of scarcity.

One parts supplier characterized it as Tata throwing out everything the auto industry had thought about cost structures in the past and taking out a clean sheet of paper and asking, "What's possible?" As they built Tata's new car, the guiding philosophy was: Do we really need that? A powerful strategic intent makes such questioning not only permissible, but necessary.

We've looked at powerful and successful examples of strategic intent. When strategic intent is absent, however, a company can lose focus and drift. In a crisis, a company with no strategic intent it can collapse.

Let's turn to what happens when, in business, a company refuses to articulate a powerful vision. When it refuses to state its strategic intent.

Digital Equipment Corporation is an example of a company that refused to make the hard choices necessary for coherent strategy and found itself paralyzed, unable to even articulate a coherent strategic intent. In 1992, the company was faced with the necessity of charting its strategic direction in a chaotic electronics industry.

The company could not decide on one of three directions advocated by passionate adherents within the senior leadership: whether to manufacture chips or to offer customers consulting solutions or to build computers. So the company compromised. It issued this statement: "DEC is committed to providing high-quality products and services and being a leader in data processing."

This statement is a pretense. It's like whitewash on a rotting fence. Its vague language and lack of focus is an indicator of faltering leadership. It was surely not designed to rally the troops at a time of company crisis. Six years after this debacle, the company was swallowed by Compaq.

Let me issue a caveat here to note that a powerful, focused strategic intent is not sufficient for securing the ends of your strategic plan. Misguided intent can be just as bad as no intent at all.

Here, an example from business is the proud company Levi Strauss, makers of possibly the most famous blue jeans in history. Under CEO Bob Haas, who assumed command from 1984 to 1999, Levi's adopted a strategic vision that was nothing short of bizarre, according to some observers.

Competitive intelligence expert Ben Gilad contends that "Levi's was a classic case of a leader with a vision, but the vision did not match reality, and the leader did not let that obstruct his actions."

The management had adopted a vision that seemed to have nothing to do with selling jeans. After a promising turnaround in 1984, Levi's market share plummeted from 1990 to 2000 from 48 percent down to 17 percent. Levi's was busy looking inward to "re-create capitalism in Bob Haas's humanistic image of utopia," according to Ben Gilad. This strategic intent completely forgot about customers: In 1998, the company delivered its back-to-school line to its leading vendor, J.C. Penney, 45 days late.

The strategic intent had little to do with the purpose of the business. Another example on a far greater scale than a single company comes from Imperial Japan in the 1930s.

We can look at the grandiose Japanese strategic intent of the late 1930s for a lesson in strategic intent gone awry. Japan wanted to rectify many of the perceived injustices of the colonial period in Asia, Southeast Asia, and the Pacific. Imperial Japan envisioned an Asian region free of the western powers, but under its own leadership.

This region was to be called the Greater East Asia Co-Prosperity Sphere. Japan's Prime Minister Fumimaro Konoe was the architect of this forced would-be economic alliance.

This alliance was purported to be a new international order that sought a euphemistic "co-prosperity" for countries throughout Asia. This, of course, was really a front for Japanese imperialist ambitions and led to the establishment of puppet regimes in every place the Japanese were ascendant.

But every student of history knows now that Japan overreached. It did not have the capabilities to match its ambitions. While its strategy worked, for a time, in the long run it was not tenable.

As a final example of a powerful and successful statement of strategic intent, consider this powerful statement by one of America's most revered leaders— Abraham Lincoln.

President Lincoln grappled with the greatest trial of any president in American history. He faced the real possibility of the dissolution of the country by bloody civil war. He was forced to wage war against his countrymen. But he did not wage war simply and reactively and as a mere technical process.

Lincoln waged war with strategic intent of maintaining the union as a country free for all men, breathing life into those ideals put to paper almost a century earlier. These were ideals he so eloquently framed already two years before he became president, during his first speech as a candidate for the U.S. Senate in 1858:

> A house divided against itself cannot stand. I believe this government cannot endure, permanently, half slave and half free. I do not expect the Union to be dissolved—I do not expect the house to fall—but I do expect it will cease to be divided. It will become all one thing or all the other.

And then, in one of the most powerful expressions of strategic intent ever articulated. The Gettysburg Address, delivered as a eulogy for those who died in battle, begins with the famous words, "Four score and seven years ago our fathers brought forth on this continent, a new nation, conceived in Liberty, and dedicated to the proposition that all men are created equal." And the Gettysburg Address concludes with a ringing statement of strategic intent: "We here highly resolve that these dead shall not have died in vain—that this nation, under God, shall have a new birth of freedom—and that government of the people, by the people, for the people, shall not perish from the earth."

From foreign policy, to social policy, to business, to sports, to myth and legend, to the preservation of the Union, strategic intent provides a powerful impetus to drive cogent strategy and motivate people to implement the strategy.

Strategy without strategic vision is just soulless technique, a great flurry of activity akin to that of a treadmill. We see this too often, as part of the strategic masquerade.

There is nothing courageous about making a bold pronouncement in vague language. Sloganeering in the language of market leadership or hat-tipping to shareholder wealth or to the pursuit of excellence.

Lack of strategic intent means a loss of focus and the routinization of process. "Continuous Improvement" is neither strategic intent nor a strategy. "Being the best I can be" is neither a strategic intent nor a strategy.

We've seen that articulating a strategic intent requires boldness, grounded in a strategic and accurate assessment of reality. It means charting a course and closing off some options because you have elected consciously to pursue one goal with single-minded fervor.

With regard to strategic intent in our own lives, too often we perhaps think too modestly—we look only at our resources and we trim our ambitions accordingly.

We can't all be Abraham Lincoln or Martin Luther King, Jr. But we can—and we should—set seemingly impossible goals, acquire the necessary resources, and develop a strategy to attain our goals.

The Core and the Rise of Strategic Planning
Lecture 7

E very firm must have a core mission—a reason for its existence, a mission for which it alone is suited. From the concise articulation of that mission, strategy emerges in a process, either aimless or thoughtful. In this lecture, we trace the history of strategic planning and look at some of the problems that plagued its early development. We then learn a six-step strategic planning process that serves as a useful framework for any strategy development.

A Founding Myth

- The founding myth of the French Foreign Legion is drawn from the story of the brave Legionnaires who fought at Camerone in Mexico in 1863 and the respect accorded them by their opponents, the Mexican nationalists. The values and mission of the Legion spring from this beginning and are reflected in its motto and its code of honor.

- Every organization should have a founding myth that exemplifies its code or mission, one that is substantial and inspiring and captures the spirit of the organization. Think of Apple Computer's founding myth of two young men in a California garage starting the computer revolution in 1975.

The Mission Statement

- The founding myth should inform the organizational mission statement, which anchors strategy and serves as the basis for strategic intent. This statement should be bold, lofty, and inspiring, like that of the Coca Cola Company: "To refresh the world; to inspire moments of optimism and happiness; to create value and make a difference."

- But mission statements—and the strategies they engender—can often be mundane, uninspiring, or routine. **Henry Mintzberg**, one of the great strategist academics of the past 20 years, has a special place in his heart for the elegant, different, and exciting strategy. He says: "The most

After World War II, military methods of strategic planning were applied to business on the assumption that valuable lessons might be learned from the titanic logistical operations involved in defeating Germany and Japan.

interesting and most successful companies are not boring. They have novel, creative, inspiring, sometimes even playful strategies."

- Equal Exchange, a small coffee company based in Massachusetts, has the mission statement: "Fairness to farmers. A closer connection between people and the farmers we all rely on." From this statement, the company has laid out a series of achievable objectives, a superb example of defining a mission that supports strategic planning.

The History of Strategic Planning

- Strategic planning began in the military. Marshaling resources, training and arming soldiers, planning maneuver on the battlefield—all these activities require forethought and planning.

- Prior to the Napoleonic era, planning was the province of the general or the monarch, with advice from his trusted confidantes. The development of military staff planning began with the Prussian general staff in 1807.

- The idea of formal planning made its way slowly into the business world after World War I. The Harvard policy model, developed in the 1920s, was more of a general call to action than an actual methodology, but it charted a direction in thinking that would be joined with military methods of planning in the post–World War II era.

- In the wake of World War II, financial difficulties and administrative chaos at Ford Motor Company prompted the hiring of 10 former military officers. These men introduced advanced planning, organization, and management control systems, along with fiscal and process discipline, to the world of business and charted the course of American strategic business thought for the next 20 years.

- But American corporations began to base their strategic plans primarily on financial data, collating figures from the previous year, preparing spreadsheets, making forecasts, and setting budgets. Planning became little more than a budgeting exercise conducted once a year. The problems with this kind of planning remained hidden by the dominance of American productive might in the postwar world.

- Robert McNamara, the former leader of the team at Ford, introduced a model of strategic planning as secretary of defense in the Kennedy administration. Throughout the 1960s, the gospel of strategic planning spread and became embedded in American corporations as a standard management tool.

- In the decade of U.S. industrial dominance, the distorted results yielded by early strategic planning didn't matter much. But as the 1970s dawned, the challenge of the Japanese and the power of the Arab oil states revealed the poverty of the current planning model. Among other things, it ignored human irrationality in decision making and the actions of other players in the great games of politics and commerce.

Identifying the Problems of Planning

- Henry Mintzberg identifies three fallacies that have worked against planning since its inception.

  o First is the fallacy of predetermination. We believe that we can know the future, and this leads us to the "predict and prepare" line of thought. But of course, we can't predict the future, and basing our plans on this single line of thought can be disastrous.

  o Second is the fallacy of detachment. This refers to the tendency of planners to remove themselves from the scene of the action. This is strategic formulation detached from implementation.

  o Third is the fallacy of formalization. This is the ossification of strategy and a "binder" mentality: The strategic plan is in a binder on the shelf. It begins to be detached from reality, and as time passes, it represents less and less of what the company actually does.

- Beginning in the late 1970s, business thinkers began to focus on strategy and how decisions were made, and they began to connect this process of thinking to the real world, where strategy is played out.

- Marking this new thinking was the 1978 publication of "The Evolution of Strategic Management," an article by McKinsey and Company, a global management consulting firm. In it, McKinsey identified the phases of ineffective planning that had plagued American industry and left it vulnerable to new challenges. The article called for changes in the way we think and the way we conceive of planning.

  o The first phase identified by McKinsey was the financial planning phase of the 1950s. Here, planning was viewed as almost a purely financial problem and was conducted as an annual budgeting exercise.

  o The second phase was forecast-based planning, which recognized that deeper thinking is necessary about resource allocation and development of key issues.

o The third phase was externally oriented planning. This kind of planning was even better because it looked outward to how the firm interacts with the external environment of competitors and other businesses.

o The final and highest phase was strategic management itself. Here, we aim to weld strategic planning and management into a single process in pursuit of that lodestone—the linking of strategy conception with execution. This means diffusing the ability to think strategically throughout the entire organization—a worthy goal.

Strategic Planning Today: A Six-Step Process

- The strategic planning process offers incredible benefits if we pursue it correctly. The following six steps constitute one version of the process: mission, objective, situation analysis, strategy formulation, strategy implementation, and control.

- The first step in the process is to define your mission; as we saw at the beginning of this lecture, this is the core that guides you. Your mission is what you look to in setting your objectives.

- The objectives established in the second step are chosen based on some notion of wanting to fulfill your mission. They should be clear, concise, achievable, and in some sense, measurable.

- The third step, the environmental scan, is pivotal for most firms, and it is the most involved. Look at both the external and internal environments in which your firm functions. On a personal level, evaluate the external factors that impinge on you with respect to your objectives.

- The fourth step is the actual formulation of strategy. Decide what you will actually do to get from where you are to where you want to be. Allocate resources and connect your management decisions with the people who will implement the plan.

- The fifth step is implementation of strategy, and here is where many companies fail because they do not follow the military dictum to "supervise and refine." This means not to simply issue orders and assume that they'll be carried out.

- The sixth step, control, involves developing a control mechanism to evaluate whether or not the plan is working. When the control or monitoring system tells you that something is amiss in your strategy, you can then circle back to your environmental scan to discover whether the relevant environmental factors have changed.

Planning Points to Remember
- As you think about your own strategic planning process, it's essential to remain rooted in your mission and to remember what constitutes a good strategy. You don't want to do things just like everyone else. As Harvard business professor **Michael Porter** told us, strategy means doing things differently.

- Strategic planning also takes time. In Porter's view, the proper timeframe for strategic planning may be a decade or more. The timeframe of a single budget or planning cycle is typically not enough for a strategy to be successful.

- Planning far in advance has other advantages, too. As Porter noted, a long-range plan "fosters improvements in individual activities and the fit across activities, allowing an organization to build unique capabilities and skills tailored to its strategy."

- As you enter into the strategic planning process, this idea of seeking competitive advantage by doing things differently should inform your thinking every step of the way.

- With a core sense of mission, anyone can develop a competent and effective strategy using the basic strategic planning process—whether for business or the accomplishment of personal goals.

Names to Know

Mintzberg, Henry (1939–): Mintzberg is a noted business professor and theorist whose sometimes contrarian notions frustrate his contemporaries through their brilliant insights and counterintuitive propositions. He appeared at number 30 on the 2009 Forbes biennial global ranking of management thinkers.

Porter, Michael (1947–): Possibly the most influential scholar on business strategy in the last 30 years, Porter became one of Harvard University's youngest tenured professors at age 26. His work in the field of corporate competition and strategy formulation transformed business education worldwide, and he commands speaking fees of more than $70,000 per lecture.

Suggested Reading

Abrahams, *101 Mission Statements.*

Ansoff, *Strategic Management.*

Kiechel, *The Lords of Strategy.*

Mintzberg, *The Rise and Fall of Strategic Planning.*

Porter, *On Competition.*

Questions to Consider

1. The lecture notes that mission statements can be mundane, uninspiring, routine, and forgotten. They can also be nonexistent. Do you have a mission statement, an articulation of your purpose in life? If not, craft one now. If so, ask honestly, as Mintzberg suggests we do, whether it inspires you.

2. Evaluate your company's mission statement and assess whether what your company actually does is aligned with the company's stated mission. Try to understand and measure the difference between slogan and action.

3. The strategic planning process of mission, objective, situation analysis, strategy formulation, implementation, and control provides a clear blueprint for any organization and any individual to assemble a focused, effective strategy. Use the six steps of the process right now to sketch the outlines of your own personal strategy with regard to a long-term goal.

4. Do you understand the difference between "mission" and "objective"? The mission is your reason for being, how you conceive of your purpose, whether as an individual or as a firm. The objectives are goals set to fulfill that mission. For instance, if you conceive of your mission on this earth to heal the sick, what might be the objectives you would set for yourself in order to fulfill that perceived mission?

The Core and the Rise of Strategic Planning
Lecture 7—Transcript

Every firm, every organization, must have a core–a sense of mission. This is different from strategic intent, which we talked about in our last lecture. Even an organization that lacks strategic intent must have a reason for its existence. What we talked about last time is where you want to go: your vision.

This time, we're starting with the core of Who You Are, and how that core sense of mission can also inspire and inform the entire process of strategic planning. Google, for example, says its mission is: Organize the world's information and make it universally accessible and useful. To identify a core mission, it's not enough to point to a process or to the firm's activities as the reason for its existence. That's tautological. It's like saying we deliver a speech for the purpose of being heard, or jogging for the purpose of saying that we ran.

No, each of us must have a core mission in this life for strategic thinking to make any sense at all. Likewise, for firms or sports teams, or for armies to have a meaningful and effective strategy—for that strategy to have any purpose at all—they must have one or more core ideas or values; better yet, a founding myth that encapsulates that core and fires the imagination. From that core mission, we can then talk about planning to achieve specific objectives.

Planning as a management tool for business began in the 1920s at Harvard and blossomed after World War II into strategic planning. But planning has been an integral part of military operations for hundreds of years. For an example, let's go to Mexico in 1863. At that time, most eyes were on the East Coast of the United States. There, a titanic struggle between two great armies was playing out in the American Civil War in a place called Gettysburg.

But here, along a dusty Mexican road between Vera Cruz and Palo Verde, few people in the world knew or cared what was happening, even as a legend was being born that would carry half a world away and inspire subsequent generations of warriors.

Mexico was ruled by the French under an appointed emperor, Maximilian. The French were fighting Mexican nationalists under Benito Juarez.

On the morning of April 30 a column of French Foreign Legionnaires went on patrol to guard a convoy of gold and munitions travelling to the town of Puebla. The column consisted only of 62 soldiers and three officers. It was commanded by Captain Jean Danjou.

This band of soldiers was attacked suddenly at 7:00 a.m. by a superior force of Mexican infantry and cavalry. The Legionnaires fell back under the Mexican onslaught to a little walled hacienda called Camerone. More Mexican cavalry arrived, and their ranks swelled to 2000 men at arms. They outnumbered the French 30 to 1.

As the casualties mounted, the French retreated to a farmhouse, fought room by room as ammunition dwindled, and they fought with bayonet. And minute by minute, unknowingly, with their bravery they began constructing a legend, a powerful larger-than-life myth that would serve as the unshakeable core of their organization for more than a century.

When only three Legionnaires were left standing, the Mexican soldiers swarmed over them, ready to club them to death. But the Mexican commander, Colonel Milan, stopped the battle, and with tears streaming down his face pleaded with the remaining French to surrender. And they agreed—if they could tend to their wounded and to their fallen commander, and receive safe passage home.

Colonel Milan's response reflects the respect that men at arms have for each other and the almost mystical bond of shared near-death experience for men who fight from sense of honor.

Colonel Milan spoke these words: "What can I refuse to such men? No, these are not men, they are devils." This became the founding legend of the French Foreign Legion. Forged in battle and seared into the consciousness of all who join *La Légion étrangère*.

Once perceived as a band of brigands, ruffians, and criminals in hiding at its founding in 1831, the legion was suddenly transformed. Its real beginning came at Camerone. Its values and mission spring from this beginning and are reflected in its motto—*Honneur et Fidélité*—and its Code of Honor, which every Legionnaire must memorize.

> Légionnaire, you are a volunteer serving France with honour and fidelity.

> Each legionnaire is your brother in arms whatever his nationality, his race or his religion might be. You show him the same close solidarity that links the members of the same family.

> Respectful of traditions, devoted to your leaders, discipline and comradeship are your strengths, courage and loyalty are your virtues. The mission is sacred, you carry it out until the end and, if necessary in the field, at the risk of your life."

The French Foreign Legion became a sacred warrior band, bound by honor and fidelity.

Now that is a founding myth, and every company, every firm, every organization, ought to have a founding myth that exemplifies its code or mission. Perhaps not one as extreme as that of a warrior band, but one that is substantial, inspiring, and captures the spirit of the organization, one that breathes life into the dream.

Think of Apple Computer's founding myth of two guys in a California garage starting the computer revolution in 1975, or Henry Ford's can-do attitude and drive to make a car for the common man early in the 20th century.

And the myth should inform the company mission statement. A founding myth should inform your personal mission statement as well. It's from this statement that your strategy grows. The mission statement anchors your strategy and serves as the basis for your strategic intent. The mission statement is bold and lofty and inspiring.

For example, here is the declared mission of Coca Cola: To refresh the world; to inspire moments of optimism and happiness; to create value and make a difference.

But mission statements can be mundane, uninspiring, routine, forgotten. Often a company becomes lodged in its routine. Its heritage is lost, its environment sterile and devoid of emotional power. Look hard at the mission statement before you think more about strategy. If the statement is laden with jargon, if it's dull, if it talks about "increasing shareholder wealth," if it talks in vague terms about market leadership, if you can't even tell what the company does by reading the statement, then there is a tremendous problem right there.

The founding myth and the mission is the wellspring from which planning emerges. It sets the direction and the tone for the objectives. One of the great strategist academics of the past 20 years is the iconoclast Henry Mintzberg, at Canada's McGill University. Mintzberg has a healthy skepticism about the ways of strategic planning, and the ways it can go wrong. And he has a special place in his heart for the elegant, different, and exciting strategy—a strategy that that doesn't bore.

Mintzberg once said that:

> Thinking about [strategy] shouldn't make you reach for the snooze button, but in the world of strategy everybody has become so serious. If that gets us better strategies, fine. But it doesn't; we get worse ones—predictable, generic, uninspiring, dull … [strategy] has to inspire. So an uninspiring strategy is really no strategy at all.
>
> The most interesting and most successful companies are not boring. They have novel, creative, inspiring, sometimes even playful strategies. By taking the whole strategy business less seriously, they end up with more serious results—and they have some fun in the bargain.

Here's an example of an inspiring mission statement. The product is coffee, and the company is Equal Exchange. Based in Massachusetts, this little company charted a unique course in marketing in 1986. They sell a variety of products, but their core business is coffee. The essence of their vision and mission is: "Fairness to farmers. A closer connection between people and the farmers we all rely on."

They didn't want just to sell coffee. They wanted to change the world with how they sold coffee, and they wanted to do it in an inspiring way. With mission in-hand they took the next step and laid out a series of achievable objectives: Help farmers and their families gain more control over their economic futures; provide high-quality foods to nourish the body and the soul; put company control in the hands of the people who did the actual work; establish a community of people who believe that honesty, respect, and mutual benefit are integral to worthwhile endeavor.

This is a brilliant exposition of mission and the establishment of objectives. All of Equal Exchange's marketing carries its message. Look at a package of Equal Exchange coffee: Everything about it speaks to the company's mission. "Whole bean, organic, mind, body & soul." This is mission-focus at its best—a superb example of defining a mission that supports strategic planning.

Now, we can locate the beginning of strategic planning in the military. The marshaling of resources, the training of soldiers, the arming of soldiers, their maneuver on the battlefield—all of this requires forethought and planning.

Prior to the Napoleonic era, planning was the province of the General, or the monarch, with advice from his trusted confidantes. The development of military staff planning saw its beginnings in Prussia during the Napoleonic era.

This was the beginning of the most famous military planning staffs—the Prussian general staff, which came into being in 1807 at the order of King Frederick William III. This became a full-time body guiding the Prussian Army and it was established by law in 1814. This was the first general staff in history.

It was at this juncture in history it was recognized that preparatory staff work was just as essential to wartime operations as was battlefield leadership.

The idea of formal planning made its way slowly into the business realm after World War I. There were early efforts in the 1920s at Harvard University with what was called the Harvard Policy Model. This was a planning method that was more of a general call to action than an actual methodology. Although it amounted to little more than a general atta-boy approach, it did lay important groundwork and charted a direction in thinking that would be joined later with military methods of planning in the post-World War II era.

Ford Motor Company was in financial trouble after World War II and was in administrative chaos. The head of the company—Henry Ford II— knew something new and radical was needed to change the fortunes of the company. His company had been producing vehicles for the military throughout World War II. So he looked to the military.

Ford thought that if the United States Army could conduct the successful invasion of Normandy, race across France and defeat Hitler's Germany, and defeat Imperial Japan, with all of the titanic logistical operations involved in fielding an army of 12 million men, surely there was something in military methods that could help Ford Motor Company overcome its management problems.

Ford looked to the U.S. Army Air Force Office of Statistical Control. He hired 10 former wartime officers who became known as the Whiz Kids. They brought with them advanced planning, organization and management control systems, and they imposed fiscal and process discipline. The man who emerged as leader of the Whiz Kids was Robert McNamara, and he was quickly tapped as a future leader of Ford. He started as manager of planning and financial analysis, and he advanced through a series of top-level management positions. By 1955, McNamara was the General Manager of Ford Division.

These managerial methods stopped the company's losses and brought order to Ford's administrative chaos over the next 15 years. And perhaps wittingly, the Whiz Kids charted the course of American strategic business thought for the next 20 years. Call it the "rise of strategic planning."

But American corporations began to base their strategic plans primarily on financial data—collating the financial figures from the previous year, preparing spreadsheets, making forecasts based on those figures, and then setting the budget. Planning had become little more than a budgeting exercise conducted once a year, all with the illusion of precision.

The planners began moving farther and farther from the mission of the company and focused on budget numbers as a substitute for engagement with reality. But the problems with planning were hidden. They were hidden by the dominance of American productive might. In the post-war world, America had few competitors. American industrial supremacy served to hide whatever defects planning had, on into the 1960s—defects that would loom ever larger as the years passed.

Flush with success at Ford, the Whiz Kids went to Washington at the beginning of the 1960s. Robert McNamara joined the presidential administration of John F. Kennedy as Secretary of Defense. He determined that strategic planning would be elevated to the highest organizational levels of government and created a high-priesthood of planners who reported directly to him—Daniel Ellsberg, Alain Enthoven, Charles Hitch, and Adam Yarmolinsky.

McNamara's model of strategic planning has been applied to many other public sector organizations over the years, and it does seem to have a kind of internal logic to it. It appears to work—though only if you exclude many crucial variables. Through the 1960s, the gospel of strategic planning spread and became embedded in the American Corporation as a standard management tool in virtually every *Fortune* 500 company and many smaller companies. Firms would create complex and meticulously wrought plans based on elaborate forecasts of company performance in the economy and in specific markets. But early strategic planning ignored more than it encompassed. It yielded distorted results.

In the decade of U.S. industrial dominance, it didn't matter as much. But as the 1970s dawned and complexity imposed itself, the challenge of the Japanese and the power of the Arab oil states revealed the poverty of the current planning model. Among other things, it ignored human irrationality in decision making and the actions of other players in the great games of politics and commerce.

Even McNamara, in later years, recognized the flaws in this early form of planning and that even the best plan, the most securely rooted in data and rational calculation, may prove useless in the face of the inevitable irrationality of human behavior and unpredictability of the external environment.

If we recognize the pitfalls in early strategic planning, perhaps we can correct and build a better model. Henry Mintzberg identifies three fallacies that have worked against planning since its inception.

First, the fallacy of predetermination. We believe we can know the future, and this leads us to the "predict and prepare" line of thought. But of course, we can't predict the future, and basing our plans on this single line of thought can be disastrous.

Second is the fallacy of detachment. This refers to the tendency of planners to remove themselves from the scene of the action. This is strategic formulation detached from implementation.

Third is the fallacy of formalization. This is the ossification of strategy and a "binder" mentality. The strategic plan is in a binder on the shelf. And there it stays. It begins detached from reality and, as the days and weeks pass, it becomes even less of a representation of what the company actually does. The more elaborate the plans, the more elaborate their failures.

So, this leads to an obvious question: If strategic planning has such an ignominious track record and seems fruitless in hindsight, then why do we speak of it except as an unfortunate historical hiccup? Just this: Beginning in the late 1970s, the best business thinkers began to think about strategy and how they made decisions, and they began to connect this process of thinking to the real world, where their strategy is played out.

Marking this new thinking was the publication of a powerful article in 1978 by McKinsey and Company, the global management consulting firm. The McKinsey article was called "The Evolution of Strategic Management." It traced the evolution of effectiveness of strategic decision making. McKinsey identified the phases of ineffective planning that had plagued American industry and left it vulnerable to new challenges. The article called for changes in the way we think and the way we conceive of planning.

Let's look quickly at these phases so we can understand how we reached our present point. The first phase was the 1950s Whiz Kid phase—the financial planning phase. This viewed planning as almost a purely financial problem and was conducted as an annual budgeting exercise. We've seen how this is inadequate, and yet this focus lingers on in some businesses because it's easy.

The second phase was forecast-based planning, which recognized that deeper thinking is necessary about resource allocation and development of key issues.

The third phase was externally-oriented planning. This kind of planning was even better because it looked outward to how the firm interacts with the external environment of competitors and other businesses.

The final and highest phase was strategic management itself. Here, we aim to weld strategic planning and management into a single process in pursuit of that lodestone—the linking of strategy conception with execution. This means diffusing the ability to think strategically throughout the entire organization—a worthy goal. This, of course, is easier said than done. It's rarely accomplished because of natural inertia, the distribution of power, and the unity of effort that is needed.

This brings us to the state of strategic planning today. For our purposes, the strategic planning process offers incredible benefits if we pursue it correctly. Here I offer a six-step strategic planning process—six steps to the crafting of competent strategy. Here, we learn the steps in constructing a competent basic strategy. How to develop a strategy in building-block form.

This strategic planning process is one version of planning. It's not the only process. Every competent firm has its own version of this process. It may be five steps, it may be seven. But these are the main steps. Two of them we've covered in this lecture, the remainder we'll be covering in later lectures. They are mission, objective, situation analysis, strategy formulation, strategy implementation, and control.

First, your mission. I began this lecture with a dramatic call to action. Your mission is your core that guides you. Define your mission now. Can you do it in a few short sentences? Or even one sentence? You'd be surprised how many people take this for granted, in both their personal and professional lives. Entire companies can take this for granted, never looking to their mission to guide them in setting of objectives.

The second step is the setting of objectives. You choose these based on some notion of wanting to fulfill your mission. They should be clear, concise, achievable, and in some sense measurable. You want to see progress toward your mission. You can measure your progress and the effectiveness of your strategy: number of meals served, number of satisfied clients, average test scores increasing, market-share targets are met, revenues are increasing, the hill is taken from the enemy, you complete med school, you complete your first tour in the Peace Corps.

The third step is pivotal for most firms, and it is the most involved. This is the environmental scan. We look at the environment in which our firm functions, both the external environment and the internal environment. On a personal level, we evaluate the external factors that impinge on us with respect to our objectives.

We devote several upcoming lectures to the scanning of our environment— what to look for and how to look for it. It's common sense that we should develop knowledge about our own capabilities and resources and then evaluate them against the outside environment to see if we can actually do what we intend to do. But as we saw in our discussion of strategic planning's history, common sense isn't all that common.

The fourth step is the actual formulation of our strategy. We decide what we will actually do to get from where we are to where we want to be. We decide the when, where, and how much of our plan. We allocate resources and we connect our management decisions with the folks who implement the plan.

The fifth step is implementation of our strategy, and here is where many company's fail in their strategic efforts.

The military has a dictum for its officers when directing the soldiers: "supervise and refine." This means not to simply issue orders and then assume they'll be carried out as issued. Experience shows us that too many dissonant factors can disrupt even the best of plans—the variables can wreak havoc on our work. We must constantly supervise and refine during the implementation phase, and this leads us to the final step of the strategic planning process: control.

Control is just what it sounds like. We develop a control mechanism to evaluate if our plan is actually working. Is our plan getting the results we want? If not, why not? We're already familiar with control mechanisms; they're all around us. In university classes, the control mechanism is regular examinations to verify that both learning and teaching strategies are working. In manufacturing, the quality control department is a method of control and evaluation that helps a firm discover systemic deficiencies. The Japanese concept of *Kaizen*—or continuous improvement—is a form of control. When our control or monitoring system tells us that something is amiss in our strategy, we can then circle back to our environmental scan to discover if the relevant environmental factors have changed.

As we think about our own strategic planning process, we should remember to remain rooted in our purpose—our mission. And we should remember what constitutes a good strategy. We don't want to do things just like everyone else. We don't want to be yet another me-too offering in the marketplace, undifferentiated in any meaningful way.

We are not filling out a checklist. We want to remember our definition of strategy from Michael Porter—it means doing things differently. This is one of the most incredibly useful takeaways that the world of strategy can offer us, and it comes from his powerful 1996 article in *Harvard Business Review*: "What is Strategy?" What does it take to be different? Creating different products or producing old products in unique ways. It means taking resources largely available to everyone, and assembling them in a way that yields competitive advantage.

It also takes time. In Michael Porter's view, the proper timeframe for strategic planning may very well be a decade or more. Maybe that seems impossible. Maybe for your organization, looking five years ahead is all you can do. The point is that the timeframe of a single budget or planning cycle is typically not enough for a strategy to be successful. Remember the plan recommended to President Kennedy for beating the Russians in space? Beating the Russians took literally a decade.

Planning far in advance has other advantages, too. As Michael Porter noted, a long-range plan "fosters improvements in individual activities and the fit across activities, allowing an organization to build unique capabilities and skills tailored to its strategy."

As we enter into the strategic planning process, this idea of seeking competitive advantage by doing things differently should inform us every step of the way. Strategic planning has its adherents and its detractors. It takes time. And it can take too much time, especially if the plan is never executed. Used mindlessly, the process can ignore far more than it reveals— perhaps nothing more than an annual budget exercise. Like any process, strategic planning is not perfect. But if we recognize its strengths and stay cognizant of its weaknesses, we can make use of the technique for our own benefit.

What we have discussed in this lecture is an overview of strategic planning, plus with specific attention to the core mission. We will cover the other steps of strategic planning in later lectures.

For now, be aware that anyone can develop a competent and effective strategy with this basic strategic planning process, whether for business or for the accomplishment of personal goals—if there is a core sense of mission.

Near the beginning of this lecture, I presented to you the example of the French Foreign Legion as an organization with a superb sense of self and mission derived from a conflict on a dusty battlefield 150 years ago. And what of the Foreign Legion today?

Each year, the French Foreign Legion publicly reiterates its mission and links its current Legionnaires to its founding traditions. Every April 30 at its headquarters in Aubagne near Marseille, *La Légion étrangère* celebrates the feast of Camerone in a solemn ceremony that commemorates the founding legend of the Legion. It serves as a major source of its operational effectiveness, its ability to disseminate its strategy to all levels of the organization, and a splendid example of how to link those who make the strategy with those who execute it.

Which Business Strategy? Fundamental Choices
Lecture 8

W hen we consider strategy, broadly defined, we move freely under one of two umbrellas: differentiation or cost leadership. Within those broad parameters, we can do many different things—apply tactics, adjust our focus, or concentrate resources in special ways. But always we find ourselves traveling in one of these two directions to compete against our rivals. These categories hold true in a variety of disciplines, and if given a choice, we surely want to compete through differentiation.

Strategies of Marketplace Competition
- Differentiation and cost leadership are the two main ways that businesses compete in the marketplace.

- Under these two umbrellas, we can do many different things: apply tactics, focus on different parts of the value chain, focus on a particular market segment, and so on.

Cost Leadership
- The objective of cost leadership, or the low-cost strategy, is to sell products and services at the lowest price the market will bear and make profits on volume. Businesses find ways to cut costs and to attract value-conscious customers, who are motivated primarily by low prices.

- The big-box retailer Walmart gives us an example of the low-cost strategy in action.

  o Walmart has consistently pursued an elegant business model: Make its profit on volume. Stock its shelves in volume and obtain volume discounts. Squeeze its suppliers and pass the savings on to consumers.

  o In 2007, Walmart strayed from this core strategy in an effort to attract middle-income customers with more buying power than its blue-collar base. It changed its store layout and dropped more than 300 popular low-price items, but in doing so, it alienated customers who had served as the backbone of its success. In 2011, Walmart returned to its original formula.

- Another firm tinkering disastrously with a winning low-price formula was the movie rental company Netflix. With 23 million subscribers in early 2011, Netflix decided to raise its prices and split its services into two separate entities—Internet streaming and mail order. As a result, the company almost 1 million subscribers in six months.

- Some products, particularly commodities, virtually demand a low-cost strategy. It's tough to differentiate something like cement, for example. You can't alter its features in meaningful ways to appeal to customers. This means that cement companies must compete on price, which isn't pleasant. Profit margins are low and the competition is fierce.

- Many job seekers unwittingly choose the low-cost strategy when they should be pursuing a differentiation strategy. Instead of doing the hard work of differentiating themselves, they choose the easy path of low cost, effectively advertising themselves as commodities.

- We can see similar thinking at work among professionals. If there is no differentiation among, say, chiropractors, customers will seek out the lowest price in the marketplace. But a chiropractor who has a specialty, such as athletes' low back pain, is able to charge a higher rate; he or she has moved from being a commodity to a premium product.

Low-Cost Strategy in the Military
- In World War I, all armies in the conflict competed with a low-cost strategy, delivering the same product as efficiently as possible. The result was undifferentiated strategy and tactics that yielded unimaginative warfare and pointless bloodletting. This is the military version of price competition: Gains are rare, and losses can be heavy for both sides.

- It was not until almost three years had passed before one side achieved an innovative breakthrough and differentiated itself in a major way: The invention and use of the tank broke the stalemate of trench warfare and proved to be a technological innovation that turned the tide of war. The differentiation strategy won.

- The choice here is not just about technology; it's also about people. Do you create special elite divisions of your best troops, or do you spread your best troops around, hoping to raise the quality of all of your divisions? In World War II, the Allied and the Axis powers each took different approaches.

  - Germany learned the lessons of World War I and went for differentiation. It built numerous elite divisions and used these troops either as spearheads in offensive operations or as fire brigades in defensive operations.

  - The United States and the Soviet Union took an egalitarian approach and spread their best troops evenly throughout the army. In the end, the Allies defeated Germany by pursuing a high-volume strategy using many units of roughly equal quality.

- World War II provided such a powerful example that many U.S. businesses after the war came to the view that following the low-price, high-volume strategy was the only way to compete successfully.

Differentiation
- World War II in Europe was won on a high-volume strategy, but the war in Asia ended with an extreme example of differentiation: the first use of nuclear weapons. Japan was on the receiving end, and the conclusion spread throughout Japan that differentiation is the way to win.

- In the United States, Michael Porter articulated this principle and began pointing out all the ways a firm can differentiate itself by providing something unique that is valuable to buyers beyond simply offering a low price. This difference can be thought of as a unique selling proposition (USP).

- Many firms make the mistake of unfocusing their proposition, even to the extent that it's no longer unique. They believe, mistakenly, that ambiguity is a good thing because it allows them to "do more things" for different types of people. As a result, the brand is diluted until it eventually becomes meaningless.

- Two good examples of differentiated products are provided by Rolex and Casio. Although both companies sell watches, their products are so well differentiated that they do not compete against each other. Casio offers rugged, high-tech functionality for a reasonable price. Rolex offers luxury and a message of enduring success.

- Two products in the automobile industry, the Tata Nano super compact and the Lexus LS460, offer another example of differentiation. The Nano, priced at under $3000, is pursuing a low-cost strategy, fulfilling the basic human need for transportation. The Lexus, priced at $75,000, is pursuing a premium pricing differentiation strategy.

- Differentiation means specializing; it means adding attractive features and functionality, delivering a crucial service superbly. But it also means establishing a reputation, creating an aura. Nike tennis shoes, for example, are differentiated by a carefully crafted reputation and demand a high price as a result.

Differentiation Strategy in the Military
- In military confrontation, differentiation can win the day. In the latter stages of the Cold War, the U.S. military saw a renaissance of its strategic core. This change in strategy was the development (and threatened development) of a new generation of differentiated technology and weaponry that the Soviets could not imitate.

- The Soviets were still competing in the era of intercontinental ballistic missiles, manned bombers, and submarine-launched ballistic missiles—the strategic triad. The United States competed in this way, as well, and both competed mostly on volume.

- Then, in 1983, the Reagan administration announced the Strategic Defense Initiative (SDI). This was a radical departure from the previous Cold War military balance. The United States consciously chose to use its existing advantages in basic scientific research and overall economic output to upend the strategic balance and create new sources of military advantage.

- SDI was a set of advances in stealth technology and miniaturization across an entire spectrum of weapon systems. Together, these advances fundamentally altered the balance of power and accelerated the collapse of the Soviet Union.

Differentiating a Commodity

- Determining how to differentiate a commodity is one of the most difficult tasks in business. Let's consider the commodity product coffee.

- Although different types of coffee can have different product features, Howard Schultz, the CEO of Starbucks, chose to differentiate coffee by the way it is served. Schultz pioneered the notion that he could charge more for coffee by serving it in a European-style

Both Starbucks and Equal Exchange exemplify the idea that differentiation means specializing.

coffee house that fed into the notion of "lifestyle." Starbucks, with its unique, low-key ambience, became a destination for many people, not just a stop off.

- Following its 1985 debut, Starbucks succeeded stupendously, but by 2007, it seemed to have lost its way. With Shultz no longer the CEO, Starbucks decided to change the format of its stores to make them more "inviting" to other types of customers. By switching to a less differentiated strategy, Starbucks lost its distinctiveness and began to lose customers.

- Schultz returned to Starbucks as CEO in 2008, and under his revitalization initiative, Starbucks began to regain its cachet by going back to its roots and refining its USP.

Focus
- A third path that a business can follow—an offshoot of our two main strategies—is pursuing a highly targeted market and focusing its resources on serving that tight segment, whether through cost leadership or differentiation. This is the focus strategy.

- Focus is a kind of hyper-differentiation. Examples of firms that follow a focus strategy include ethnic grocery stores and producers of ultra-high-end cars. These focused companies target the highly specialized needs of a narrow market and fulfill them better than any other firm.

- Equal Exchange is an example of a company pursuing a focus strategy.

  o The company sells fair trade coffee, which means that it guarantees its coffee is produced by farmers who receive a higher-than-market-price for their coffee beans. The expense is passed on to customers, but those who are motivated by social justice causes will gladly pay the higher price.

  o Equal Exchange has a niche/focus strategy that targets a highly specific market with sharply drawn characteristics. This market is not likely to grow substantially, but the niche has been profitable for the company.

- Another example of a focus strategy can be found in the incredible debut and rise of a soft drink called Jolt Cola. This cola was created as a reaction to the increasing health-consciousness of Americans and the desire to reduce caffeine and sugar intake. Jolt Cola went against this trend, targeting young people with a maverick streak using the slogan: "All the sugar, and twice the caffeine."

Differentiating Yourself

- Pursuing a differentiation strategy has merit over pursuing a low-cost strategy. Focusing and sharpening your strengths is a major step in developing competitive advantage—the thing that you can do better than anyone else.

- The first step is to take stock of your resources and capabilities and assess whether they match your intentions. Do you have what is called "strategic fit"? Aligning your resources and capabilities with your intentions puts you in the best position for crafting and executing a successful strategy.

- To help you achieve this, develop a personal USP, a one-sentence description of what you offer people that few others can match. Now do the same for a trusted friend and exchange the results. This is sometimes the best way of taking your personal skills inventory.

Suggested Reading

Porter, *Competitive Strategy*.

Trout, *Differentiate or Die*.

Questions to Consider

1. This lecture cites the important distinctions among the competitive strategies and the importance of choosing the right strategy to match your resources and capabilities *or* developing resources and capabilities to match our grand ambitions. Using the framework from the lecture, consider thoughtfully how you compete, personally, in your profession. Do you strive for operational efficiency, doing the same thing as everyone else, only better, faster, more efficiently? If you strive for differentiation, combining your unique skill set, experience, and expertise to offer a service that no one can match, take a moment to disaggregate and list the components of that competitive advantage.

2. Nike can charge a superior premium for its branded merchandise. Examine your first reaction to this information: Do you shake your head and comment, "It's not worth that!"? Or do you ask, "What is the magic formula that has enabled Nike to charge more for its particular brand?" Ask yourself what factors might be in play that enable your products, your firm, and your persona to increase in value with respect to people's perceptions.

3. One of the most difficult tasks in business is to convert a generic commodity into a differentiated product with premium value added. Consider coffee for a moment and how Equal Exchange created a sharply defined "persona" linked to fulfilling the desires of a particular customer base. Were you to launch your own brand of coffee tomorrow, consider how you might differentiate this common commodity in such a way that sets you apart from the plethora of other coffees on the market. What combination of attributes, service, brand, packaging, distribution, and benefits might make for a winning coffee launch?

Which Business Strategy? Fundamental Choices
Lecture 8—Transcript

Business theorists have studied competition for decades, and they have come to some robust conclusions about how we compete and what factors compel us to compete the way we do.

That's the topic of this lecture: The main types of business strategies. Our objective is to learn the major ways that firms and people compete economically with each other and how these modes of competition also apply across non-business activity. We also learn how to use this knowledge so that we might compete more effectively by obtaining what we call a competitive advantage.

After this lecture, you should have a much better idea of how to position your business and position yourself successfully in competitive situations of all kinds.

First, we look at the two main ways that businesses compete in the marketplace—this is your basic choice—what we call "differentiation" or "cost leadership." Think of these two strategic thrusts as umbrellas, and we move freely under one or the other.

Under these two big umbrellas: differentiation or cost leadership. We can do many different things: We can apply tactics, we can focus on different parts of our value chain, we can joust with our opponents in shrewd ways, we can focus on a particular segment of a market, we can concentrate our resources in special and unique ways. But always, we find ourselves traveling in one of two directions: differentiation or cost leadership.

Michael Porter introduced this quite brilliant categorization back in 1980 in a classic work called *Competitive Strategy*. Let's have a look. First, let's look at cost leadership. This is sometimes called the low-cost strategy. The objective of this strategy is to sell our products and services at the lowest price the market will bear and make our profits on volume. We find ways to cut our costs and to attract value-conscious customers. Our target customers are motivated primarily by low prices. They usually don't have much loyalty to our brand—or any brand for that matter. They'll switch to a lower-priced product immediately.

If we produce a commodity such as crude oil, we are almost locked into this strategy. Commodities are difficult to differentiate. We can't attract more customers or charge higher prices by packaging our crude oil in colorful barrels or giving it a catchy brand name or by hiring Michael Jordan for our advertisements.

Here's an example of the low-cost strategy in action. Most of us are familiar with the big-box retailer Wal-Mart. This company is one of the great icons of American Capitalist success. With 6000 stores and more than $250 billion in annual sales, Wal-Mart is the world's largest retailer. Wal-Mart has pursued almost exclusively a low-cost strategy. This has been reflected in its motto for much of its history: "Always Low Prices". Wal-Mart's brand stands for something in the minds of its customers and has resulted from a consistent pursuit of its elegant business model: Make its profit on volume. Stock its shelves in volume, and it obtains volume discounts. Squeeze its suppliers and pass the savings on to you. And you enjoy everyday low prices.

But our inclination is to tinker with a successful model—sometimes for the better. But straying from a proven strategy without sound reasons is never a good idea. For instance, Wal-Mart. Wal-Mart has strayed from its core strategy on occasion as it tries to capture more customers. Nothing wrong with that. But this just muddies up the brand. It muddles what people expect when they walk into the store.

In 2007, Wal-Mart shelved its 19-year old motto and adopted a new motto: "Save Money. Live Better." This vague catchall slogan was a blunder. In fact, it was one of a series of strategic blunders that decoupled Wal-Mart from the secret of its success. Wal-Mart wanted to attract newer middle-income customers with more buying power. But it began to alienate its base—the blue-collar workers that had served as the backbone of its success. It changed its store layout so it looked, frankly, more like a Target store. It eliminated what it thought was clutter: It dropped more than 300 popular low-price items—and prices began to creep up.

The new slogan didn't work, and even though there was a recession, the low price-items were missing, and people hated the new store layout. After three years, Wal-Mart chucked it all. In 2011, the store brought back hundreds of items and advertised the fact in its stores with signs saying, "It's back." Wal-Mart's tinkering with its formula stopped—at least for the moment. Wal-Mart went back to its roots in 2011 with its slogan: "Low prices. Every day. On everything."

Another firm tinkering disastrously with a winning low-price formula was the movie rental company Netflix. Netflix had begun offering DVD rental by mail and was trying to expand into on-demand Internet streaming media. By early 2011, it had more than 23 million subscribers. Highly successful and blessed with phenomenal growth, Netflix in late 2011 made two incredibly bad strategic decisions.

First, it arbitrarily raised its prices by 60 percent and offered a limp rationale that merely angered subscribers. Second, it split its services into two separate entities—streaming and mail order—and set up two separate websites. As a result, Netflix lost almost 1 million subscribers, a discovery that Netflix commanded very little respect as a brand. Customers shopping on price left for competitors Amazon.com, Google, and Wal-Mart, and Netflix stock dropped. The company immediately reversed track on the dual website idea, having learned, one believes, a valuable lesson about the importance of having and maintaining a core strategy at all times.

Some products virtually demand a low-cost strategy be used. These products are commodities. An example of product that demands a low-cost strategy is cement. Cement is a commodity. It's tough to differentiate cement. You can't alter its features in meaningful ways to appeal to customers—you can't sell scented cement, or sell it in colorful individually packaged servings, or sell it with a freshness date-stamp, or such like. This means that cement companies compete on price. This isn't pleasant. Profit margins are low and the competition fierce.

Now, let's translate the low-cost strategy to the individual person competing, say, in the job market. When people search for a job, many of them unwittingly choose a bad strategy. They pursue a low-cost strategy when they should be pursuing a differentiation strategy. Picture a job-hunter going into an interview. She walks in with a sign around her neck that says, "Hire me, I'll work for less."

This unfortunate soul is pursuing what is called a low-cost strategy. It means that she is competing on price, and nothing else. Her "price," of course, is her salary. It means she'll work longer hours for less pay. She unwittingly advertises herself as a commodity. Instead of the hard work of differentiating herself, she chooses the easy path of low cost, slashing her salary demands. She tries to undercut his competition by offering more of the same, but for less.

This seems foolish, doesn't it? Why would anyone want to compete this way? "Everyday Low Wages". And yet many people do. Especially newly minted college graduates. And even, at times, the more experienced of us. Even many professionals fear to differentiate themselves, believing they may lose the stray walk-in customer. Take a chiropractor, for instance.

The old joke about chiropractors is that anyone with a back is a customer. Such an approach is a textbook low-cost strategy. With no differentiation between chiropractors, customers will seek out the lowest priced in the market. Thus chiropractors are at the mercy of the dictates of supply and demand. They charge what everyone else charges—maybe a bit less.

But what if you're a chiropractor and you specialize in, say, athletes' low-back pain? Suddenly, your hourly rate went up. Sure, you've lost the occasional walk-by and a host of non-athletes. But every athlete with low-back pain will seek you out. You have moved yourself from a commodity to a premium product. You have moved yourself from Wal-Mart to Bloomingdale's. You have, in fact, differentiated yourself.

In the realm of the military, we also find low-cost and differentiation strategies. In World War I, all armies in the conflict competed in the same way—low cost, delivering the same product in as efficient a way as possible, undifferentiated strategy and tactics that yielded unimaginative warfare and pointlessly bloody results. Over-the-top charges into machine-gun fire and barbed wire was the norm. This is the military version of price competition: Gains are rare, and losses can be heavy for both sides.

It was not until almost three years had passed before one side achieved an innovative breakthrough and differentiated itself in a major way—the invention of and use of the tank broke the stalemate of trench warfare and proved to be a technological innovation that turned the tide of war. The differentiation strategy won.

And the choice is not just about technology; it's also about people. Do you create special elite divisions of your best troops? Or do you spread your best troops around, hoping to raise the quality of all of your divisions? In World War II, the allies and the Axis powers each took different approaches.

Germany learned the lessons of World War I and went for differentiation. It built numerous elite divisions and used these troops either as spearheads in offensive operations, or as fire brigades in defensive operations. The United States took an egalitarian approach and spread their best troops evenly throughout the army. In the end, the U.S. defeated Germany by pursuing a high-volume strategy using many units of roughly equal quality.

World War II, in turn, provided such a powerful example that many U.S. businesses after the war came to the view that low-price, high-volume was the way to compete successfully. Which brings us back to our second major strategy: differentiation.

While World War II in Europe was won on a high-volume strategy, the war in Asia ended with an extreme example of differentiation: the first use of nuclear weapons. Japan was on the receiving end, and the conclusion spread after the war that differentiation is the way to win.

In the United States, Harvard Business School guru Michael Porter articulated this principle, and began pointing out all the ways a firm can differentiate itself by providing something unique that is valuable to buyers beyond offering simply a low price.

This unique difference can be thought of as a Unique Selling Proposition, or USP.

Many firms make the common mistake of unfocusing their proposition, even to the extent that it's no longer unique. They believe, mistakenly, that ambiguity is a good thing. Why? Because they believe it allows them to "do more things" for different types of people. As a result, the brand is diluted until eventually it can become meaningless.

Think of the many companies out there that advertise themselves as offering as their product "solutions." Say what? It means absolutely nothing. Here's a simple test to show you what I mean. I call this the Adult Bookstore Test. To discover whether a slogan or USP is tightly focused and powerful, try this: If the slogan in question could be attached equally well to Colombian coffee, Joe's barbershop, a software company, an airline, and an adult bookstore, then it's likely an unfocused, generic, and ineffective slogan. Exhibit A is Grolsch Beer. This craft beer's awful longtime slogan was this: "Craftsmanship is Mastery," which could refer to power tools—or the aforementioned adult bookstore. At one time, Mobil Oil used, "We want you to live," which is a nice sentiment, I suppose, but which could apply to most any business. Companies selling a commodity with nothing to differentiate it often fall back on vague slogans with no real focus.

But there are also examples of superb differentiation. Let's look at two fine examples of differentiated products. Superficially, they're the same product performing the same function: the Rolex watch and the Casio watch. Both Rolex and the Casio digital watch are timepieces. But do they compete in the same market space? No, they do not. You don't find them sold in the same stores or through the same channels; you don't see them advertised in the same media, nor will you find the same celebrities advertising them.

Rolex and Casio do not compete against each other—they do not serve the same customers. In reality, the Casio and Rolex offerings are different products with different pricing. Let's look: Casio has offered great watches, starting at about $14 for a basic digital watch and running to more than $450 for watches in its Pathfinder series for the serious outdoorsman and $500 for its Edifice smart watches. The watches are rugged and well-made.

For instance, Casio has offered a sports watch that takes and displays barometric pressure readings, which are then converted into altitude measurements based on International Standard Atmospheric Values. A built-in thermo sensor gives reliable temperature readings. And it gives you the time in 48 of the world's cities. It's also waterproof down to 100 meters. This watch sold for $84.

Rolex is different. At the low end, the Rolex Oyster Perpetual Air-King was around $4600. At the higher end, there was the Oyster Perpetual Day-Date. Now, compare these features of the Day-Date with the Casio sports watch I just described. The Rolex is platinum, bezel set with 42 baguette diamonds, 8 round and 2 baguette diamonds set on the dial, 31-jewel chronometer movement, synthetic sapphire crystal with—and I think this is ironic—Roman numerals on the dial. Price: $71,000—for a watch using Roman numerals.

Both watch brands are differentiated quite well. They are so differentiated, in fact, that they don't even compete against each other. Casio offers rugged, high-tech functionality for a reasonable price. Rolex offers true luxury for what you expect to pay for true luxury and prestige, and a message of enduring success that never goes out of style.

Here's another example from the automobile industry. If that car is Tata Nano Supercompact, it's priced under $3000. If that car is a Lexus LS460, it's priced at $75,000. That's a gap of $72,000. What constitutes this gap between these two vehicles? One vehicle is pursuing a low-cost strategy, fulfilling the basic human need for transportation; the other is pursuing a premium pricing differentiation strategy, fulfilling a host of other needs and demands that people are willing to pay for.

Differentiation means specializing—it means adding attractive features and functionality, delivering a crucial service superbly. All of these things people will pay for. But differentiation also means establishing reputation, creating an aura. Take, for instance, tennis shoes. Not just any tennis shoes: Nike tennis shoes. Here is a product differentiated by a carefully crafted reputation. This reputation has lent incredible value to the brand and logo. In this case, Nike and its swoosh logo and the stable of celebrities that endorse the shoes. Are Nike shoes truly worth up to $200 more than its competitor shoes, even when there is really little or no qualitative difference? The answer is a resounding yes! The concept of worth has no meaning outside the people who establish worth with their preferences. So those Nike tennis shoes are worth exactly what people are willing to pay for them.

Even outside the business world, the concept of a differentiation strategy has much to recommend it. In military confrontation, differentiation can win the day. In the latter stages of the Cold War, the United States military saw a renaissance of its strategic core. This change in strategy was the development of a new generation of differentiated technology and weaponry that the Soviets could not imitate. The Soviets were still competing in the era of ICBMs (intercontinental ballistic missiles), manned bombers, and submarine-launched ballistic missiles—the strategic triad. The U.S. competed this way as well. Both competed mostly on volume.

Until about 1983, when the Reagan Administration announced the Strategic Defense Initiative. This was a radical departure from the previous Cold War military balance, which relied upon the old strategic triad. As Kennedy had done with the program to put a man on the moon, the U.S. consciously chose to utilize its existing advantages in basic scientific research and overall economic output to upend the strategic balance and create new sources of military advantage.

While the U.S. public mostly debated whether so-called "Star Wars" lasers could work just like in the movies, in reality, fixation on any single technology was never the point of strategic defense. Instead, SDI was really a set of advances across an entire spectrum of weapons systems: Advances in stealth technology and miniaturization led to the stealth bomber, the stealth fighter, cruise missile technology, neutron anti-tank weapons, and weaponized laser research. Together, they fundamentally altered the balance of power and accelerated the collapse of the Soviet Union.

Development and deployment of new technologies broke the stalemate in the late 1980s, much as it broke the World War I stalemate of trench warfare, and the World War II miasma of island-hopping in the Pacific. The decision to compete differently, in differentiated fashion, achieved victory.

That brings us to one of the most difficult tasks in business: figuring out how to differentiate a commodity. It's tough, but it's been done successfully in many cases both well-known and not-so-well-known. Let's take the commodity product coffee.

Coffee. Some people buy their coffee in plain white cans marked with the word "coffee." It's a kind of ultimate commoditization. The product has a sameness about it, as does the package. Coffee in a can is a ground-up brown bean.

Now, many people don't realize that there are two major kinds of coffee beans—Robusta and Arabica. Robusta beans yield coffee with a bitter taste, but the bean is cheaper and weathers the elements better at harvest time. Arabica offers a mellow, rich taste, but it's more expensive and less hearty in the fields. This difference between Arabica and Robusta beans hasn't proven enough to differentiate coffee in a meaningful way. Especially when the folks at Maxwell House and Folgers mix the two types of beans.

So here's how you differentiate coffee—think Starbucks. Howard Schultz, CEO of Starbucks, differentiated coffee not by the product features, but by the way it's served. He created the concept of the Eurostyle coffee house in the United States after a trip to Milan, Italy. He pioneered the notion that he could charge more for his more expensive Arabica bean coffee by serving it in a unique manner that fed into the notion of lifestyle.

Starbucks, with its unique and low-key ambience, became the "third place" for many people. By this was meant the third place in addition to home and work. Starbucks became a destination, not just a stop-off. By any measure, Starbucks succeeded stupendously following its 1985 debut. But by 2007, Starbucks had seemingly lost its way. With Howard Schultz gone for several years as CEO, others decided to do what many firms do when the goal of growth overrides all considerations of fundamental strategy.

Starbucks decided to change the format of its stores to make it more inviting to other types of customers. In New York, for instance, the idea that hundreds of people were walking by the store every hour beckoned. These people might be enticed into the coffee shop with a wider selection of food and beverage. And so deli meats were added to the mix.

And the store, once a haven for Eurostyle-craving young professionals, began to smell like a deli. By switching to a less differentiated strategy, it lost its distinctiveness and it began to lose customers. It alienated its core customers while making itself more like every other joint on the block. Deli meats?

Starbucks also missed an even bigger opportunity to deepen its identity in response to the revolution in wireless network access. What Starbucks could and should have done was immediately offer free wireless access to deepen its status as the premier third destination, comparable to home and work. However, Starbucks was slow to offer free WiFi. When it did, it was already trailing behind new competition from McDonald's and Panera Bread in embracing this important technology. Howard Schultz returned as CEO in 2008, and under Schultz's revitalization initiative, Starbucks began to regain its cachet by going back to its roots and refining its unique selling proposition.

We've looked at differentiation and we've looked at cost leadership. There's a third path that a person or a business can follow, an offshoot of our two main strategies, and this consists in pursuing a highly targeted market and focusing your resources on serving that tight little segment, whether through cost leadership or differentiation: This is the focus strategy.

Focus is exactly what it sounds like. You slice off a narrow spectrum of the market and focus on that segment. But this is much more than differentiation; focus is a kind of hyper-differentiation. Here are some examples of firms that follow a focus strategy: ethnic grocery stores, catering to the specific needs of a highly identifiable sub-segment of the grocery industry; the producers of ultra-high-end motor cars, such as Bentleys, which cost upwards of a quarter million dollars each, or Maserati sports cars. These focused companies target the highly specialized needs of a narrow market and fulfill them better than anyone else.

One of my favorite examples of a company pursuing a focus strategy is Equal Exchange Coffee, which we looked at in the last lecture. This is the for-profit firm that behaves as if it's a non-profit social conscience operation. Equal Exchange sells coffee. Not just any kind of coffee, but Fair Trade coffee. This means that Equal Exchange guarantees that its coffee is produced by farmers who receive a higher than market-price for their coffee beans.

The best part of this operation is the brilliant business model behind it. You recall that Wal-Mart contracts low-cost suppliers and passes the savings on to you? Equal Exchange Coffee pays above market prices for its coffee and passes the expense on to you.

Customers who are motivated by social justice causes, and have disposable income to spend in that way, will gladly pay the higher price. Equal Exchange Coffee has succeeded in increasing the perceived value of its product by linking it to a social justice cause. Consumers receive not only good coffee, but a clear conscience and a warm fuzzy that they're doing good in the world.

Equal Exchange has a niche/focus strategy that targets a highly specific market with sharply drawn characteristics. This market likely will not grow substantially because of that. But it is a profitable niche, even if they never get on the menu at Starbucks.

Another example of a focus strategy was the incredible debut and rise of a soft drink in 1985 called Jolt Cola. This cola was created as a reaction to the increasing health-consciousness of Americans. People at the time were reducing caffeine and sugar intake. Jolt Cola went against this trend. Jolt Cola's motto was "All the sugar, and twice the caffeine."

In retrospect, Jolt was one of the first energy drinks. It clearly positioned itself as a renegade and an alternative to the "healthier" soft-drinks on the market. It targeted young people with a maverick streak. It was a focus strategy with a highly segmented and identifiable market segment. But Jolt also lost its way, filing for bankruptcy in 2009 after getting bogged down in overly expensive packaging.

Now, how do you differentiate yourself? I hope that you have seen the merit in pursuing a differentiation strategy for yourself as opposed to a low-cost strategy. There is merit in focusing and sharpening yourself as opposed to the all-things-to-all-people approach.

This is a major step along the way to developing competitive advantage. We've used that term a lot in this lecture. It means something that you can do better than anyone else—something that is not easily replicable. It may not even be a single talent or skill. Instead, it could be a combination of activities that together give you a source of advantage. Regardless of the source of your competitive advantage, you must drill down until you discover it. Then focus on it relentlessly.

You have the advantage of being able to change yourself. By this, I mean you can specialize. You can aggregate your talents, your skills, your experiences, and you can position yourself accordingly.

Your first step is to take stock of your resources and capabilities and assess whether they match your intentions. Do you have what is called "strategic fit?" This is very much what a company does when it searches for its competitive advantage. You want to discover your own competitive advantage. You want to align your resources and capabilities with your intentions, because when you do, you have achieved the best possible circumstances for crafting and successfully executing your strategy.

To help you achieve this, I leave you with a task. I want you to develop your USP—your Unique Selling Proposition. This is another way to think about your core mission. It is your one-sentence description of what you offer people that few others can match. Think of famous product USPs: Avis—we try harder; BMW—the ultimate driving machine; Mercedes-Benz—German engineering; Bounty—the quicker picker upper; Folger's—the best part of waking up is Folger's in your cup.

To get you started on your own USP, ask yourself a series of questions: What is it I love to do? What am I good at? What category can I own? What word will people associate with me?

Now, meet up with a trusted friend who is similarly motivated as you. Interview each other and develop a USP for your friend. Your friend develops one for you. This is sometimes the best way of going about your skills inventory.

None of the fundamental strategies we've discussed fits every person or situation. That's why identifying your own fundamental strategy is one of the single most valuable steps you can take. So don't put it off. Do it now.

Your Competitive Advantage—Find the Blue Ocean
Lecture 9

At some point, we have to put into action what we've learned; we must craft a strategy that is unlike what everyone else is doing. One idea that can assist in this process is the concept of the "blue ocean," an uncontested area of the market space, in which your product or firm is differentiated in some meaningful way for your target market. In this lecture, we look at a framework to help you find your blue ocean and use it to develop your personal brand.

Madonna
- When you think of strategy, the popular singer Madonna probably doesn't spring to mind, yet Madonna has proven to be one of the shrewdest strategists the entertainment industry has ever seen.

- An unknown when she arrived in New York in 1977, Madonna made a huge and surprising impact with her first album in 1983. She seemed to have come from nowhere. But that first album was the successful result of a superb strategy developed by a superb business strategist.

- Madonna articulated her core mission, established her objectives, adopted a relentless strategic intent, and recognized that she could carve out uncontested market space by developing a USP and personal brand unlike anyone else's.

- For us, Madonna underlines the point that competitive advantage is a concept we can apply in many areas of competition. In fact, Madonna's overall success is directly attributable to precisely the kind of highly differentiated competitive advantage that we will discuss in this lecture.

A Different View of Competition
- Many people think of competition as doing the same thing as everyone else, only better. An entire industry and management mythos has

grown up around this notion, focusing on the use of best practices, benchmarking, and so on.

- However, if we do nothing else but benchmark and copy our competitors, we end up playing a game of mimicry. We offer pale imitations of our competitors' products and others offer imitations of ours. That's hardly what Madonna did to achieve stardom.

- As we said in the last lecture, our goal is to develop a USP, which is a collection of factors assembled in such a way that it constitutes a distinctive core competency and confers unique competitive advantage. This USP can become the basis for a personal brand.

- To create a USP, we start with Michael Porter's ideas about strategy—determining how we want to compete and how we will do things differently. This means choosing a generic strategy and building on it; it means assembling our resources in new and different ways.

- Madonna didn't have a checklist to tell her how to compete and she didn't benchmark herself against the competition to give crowds an improved version of the same old thing; instead, she looked at her competition in a cool and calculating way to discover her blue ocean.

- "Blue ocean" is a strategic term that first appeared in a book called *Blue Ocean Strategy* by W. Chan Kim and Renée Mauborgne, professors at INSEAD, one of the world's greatest business schools. It refers to uncontested market space carved out by shrewd competitors.

- Kim and Mauborgne showed that most companies are driven to compete in what they call "red oceans." This name evokes a steaming cauldron of competitors fighting over a shrinking profit pool—low margins, high stress, survival in the world of commodities.

- The alternative to carve out uncontested market space, to differentiate yourself, your product, or your firm in some way meaningful to your target market, that is, to find your blue ocean.

The Four Actions Framework

- Kim and Mauborgne offer the Four Actions Framework as a method to get you thinking in fresh ways about what you do each day. This model challenges the value curve, which depicts how a company is doing across an industry's accepted factors of competition. For cars, the accepted factors of competition might be price, prestige, gas mileage, size, comfort, performance, longevity, safety, and service.

- The conventional competitive model says to compete across the full range of factors, but the blue ocean strategy argues for a different approach: Ask basic questions about the industry with the intent of creating new competitive factors that appeal to unexplored market segments.

- For example, with the Nano, the Tata Group consciously chose not to compete on most of the standard features of the industry, instead betting everything on a highly differentiated price strategy that addressed an ignored market segment: consumers at the bottom of the pyramid. This was Tata's USP, which allowed the company to explore a blue ocean.

- The Four Actions Framework consists of four questions that are designed to challenge an industry's established structure and business logic: (1) Which of the factors that the industry takes for granted should be eliminated? (2) Which factors should be reduced well below the industry's standard? (3) Which factors should be raised well above the industry's standard? (4) Which factors should be created that the industry has never offered?

- We might phrase these questions as four steps—eliminate, reduce, raise, and create; these activities will enable you to create a new value curve.

The Framework in Action

- Casella Wines, the producer of [yellow tail], carved out uncontested market space for itself by thinking unconventionally to redefine the value curve for the wine industry.

- The conventional value curve for wine consisted of price, use of intriguing terminology, high-visibility marketing, aging quality, vineyard prestige, wine complexity, and wine range. Both prestige and budget wines competed on these factors.

- But Casella downplayed the traditional competitive factors and created three additional factors that other wines could not match: easy drinking, ease of selection, and fun and adventure. In doing so, the company eliminated the emphasis on wine as complex and characterized by subtleties. It even eliminated different bottle designs for red and white wines and drastically reduced its selection, at first offering just one red and one white wine.

Casella Wines discovered its blue ocean by developing new factors in the value curve of the wine industry: ease of enjoyment and fun.

- At the same time, Casella raised the level of fun of its [yellow tail] wine, putting a kangaroo in bright orange and yellow on a very simple label. It even created a unique way to present the brand name, using all lowercase letters placed in square brackets.

- [yellow tail] grew quickly, not just by taking market share from established competitors but by actually growing the market, selling to new wine drinkers attracted by Casella's distinctive willingness to highlight a single fresh, fruity wine and cut through the overwhelming number of available choices.

- With [yellow tail], Casella found a blue ocean that allowed it to prosper while other producers were suffering through a dip in the industry. As the industry recovered, Casella responded by adding a small number of additional offerings in a way that continued to reinforce its USP.

Your Personal Blue Ocean Strategy

- Your resume may show that you have lots of experience and a desire to succeed, but that is not the way to carve out uncontested market space. You find your blue ocean by applying unconventional thinking to familiar situations.

- The failed ad campaign for Diet Coke, launched and quickly pulled after six weeks in 1993, lets us imagine how this unconventional thinking might work.

  o The campaign was designed by Lintas Media Group in New York, the longtime ad agency of Coca Cola. But after the ads were pulled, Lintas lost the Coke account.

  o In the wake of that loss, it's likely that personnel at Lintas were hunkered down behind closed doors, updating their resumes and hoping that they wouldn't become scapegoats.

  o But what if the person responsible for losing the account had stepped forward and accepted the blame? Instead of being a nameless, faceless mid-level executive, he or she would have established a bold personal brand: "I'm the manager who lost the Coke account."

  o The magnitude and boldness of the statement, the high stakes involved, and the unusual stance make this selling proposition truly unique. The manager could go on to become an executive who provides insight on corporate advertising. He or she might land a book deal or a gig on CNN as a business analyst.

  o Of course, such a move would be risky, but the lesson here is that you need to untrain yourself from thinking conventionally and unharness yourself from the need for external validation of your ideas. If something is truly new and different in its nascent stages, few people will recognize it as such.

- Another opportunity for unconventional thinking comes to us from BP, the world's third-largest oil company. As we know, BP became the object of scorn during the summer of 2010 after one of its wells in the Gulf of Mexico malfunctioned and exploded.

- As an exercise at the time, I asked my students to think unconventionally about the situation. I challenged them to ignore the easy chorus of boos and ask themselves what they would do if they were on the BP team. How might they help to turn things around for the company?

- I also advised the graduating students to submit their resumes to BP. I urged them to consider what might happen if they were to join the company at its lowest point and whether they might then rise quickly in the company when it recovered.

- The idea might seem farfetched, but by joining BP when it was down, a young executive could build a feisty brand as someone who helped turn the company around.

- The easy, conventional choice is always available to you, but the rewards are commensurately small. Great strategy is about using unconventional thinking to figure out what you have to offer the world and how you can promote what you do best.

Your Personal Brand
- It's a fact that you will always be labeled by others, so it's wise to seize control of that process rather than allowing it to take shape without your input. Crafting your personal brand is one of the most important strategic activities of your life.

- Your brand is your reputation. It's what people first think when they see you or hear your name. And brands mean something: Mercedes means quality; Volvo means safety. What image or tagline does your name evoke?

- You can argue that people ought to accept you as you are and not judge you by appearances or behavior; in other words, you can opt out of branding. But if you don't take control over how you are perceived, you handicap whatever strategy you choose to pursue.

- Brand yourself consciously. Unleash your creativity in ways that stretch the boundaries of the conventional. Question the assumptions that guide individual or market competition in your industry. All this will help you establish a USP that captures a position unlike any other.

Suggested Reading

Beckwith and Beckwith, *You, Inc.*

Kim and Mauborgne, *Blue Ocean Strategy.*

Questions to Consider

1. When strategy is the topic, Madonna doesn't usually spring to mind, but she exemplifies how strategic thinking can be applied rigorously in almost any professional field to craft successful strategy. Consider other high-profile, successful professionals and identify the characteristics that you believe contributed to their accomplishments. Is the success fleeting or is it sustained? If it's the latter, can you identify the dimensions of competition in the particular field in which the individual excels? How does he or she do it?

2. Blue ocean strategy means creating new ways to compete and offers us a framework to channel our thinking in creative ways. One extremely useful exercise is to assess two competing products, one of which leads the market and the other, an also-ran. How do these products compete? In other words, what are the metrics we use to evaluate the products? Can you discover the secrets of success of one product and of mediocrity for the other?

3. Blue ocean strategy means thinking unconventionally, and most times, we have to force ourselves out of the rut of our thinking habits. It's helpful to train ourselves to look at situations not with our habitual perspective but with a keen eye for the main chance lurking within. Take

any prominent public relations disaster at a big company in the past five years and ask yourself: What opportunities lie within this ostensible wreck? If I were trying to swim in those turbulent waters, how might I make the most of the situation? What would I do if I had no choice but to deal with the situation?

Your Competitive Advantage—Find the Blue Ocean
Lecture 9—Transcript

When you think of strategy, the popular singer Madonna probably doesn't spring to mind. You probably wonder why she enters a conversation about strategy. Yet Madonna has been, throughout her decades-long career, one of the shrewdest strategists in the entertainment industry we've ever seen.

In 1977 Madonna Louise Ciccone left Ann Arbor, Michigan, where she was a relatively unknown student studying dance at the University of Michigan. She arrived in New York City with $35 to her name and carrying a determination—a focus—to make it big in the entertainment business. She had her training in dance, but little else—no musical background and no contacts in the industry. This hardly seems a formula for success. But we now recognize a great legend when we see one, and how that contributes to an enduring and consistent sense of mission.

Which is exactly why Madonna's career teaches us much about key facets of strategy—focus, strategic intent, adaptability, and sustainable competitive advantage. Madonna's relentless drive and shrewd instincts about the music business led her to identify the pathways and gatekeepers of the industry. She then focused on those pressure points, especially the DJs of New York clubs, whom she correctly recognized as holding the keys to popularity and eventual success.

Madonna gives the lie to the instant success or "discovery" myth—her hard work was legendary. Her relentless networking and developing of contacts was paralleled by her conscious development of a unique style. Her style was unlike others of the time and would soon set the trend for an entire generation of teenage girls.

Madonna burst onto the national and international scene with her first album, *Madonna.* The impact was sudden and, to the world at large, a huge surprise. She seemed to have come from nowhere. But her first album was the successful result of a superb strategy developed by a superb business strategist. Madonna articulated her core mission, established her objectives, adopted a relentless strategic intent, and recognized that she could carve out uncontested market space by developing a unique selling proposition and personal brand unlike anyone else's.

Madonna's first album was incredibly successful, but she was only at the start of her amazing career. She brazenly articulated her strategic intent in her debut on the television music show American Bandstand, when host Dick Clark asked her: "What do you really want to do when you grow up?" Madonna answered: "Rule the world." She went on to star in several films, and her second album *Like a Virgin* sold more than 3 million copies. Her third album *True Blue* sold 24 million copies.

As the 1990s unfolded, Madonna's popularity continued. She developed professionally in addition to her singing, and she became a true renaissance business woman. She developed acute interests in intellectual property, book publishing, music production, concert production, motion pictures, business management, art direction, and—perhaps most important—manager of her personal brand.

"I'm tough," she said in 1985. "I'm ambitious, and I know exactly what I want." This was just eight years after she arrived in New York with a pocketful of small bills.

What's the Madonna secret? Is there a Madonna secret? There must be—after all, Madonna is not the most attractive star in her various worlds; she is not the best dancer; she is not the best singer. But Madonna has no equal in assembling all of the entertainment success factors into a strategic position unique and powerful. Her strategic position has proven unassailable. While other acts have come and gone since 1983, Madonna has remade herself and remade herself again.

Madonna has a shrewd business acumen that most businesses should envy. She maintains her competitive position by way of a series of shrewd competitive moves that are coolly calculated. They keep her at the cutting edge of pop culture as a leader and trendsetter in that culture. Her 2009 tour ended having grossed more than $400 million from 85 sold-out concerts attended by thousands of new fans who weren't even born when her first album debuted.

Madonna is not just another singer. She has a superb personal brand, enormous brand equity, and incredible competitive advantages, carefully nurtured over a long period of time. Madonna offers a superb, if perhaps surprising, example to make the point that competitive advantage is a concept that we can apply in many areas of competition. In fact, Madonna's overall success is directly attributable to precisely the kind of highly differentiated competitive advantage that is the topic of this lecture.

Now, many firms—many people—tend to think of competition as doing the same thing as everybody else, only better. An entire industry and management mythos has grown up around this notion: best practices, benchmarking, techniques designed to squeeze just a bit more savings from this process, perhaps save valuable seconds from that process. And that's fine, but it's just running in place; it's not strategy, and these kinds of activities certainly don't gain us lasting and powerful competitive advantages.

Think carefully here—if we do nothing else but benchmark and copy our competitors, we end up playing the great game of mimicry. We offer pale imitations of our competitors' products and others offer imitations of ours. Is this what Madonna did to achieve stardom? Hardly. If she had merely imitated predecessors like Donna Summer from the disco era, we'd not be talking about her.

Let's think differently about competition and what it means to compete effectively. Let's devise a way to differentiate our product, our company, ourselves. Our goal is to develop a Unique Selling Proposition, which is the collection of factors assembled in such a way that it constitutes a distinctive core competency and confers unique competitive advantage. We've called this a Unique Selling Proposition, and that Unique Selling Proposition can become the basis for our personal brand.

We can go about the business of creating a Unique Selling Proposition for our product or ourselves by starting with Michael Porter's notion of strategy—determining what we're trying to do with strategies, determining how we want to compete, and determining how we will do things differently.

This means choosing a generic strategy and then building on it; it means assembling our resources in new and different ways than our competitors. We can do this in any number of ways, and this is where the spark of creativity and innovation ignite the best and most successful businesses and endeavors.

Madonna didn't have a checklist to tell her how to compete. In the early New York years before her first solo album, she was a backup dancer for other acts and a singer in two different bands. And she didn't benchmark herself against the competition to give crowds an improved version of the same old thing; she looked at her competition in a cool and calculating way to discover her Blue Ocean.

Blue Ocean. This might sound like the title for a song, but Blue Ocean is a strategic term that first appeared in a 2005 book called *Blue Ocean Strategy*. W. Chan Kim and Renée Mauborgne, professors at INSEAD, one of the world's great business schools, introduced us to the notion of the Blue Ocean—uncontested market space carved out by shrewd competitors.

Kim and Mauborgne showed that most companies are driven to compete in what they called "red oceans." This is an apt name, as it evokes the specter of a steaming cauldron of competitors fighting over a shrinking profit pool. Low margins, lots of stress, surviving in the world of commodities.

The 17th century philosopher Thomas Hobbes described a world of unfettered competition as a "War of all against all ... where life is solitary, poor, nasty, brutish, and short." Red Ocean competition might not be quite that bad, but surely there must be something better.

The alternative to this unpleasant scenario is to carve out uncontested market space; to differentiate yourself or your product or your service or your firm in some way meaningful to your target market; to find your Blue Ocean.

Here is one way we can do this—it's not a checklist and it's not a formula. It's a method to get you thinking in fresh and different ways about what you do each day.

Kim and Mauborgne offer what they call the Four Actions Framework. This model challenges what they call the value curve. This value curve depicts how a company is doing across an industry's accepted factors of competition. For instance, take automobiles. The accepted factors of competition might be price, prestige, gas mileage, size, comfort, performance, longevity, safety, and service.

The conventional competitive model says to compete across the full range of factors. Blue Ocean strategy argues a different approach. Instead, ask basic questions about the industry with the intent of creating new competitive factors that appeal to unexplored market segments. For example, the Tata Nano, consciously chose not to compete on most of the standard features of the industry, instead betting everything on a highly differentiated price strategy, addressing the most ignored market segment in India—the segment at the bottom of the pyramid. This was Tata's Unique Selling Proposition, which allowed the company to explore a Blue Ocean. Other examples include Chrysler's creation of the minivan format and Toyota's willingness to create a gasoline-electric hybrid car that did not look or perform like existing cars.

So let's look more closely at the Kim-Mauborgne model for creating uncontested market space. What they call the Four Actions Framework consists of just four questions. It is designed to challenge an industry's established structure and business logic. Here are those questions: Which of the factors that the industry takes for granted should be eliminated? Which factors should be reduced well below the industry's standard? Which factors should be raised well above the industry's standard? Which factors should be created that the industry has never offered?

Eliminate, reduce, raise, create—these four steps enable you to create a new value curve. It may appear simple enough. But its simplicity is deceptive. To develop and then to implement a new value curve requires boldness. It also means that the usual external validation you receive will be absent.

This is not a checklist or some kind of 12-step program to attain something that already exists. It requires a brain-stretch. It requires creativity and thinking outside of the proverbial box. It requires that we offer new factors of competition and that we decide consciously not to compete in some of the standard categories.

Let's take an example of how this works. We look now at [yellow tail] wine, produced by Casella Wines. [yellow tail] is an Australian wine that carved out Blue Ocean uncontested market space for itself by thinking unconventionally to redefine the value curve for the wine industry. The conventional value curve consisted of these factors: price, use of intriguing terminology from the wine industry, high-visibility marketing, aging quality, vineyard prestige, wine complexity, and wine range. All prestige wines and all budget wines competed on these factors. The prestige wines at the high end, and budget wines at the low end. But [yellow tail] changed this entire strategic profile.

Casella Wines brought [yellow tail] from Australia to the U.S. in 2000, and by 2003, it was the United States' number one imported wine. How did it achieve this, even in the midst of a worldwide wine glut? By carving out uncontested market space, Casella downplayed the traditional competitive factors and created and excelled on three additional competitive factors that other wines could not match. Those factors are easy drinking, ease of selection, and fun and adventure.

A selling proposition that was uniquely compelling and new. [yellow tail] eliminated the emphasis on wine as complex, properly aged, and characterized by subtleties such as tannins and oak. [yellow tail] even eliminated the use of different bottle designs for red and white wines. [yellow tail] drastically reduced selection, at first offering just one red wine (a Shiraz) and one white wine (a Chardonnay).

Conversely, [yellow tail] raised the level of fun, putting a kangaroo in bright orange and yellow on a very simple label and providing some salespeople with outfits from the Australian outback. [yellow tail] even created a new way to present the brand name, using all lower case letters placed in square brackets—a unique look that was different from anything that had come before.

[yellow tail] grew quickly, not just by taking market share from established competitors offering either bottom-end jug wine or higher-priced bottled wine. Instead, [yellow tail] grew quickly by actually growing the market, selling to new wine-drinkers attracted by [yellow tail]'s distinctive willingness to highlight a single fresh, fruity wine. A wine that could cut through the overwhelming number of choices with a taste and brand that even newcomers could appreciate.

With [yellow tail], Casella Wines found a Blue Ocean that allowed it to prosper while other wines were suffering through a dip in the industry. And as the industry recovered and grew over the years, [yellow tail] responded by adding a very small number of additional offerings in a way that continued to reinforce its unique selling proposition.

This is just one way to conceive of your strategy, and you can see that it fits into the overall framework we've been discussing throughout these lectures—doing things differently.

Let's look at this concept of Blue Ocean strategy at a personal level. How do you compete in your "industry?" What are the factors you compete on against others? What makes you unique, special? Anything at all? Or do you compete just like everyone else? Your résumé looks like everyone else's. You do the same thing, only better. You're motivated, driven to succeed, have a great work ethic, have lots of experience. This is not the way to carve out Blue Ocean uncontested market space.

You can go about carving out Blue Ocean by applying unconventional thinking to familiar situations. You question your assumptions. You change the assumptions. You ask yourself what might be possible if ….

Here's an open-ended example. Back in 1993, Coca-Cola Company launched a new ad campaign for its popular Diet Coke brand. Everyone knows and loves Diet Coke. The campaign was designed by longtime Coke ad agency Lintas New York, one of the largest and most prestigious ad agencies it the world. It launched in January to great fanfare.

It featured the catchy slogan: "Taste it All." If you don't remember this slogan or this campaign, it's because Coca-Cola hated it and pulled the ads after just six weeks. Coca-Cola fired Lintas New York as its ad agency. Lintas lost the Diet Coke account—an account worth $95 million per year in billings.

Think—they lost the Coke account, an account for one of the most valuable brands in the world. Now, imagine the scene in the Lintas building after the announcement. Do you think that folks are striding down the halls, chipper and with big hellos for everyone? You think people want to be seen? Of course not. Doors are closed and executives are hunkered down, updating their résumés and information about their contacts. Upper management is looking for scalps. Who takes the fall for this debacle? In the usual run of things, nameless and faceless mid-level executives are fired as scapegoats.

Who was responsible for the debacle, do you think? Do you think that person or persons stepped forward and raised their hand to accept responsibility? "Lost the Coke account? That was my mistake." Of course no one did that. Instead, the blame-shifting began. Good luck finding that creative team who actually assembled the failed ad campaign. Our natural reaction to such a scenario is perhaps to think, "I'm glad I'm not part of that cluster." But think what you would do in such a scenario. Would you hunker down in conventional fashion? Would you distance yourself from the disaster and hope the grim reaper selects someone else for sacrifice?

Ask yourself this: What might happen if someone stepped forward and accepted full responsibility? "That was my idea. That was my project. I was responsible." I would have done it. What an opportunity! "That was my work that lost our $95 million account. I'm the guy who lost the Coke account." Instead of one of the nameless faceless executives who were fired, I'd seize this chance to establish a bold personal brand. A brand that could not be imitated. A brand with an incredibly memorable tag line. A truly once in a lifetime chance. An incredibly powerful USP. "I'm the guy who lost the Coke account." Is it a brand of failure? Not at all. The magnitude and boldness of the statement, the high stakes involved, and the unusual stance make this selling proposition truly unique. You can have a book deal and you can be on Oprah's Book Club. You can become the executive who provides insight on big-time corporate advertising. You land a gig on CNN as a business analyst. You offer yourself as a visionary who can see beyond the big rejection from Coke. Risky? Sure! And 99 percent of people would hunker down and accept the situation as dire and do the expected thing. Again, where others see only obstacles, train yourself to see opportunity.

Was this scenario outlandish? Surely. And I used it to make the point that you can find opportunity in the most absurd situations, and the most mundane of situations. The key is to untrain yourself from thinking conventionally and to unharness yourself from the necessity of external validation of your ideas. If something is truly new and fresh and different at its nascent stages, before it actually has form, few people will recognize it as such.

Here's another example of unconventional thinking. BP is a global oil and gas company based in London, whose slogan is "beyond petroleum." The world's third-largest fossil fuels company, BP became the object of scorn during the entire summer of 2010 after one of its wells, the Deepwater Horizon, malfunctioned and exploded. The resulting three-month long oil leak at the bottom of the Gulf of Mexico threatened to become an environmental disaster of unparalleled scale. As days turned into weeks, the public trust in BP—such as it was—plummeted.

The oil company struggled to contain both the oil gushing into the Gulf and its increasingly battered reputation, which suffered even more as a result of several public relations gaffes by senior BP leadership. Few would have said that BP was an attractive company to work for during that catastrophe.

Or was it? It was then that I asked my students to think unconventionally about the situation. I asked them: Did BP intend to blow a hole in the floor of the Gulf of Mexico? Of course not. BP did not even own or directly operate the drilling rig that failed. Is BP an "evil company?" Of course not. A company may be expected to assume ultimate responsibility for operations conducted on its behalf, but BP was not omniscient. Apart from this one incident, BP did not appear to deserve any special scorn when compared with other companies in the oil business.

So, when BP's fortunes dipped and hit seeming rock bottom in the summer of 2010, I put a challenge to my students. I challenged them to think differently about the situation. I asked them to go beyond the hand-wringing and sloganeering of the moment, to look past the photos of oil-covered birds. I asked them not to join the easy chorus of boos and to do something quite difficult: I asked them to answer some questions. What would I do if I were on the BP team? How might I help turn things around at BP if I were on that team?

Then I suggested that they do this: As BP's fortunes completely bottomed out, I urged my graduating students to consider submitting their résumés to BP. To think about joining a company when it's down and what that actually might mean to them professionally. I asked them to think about the future beyond a single summer oil spill and what might happen with this company the next year and the next. I asked them what might happen if they were to join the company at its lowest point, and to consider whether they might then rise quickly within that company as it quickly recovers.

If you join a company when it's down, you consciously swim against the tide, you test yourself and your skills. In the process, you build a feisty brand. You become known as the gutsy young executive who charged aboard to save the ship when everyone else was jumping off the ship or shunning the company. And if you help turn that company around, you participate in helping to build the lore of the company, perhaps even a new legend—one that you're part of. "He jumped into the fire and he turned BP around."

Farfetched? Much less farfetched than two guys in a garage in Northern California jump-starting the computer revolution with a company they called Apple. The conventional alternatives are always available, like soldiering in an unmarked cubicle in a multinational company, as one of the masses of the latest intake of graduates, or a mid-level manager who doesn't rock the boat.

You always have the easy choice of the conventional. It's safe. It's predictable. And the rewards are commensurately small. But great strategy is about unconventional thinking. This process of unconventional thinking is a part of figuring out what it is that you offer the world. It's part of discovering and promoting who you are and what you do best. It's part of establishing your Unique Selling Proposition and personal brand. It's what sets you apart, what gives you a story to tell, what sharpens the details of your persona.

The personal brand is a tangible example of strategic thinking in action. Most people are oblivious to the concept of the personal brand. Many people in humanities departments in higher education even have an intense bias against the notion of "branding" persons. "I'm a human being, not a product." It's just a matter of terminology. Everyone brands, we just call it something different. In the liberal arts, it's called "individualism," or having a story to tell. But regardless of what you call it, it serves the purpose of sending a message of what you are all about.

Whatever else you do, recognize and accept that you have a personal brand that is yours to cultivate or neglect. Either way, you will be labeled. Isn't it better to seize control of that process than to allow it to just grow of its own accord?

This makes sense as one of the most important strategic acts of your life, to seize control of your public face, your personal brand, your persona. For strategic purposes and for your own success, realize that you are branding yourself every single day whether you know it or not. You can decide to not participate actively in the branding process. That just means that the branding process moves steadily forward without your direction or even conscious input. It's important that you take control of that process rather than let it unspool on its own. Rather than allow others to brand you.

Your brand is your reputation. It's what people think first when they see you or hear your name. Brands mean something: Mercedes means quality; Volvo means safety; Wheaties means a "breakfast of champions"; Allstate means "you're in good hands"; "Intel Inside" means a computer you can trust.

What image or tagline does your name evoke? Hard-working, punctual, always making others around her better, lazy, he's always a mess in a rumpled suit, she's sharp as a tack, he has it all together. You can choose to opt out from branding and instead argue how people ought to accept you as you are and not judge you by appearances or behavior, how people ought not to pay attention to your hair, your clothing, your speech, your hygiene.

You can choose to go that route, but unless you are in the business of social change, that is anything but strategic behavior. It's time to move from the realm of what other people ought to care about to the realm of what they do care about, and consider what you should do to seize control over how you are presented. If you don't get this part right, you handicap whatever strategy you choose to pursue.

So brand yourself consciously. Like the Pennsylvania firm High Concrete Group—"We build high concrete structures." Like the old Federal Express slogan—"When it absolutely, positively, has to be there overnight." Like Madonna.

So, always be looking toward your own Blue Ocean. Unleash your creativity in ways that stretch the boundaries of the conventional. Question the assumptions that guide the industry, whether at your individual competitive level or at the firm level. Establish a Unique Selling Proposition that captures a position unlike any other.

Do I know what your challenges will be? Of course not. And neither do you. That's the nature of an inherently chaotic and unpredictable world. But we can eliminate some of what is commonly done, reduce standards in some ways, raising standards in other ways, and we can seize—and even create— new opportunities.

One way to explore a route to our own Blue Ocean is to utilize analysis in a systematic way, to explore our external environment for opportunities, and to take our own internal pulse and discover where we're strong, where we need improvement, and what we need that we don't yet have.

Our next lecture takes us on an exploratory journey to discover how specific tools of analysis can help us find our own Blue Ocean by learning to make better assessments of ourselves and the world around us.

Strengths, Weaknesses, Opportunities, Threats
Lecture 10

S trategic thinking means acting from knowledge, not emotion or preconceptions. In this lecture, we examine four tools to help you acquire and analyze information so that your plan and resulting actions will have the intended effect. We also look at a case study of an independent bookstore that was challenged by a megastore but eventually adapted and outlived its larger competitor.

Copperfield's Books and the Great Wheel of Business

- Copperfield's Books was founded in 1981 in northern California and grew over the next 13 years. But in 1995, stagnation set in; Copperfield's saw its profits begin to decline and was forced to close stores.

- Although Copperfield's still offered the same product in the same venues, the environment in which it was operating—consisting of competitors, customers, and market forces—had changed radically. The "great wheel of business" was turning, heralding the advent of mega-bookstore chains, Amazon.com, and e-readers.

- To survive these powerful new external forces, Copperfield's would have to change the way it did business, the product mix it offered, and the selling experience itself. It would need to look beyond whatever strategic planning it might have done previously and engage in a strategic analysis of how to survive and prosper under new conditions.

- Strategic thinking means setting aside our impressionistic view of the world and thinking rationally about causes and effects, actions and reactions. It means imposing order on what we see, filtering out static and letting in information we can use in an orderly, logical fashion.

- The business world has developed numerous tools of analysis that aid businesspeople in making sense of what they do and how and when they should do it. We can use those tools for ourselves in our personal lives and in achieving our professional goals. In this lecture, we'll learn about four tools of strategic analysis: PEST, five forces, value chain, and SWOT.

PEST

- A PEST (political, economic, social, and technical) analysis is a scan of the external environment. Let's look at each of these factors in turn.

- The political environment affects all of us in ways we may not even suspect. In a macro-sense, that environment includes the national, state, or local government's leadership and bureaucracy. In a personal sense, it describes the web of power relationships we deal with in our lives at work and at home.

  o With your mission and objective in mind, explore the power relationships that affect you. Ask yourself what power relationships hinder or help you and what legal regulations, such as zoning or tax laws, affect you.

  o The political climate is like a powerful tide that shifts first one way and then the other. For example, new medical instruments for surgery may be regulated more or less stringently at different times. It makes sense to ascertain which way the tide is shifting and to figure out ways to swim with the tide instead of against it.

- Business is conducted within an economic environment that either supports or doesn't support what we want to do. In starting a consulting business, you should ask basic questions, such as: Do enough customers exist who are willing to pay your fee? Does the economic environment favor you or your competitors? Such questions may clarify your thinking with a dose of reality.

- In looking at the social and cultural environment, find out what trends and fads are in play. What substantial and rooted long-term cultural factors should you consider? Can you identify tomorrow's trends based on today's indicators?

- Finally, in the technological environment, ask whether technology supports what you want to do or whether it poses a threat.

Five Forces
- Michael Porter's five forces model is a tool that can be used—with minor tweaking—to evaluate the forces impinging on virtually any competitive situation, from the computer industry to personal romantic relationships.

- The five forces of competition are: buyer power, supplier power, intensity of rivalry, threat of substitutes, and threat of new entrants. These forces compel you to answer a series of questions about your industry and your place in that industry.

- How much power do your customers have over you? How much power do your suppliers have over you? How intense is the rivalry with others in your industry? Are you forced into constant battles with them that affect your profit margins? How easily can your buyers switch to substitute products? What is the danger of new entrants in your industry?

- As we saw, Copperfield's Books was faced with the challenge of powerful new forces in the competitive environment. These forces threatened not only Copperfield's but other brick-and-mortar booksellers, as well, even the big ones. How did they contend with the five forces of competition?

  o The power of customers was significant. Buyers could purchase identical books from a wide variety of retailers. Price was a major consideration, and there was not much loyalty to individual stores.

  o The power of suppliers—that is, publishers—exerted a disproportionately negative impact on independent bookstores, such as Copperfield's. Chain bookstores could order in massive volume and receive discounts from publishers that were unavailable to independents.

○ The rivalry among players in the retail book industry was intense. Although bookselling is basically a mature industry with low growth rates, there was a surge of megastores and consolidation.

○ Booksellers also faced the threat of substitutes. People can get books from libraries, online, and from many stores that don't specialize in books. Increased competition also comes from other forms of entertainment, such as television or computer games.

○ For independent booksellers, the threat of new entrants was low. Entering the market requires a good deal of capital, and the industry itself is unattractive, offering low profit margins and growth rates.

• A five forces analysis of the industry would have told Copperfield's that it was time to consider a change in business model to cope with the variables that seemed to be trending in a negative direction.

Value Chain
• Value chain analysis can tell you a great deal about your internal strengths and weaknesses. This method divides your firm into its value-producing activities, with the aim of evaluating what makes the firm strong and what makes it weak.

• This type of analysis can be applied to almost any complex series of activities. We can disassemble a football team, an automobile company, an army platoon, or our own series of activities and evaluate how each part contributes to the whole. Let's take a football team as an example.

○ The overall performance of a football team is captured in its won-loss record and in the final scores of games it plays, but looking at these measures doesn't tell us anything specific. In fact, these measures can hide the contributions of the individual components that actually give the team its strengths and weaknesses.

○ If we analyze the separate activities of the offense and defense, we begin to get a clearer picture of the team's strengths, player by player. We disassemble the team and staff and look at the individual contributions of the players; the leadership, strategy, and tactics of the coaches and quarterback; the personnel decisions; and so on.

o   This assessment is conducted with the mission and objectives in mind, that is, winning the championship, scoring points, or preventing the other team from scoring.

• Another example of a value chain is your personal value chain—the things you do to accomplish your self-defined mission. What are these functions and how well do you perform them?

• Both firms and people outsource the functions they cannot do well and retain the functions that constitute core strengths. For instance, Borders contracted with Starbucks to operate the cafes inside its bookstores. Most of us, as individuals, outsource such functions as clothing manufacture so that we can concentrate on our strengths.

SWOT

• The value chain analysis assesses internal strengths and weaknesses, while the five forces and PEST analyses show us external threats and opportunities. The SWOT (strengths, weaknesses, opportunities, threats) analysis brings the internal and external together.

• Let's think of SWOT with respect to Copperfield's Books. The changing external environment meant that an old strength of the brick-and-mortar bookstore—thoughtful selection—had been transformed into a weakness—relative lack of choice.

• In the retail book industry, the external threats loomed large and attacked Copperfield's weaknesses. The opportunities all seemed to be in favor of the big-box bookstore and the almost simultaneous rise of online bookselling. The changing external environment ensured that Copperfield's would fail if it did not alter its business model.

• This example shows us what happens if we focus only on what we do to the exclusion of what others do and to the exclusion of macro-factors that change the very assumptions that support our strategy.

- The obvious move for Copperfield's was to offer book buyers something attractive in the store that they could not receive elsewhere. Thus, Copperfield's crafted a persona that was uniquely local in flavor, offering local book buying and socializing experiences to its clientele that were unavailable either online or in the megastores.

- Borders was one of the apparent victors in the competition with the independents, but then, it failed to respond to further changes in the external environment. Instead of recognizing the potential of the Internet, the company outsourced online sales to Amazon; it also missed the growing importance of the e-reader and gave up the opportunity to become a destination when it lost a Starbucks contract to Barnes and Noble.

Changes in the world of bookselling meant that independent bookstores would have to engage in strategic analysis and develop new strategic plans to survive.

- Every bookstore at the time faced the same competitive pressures as Borders, but it was the response to those pressures that made the difference between success and failure.

- New technologies and new ways of doing business did not mean that traditional bookstores would go out of business, but to sustain themselves into the 21st century, such stores would have to find a new business model. Many independent bookstores, including Copperfield's, have adapted themselves to provide services to a distinct clientele.

- It's clear, then, that the tools of strategic analysis can give us the crucial intelligence we need to evaluate strategic direction and to change it if need be. This willingness to adapt to external realities is the key to business success and, in some cases, to survival.

Questions to Consider

1. Evaluate the external environment that affects you to assess the opportunities and threats you face with regard to your mission and objectives. Then, using value chain analysis, conduct an honest inventory of your personal strengths and weaknesses as they relate to that external environment. What actions do your results suggest?

2. Think of the digital revolution and how it brings such companies as Apple and Amazon into conflict—in this case, in the field of the e-reader and e-tablet. Using the PEST analysis technique, identify what changes in the external environment drove these two companies into competition.

3. Consciously apply the value chain concept to analyze a business or sports situation and then explain the result. What does your analysis suggest as a strategy for the company or team?

Strengths, Weaknesses, Opportunities, Threats
Lecture 10—Transcript

Copperfield's Books was founded in 1981 in Northern California and, at first it seemed to be doing everything right. Copperfield's was doing what an independent bookstore ought to be doing. Popular, profitable, and growing, it enjoyed 13 straight years of growth.

There seemed to be no reason to change the winning formula. From the perspective of the internal workings of Copperfield, everything functioned smoothly and well. But in the outside environment consisting of competitors and customers and market forces, the world was changing rapidly and radically.

In 1995, stagnation set in, and Copperfield's Books saw its profits begin to decline. It was forced to close stores. It still offered the same product in the same superb venues, but apparently, something had changed. It was the outside world that had changed. It is this changing environment and how we respond to it that we focus on in this lecture.

The business world is always changing, evolving in unexpected ways. I like to view the business world as a Great Wheel that turns slowly. This Great Wheel of Business constantly turns and it brings change—slow change, sudden change, many changes. We can't ignore this great wheel of business. We can't pretend that it doesn't affect us. It falls to us to determine what changes are important to us and to our business; it falls to us to figure out how best to cope with those changes.

We began with the tale of Copperfield's Books, emblematic of the independent bookstore in modern America. But this bastion of Americana was about to face its greatest challenge in the mid-1990s as the book retailing industry was to undergo tremendous upheaval—such upheaval that Hollywood even made a feature film about the book business.

The changing character of the book business in the 1980s and 1990s was told in cinema in the film *You've Got Mail* that featured Tom Hanks and Meg Ryan. This 1998 film tells the story of a small bookstore being forced out of business by a big-box bookstore similar to Borders or Barnes & Noble. The film depicts the Great Wheel of Business as it turns and forces people and companies to adapt to the external world.

One new feature of this changing competitive environment was the arrival and continuing expansion of Borders, which itself began as a used bookstore in Ann Arbor, Michigan, in 1971. Borders reached its peak in 2003. With 1200 stores, each filled with thousands of new titles, Borders was the heavyweight of the bookselling industry, rivaled only by Barnes & Noble.

Copperfield's Books, on the other hand, was one of many small and medium-sized independent bookstores. These stores faced dramatic changes in the competitive environment that threatened their very existence. Suddenly, people had alternatives to buying books at Copperfield's—they could go to the newly arrived mega-bookstore chains, offered by Borders and Barnes & Noble. People could buy books on the internet with a new online firm called "Amazon.com." Books could be delivered to their doorstep more cheaply and from a much wider selection. If this wasn't enough, suddenly, something appeared on the horizon called the "e-reader." This meant that the actual physical product that Copperfield's sold might begin to disappear.

To survive these powerful new external forces, Copperfield's would have to change the way it did business, the product mix it offered, and the selling experience itself. It would need to look beyond whatever strategic planning it might have done previously, and engage instead in a strategic analysis into how to survive and prosper under new conditions.

Strategic thinking means setting aside our impressionistic view of the world and thinking rationally about causes and effects, actions and reactions, and then, making our way successfully to our goals while others drift and bob on a sea of chaos. This means imposing order on what we see. It means filtering out static and letting in information we can use in an orderly, logical fashion.

Let's start thinking about the world around us and how we can best assess and marshal our capabilities to take advantage of the opportunities that present themselves. The business world has developed numerous tools of analysis that aid business people in making sense of what they do, how they do it, when they do it. We can use those tools for ourselves in our personal lives, and in achieving our professional goals.

Today, we learn about four tools of strategic analysis, what they do, how to use them, and how they benefit us in crafting prudent strategy. The tools are: PEST analysis; five forces analysis; value chain analysis; and finally, looking at all our strengths, weaknesses, opportunities, and threats taken together, an analysis known in business schools as the SWOT.

First, a scan of our external environment, known as PEST. PEST is an acronym that stands for political, economic, social, and technical. Attention to all four ensures the most comprehensive evaluation of the factors that may impinge on us in the pursuit of our goals. Through PEST, we discover if factors in these four realms help or hinder us; we discover opportunities we can seize; we learn of threats we must deflect—threats and opportunities we otherwise would have missed.

One caveat: We cannot do a meaningful PEST analysis without our mission and objectives in mind. We must anchor our analysis in what it is we are and what we want to achieve. Only with this analytical anchor will the analysis take on meaning.

For instance, take our bookselling example. The bookselling industry faces a variety of economic and technical pressures that differ dramatically from the types of political pressures faced by, say, the automobile industry or the pharmaceutical industry. Consequently, a PEST analysis for Copperfield's books would be focused accordingly.

Our political environment affects all of us in ways we may not even suspect. In a large, macro-sense, that environment, our nation's, our state's, or our local government's leadership and bureaucracy. In a personal sense, it describes the web of power relationships we deal with in our lives at work and at play.

With our mission and objective in mind, we explore the power relationships that impinge on us. We ask the question, what power relationships hinder me? Which ones can assist me? What are legal regulations that affect me, everything from business zoning in local neighborhoods to tax laws to protection of intellectual property. For example, physical bookstores may face different tax policies than online booksellers, and later, a common policy may be imposed that treats both the same.

The political climate is like a powerful tide that shifts first one way and then the other. For example, new medical instruments for surgery may be regulated as stringently as pharmaceuticals, and subject to a very long waiting period for government approval, or they may be less regulated. It makes good sense for us to ascertain which way that tide is shifting and when. And it makes sense for us to craft ways to swim with the tide instead of against it.

We conduct our business within an economic environment and this supports what we want to do, or not. If we want to start our own consulting business, we should ask basic questions, such as, are there enough customers out there willing to pay my fee? Questions like these may give us pause and clarify our thinking with a dose of hard-nosed reality.

How much capital do we need to achieve our needed capability? Does the economic environment favor me over my competitors, or the converse? What trends and fads are in play in the social and cultural environment? What substantial and rooted long-term cultural factors must I consider? Can I identify tomorrow's trend based on today's indicators? Am I looking over the horizon at tomorrow's implications over what is happening today? Does the tech environment support what I want to do? Or are there threats I have to consider? In Copperfield's case, longer term threats that might have given pause were the increasing popularity of online bookselling, and taking even a longer perspective, the advent of the e-reader.

Let's move to a tool of analysis that focuses on our own industry. One of Michael Porter's most famous contributions is his technique for analyzing the forces that impact competition within an industry. This technique is called the five forces model. We can use this model—with minor tweaking—to evaluate the impinging forces of virtually any competitive situation, from the computer industry to our personal occupation—even to personal romantic relationships.

The five forces of competition are: buyer power, supplier power, intensity of rivalry, the threat of substitutes; and the threat of new entrants. These forces compel us to answer a series of questions about our industry and our place in that industry.

How much power do our customers have over us? How much power do our suppliers have over us? How intense is the rivalry we have with others in our industry, in our field? Are we forced into constant battles with them that affect our profit margins? How easily can our buyers switch to substitute products? Orange juice instead of apple juice. The electronic books and other electronic media instead of physical books.

What is the danger of new entrants into our industry? Copperfield's Books was faced with the challenge of powerful new forces in the competitive environment. These forces threatened the position of not only Copperfield's, but of the other brick and mortar booksellers, too, even the big ones.

So how did Copperfield's and Borders contend with the five forces of competition? Let's take a look. First, the power of buyers—the bookstore customers. Customers had tremendous power at the time—they could purchase identical books from a wide variety of retailers. Price was a major consideration, and there was not much loyalty to stores offering similar products in a similar format.

Next, the power of suppliers to bookstores—the major publishers. Both Copperfield's and Borders obtained books from publishers, but the big chains could order in massive volume and receive big discounts that were unavailable to independents. The power of publishers exerted a disproportionately negative impact on independent bookstores such as Copperfield's.

Next, the intensity of rivalry among the players in the retail book industry. This is a hotly contested market; there is lots of rivalry. There was a surge of mega-stores and consolidation, but it is basically a mature industry with low growth rates.

What about the threat of substitutes? People can get their books in many places: in libraries, online, online from libraries, and in many stores that don't specialize in books. And books face increased competition from other forms of entertainment—television, radio, Internet, computer games, movies, and such like. If books get too expensive, people switch.

Finally, the threat of new entrants. There is little or no room for new players in this market. It requires much capital. And to be frank, it is an unattractive industry, with low profit margins and low growth rates.

This analysis of the industry would have told Copperfield's that it was time to consider a change of business model to cope with the exogenous variables that seemed trending in negative direction. The correlation of forces was moving against the undifferentiated little bookshop around the corner that offers a limited selection of high-priced books, and nothing else.

The five forces analysis tells us clearly that we must change something in the way we do business, or we won't be in business much longer.

Value chain analysis is a tool that can tell us a great deal about our own internal strengths and weaknesses. The value chain is a method of analysis that takes apart the firm, divides the firm into its value-producing activities. The point is to evaluate what makes our firm strong and what makes it weak as it, say, manufactures a product. We call this a "chain" of activities because it is a series of processes, all of which add value to a product.

We can apply this type of analysis to most any fairly complex series of activities. We can disassemble a football team, an automobile company, an army platoon, or our own series of activities, and we can evaluate how each part contributes to the whole. Let's take as an example a football team.

The overall performance of a football team is captured in its won-loss record and in the final scores of games it plays. If other teams score 7 to 8 touchdowns per game against us, and we score 7 to 8 touchdowns as well, we can observe that our defense is terrible, and our offense is great. But this does not tell us anything specific. In fact scores of games and overall record can hide the contribution of the components that actually provide team strength or team weakness.

If we analyze the separate activities of the offense and defense, we begin to get a clearer picture of the team's strengths, player by player. Many fans already do this type of value chain analysis with their favorite sports teams. Sophisticated fans don't stop with the won-loss record or the scores of games; these fans delve deep into the issue to discover the impact of other factors.

Without even knowing it, these fans are conducting a type of value chain analysis. They disassemble the team and staff and look at their contributions, the contributions of the players, whether tight ends, wide receivers, running backs, the backfield defense, the generalship and strategy and tactics of the coaches and quarterback, the personnel decisions, the scouting reports for the games. They search for the root causes of dysfunction in their favorite team. Could it be the offensive line? The defensive line? What about the head coach, the general manager or the owner? And what about the fans?

Each of these factors we evaluate according to our own internal calculation. When it's done formally, we can call it value chain analysis. We assess the contribution of the processes that make up the whole, and we do it with the mission and objectives in mind—we want to win the championship, to score points, to prevent the other team from scoring.

Another example of a value chain is your personal value chain—the things that you do to accomplish your self-defined mission. What are these functions and how well do you do them? We are fortunate in an advanced economy that most of us specialize in pursuing our goals while living fairly comfortable lives. Contrast this with the value chain of a U.S. pioneer in, say, the early to mid-19th century.

Such pioneer men and women living on the frontier survived in a much different and simpler economy than we enjoy today. Rather than enjoying the wide variety of goods we take for granted, a primitive and much less communal lifestyle meant that mere survival occupied the value chain functions—building shelter, making clothing, obtaining food, providing security—all of this absorbed time.

It also led to a lower standard of living in that people simply do not possess top notch skills in all of the value-producing functions that yield the necessities of life—things like clothing, shelter, food, security. And just as we cannot do everything well, neither can business firms.

Both firms and people outsource the functions that they cannot do well and retain the functions that constitute core strengths. For instance, Borders had added some cafes inside its bookstores but later decided to approach Starbucks about operating those cafes instead. We, as individuals, outsource functions such as clothing manufacture and the farming of vegetables so that we can concentrate on our strengths.

So, we can see how value chain analysis can be quite revelatory, zeroing in on what we must change and what we should continue. Now, here is where we match our internal analysis with our external analysis. The value chain assesses our strengths and weaknesses. The five forces in our industry and a scan of the broader PEST environment show us our external threats and the opportunities. We can now list these strengths and our weaknesses and match them against the external opportunities and threats. Do our strengths match the opportunities available? Do our weaknesses make us vulnerable to the most salient threats?

The tool for bringing these together is called the SWOT, which stands for strengths, weaknesses, opportunities, and threats. Think of the SWOT with respect to our original example: Copperfield's Books. The changing external environment meant that an old strength of the brick and mortar bookstore had been transformed into a weakness (relative lack of choice).

In the retail book industry, the external threats loomed large and attacked Copperfield's weaknesses. The opportunities all seemed to be in favor of the big-box bookstore and the almost simultaneous rise of online bookselling, which together spelled the end of the independent bookstore as we knew it in the late 1980s. The changing external environment ensured that Copperfield's Books would ultimately fail if it did not alter its business model.

This clear example shows us what happens if we focus only on what we do to the exclusion of what others do, and to the exclusion of macro-factors that change the very assumptions that support our strategy. And so Borders, Barnes & Noble, and Amazon.com seemed to win as hundreds of small bookstores closed their doors for the last time. The Great Wheel of Business turns, and it does not care if we cope with the changes. It turns inexorably, and it is up to us to figure out what changes are afoot and how to best cope with those changes and chart a new strategic direction.

The obvious move for Copperfield's was to offer book buyers something attractive in the store that they could receive no other place. So Copperfield's nimbly crafted a persona that was uniquely local in flavor and that offered local bookbuying and socializing experiences to its clientele that were unavailable either online or in the mega-stores. Copperfield's survived. Meanwhile, the Great Wheel of Business continued to turn. The same factors that assaulted the independents, like Copperfield's Books, soon began to undermine the powerful Borders chain.

Borders had been the apparent victor in the 1990s and was seemingly unstoppable. But Borders did not respond to further changes in the external environment. Borders committed serious strategic errors—errors that its fraternal big-box competitor Barnes & Noble largely avoided.

Let's see what happened to Borders. First, Borders failed to recognize its vulnerability to the Internet. Borders refused to embrace the new technology. Instead of recognizing the potential and adapting to the new wired and connected world, Borders outsourced the sale of many of its books online from 2001 to 2008 to Amazon. By contrast, Barnes & Noble, had experience with mail order sales dating back to the 19th century, recognized an opportunity to transition from mail-order catalogs to online selling.

Borders also missed the growing importance of the e-reader. While Amazon introduced the Kindle in 2007 and a second generation in 2009, Barnes & Noble introduced the Nook in 2009, and Apple entered the same market space with its iPad in April 2010. Borders ignored the threat until too late; it partnered in 2010 with "Kobo," a bargain e-reader, whose majority owner at the time was the Canadian big-box retailer Indigo Books and Music. It was a me-too effort—almost an afterthought.

So first, we saw how the big-box retailer displaced the little independent bookstore, and in the same dynamic, the online booksellers later began to displace the big-boxes with a larger selection of books at lower prices.

Perhaps Borders was still consolidating its position and looking to shorter term goals like "growth" and "excellence" Borders neglected the one advantage it still carried as a brick-and-mortar bookseller—a place for people to gather. Big box was a place where you could go, where you could sit, where you could sip great coffee and meet others of like mind. But Borders did not recognize this aspect of the brick-and-mortar bookstore as a crucial, life-and-death source of advantage, as it turned out.

This lack of perspicacity was evidenced when it lost a Starbucks contract to Barnes & Noble. Instead of signing Starbucks, Borders ended up with Seattle's Best, which is the wholly-owned subsidiary of Starbucks that focuses on coffee without the full coffeehouse experience.

Annie Lowrey, a business writer for the *New York Times* captured the essence of the issue and how Barnes & Noble's response differed from Borders': "It's very, very hard to compete unless you are offering a very boutique experience." "Barnes & Noble at least has built a business that recognizes the trends in bookselling—toward the Internet, toward e-readers, toward a more boutique retail experience, away from big-box stores."

Borders had locked itself into a big box. Borders had opened too many stores, it had signed too many long-term leases, and this meant that underperforming stores could not be closed. Borders was trapped in an unprofitable and ultimately a self-damning situation.

Borders says that a host of factors led to its demise, including the turbulent economy; the move away from brick-and-mortar stores to online retailers; and the rise of e-readers, like Amazon's Kindle, Apple's iPad, and the Nook of rival Barnes & Noble.

But every bookstore faced competitive pressures—the same competitive pressures. It's the response to those pressures that means success or failure.

The changes in the industry in the mid 1980s into the 21st century have challenged booksellers of every type. New technologies and new ways of doing business meant that bookstores would have to evaluate how they did business. No, it did not automatically mean that the traditional bookstore would go out of business. But it did mean that the traditional bookstore would have to reinvent itself as something special.

To survive, it would have to find a new business model to sustain itself in the 21st century. It would have to recognize that the brick-and-mortar model of bookselling would have to offer something more than books—it would have to offer unique products and a unique customer experience.

As for the independent bookstores that were supposedly doomed back in the 1990s: A substantial number of them are still doing well, but only because they adapted. Many have diversified into selling things like coffee and alcohol and rare books, as well as offering regular talks, book groups, and classes—all to provide tailored services to a distinct clientele. They have differentiated themselves in ways to provide a distinctive service. In the end, this is what Copperfield's did, and what Borders did not do.

Another turn of the Business Wheel has left Borders a memory, and a case study for thousands of MBA students to learn how not to craft and implement strategy. The mega-bookseller that threatened Copperfield's could not survive in a world with new and multiple channels for book delivery; Borders went bankrupt in 2011.

And Copperfield's? Ironically, it has survived Borders. And it has grown to seven stores in Northern California. Copperfield's Books remade itself into a unique place that transcends the bookstore as simply a location to purchase undifferentiated stock off the shelf. It offers rare and antiquarian books; it offers author events, writing workshops, the purchasing of used books from customers, and online access to bookbuying. Late, but not too late— Copperfield's adapted its internal processes to accommodate the changing external environment.

We have seen how the tools of strategic analysis can give us the crucial intelligence we need to evaluate our strategic direction, and to change that direction if need be. This willingness to adapt to external realities as revealed to us by our analysis is the key to business success, and in some cases, to survival.

Avoid the Pathologies of Execution
Lecture 11

W hen we craft strategy, we try to impose order on a chaotic reality. Our strategy is, in fact, an attempt to create a system to deal with that reality and channel it in our best interests. But even with a superb strategic vision and the formulation of prudent strategy, the best-laid plans can go awry for many reasons, including those we examine in this lecture: lack of responsibility, overreach, communication and coordination breakdown, poor intelligence, and inertia.

Operation Market Garden
- In September 1944, British Field Marshal Bernard Montgomery conceived of a plan known as Operation Market Garden for the final push of the Allies into Germany that would end World War II. The complex plan called for air and ground forces to seize a series of six bridges behind enemy lines to reach the town of Arnhem.

- But Operation Market Garden was freighted with a built-in disadvantage that dooms even the best of plans: It required everything to go right, and as we know, that usually doesn't happen.

- The Allied high command believed that the German resistance had broken. It seemed that most of the enemy troops were fleeing and they seemed to have no tanks. What the allies didn't know was that two powerful panzer divisions were assigned to the area to rest and refit, one of them at the ultimate objective: the town of Arnhem.

- The complexity of the plan led to multiple blunders, and after nine days of battle, the Allies were forced to withdraw. How could such seasoned veterans bungle the planning so badly?

- The Allies underestimated German capabilities and overestimated their own capabilities. Based on these estimates, they created a plan that was too tightly wound, with too many objectives, too many moving parts, too much necessary coordination, and a heavy dose of wishful thinking that blinded the planners to red flags.

- Operation Market Garden is an example of overreach, which occurs when capabilities and strategy don't align. Overreach, along with omission of responsibility, breakdown of communication, poor intelligence, and inertia, is one of the pathologies that can interfere with the implementation of our chosen strategy.

Pathologies of Execution
- Let's begin with omission of responsibility. In strategy, and many other areas of life, nothing happens when no one is responsible. This is as much a failure of strategic leadership as it is a disconnect between strategy and implementation. Those responsible for strategy refuse to connect planning to the assignment of specific tasks. The most obvious manifestation of this pathology is the gap we often see between planning and execution.

- Second is the pathology of overreach. As we saw, in Operation Market Garden, the British had ambitious goals and clearly articulated objectives, but they did not have the capabilities to carry them out. And they compounded their problem by not accurately assessing the Germans' capabilities for interfering with the strategic plan. Another example of overreach occurred in what became known as the Battle of the Bulge.

  o In December 1944, the Allies believed that Germany was on the brink of defeat, but Germany was planning a breathtaking offensive in the Ardennes Forest.

  o Like Operation Market Garden, Germany's plan required that everything to go right for it to succeed, but in the end, the Germans were not powerful enough to accomplish their bold objectives within the necessary timetable. The plan underestimated enemy capabilities to interfere with its execution.

- The third pathology that can doom execution of a strategy is the breakdown of communication and coordination. Even with plans that are clearly articulated, constant communication is critical, especially if the plans involve many participants and moving parts.

  - The well-known Charge of the Light Brigade, which took place during the Crimean War in 1854, serves as a stunning example of poor communication in execution.

  - The British were fighting the Russians at the port of Balaklava on the Crimean Peninsula. The overarching strategy of the units involved was to support the siege of Sevastopol and seize Balaklava, a nearby port. The tactics designed to execute this strategy seemed sound.

  - As the British pursued the retreating Russians, however, their commander issued a vague order that the British cavalry should "advance rapidly to the front… to prevent the enemy [from] carrying away the guns."

  - Unfortunately, the order did not specify which guns the commander had in mind; thus, the Light Brigade charged off in the wrong direction, directly toward a mass of Russian guns in place at the far side of a valley.

- The fourth pathology that hinders execution of strategy is poor intelligence. The British raid on the French port of Dieppe in 1942 is our example here, although it could easily serve as the example for a number of other strategic pathologies. This operation shows much of what is wrong with strategy that is based on an unclear objective, sabotaged by loss of institutional control, and supported by poor intelligence.

  - To this day, the point of the Dieppe raid is still not quite clear. In hindsight, the operation was assigned as a mission, ostensibly to "learn lessons" in how to conduct an amphibious invasion.

The fiasco at Dieppe during World War II was caused by faulty intelligence; British planners were forced to use holiday snapshots to assess the conditions of the beach for landing.

o   Planning for the operation was lengthy and sporadic. At one point, British high command canceled the raid, but Lord Mountbatten, then chief of British Combined Operations, resurrected it and pushed it forward without authorization. He had neither enough resources nor access to intelligence.

o   Mountbatten's planners were forced to use unreliable intelligence that was months old. The British knew nothing about hidden German gun positions on the cliffs, and they had assessed whether tanks could navigate the beach by closely examining holiday snapshots.

o   During the attack, only 15 tanks made it off the beach, and these were quickly repulsed. Naval support was insufficient, and for political reasons, the British had elected not to bomb the German positions so as not to alienate the French with civilian casualties.

- After the fact, veteran memoirs and other accounts showed that the Germans had known about and been preparing for the anticipated Allied landings for weeks.

- The Dieppe raid deserves detailed study to understand how a plan can spiral out of control and be negatively influenced by a host of factors, many of them controllable.

- The last pathology we will look at in this lecture is inertia. We often think of inertia as resistance to change, the tendency for a body at rest to stay at rest, but it's also the tendency for a body in motion to stay in motion in a particular direction on a fixed course.

  - Strategies are difficult to craft and even more difficult to implement. Given the investment that goes into a major strategy adoption and implementation, the impetus for a firm and the people involved is to stay the course. This is especially true when egos and careers are invested in a course of action, even if the strategy is failing.

  - When lives are at stake, changing course becomes an even more urgent matter, and the pathology can sometimes take on horrific proportions, as it did in 1916 in the Battle of the Somme.

  - The battle began with a British offensive designed to steamroll the Germans and break the stalemate of trench warfare to reach open ground. The plan called first for an artillery barrage to obliterate German positions, destroy barbed wire entanglements, and demolish the German artillery; the British would simply walk in to occupy the newly won territory.

  - But none of that happened. A seven-day artillery barrage gave the enemy adequate notice of what was to happen, and the German defenses proved incredibly durable.

  - It was obvious that the preconditions for the successful execution of British strategy had not been met, yet the commander of the British

Fourth Army, General Sir Henry Rawlinson, let inertia take over and ordered the attack to proceed.

o The British emerged from their trenches and marched over open ground under machine gun and artillery fire; by the end of the day, they had suffered 60,000 casualties.

Control

- It's essential to create a control mechanism in order to massage a strategy to successful completion. For example, Jack Welch, the CEO of General Electric, famously devoted an entire week during each of his 20 years as CEO to reviewing the operating plans of each of his company's units for that year.

- Strategy is not like an aircraft autopilot. We can't publish a strategy, put it on a shelf, and sit back to wait for good things to happen. We must follow through. We must assign responsibility, avoid overreach, maintain clear communication, nurture effective intelligence, and reject inertia in the face of new information. In short, we must remember that strategy is a process, not a single event or decision.

- This means that identifying the specific action steps of a strategy cannot be omitted from the strategic process. A decision will not take effect unless action commitments are built into the decision from the start. If a decision is no one's specific work and responsibility, it's likely that nothing will happen.

- Grand strategy must be translated into the proper action steps at the lower unit level, but this does not happen on its own. It happens with follow-through, checks and balances, and control. Strategic leadership includes execution and should include some informal "management by walking around."

- Execution is ultimately a function of strong and bold leadership, a propensity to take responsibility, and a system of control to bring the strategy to completion. Conversely, strategy even at the very highest levels, is ultimately a function of thoroughgoing execution. We can move forward with successful strategic execution by recognizing and avoiding the pathologies that plague us every step of the way.

Suggested Reading

Charan and Bossidy, *Execution.*

Drucker, *The Effective Executive.*

Harvard Business School Press, *Executing Strategy for Business Results.*

Questions to Consider

1. Can you think of a time, in either your personal or professional life, when you were too optimistic about the results you expected? Evaluate that experience to discover if part of the reason was that your plan was too tightly wound and had no margin for error.

2. What are some examples in your experience that illustrate the five pathologies that lead to poor execution of strategy: lack of designated responsibility, overreach, communication breakdown, poor intelligence, and inertia? Would recognition of any or all of these have changed what you did and, as a result, changed the outcome?

3. What kind of control mechanism do you employ to mitigate the risk of the five pathologies that hinder strategy?

Avoid the Pathologies of Execution
Lecture 11—Transcript

When we craft strategy, we try to impose order on a chaotic reality. But even with a superb strategic vision and the formulation of prudent strategy, the best-laid plans can go awry. Let's start with an example that seemed like a good idea, and on paper, carried a strategic elegance, full of daring and *élan* to propel it forward.

It was September of 1944 during World War II, and "Operation Market Garden" seemed like the right plan at the right time, especially to the man who conceived it. The allies had raced across France and were right at the German border, poised to make the final push and end the war.

But the allied offensive against Germany had run out of gas—literally. Supplies were scarce. So British Field Marshal Bernard Montgomery conceived of Operation Market Garden.

Montgomery wanted all fuel supplies given to him for his plan. The operation was to flank the Germans to the north where Belgium meets Holland. He wanted to cross the Lower Rhine River in Holland, going around the German line of defenses opposite the Maginot Line and thrust into Germany. An exciting plan! A neat reversal of how the Germans had gone around the Maginot Line itself at the beginning of the war.

But Operation Market Garden was freighted with a built-in disadvantage that dooms even the best of plans: The plan required everything to go right, and that's just not going to happen.

The Second Law of Thermodynamics tells us that. It tells us that if left to themselves, all systems tend toward entropy and disorder. Systems tend to break down and return the status quo to chaos. When our strategy becomes more and more complex—when we set up a complex system to execute our plans—it incorporates more and more variables. This means that more and more things have to go right for our strategy to work. The popular wisdom of Murphy's Law is not a bad guide when we consider how our strategy might go awry. Whatever can go wrong will go wrong. Usually in the worst possible way.

And thus it was with Operation Market Garden. It sounded good. Airborne troops parachute in to seize a series of six bridges behind enemy lines all the way up to the final bridge over the Rhine at the town of Arnhem more than 60 miles away.

There were six water obstacles the allies would have to cross. All six bridges would be seized simultaneously. Four divisions of airborne troops would be dropped to seize these bridges. The last bridge at Arnhem would be seized and held by airborne troops for four days until ground forces could fight their way through to them over a distance of 62 miles through enemy territory.

How does this sound to you so far? For the ground attack, the allies would advance their tanks along a single highway that was two lanes wide and was raised above the flat terrain around it. The ground on either side was too soft and mushy to support vehicles of any kind, and it was crisscrossed with dykes and drainage ditches. Tanks and trucks couldn't leave the road.

What about intelligence on the enemy? What can we expect from them? It seemed to the Allied High Command that the German resistance had broken. It seemed that most of the enemy troops were fleeing, and it seemed that they had no tanks. Montgomery was convinced that the allies would face limited resistance on their route up Highway 69. And the German defenders would be spread out over the entire length of the road, trying to fight pockets of airborne forces.

What the allies didn't know—and later, would not believe—was that two powerful SS Panzer Divisions were just assigned to the area to rest and refit, one of them right at the ultimate objective: the town of Arnhem. But Montgomery dismissed intelligence reports about the 9th and 10th SS tank divisions. He refused to change plans for the drop of 1st Airborne Division at Arnhem, right on top of a waiting SS Panzer Division, one of the most powerful formations in the German army.

A British intelligence officer, Major Brian Urquhart, believed the plan was critically flawed, and he tried to persuade his superiors to modify or abort the operation—both aerial reconnaissance and the Dutch resistance confirmed that the German tanks were there. He was ignored and ordered out of the country on "sick leave."

What did the Germans know about the plan? Not much until quite early in the fighting, when the Germans recovered a copy of the Market Garden plan from a dead American officer who should not have been carrying it into combat.

The plan was complex and led to blunders: Instead of landing near the bridge at Arnhem, they were dropped eight miles away. Insufficient transport meant that the force could not be dropped all at once; they would be brought in over three days, feeding them into the battle in penny-packets. Air-to-ground radios did not work, and so the allies could not even be resupplied. After nine days of battle the allies withdrew, evacuating the troops they could rescue.

It was a catastrophic defeat. A disaster. Of the 10,000 soldiers dropped into Arnhem, only 2163 escaped. Why? How could smart, experienced, war-seasoned veterans bungle so badly?

The allies underestimated German capabilities and overestimated their own capabilities. Based on these estimates, they created a plan that was too tightly wound with too many objectives, too many moving parts, too much necessary coordination, and a heavy dose of wishful thinking that blinded the planners to red flags.

What did Field Marshal Montgomery have to say after the bullets and shells had stopped? "It was a bad mistake on my part—I underestimated the difficulties of opening up the approaches to Antwerp ... I reckoned the Canadian Army could do it while we were going for the Ruhr. I was wrong."

And yet, even after this defeat, Montgomery stubbornly held to his incredibly flawed plan. As is the case with human nature, Montgomery evoked the "if" clause.

He offered this:

> In my prejudiced view, if the operation had been properly backed from its inception, and given the aircraft, ground forces, and administrative resources necessary for the job, it would have succeeded in spite of my mistakes, or the adverse weather, or the presence of the 2nd SS Panzer Corps in the Arnhem area. I remain Market Garden's unrepentant advocate.

In other words, if everything had gone according to plan, the over-complicated plan would have worked. In the business world, consultants tasked with strategy can claim the same thing: The strategy I offered would have been fine, but the company failed to execute properly.

Operation Market Garden is an example of overreach. Overreach occurs when our capabilities and strategy don't match—they don't align with each other. Overreach is one of the pathologies that can interfere with the implementation of our chosen strategy. Much of what goes wrong in strategy occurs because of bad planning and poor execution. If you had to choose, which would you rather have: a well-executed bad plan or a good plan poorly executed?

Even with crisp execution and follow-through, a superb strategy may still fail due to reasons outside our ability to predict or adapt to. Clausewitz called this "friction." But often, we find a disconnect between strategy formulation and its execution. It's common in politics, for example, where the general policies are often created by people with no connection to the implementation. Other times, this separation of planning and execution is a more artificial distinction—much of the strategy might be executed by the folks who plan it. Either way, we can find a continuous spectrum of activity that takes us from the situation room to the battlefield.

And regardless of whether you're facing a distinction between strategy and execution that is large or small, there is enough of a sameness to failed strategy in all walks of life to discern some patterns of failure. Five main causes of strategic failure we can consider here are omission of responsibility, overreach, breakdown of communication, poor intelligence, and inertia. Let's look at each.

First, the omission of designated responsibility. In strategy, nothing happens when no one is responsible. This is like many other things in life. This is as much a part of failure of strategic leadership as it is a disconnect between strategy and its implementation. Some people have difficulty making the connection between planning and executing plans. A former business colleague of mine had this problem. He was a former high-ranking military officer, but apparently one who plied his trade on the staff side of the house rather than as a leader of troops. His modus operandi exemplifies this common disconnect in strategic implementation. He spoke well, he knew all of the Pentagon jargon, he seemed personable enough, he would hold a meeting that held all of the trappings of a real meeting where bold initiatives would be discussed. And then nothing would happen.

Nothing happened because he shrank from the most obvious duty of strategic leadership—he refused to connect planning to the assignment of responsibility. And this meant, de facto, that he refused to accept the mutual responsibility of assigning specific tasks. With his fingers crossed, he hoped something good would happen. If it did, it was hit or miss and it sprang from the initiative of other people.

This is a defensive and damage-limitation mode of faux leadership. Its most obvious manifestation is the gap between planning and execution, the omission of designated responsibility. This utterly crucial step is left to happenstance. For the military in time of peace, or businesses without severe external threats, this type of pathology may be tolerated. But, in time of war, or whenever survival is at stake, it becomes fatal.

Second is the pathology of overreach. We saw how the British overreached in Operation Market Garden in 1944. They had ambitious goals, clearly articulated objectives, but they did not have the capabilities to carry it off. And they compounded their problem by not accurately assessing the Germans' capabilities of interfering with the strategic plan. In fact, it was almost as if the strategy was to be crafted and executed without German interference, as if the Germans would play a passive role—powerless to interfere with British aims.

Another example of overreach occurred just three months later in the Ardennes forest. In what became known as the Battle of the Bulge. In December of 1944, Germany was on the brink of defeat in World War II. Or so she seemed. The Russians were closing in the East, and in the West, Americans were debating whether the war might be over by Christmas.

But in Germany, the view was different. Germany planned a breathtaking offensive in the Ardennes forest of Belgium that sought to gain strategic military and political objectives. The intent was clear. The operation was called "Watch on the Rhine." Three powerful German armies were to blast through the Ardennes forest, just as they had done in 1940. The offensive would split the American and British lines, seize the strategic port of Antwerp, and buy the Germans time for the Anglo-Russian alliance to crumble.

No one can accuse the Germans of timidity. It was a bold plan. But again, just as with the British in Operation Market Garden, the plan required everything to go right for it to succeed. The Germans needed bad weather to keep the influence of Allied air superiority to a minimum. And they needed to succeed before Allied reinforcements could arrive.

On December 16, 1944, the Germans hurled the last of their strategic reserves into battle, three great armies of a quarter-million men—powerful, yes, but not powerful enough to accomplish the bold objectives within the necessary timetable. After initial success, the lack of sufficient capability and a vigorous American counterattack stopped the offensive and rolled it back.

And as with Market Garden, the Germans did not have the wherewithal to accomplish their bold objectives. Like Market Garden, the plan underestimated enemy capabilities to interfere with the execution of the plan, and it failed. Overreach, lack of responsibility.

The third pathology that can doom execution of a strategy is the breakdown of communication and coordination. Generals themselves do not execute strategy. Their junior officers and soldiers execute the plan. But even with the best intent, even with plans clearly articulated, constant communication is critical, especially in executing a plan with many participants and many moving parts.

We sometimes think of "poor communication" as a euphemism for two people who just can't get along. Often that's true, and it can cascade. It can cascade into an implementation of our strategy where coordination is upended, and sometimes the exact opposite of what we intend happens. In the following example, poor communication in execution leads to a grotesque inferno on the battlefield—such a debacle that it is immortalized in verse by Great Britain's poet laureate Alfred Lord Tennyson. Now, when they compose poetry about your strategic failure, you know it's bone-headed; you know you have a candidate for the strategic hall of shame.

Here, I talk about the example of the Charge of the Light Brigade during the Crimean War in 1854. The location was the port of Balaclava on the Crimean peninsula. The British were fighting the Russians, and the overarching strategy of the units involved was to support the siege of Sevastopol and to seize Balaclava, a nearby port. The tactics designed to execute this strategy seemed sound. In fact, the British performed admirably in their land operations. But it was in their execution of this action that incredible failure followed—failure that led to a famous poem and several films by the same name: *The Charge of the Light Brigade*.

As the British pursued the retreating Russians, the commander, Lord Raglan, looked over the battlefield from a good vantage point on a low mountain. He gave an order that was scribbled in pencil by General Richard Airey and given to an eager messenger. This messenger, a Captain Nolan, galloped down the mountain and excitedly rode up to Lord Lucan, who was commanding the Heavy Brigade and the Light Brigade.

The order was vague. It stated that the British cavalry should sweep the cannon from the ridge. But it did not say which ridge. And the cavalry on the field below could not see the cannon. Here, in fact, is the actual order: "Lord Raglan wishes the Cavalry to advance rapidly to the front, follow the enemy, and try to prevent the enemy carrying away the guns."

When Captain Nolan rushed up to Lord Lucan to present the order, he added his own urgency to the message. He urged the cavalry to attack immediately. When Lucan asked Nolan which guns, Nolan responded with a wide sweep of his arm, gesturing at the mass of Russian guns at the end of the valley, a mile away.

And this is how the 600 lancers, dragoons, and hussars of the Light Brigade formed up at the valley mouth and rode at a trot down the valley floor for a mile, with Russian cannons on the heights to either side blasting them and cannons awaiting them at the end of the valley. They accelerated to a gallop through a storm of shot and shell.

A journalist on the scene, William Howard Russell, described it this way:

> They swept proudly past, glittering in the morning sun in all the pride and splendor of war. We could scarcely believe the evidence of our senses! Surely that handful of men [were] not going to charge an army in position? Alas, it was but too true—their desperate valor knew no bounds, and far indeed was it removed from its so-called better part—discretion.

Up on the mountain, Lord Raglan and his staff looked down in horror as the scene unfolded below, as the Light Brigade went the wrong way. It plunged into the valley, and into immortality. Rarely has the execution of strategy been so publicly short-circuited by miscommunication. The actual order that triggered this debacle now resides in the National Army Museum in London—a mere note of 8 lines, and a vivid reminder of how small a fatal breakdown of communication can be.

The fourth pathology that hinders our execution of strategy is poor intelligence. Let's look at a strategic failure from 1942 that isn't emphasized much in history books. Certainly, the British would rather forget this horrendous fiasco. I cite this British raid on the French port of Dieppe as an example of strategy poorly executed because of faulty intelligence and poor counterintelligence. But the Dieppe Raid in August 1942 across the English Channel can just as easily serve as the example for a number of other strategic pathologies. This operation shows much of what is wrong with strategy that is based on an unclear objective, sabotaged by loss of institutional control, and supported by poor intelligence.

To this day, the point of the Dieppe Raid is still not quite clear. In hindsight, the operation was assigned a mission, ostensibly to "learn lessons" in how to conduct an amphibious invasion. But at the time, the strategic purpose was vague. Planning for the operation was lengthy and sporadic. British High Command canceled the raid, scheduled for July 5, because of bad weather and the loss of surprise. But the raid had taken on a life of its own. It quickly became a "prestige project" to serve the ambitions of a single man, Vice-Admiral Louis Lord Mountbatten, then Chief of British Combined Operations. Lord Mountbatten resurrected it, called it Operation Jubilee, and pushed it forward as a personal project without authorization. He had neither permission nor access to enough resources, nor access to intelligence.

Because it became Mountbatten's personal project, his planners were forced to utilize intelligence that was months old. And that intelligence on the area was poor and unreliable. The British knew nothing about hidden German gun positions on the cliffs. British planners had assessed the slope of the beach and whether tanks could use it by closely examining holiday snapshots.

The planners completely misjudged British capabilities in executing the attack. In the attack, tanks sank in the soft, pebbly beach and few could breach the high sea wall. Only 15 tanks made it off the beach, and these were quickly repulsed. Naval support was completely insufficient and for political reasons, the British had elected not to bomb the German positions so as not to alienate the French with civilian casualties.

While British intelligence was seriously flawed, German intelligence exposed the operation early-on. After the fact, veteran memoirs and many accounts of interrogated German prisoners, German captors, and French citizens all show that the Germans had been preparing for the anticipated Allied landings for weeks. The Germans were on high alert for the attack on August 19 and well-prepared to defend against it.

The British assault began at 5:00 am, and after just six hours, such disaster loomed that the Allied commanders were forced to call a retreat.

The Germans who defended Dieppe were outnumbered 5-1, and yet they achieved a great victory. Of 6000 men attacking, the allies lost 3300 killed or captured. Germans casualties were approximately 600.

The Dieppe Raid deserves detailed study to understand how a plan can spiral out of control and be negatively influenced by a host of factors, many of them controllable. The raid, despite all of the shortcomings that were recognized at the time, continued to move forward as if it were preordained and beyond the power of human beings to stop, even if human rationality concluded that it should be. In fact, the Dieppe Raid's rigidly inflexible qualities lead us into the final pathology that causes poor strategic execution.

We next examine the pathology of inertia—or more colloquially, throwing good money after bad. We think of inertia as the tendency for a body at rest to stay at rest. It's the tendency for the status quo to remain in place. Inertia is resistance to change. But inertia is also the tendency for a body in motion to stay in motion in a particular direction on a fixed course. Employees can stay on a particular promotion track merely because of organizational inertia. Strategy can be like this—paradoxically, bad strategy in particular. There are good reasons for this.

Strategies are so difficult to craft and even more difficult to implement. Given the investment that goes into a major strategy adoption and implementation, the impetus for a firm and the people involved is to stay the course. This is especially true where egos and careers are invested in a course of action, even if the strategy is failing. It's not human nature to just let go of what economists call "sunk costs" and focus only on "prospective costs" to come in the future, even though it's only the prospective costs that we still have any ability to influence. For example, in 2008, the investment bank Lehman Brothers refused to change course for months after the bankruptcy of Bear Stearns had made clear that a continued strategy of high-leverage reliance on mortgage-backed securities could be punished most severely by investors. Lehman Brothers went into bankruptcy that same year.

When lives are directly at stake, changing course becomes an even more urgent matter and the pathology can sometimes take on horrific proportions, as it did in 1916 in the Battle of the Somme. The Battle of the Somme during

World War I began with a British offensive on July 1 designed to steamroll the Germans and to break the stalemate of trench warfare to break through to open ground.

The plan called first for a crushing artillery barrage to obliterate the German positions, destroy barbed wire entanglements, and demolish the German artillery; the British would simply walk in to occupy the newly won territory.

But none of this happened. A seven-day artillery barrage gave the enemy adequate notice of what was to happen. But the German defenses proved incredibly durable, and they remained almost intact. This fact was known to the British. It was obvious that the preconditions for the successful execution of British strategy had not been met. So the commander of the British Fourth Army, General Sir Henry Rawlinson, was faced with this decision: To pursue a strategy that vitally depended for its success on the destruction of enemy defenses when these enemy defenses were left almost intact. Inertia took over. Rawlinson let bravado carry the day; he gave the order for the attack.

The British emerged from their trenches and they marched slowly over open ground under machine gun and artillery fire, and by the end of the day, they had suffered 60,000 casualties. This was 20 percent of the entire British force that attacked that day.

Military historian Geoffrey Regan described the bloody battle this way: "Rawlinson must have known that this would happen and that he could prevent it. But this would have called into question the whole strategy on which the British plan was based." Instead, he let the attack go ahead even though he knew that the plan had already failed—that the strategy had failed. "When the horrendous casualty figures came in, Rawlinson ordered his staff to destroy all the notes he had issued as a guide to the officers leading the attack." Suicidal inertia, faux leadership that fails to assign responsibility, overreach, communication breakdowns, and acting on the basis of unreliable and outdated intelligence.

We've focused on military examples to highlight possible consequences of these pathologies as clearly as possible. Recognition of these difficulties is only halfway to their solution. The rest of the solution is to be found in control. We must create a control mechanism so that we may massage a strategy to successful completion. For example, Jack Welch, the CEO of General Electric, famously devoted an entire week during each of his 20 years as CEO to reviewing the operating plans of each of his company's units for that year.

Strategy is not like an aircraft autopilot. We can't publish our strategy, put it on a shelf, and sit back to wait for good things to happen. We must follow through. We must assign responsibility, avoid overreach, maintain clear communication, nurture effective intelligence, and reject inertia in the face of new information. In short, we must remember that strategy is a process, not a single event or decision. This means that identifying the specific action steps of a strategy cannot be omitted from the strategic process. A decision will not take effect unless action commitments are built into the decision from the start. If a decision is no one's specific work and responsibility, it's likely nothing will happen.

Grand strategy must be translated into the proper action steps at the lower unit level. This does not happen on its own. It happens with follow-through, and checks and balances, and control. Strategic leadership includes execution and should include some informal "management by walking around." Execution is ultimately a function of strong and bold leadership, a propensity to take responsibility, and a system of control to bring the strategy to completion. Conversely, strategy even at the very highest levels is ultimately a function of thoroughgoing execution.

We can move forward with successful strategic execution by recognizing and avoiding the pathologies that plague us every step of the way and by following through with the action steps of our plan.

Tactics of Combat as Problem-Solving Tools
Lecture 12

The language of combat is all around us, in business, sports, politics, and elsewhere. But rather than simply adopting the machismo of war words, we can learn something about strategy from the actual techniques of martial combat. In fact, with judicious thought, we can apply the tactics of war and strategy as problem-solving tools relevant to business and our personal lives.

Definitions Revisited

- Let's begin by revisiting a terminology issue: the difference between strategy and tactics. This difference often seems slippery to many people, and there's a good reason for this confusion.

- In simplest terms, a strategy is an overall plan while tactics are the actions we take to execute the plan. This distinction has a long tradition in strategic planning that goes back to the military but leads to an unfortunate conclusion that strategy refers to the big things and tactics, to the details.

- However, when we embark on a strategy, there is no way to know in advance which details are insignificant and which may loom large as important strategic milestones. Our intended strategy merges imperceptibly into our emergent strategy through the process of strong and crisp execution and responses to what our competitors do.

- Perspective also plays a major role. Strategic theorist **Richard Rumelt** put it this way: "One person's strategy is another's tactics—that is, what is strategic depends on where you sit." For instance, from the overall perspective of corporate strategy, business units are expected to execute tactics. But from the perspective of a single unit within the business, these tactics for the company are likely part of its strategy.

- The important point to remember is that execution is the neglected child of strategy and that follow-through in execution—tactics—is a more important part of strategy than the publication of the strategy in a handsome binder.

- For this lecture, we'll call these techniques strategic maneuvers. As we use them, let's keep our eyes open for opportunities to change direction, to abandon plans gone awry, to follow up victories with more victories, and to allow our realized strategy to emerge from the flurry of actions and responses that play out in the real world.

Strategic Maneuvers

- Many of the strategic maneuvers used on the battlefield have a long history, which suggests both their conceptual durability and the constancy of human nature.

- Principles of maneuver can be applied at the level of the army, with its thousands of armed combatants, down to the level of the individual soldier.

- Maneuvers have their counterparts in other venues, such as business and sports. In fact, the lines between these venues are different only in the level of conflict and degree of violence involved.

- Maneuvers can be faster than the speed of conscious thought. In the sport of fencing, for example, the attacks and defensive maneuvers of the two opponents create a dynamic and fluid combat situation. Each opponent must be ready to abandon the line of attack he or she has created and pursue other advantages that present themselves.

- Fencing, and the speed at which it takes place, helps us understand a broader fact about conflict and competition: What actually occurs in competition is often not the result of a carefully wrought strategic plan but the swift and flexible application of martial principles at the place and time demanded of the situation.

- It's also important to remember that not every maneuver or attack is appropriate in every situation. Maneuvers must make sense in the overall plan and in the context of the ongoing battle, events that have already occurred, and current capabilities.

The Frontal Assault

- Frontal assault is, obviously, an all-out attack on the enemy's front. Usually, the enemy has chosen the location where the battle will take place and is well dug in.

- If you believe that frontal assault is the only option open to you, then you can act to mitigate the disadvantages of this maneuver. Consider, for example, D-Day, the Allied invasion of western Europe, launched on June 6, 1944.

  o The Allied landings in western France were the deadliest kind of frontal assault—against a well-prepared and well-entrenched enemy across unfriendly terrain.

  o The French coast was the Allies' only choice for the point of attack, and the Germans knew it. But the Allies were still able to shroud the exact time and location of the assault from the Germans with an elaborate deception campaign.

- In business, the frontal assault pits one competitor against another; its manifestation is the price war. Often, the only winners in these engagements are the consumers.

- Unless other mitigating factors can be brought to bear, attacking a strong and well-prepared enemy is foolhardy. It goes against every principle of competition we have studied. This is true in professional conflict and on a personal level.

The Indirect Approach

- The indirect approach is a strategic contribution offered by **Sir Basil Liddell Hart**, a British strategist of the early and mid-20th century. In his book *Strategy*, Liddell Hart notes that seven out of eight frontal assaults in the American Civil War failed. He also observed that when the art of indirect approach was used, it demonstrated great utility both in achieving objectives and minimizing damage to the attacker.

- In mobile warfare, where maneuver can be used to great effect, a technique of the indirect approach is to keep an opponent guessing about your intermediate objectives as you advance. By keeping two equally attractive objectives in the strategic scheme, you impose indecisiveness on your opponent, compelling a split in forces in a futile attempt to defend everything.

- William Tecumseh Sherman's 1864 Georgia campaign in the Civil War offers an excellent example of keeping the enemy in suspense about successive objectives. The Southern forces, led by General Joseph Johnston, were never able to fix Sherman's objectives along his march.

- In business, Honda Motor Company successfully used the strategy of indirect approach in developing its expertise as the world's leading manufacturer of small internal combustion engines. This technological leadership laid a platform for Honda's horizontal expansion into automobiles and caught American carmakers napping.

Turning the Flank
- Turning the flank is a maneuver that attempts to dislocate the enemy by moving to either of its flanks. The flanking movement requires a response from the enemy, which usually disrupts its operations.

- Napoleon crafted much of his reputation by maneuvering against the flanks and into the rear of the enemy. In the Korean War, General **Douglas MacArthur** used the technique in his amphibious landing at Inch'ŏn.

- In the Civil War, General Sherman maneuvered against the enemy flanks many times in his 1864 campaign against the South in Georgia. Repeatedly, Sherman maneuvered to turn the flank of Joseph Johnston's army, forcing the Southern general out of his prepared defensive positions and into successive retreats.

- On the Southern side, General **Robert E. Lee** achieved his greatest victory in 1863 at Chancellorsville by means of the flank attack, accompanied by the force multiplier of surprise. Lee launched a distracting demonstration attack on the Union front while Thomas Jackson—Stonewall—maneuvered to the unsuspecting Union right flank, surprising and routing the Union troops.

- In business, attacking the flank can take many different forms, depending on the product or service offered and the various alignments of power relationships. Attacking the flank can mean, for instance, carving out market space by specializing in a narrow niche of a major competitor, as we saw in retail bookselling.

Robert E. Lee's flank attack at Chancellorsville caught the Union troops completely by surprise and resulted in the general's greatest victory.

- Royal Crown Cola failed in a frontal assault against Coke and Pepsi in the early 1960s, but the company might have been successful had it pursued a flanking course.

  o Royal Crown went nationwide with the first diet soft drink, Diet Rite Cola, in 1962. This flanking move caught the major colas by surprise, and by the end of the decade, Diet Rite was the best-selling soft drink in the United States.

  o By concentrating its resources on market leader Diet Rite, RC could have solidified its position. But the company didn't anticipate its market leadership in diet soda and chose to squander the opportunity.

- o Rather than show flexibility and follow up on a clear winner, RC decided to compete on both fronts and let the market make the choice, with disastrous results. Increased competition appeared with the introduction of Diet Coke, and without strategic support, Diet Rite faded.

Rear Area Battle

- Rear area battle is a concept of 20th-century warfare, whose operative idea is to sow confusion in the enemy's ranks behind the lines by creating the impression that no ground is safe. This technique forces opponents to expend resources defending ground they thought they had already won.

- In warfare, at the start of hostilities, commandos with various deadly skills infiltrate into the enemy's rear areas, where support and supply bases are maintained. These commandos disrupt communications and supply and even assassinate enemy commanders, sowing confusion and suspicion.

- During World War II, the French Underground worked tirelessly against occupying German forces, and in Russia, partisans took up arms against the invaders, forcing the Germans to divert troops from the front lines to guard supply depots and convoys.

- Just as important as the operational aspects of rear area battle is the psychological impact when your opponent realizes that you have penetrated its lines. In World War II, at the start of the Battle of the Bulge in 1944, the Germans managed to drop commandos wearing American uniforms behind Allied lines in an effort to sow confusion in the American ranks.

- Rear area battle is also used in presidential political campaigns as candidates strike and counterstrike at one another's home bases—with advertising, personal appearances, and surrogate campaigners. This move forces opposing candidates to redirect their resources to areas they thought were already secure.

- This technique has been used throughout history to take pressure off other areas of the front. In 1864, for example, the Confederacy launched a raid on the Northern capital at Washington, territory that was considered secure by the Union, in an effort to relieve the pressure on Southern forces at Cold Harbor.

- Rear area battle is often used in international business operations, as when Fujifilm attacked Kodak in its home market in the United States in the 1980s, slowly winning market share and igniting a price war. Kodak responded with a counterattack in Japan, forcing Fujifilm to reexamine operations in its home base.

Which Maneuver to Use?
- Which strategic maneuver should you use? The answer depends on a variety of factors: your position in relation to your opponent, your resources, your capabilities, your ability to accept risk, your strategic intent, and so on.

- Successful strategic implementation means knitting tactical engagements together into a coherent whole. Tactics without an overarching strategy means aimless conflict. Even if you know you likely would win a given encounter, shrewd strategic decision making means not fighting battles that do not advance your strategy.

Names to Know

Lee, Robert E. (1807–1870): Offered command of the Northern army at the outset of the American Civil War, Lee instead sided with his home state of Virginia and created a legend in the subsequent four years as one of the greatest battlefield generals in American history.

Liddell Hart, Basil (1895–1970): Fighting in the Great War imbued this great military thinker with a revulsion toward static attritional warfare and led to his theorizing on the great potential of the armored tank. Liddell Hart extended his strategic theorizing into other realms and penned a work called *The Lawn Tennis Masters Unveiled.*

MacArthur, Douglas (1880–1964): MacArthur's personal magnetism, larger-than-life personality, and extravagant ego led him to incredible success in war for a decade and to ultimate political ruin shortly after his masterstroke at Inch'ŏn during the Korean War.

Rumelt, Richard (1942–): Rumelt is a rousing scholar and consultant whose direct and concise writing on strategy is powerful in its simplicity and elegance, cutting through the static that permeates strategic thinking. Beginning his career in the field of electrical engineering, he slowly developed a reputation as a management guru and advocated that there are only two ways for companies to succeed for the long-term: They must either invent their way to it, or they must exploit some change in their environment.

Suggested Reading

Buskirk, *Frontal Attack.*

Johnson, Whitby, and France, *How to Win on the Battlefield.*

Ries and Trout, *Marketing Warfare.*

Questions to Consider

1. Often, many of us respond to challenges or problems in the same way every time they arise, ignoring the various tactical options open to us in favor of habitual and comfortable responses. Do you always respond to problems in the same way, or do you select a tactic from a menu of options? From the options provided in this lecture, consider at least one or two that you have never used and attempt to implement them at the first opportunity.

2. Consider various historical scenarios and evaluate them with an eye to exploring what options were available to the contenders that might have yielded a different outcome. For instance, what were General Robert E. Lee's options on the third day of the Battle of Gettysburg?

3. Rear area battle might be one of the least used tactics, yet it is very effective in certain situations, especially in business, where office

politics offers fertile ground for exploiting this tactic. Can you think of ways to outmaneuver your opponents by creating new threats in areas they thought previously secure?

Tactics of Combat as Problem-Solving Tools
Lecture 12—Transcript

In business and in sports and in politics, there is a pervasive language of war and of conflict. We talk of market penetration, of invading new markets, we outflank our opponents, we get ambushed in office meetings, we form alliances and we engage in battle against alliances, we conduct "hasty retreats" when facing a superior foe, we "arrange a truce" or "make peace" with our rivals. Perhaps it's only natural that we should speak this way. There is a reason. Ours is a world of conflict and cooperation. And sometimes the cooperation seems only a prelude to conflict.

Rather than simply adopting the machismo of war words, we can go beyond the surface similarities. We can study and learn something about strategy from the actual techniques of martial combat. Here, we look at some of the tactical techniques utilized by the military and codified in military manuals worldwide.

Successful strategic implementation means following through with crisp execution—it means knitting together your tactical engagements in the service of your master plan.

Let's re-visit a terminology issue right at the start. The difference between strategy and tactics. The difference between strategy and tactics has always seemed slippery to many people. Sometimes the terms seem to be used interchangeably. There's a very good reason for this confusion. In simplest terms, a strategy is the overall plan while tactics are the actions you take to execute the plan. This distinction has a long tradition in strategic planning that goes back to the military. This leads to an unfortunate conclusion that strategy refers to the big things and tactics to the details.

But as we embark upon our strategic journey into a future that is unsure, there is no way for us to know in advance which details are insignificant and which may loom large as an important strategic milestone for us. Our intended strategy merges imperceptibly into our emergent strategy through the process of strong and crisp execution and responses to what our competitors do.

Perspective also plays a major role. Strategic theorist Richard Rumelt put it this way: "One person's strategy is another's tactics—that is, what is strategic depends on where you sit." For instance, from the overall perspective of corporate strategy, business units are expected to execute tactics. But from the perspective of a single unit within the business, these tactics for the overall company are likely part of the strategy for the business unit, There may be subunits to execute the tactics of that unit strategy, what from the top level might be regarded as logistics or operations.

The important point to remember is that execution is the neglected child of strategy, and that follow-through in our execution—our "tactics"—is a more important part of strategy than the publication of our strategy in a handsome binder. So let's call these techniques strategic maneuvers. As we employ them, let's keep our eyes open for opportunities to change directions, to abandon plans gone awry to follow-up victories with more victories, and to allow our realized strategy to emerge from the flurry of actions and responses that play out in the real world.

Generals use a variety of strategic maneuvers on the battlefield to engage the enemy. Many of these maneuvers have a long history, some thousands of years old, which suggests their conceptual durability as well as the constancy of human nature. Maneuvers effective in the 1st century B.C. can be just as effective in the 21st century because the challenges, at bottom, remain the same—dealing with human nature in conflict.

These principles of maneuver can be applied at the level of the army, with its thousands of armed combatants, down to the level of the individual swordsman. Moreover, these maneuvers have their counterparts in other venues, such as business and sports. In fact, the lines between these separate venues are blurred and are different only in the level of conflict and the degree of violence.

And the maneuvers can be faster than the speed of conscious thought. Think for a moment of an individual swordsman. Today's elegant modern-day sport of fencing using the tip of a foil to touch a midsection, the saber to touch anywhere on the upper body, or the tip of the épée to touch anywhere on the body, are all direct descendants from military training rapier.

As a young college fencer, I found that one learns the same attacks and defensive maneuvers utilized by warriors in centuries past—warriors who played for the much higher stakes of life and death. Let's take a closer look now at some of these maneuvers.

Fencing is an elegant sport, a sport of strength, endurance, speed, and guile. This is a sabre; this is a cutting and thrusting weapon. We want to score touches on our opponent. The target area of our opponent is everything above the waist: the torso, the arms, wrists, and the head. Protection is essential.

Our basic attacks are the chest (or belly cut), the flank cut, and the head cut (straight on or to either cheek). I can also lunge and thrust with the point of the blade. My opponent attempts to parry these attacks; he parries the flank cut, he parries the chest cut, he parries the head cut. I want to deceive my opponent. I want him to develop tendencies so that he exposes himself to my attack. In this case, an attack to the wrist. A flank cut; parried. A chest cut; parried. Flank cut; parried. Chest cut; it was a feint! Cut to the wrist!

The same technique for the head cut. Head cut; parried. Head cut; parried. Head cut; it was a feint! Cut to the chest! And these are just a few of the deception techniques we can use. Sabre fencing, of course, is much more than hand movement; we incorporate mobility. In this case, the lunge. And finally, we conclude our brief demonstration with a running attack, called a *flèche* attack. Now, in all of this, your opponent's responses combine with learned martial principles to create a dynamic and fluid combat situation. It is from this interaction of strategic maneuvering that the final result emerges.

Of course, there is no checklist for successful fencing, much less for actual conflict. You may go into your conflict with a checklist, always beginning in the "en garde" position, but you will surely be left behind when dealing with an experienced opponent. You must be ready to abandon your line of attack to create and pursue other momentary advantages that present themselves, and to exploit them with follow-through.

Fencing, and the speed at which it takes place helps us understand a broader fact about conflict and competition. After the battle or series of battles, in hindsight we might identify a strategy pursued that actually did not exist in your prior intent. This is an important point to remember in studying the great battles and great business moves of history. What actually occurred was often not the result of a carefully wrought strategic plan, but the consistent, swift, and flexible application of martial principles at the place and time demanded of the situation.

With this fact in mind, let us examine some of these martial principles and strategic maneuvers. Let's first recognize that not every maneuver or attack is appropriate in every situation. It must make sense. It must make sense in the overall plan; it must make sense in the context of the ongoing battle; and it must make sense given what has already occurred and our current capabilities. It must have strategic fit.

An example of the elusiveness of victory and the quest for strategic fit comes from the Vietnam War. Colonel Harry Summers authored a book about the War, a Clausewitzian analysis of U.S. performance. After the War, Colonel Summers was in a delegation dispatched to Hanoi. In the airport, he got into a conversation with a North Vietnamese colonel named Tu who spoke some English. They spoke of their recent conflict, as warriors might do. Colonel Summers said: "You know, you never defeated us on the battlefield." Colonel Tu considered his response, then replied: "That may be so. But it is also irrelevant."

Colonel Tu's point was not cavalier. He described how a powerful opponent, the United States, had pursued a strategy of limited war against a weaker combatant pursuing a strategy of total war. A powerful opponent that had a muddled strategic intent with unclear objectives battling an enemy with clear intent and objectives and pursuing tactics designed to exploit weakness.

The weapons, the places, and the times may change, but conflict at its most visceral is still human versus human. And so it's useful for us to learn about some of the more venerable attacks and examine their applicability in venues other than the actual battlefield.

Some techniques of maneuver and attack are familiar to most people. Others not so well-known. The best strategic maneuver, of course, is one that Sun Tzu recommended more than 2000 years ago. Sun Tzu urged us to consider techniques that would yield bloodless victories. He said: "To fight and conquer in all your battles is not supreme excellence; supreme excellence consists in breaking the enemy's resistance without fighting."

More often than not, we are not blessed with the kind of acumen or situation that allows us the luxury of winning without battle. And so here we look at four techniques that can yield victory, if applied judiciously and at the proper place and time: the frontal assault, the indirect approach, turning the flank, and rear area battle.

The frontal assault we've already met when discussing the trench warfare of World War I, and is exactly what it sounds like—an all-out attack on the enemy's front. Usually, the enemy is well dug-in. The opponent has chosen the location where the battle will take place. You have tremendous disadvantages when making a frontal assault.

The natural question that arises here is, why use this maneuver? Is there ever a time when a frontal assault is a good idea? Perhaps. If it is the last thing a competitor expects and believes you will do. Even if it's fully expected, it may be the only option available. There may be no other way to oust an enemy from a strongpoint.

In the 8-year Iran–Iraq war in the 1980s, the Iranians launched human-wave frontal assaults on the better-equipped but outnumbered Iraqis.

If you believe your frontal assault is the only option open to you, then you can act to mitigate the disadvantages. I commend to you the example of D-Day, June 6, 1944: The invasion of Adolf Hitler's fortress Europe. The Allied landings in Western France were a frontal assault, the deadliest kind—against a well-prepared and well-entrenched enemy across unfriendly terrain.

The allies chose the French coast as their point of attack, as the Germans knew they would. There was really no other choice. But the allies still had flexibility as to the time and the exact location. These were the factors that the allies desperately needed to shroud from the Germans. The allies elected to obfuscate the true landing place and time with an elaborate deception campaign.

In business, the frontal assault pits one competitor against another—the manifestation of the frontal assault is the "price war." Especially when the two businesses compete on price rather than quality or premium brands or service. Take the discount retailer Wal-Mart. It fought and won a frontal assault on K-Mart in the 1990s. How does one attack Wal-Mart? Or the big cola companies Coca-Cola and Pepsi? With a frontal assault?

Royal Crown Cola actually tried a frontal assault on the Big Two colas in the late 1960s. Way back in the 1930s, Royal Crown was the number two soft drink in America ahead of Pepsi. RC Cola is, in fact, a part of Americana, at least in the American South. The "workingman's lunch" was an RC Cola and a Moon Pie, and even yielded a popular song in the 1950s *Gimme an RC Cola and a Moon Pie*. It remains an expression that to this day has traction in the American South. This kind of word of mouth advertising and embedding in the popular culture is considered gold in the marketing world.

But RC overreached. By the late 1960s, Royal Crown was America's number three cola and elected to take on the Big Two. It hired a big city advertising agency—Wells, Rich, Greene—led by one of the highest paid advertising executive in the country, Mary Wells. With reckless bravado, Wells made this announcement: "We're out to kill Coke and Pepsi. I hope you'll excuse the word, but we're really out for the jugular."

But RC was in no position to attack the market leaders in a frontal assault. At the time, Pepsi alone was selling four times as much as RC Cola. RC dissipated its resources promoting its mainline cola at a time when it had all the elements in place for a different and perhaps more successful strategic maneuver. A maneuver we'll talk about in a moment.

Frontal assaults between major corporations can devastate the contenders. The only winners in such a venture are consumers. So, you and I should be grateful when firms decide to assault each other directly, because the only immediate winners in a price war are consumers. To take an extreme example, in 1992 airlines engaged in a price war so devastating that some observers said airlines lost more money than the total profits earned by the industry since its very beginning.

Unless other mitigating factors can be brought to bear, attacking a strong and well-prepared enemy is foolhardy. It goes against every principle of competition we have studied and will study. This is true in professional conflict on a personal level as well. A direct frontal assault on a well-entrenched opponent, especially in public, has a good chance of ending in disaster for the attacker, unless the stage is carefully prepared beforehand and other, mitigating factors are on your side—such as timing, location, surprise, and deception.

Generally speaking—which is to say most of the time—it's much better to pursue another tack. The indirect approach is one such technique. The indirect approach is a technique that thwarts your opponent's expectations. Your opponent would like nothing better than to have you hurl yourself onto his carefully prepared position. Some enemies are just too strong to tackle head-on—like Wal-Mart.

The indirect approach is a strategic contribution offered by Sir Basil Liddell Hart, a British strategist of the early and mid-20th century. In his book *Strategy* Liddell Hart notes that seven out of eight frontal assaults in the American Civil War failed. He also observed that when the art of the indirect approach was used, it demonstrated great utility both in achieving objectives and in minimizing the damage to the attacker.

It makes no sense to wear ourselves out on an opponent entrenched in a powerful position. This could be called the "blitz-grinder," which was how the Russians viewed their defensive preparations at the Battle of Kursk in 1943. The Soviets had prepared extensive defensive belts over a period of months. These successive belts of defenses wore down the massive German offensive so that it never did achieve a breakthrough.

In mobile warfare, where maneuver can be used to great effect, a technique of the indirect approach is to keep an opponent guessing as to your intermediate objectives as you advance. In this way, by keeping two equally attractive objectives in the strategic scheme, you impose indecisiveness on your opponent and, in the best case, you compel him to split his forces in a futile attempt to defend everything.

William Tecumseh Sherman's 1864 Georgia campaign in the American Civil War offers us an excellent example of keeping the enemy in suspense as to successive objectives. Sherman faced retreating Confederate General Joseph Johnston, and Southern forces were never able to fix Sherman's objectives along his route of march.

In business, we can look to Honda Motor Company for an excellent example of the strategy of indirect approach. In Japan, Honda is known as a motorcycle manufacturer, but abroad it's known for its automobiles, and it is, in fact, the third largest carmaker in the United States. But in the 1950s, Honda developed its expertise as the world's best—not in motorcycles or automobiles. No—Honda became the world's leading manufacturer of small internal combustion engines. And it still is. American carmakers saw Honda as a Japanese maker of small motorcycles and ignored Honda's growing expertise in designing the finest small engines in the world—engines that powered everything from snow-blowers, to chain saws, to lawn mowers, to generators, to outboard motors. This technological leadership laid a platform for Honda's horizontal expansion into automobiles.

Honda's indirect approach caught American carmakers napping. They did not see the immediate threat of a new carmaker on the horizon with new ideas about smaller auto design, higher gas mileage, and reasonable price.

Our next strategic maneuver is turning the flank. Turning the flank is a maneuver that attempts to dislocate the enemy by moving to either of his flanks. It is a specific type of indirect approach focused on the opponent's sides. The flanking movement requires a response from the enemy, which usually disrupts its own operations.

Napoleon crafted much of his reputation by maneuvering against the flanks and into the rear of the enemy. In the Korean War, General Douglas MacArthur's amphibious landing at Inchon was an important example.

In the Civil War, General Sherman maneuvered against the enemy flanks many times in his 1864 campaign against the South in Georgia. Repeatedly, Sherman maneuvered to turn the flank of Joseph Johnston's army, forcing the southern general out of his prepared defensive positions and into successive retreats.

On the other side of that war, Southern commander-in-chief General Robert E. Lee achieved his greatest victory in 1863 at Chancellorsville by means of the flank attack, and he accompanied his flank attack by the force multiplier of surprise and a bit of deception.

Lee combined a distracting demonstration attack on the Union front while his trusted lieutenant general, Thomas Stonewall Jackson, maneuvered quickly and surreptitiously to the unsuspecting Union right flank. Jackson attacked and completely surprised and routed the Union troops relaxing in their bivouac. In the 2003 motion picture *Gods and Generals*, this battle is given a stunning portrayal.

In business, attacking the flank can take many different forms, depending on the product or service and the various alignments of power relationships. Attacking the flank can mean, for instance, carving out market space by specializing in a narrow niche of a major competitor. Take retail bookselling, for instance. The specialty bookseller will always outcompete the general interest bookseller within the narrow parameters defined by the niche market. Another example is specialty retail clothing stores for the "large man."

And finally, going back to our Royal Crown Cola example, we saw how Royal Crown attempted to take on the Big Two colas, and wore itself out promoting its mainline cola against Coca-Cola and Pepsi. RC could have pursued a different course, one that could have been wildly successful.

In 1962, Royal Crown went nationwide with the first diet soft drink in the United States: Diet Rite Cola. This flanking move caught the major colas by surprise, though Coke responded with TaB and Pepsi came out with Diet Pepsi. By the end of the 1960s, Diet Rite was the largest selling soft drink in the United States and accounted for almost half of Royal Crown's earnings.

This was the moment of strategic decision for Royal Crown. By concentrating its resources on market leader Diet Rite, RC could have solidified its position. RC did not anticipate this development, its market leadership in diet soda. It did choose to squander the opportunity.

Rather than show flexibility and follow-up on a clear winner, it decided to compete on both fronts and let the market choose for them, with disastrous results. Increased competition appeared in 1982, with the introduction of Diet Coke, and without strategic support, Diet Rite faded and eventually slipped to less than 4 percent of the diet soda market. Such are the results of choosing the wrong strategic maneuver—in this case, electing a frontal assault over following-up on a successful flanking maneuver.

Similar to the indirect approach and turning the flank is the maneuver called Rear area battle. Rear area battle is a concept of 20th century warfare, whose operative idea is to sow confusion in the enemy's ranks behind the lines by creating the impression that no ground is safe. It forces an opponent to expend resources defending ground that it thought it had already won. There is a large psychological component to this strategic maneuver.

In warfare, at the commencement of hostilities, commandos with various deadly skills infiltrate into the enemy's rear areas where the enemy maintains its support and supply bases. These commandos disrupt communications and supply, and even assassinate enemy commanders, sowing confusion and suspicion.

I had the chance to interview a Hungarian defector during the Cold War, a member of an elite commando unit. Hungary, of course, was a member of the Warsaw Pact. These commandos were known as Spetsnaz (or spetsialnoye nazhacheniye). This soldier's mission, at the commencement of hostilities, was to be inserted behind our lines and attack critical military installations.

During World War II, the French Underground worked tirelessly against occupying German forces, sabotaging railways and supply lines, aiding downed allied pilots, and providing the allies with valuable intelligence.

In Russia, too, partisans took up arms against the German invaders and increased the defensive burden, forcing the Germans to use troops to guard supply depots and convoys, diverting these badly needed soldiers from the front lines.

Just as important as the operational aspects of rear area battle is the psychological impact on your opponent when he realizes that the enemy has penetrated the lines and is behind him.

In World War II at the start of the Battle of the Bulge in 1944, the Germans managed to drop commandos wearing American military police uniforms behind Allied lines. The famed Commando Otto Skorzeny spearheaded the operation, which was designed to sow confusion in the American ranks as the Germans pressed forward in their last major offensive of the war.

Rear area battle can have a powerful impact on an enemy. Again, one psychological thrust is that the enemy is compelled to deploy forces to defend or to regain territory that he believed he had already won and secured. The psychological dislocation is tremendous as rear area battle sows insecurity in the mind of the enemy.

This type of action is used in presidential political campaigns as candidates strike and counterstrike at each other's home bases—with advertising, with personal appearances, and with surrogate campaigners who represent the candidate on the campaign trail.

We often hear of how one candidate is campaigning in a state thought to be solidly in the other candidate's camp. This has the intended effect of disrupting the plans of the other campaign, to force it to redirect resources into areas it thought already secure. Rear area battle or threat has been used throughout history to take pressure off other areas of the front.

In the summer of 1864, the Confederacy launched its famous raid on Washington. The South was facing a war of attrition against the North, which it could not hope to win. Ulysses S. Grant was pressing his opposite number at Cold Harbor. To relieve the pressure, General Robert E. Lee formed the

Army of the Valley—10,000 men under General Jubal Early. Lee sent Early north with orders to attack the Union capitol, Washington, D.C.

Washington was less strongly held than at other points in the war, and Early marched his troops hard. If not for a delaying battle by northern troops at Monocacy, Early's raid might have truly threatened the northern capitol. As it was, the intent of the raid was to force Union General Grant to divert troops from his pressure on the south to prevent the seizure of the capitol; to defend new territory—territory that was considered secure but was now suddenly threatened.

As an interesting historical aside, it was during Jubal Early's famous raid that Abraham Lincoln became the only incumbent U.S. president to ever come under direct fire by an adversary. As Lincoln watched from the stockade parapets that surrounded Washington, confederate Minié balls whizzed by his head. He was pulled down behind cover by a young captain, shouting, "Get down you fool." That young captain would later achieve fame in the U.S. judiciary—he was Captain Oliver Wendell Holmes, later Justice of the United States Supreme Court.

Rear area battle is used in business quite often, especially in international operations. If we conceive of companies having a "home base" or "home market," then the analogy becomes clear. For example, in the 1980s, Kodak found itself under assault by Fujifilm in its home market. Fujifilm attacked Kodak in the United States, slowly winning market share at Kodak's expense and igniting a price war. This was a combination frontal assault combined with attacking Kodak's secure U.S. bases.

Kodak responded with a counterattack in Japan, forcing Fujifilm to re-look at operations in its home base. Kodak compounded its attack with lawsuits and complaints to the GATT and, later, the World Trade Organization, charging unfair and illegal Japanese trade practices.

Kodak was quite explicit in its aggressive attitude toward Fujifilm. In 1998, Eric L. Steenburgh, Kodak's assistant chief operating officer offered this belligerent statement of Kodak strategic intent toward challenger Fujifilm: "Smack them until they figure it out."

250

So which strategic maneuver should you use? "Smack them until they figure it out?" Or some technique that has a chance of winning the day without a fight? Frontal assault, indirect approach, attack the flank, or take the fight to the rear area of the battle? That depends. It depends on your position vis-à-vis your opponent, on your resources, on your capabilities, on your ability to accept risk, on your own strategic intent, and in the implementation of your strategy, it depends on how your opponent responds to your initial and subsequent moves. It also depends on your boldness, on your analytical acumen, and on your ability to see through the fog of conflict in a detached and objective manner, and to keep your long-term strategic objectives front-and-center.

Successful strategic implementation means knitting together your tactical engagements into a coherent whole. Tactics without an overarching strategy means aimless conflict—perhaps even a string of meaningless tactical victories that weaken you, and do not advance your agenda. Even if you know you likely would win such an encounter, shrewd strategic decision making means not fighting battles that do not advance your strategy.

Shock of the New—Inflection Points
Lecture 13

We often become so ingrained in our ways of doing things that we forget that change is more common than stability. We accommodate small changes with relative ease, but occasionally, a game changer arrives, a major change that alters the landscape radically and quickly. Such transformations are known as strategic inflection points. In this lecture, we look at the types of changes businesses must make in the face of strategic inflection points.

The Strategic Inflection Point

- The term "strategic inflection point" was introduced by Andy Grove in 1996 in his book *Only the Paranoid Survive*. It refers to a dramatic change in our environment that makes us alter the way we do things or risk extinction. Such major changes compel us to change our strategy.

- Competitive advantage is conferred on those companies and individuals who can be the first to recognize and respond to a major change in the environment that affects their activities. Identifying changes in the overall environment and specific industries goes back to the PEST and five factors analyses we discussed earlier.

- Of course, competitive advantage is temporary. The knowledge diffuses quickly among practitioners, becoming "best practice," and the brief competitive advantage of one soon becomes the new competitive parity of all.

- Strategic inflection points can occur in business, sports, politics, and the military. Sometimes, an inflection point affects several of these realms. We also face our own strategic inflection points, forcing us to rethink our strategic plans.

Inflection Points in Business

- In the business world, strategic inflection points are usually manifested by technological advances or shifts in the competitive environment so severe that they change the rules of the competitive game.

- Inflection points may also be the result of sharp changes in customer preferences, changes in the regulatory environment, or dramatic increases in the value of certain raw materials.

- Despite the eventually monumental impact of a strategic inflection point, it may not at first be immediately apparent to everyone. In fact, Grove tells us that these changes hit corporations in such a way that those in senior management usually recognize them last.

- The demise of silent films in the early 1930s provides an example of how a strategic inflection point can alter the business landscape. Within a decade of the introduction of talking films, silent film production had ceased.

- A more recent example in business is the tremendous strategic inflection point sustained by the airline industry when the regulatory environment changed in 1978. In fact, the effects of this change are still being felt, both by the industry and by passengers.

  o Deregulation of the airline industry proved a bounty to the American consumer, but the airlines seemed unaware of the implications of this change for their survival. The removal of government control over fares, routes, and market entry of new airlines created a radically new environment that challenged the airlines in ways they had not contemplated.

  o This powerful strategic inflection point should have left the legacy airlines scrambling to develop new business models, but most continued doing business as usual.

- A final example from business is the bittersweet tale of the camera and film companies Kodak and Polaroid, which dominated their industry in the United States until the end of the 1980s.

  o The digital imaging revolution radically changed the film industry within a phenomenally short period of time. Both Kodak and Polaroid were challenged, and neither had the ability to respond correctly to the fact that the era of chemical film was ending.

  o Polaroid went bankrupt in 2001, although it emerged in a new incarnation in the late 2000s. Kodak sought the shelter of bankruptcy at the beginning of 2012 while it reorganized; it has since shown signs of trying to reinvent itself.

What Changes Must Be Made?

- If an inflection point has made the business model inadequate for the future, what fundamentally must change, and how do we change it?

- To answer this question, let's take the case of Richard J. Harrington, who became CEO of Thomson Corporation—a grab bag of publishing ventures—in 1997 and saw the looming reality of major industry changes.

- Although the business he took over was doing quite well, with almost $9 billion in yearly revenue, Harrington saw the inevitability of change wrought by emerging technology and realized that his firm's business model would generate less and less revenue in a fast-approaching future.

- Harrington determined that Thomson would not be left behind by the looming inflection point. He was willing to take a short-term hit in earnings and assume the costs of tooling up for the future demands of a new business model focused on electronic publishing.

- The firm spent $7 billion over the next several years to buy more than 200 businesses, and it shed more than 130 of its regional newspapers. In a business culture oriented toward short-term earnings, this was a bold move. Within five years, Thomson had transformed itself and was threatening Elsevier's top position in professional publishing.

Inflection Points in Sports and Games

- In sports, the strategic inflection point emerges most often in the form of rule changes that dictate changes in strategy. Sometimes, the inflection point we identify retrospectively was the result of a series of smaller changes.

- An example of this gradual process comes from chess. Until the 15th century, the queen in chess was a relatively weak piece, but through gradual changes in the game's rules, the queen emerged in the 16th century as the most powerful piece on the board. The changed status of the queen required a transformation of strategy and tactics in the game.

- In professional football, seemingly minor changes in the rules have transformed the game and changed the types of players recruited for certain positions.

Inflection Points in Politics

- Inflection points are difficult to exploit in politics, partly because political operatives play the game constantly, regardless of the stage of the election cycle.

- One minor political inflection point was the change from unlimited successive terms for the president to two consecutive terms. In one sense, the change merely codified what had been a tradition among presidents from Washington down to Franklin Roosevelt. But the change also forced presidents in their second terms into lame duck status.

- Consider also the process by which we nominate candidates from major parties. The power here has shifted from the party conventions to the primaries, where delegates to the convention are won. The states now jockey to schedule their primaries ahead of others so as to garner more influence. Interacting with these factors is the candidate's campaign, which must decide where and how to compete.

- New technologies can present politicians with inflection points, as well. In U.S. presidential politics, think of Franklin Roosevelt's use of radio, Kennedy and Reagan on TV, and perhaps, the Internet in Obama's campaign for the presidency in 2008. The lesson here is: Even those who aren't in a technology sector may experience an inflection point based on new technology.

Inflection Points in the Military

- In military conflict, technology can yield a temporary competitive advantage to the side that most quickly recognizes and adapts to the changes it brings.

- A famous example is the launch of Western Christendom in the Crusades during the period 1095–1291. Knights and peasants repeatedly marched east to liberate the Holy Land from the domination of Islam. Such a clash of cultures has historically entailed a dramatic change to which people and organizations must adapt or perish.

In the First Crusade, the Arab armies faced the most effective fighting forces in the Holy Land, armed with superior technology.

  o The Crusades represents the dramatic collision of Western and Eastern cultures. In the best of circumstances, cultures have difficulty meshing; suspicion is generally the first response in a culture clash. In this instance, the two great cultures touched in the most heated of circumstances: Holy War.

  o The Arabs and Turks of the Middle East first faced this inflection point in 1095. The success of this First Crusade was at least partly the result of the surprise in military tactics and strategy used by the Frankish knights against the Saracens.

  o Superior European military technology presented the Arab armies with a strategic inflection point. Suddenly, the Muslim armies faced an enemy outfitted with armor, crossbows, and powerful horses and possessing effective siege machines. The crossbow alone was an extreme technological game changer.

- In another example, from the 13th century, the Europeans were on the receiving end of the surprise. The Mongols, under Batu Khan (a descendant of **Genghis Khan**), conquered several Hungarian armies in southern Europe in 1241 and were on the verge of sweeping into Austria when they were challenged by an army under King Béla of Hungary.

  o The Mongols annihilated the Hungarians, but the death of the Great Khan Ögödei in December of 1241 broke the tempo of their invasion.

  o The Europeans had slammed into the same kind of inflection point that had given them victory over the Saracens in the Holy Land 150 years earlier. The Mongols evidenced speed and used unique supply techniques, as well as spies and scouts. Unlike the Europeans, they protected their leaders, who observed the battle from a distance and made tactical decisions.

  o In the end, it was fortune, not Europe's adaptation, that stopped the Mongols from attacking Italy and Germany and, perhaps, conquering all of Europe.

Personal Inflection Points
- According to Grove, one of the biggest problems with the inflection point is distinguishing it from garden variety changes, especially given that our disposition is to resist change. You don't want to dismantle everything in response to a small change, but you also don't want to be oblivious to changes that may be significant.

- How do you recognize a strategic inflection point as distinguished from a historical hiccup? Grove gives us some warning signs.

  o If the firm you're dealing with gives signs of having "shifted," you may be experiencing an inflection point.

o If your attention is suddenly drawn away from a lifelong competitor or a single company that has held you captive, and you're worried about someone or something new, then a threat may be brewing.

o Grove's final test is the "silver bullet" question: Where would you aim if you had only one bullet? If you have been aiming in one direction, but suddenly you change the direction of your pistol, that's a key signal that you may be dealing with something more than a minor change in the competitive landscape.

Name to Know

Genghis Khan (1162–1227): Genghis Khan forged an empire as great as any in world history and, in the process, revolutionized warfare of the 13th century, conquering all of Asia and part of Europe. Despite his deserved reputation for ruthlessness, somewhat paradoxically, he introduced the notion of religious tolerance throughout his empire.

Suggested Reading

Christensen, *The Innovator's Dilemma.*

Grove, *Only the Paranoid Survive.*

Stark, *God's Battalions.*

Questions to Consider

1. The strategic inflection point is not always obvious, and if it comes when times are flush for a company, it may be ignored. What are some of the ways that a company might overcome blindness to potential strategic inflection points in an industry?

2. It's useful if we conceive of the strategic inflection point as a rule change, perhaps technological, educational, or political. Companies and individuals who spot these rule changes most quickly and offer a bold response can steal a march on more cautious competitors. Evaluate the rules, both written and unwritten, of your competitive interactions,

and assess how those rules affect how you behave. Is your behavior prudent and rational, or can you contrive a new initiative, a newly crafted mode of behavior, within the current rule structure to achieve competitive advantage?

3. It isn't unthinkable that you can find your own temporary inflection point by maneuvering in the space offered by the rules of your game. Few of us do this kind of analysis, which makes it particularly rewarding. What do the rules allow that isn't being done? If you take advantage of this loophole, will it yield you an advantage?

Shock of the New—Inflection Points
Lecture 13—Transcript

Here is an eminently cool phrase that we in the business education community get to use often. It's jargon, yes, but it's jargon that all of us can utilize in a host of situations. The phrase? The strategic inflection point.

Because the strategic inflection point is a concept that captures much of what surprises us in the world in the most profound ways.

The strategic inflection point is a term popular in business, but we apply to a wide range of phenomena. It was introduced by Andy Grove in 1996 in his book, *Only the Paranoid Survive*. He, in turn, being trained as an engineer, got the concept from mathematics, where an inflection point refers to any place where a positive curve turns negative, or a negative curve turns positive.

The strategic inflection point is a dramatic change in our environment that makes us alter the way we do things, or risk extinction. This isn't minor change that suggests we tweak our procedures. It is major change that demands we rethink everything. This shifting of tectonic plates gives us no choice. It requires us—it compels us—to change our strategy. For Intel, a strategic inflection point came when low-cost memory chips from Japan forced Intel to abandon memory chips and focus its business on microprocessors instead.

Strategy presents us with paradoxes. The strategic inflection point is no different. As with so many things in hindsight, the major changes that seem to alter the fundamentals of the way we do everything appear obvious. Looking backward, history takes only one course—the path actually chosen. We tend to think that history as it unfolded was, in some sense, inevitable. We forget the many alternatives that were available at the time.

Competitive advantage is conferred on those companies and individual people who can do these two things well—be the first—to recognize a major change in the environment that affects their activities. And they must be the first to respond to that change correctly.

So, to gain a competitive advantage, the recognition and the response must be ahead of competitors and it must be correct.

Now, the change doesn't have to be as monumental as an inflection point. It can be something that pushes what we consider "best practices" outward. Identifying changes in your overall environment and your specific industry goes back to the PEST scan and the Five Factors scan we discussed three lectures. In those cases, the firm, or army, sports team, or individual that first develops the best response to the changed environment may win a competitive advantage. It's temporary, of course. "Best practices" means that the knowledge diffuses quickly among practitioners, and the brief competitive advantage of one soon becomes the new competitive parity of all. This is guaranteed by what I like to call the "Cult of Efficiency," driven by the fact that even companies without a real strategy typically want to be efficient.

Strategic inflection points can occur in business, sports, politics, and in the profession of arms. It is something new, which cannot be ignored. Sometimes, an inflection point affects several of these realms. Oftentimes, we face our own strategic inflection point and we have to rethink our strategic plans, perhaps even scrap them and start anew.

In the business world, the strategic inflection point is usually manifested by technological advances or shifts in the competitive environment so severe that they change the rules of our competitive game. Two examples we've already discussed are big-box bookstores, and electronic reading devices that threaten publishers and sellers of printed books and information.

These changes can also be a sharp change in customer preferences, the introduction of a changed regulatory environment, or the dramatically enhanced value of certain raw materials. Despite the eventually monumental impact of a strategic inflection point, it may not be immediately apparent to everyone. In fact, Andy Grove says that the change hits the corporation in such a way that those in senior management usually recognize it last. The common element in all of these changes is that they require a fundamental change of strategy on the part of the firm, or the firm faces extinction.

The film industry of the early 1930s provides both corporate and personal examples of how a strategic inflection point can alter the business landscape. The silent film era in Hollywood began in the early 1900s and lasted until 1927, which is considered the dawn of the talking film industry. Within a decade, silent film production had ceased.

What now seems the most natural progression in the world was not wholeheartedly welcomed in the mid-1920s. In fact, the revolution that sound film was about to make wasn't even recognized as such. Harry Warner, of Warner Brothers, famously remarked in 1927 "Who in the hell wants to hear actors talk?"

A famous actor of the time, Ronald Colman was dismissive and called the talking motion picture a "temporary digression." Colman sniffed: "I am not sympathetic to this 'sound business.' I feel, as many do, that this is a mechanical resource, that it is retrogressive ... in short, that it does not properly belong to my particular work."

Colman soon changed his mind, but fellow performer Charlie Chaplin had a much stronger sense of mission and a global brand to protect, declaring in 1930: "I shall never speak in a film. ... I am a mime, and all the nuances of my art would be destroyed if I were to accompany them with words or sound effects." He released the silent film *City Lights* in 1931 with great success, created a hybrid film in 1936 called *Modern Times*, where other actors spoke, but his own character only made some nonsense sounds.

When Chaplin finally recognized the strategic inflection point in 1940, he did so brilliantly, using his voice and other talents to mock Adolf Hitler in *The Great Dictator*, which became his most profitable film. This resistance to change is not unique to the revolution in motion pictures of the 1920s. It appears endemic to how most people view change and innovation.

A more recent example in business is the tremendous strategic inflection point sustained by the airline industry when the regulatory environment changed dramatically in 1978. The effects of this inflection point are still being felt, both by the industry and by passengers. It changed the way we fly, and even how we conceive of flying.

Deregulation of the airline industry beginning in 1978 proved a bounty to the American consumer, but the airlines seemed unaware of the deep implications for their very survival. The airline deregulation act created a radically new regulatory environment that challenged the airlines in ways they'd not contemplated.

It removed government control over fares, over routes, and over market entry of new airlines in commercial aviation. This powerful strategic inflection point should have left the legacy airlines scrambling to develop new business models. But most airlines continued doing business as usual with the old model, routines, and repertoires. They seemed oblivious to the inflection point, to the necessity of modifying strategy in accord with the dictates of the new environment—except for Southwest Airlines. Offering its first flights in 1971, this regional airline specialized in point-to-point travel instead of hub-and-spoke operations, refused baggage transfers from other airlines, and offered unreserved seating.

In short, the legacy carriers refused to recognize or simply could not recognize how to make money in the changed regulatory environment, completely misreading the implications for the future of air travel in the midst of this strategic inflection point.

A final example from business is the bittersweet tale of one of America's most beloved and iconic brands. This is the firm that brought us the phrase to share a "Kodak moment." Kodak and Polaroid were two iconic camera and chemical film companies that dominated their industry in the United States until the end of the 1980s. The digital imaging revolution radically changed the industry, and new competitors emerged, manufacturing film-less digital cameras. The change in the industry was phenomenally fast, with demand for film plummeting. Both companies were challenged, and neither had the ability to respond correctly to the fact that the era of chemical film was ending rapidly.

Neither could believe the market was changing as rapidly as it actually was. Kodak, especially, believed that it had an additional decade of film sales in developing countries before the digital revolution could possibly take over.

Kodak flailed helplessly throughout the 1990s as the digital revolution engulfed it.

Both companies bet wrong. Polaroid went bankrupt in 2001, and Kodak was left at the end of 2011 selling off more than 1100 digital-imaging invention patents to generate cash flow and seeking the shelter of bankruptcy at the beginning of 2012 while it reorganized. This is not necessarily the end for Kodak. It holds a reservoir of intellectual property potentially worth millions, and it has shown signs of trying to reinvent itself.

After all, Polaroid eventually emerged from bankruptcy in a new incarnation in the late 2000s. Most recently, that company seemed to go in an entirely new direction—in early 2010, Polaroid partnered with the pop music diva Lady Gaga, and the company appointed her as the company's creative director. So there's hope for Kodak, even as the firm leaves folks scratching their heads asking, what happened to this once-powerful company?

The great irony is that Kodak invented the first digital camera in 1975. Scholars for decades to come will ponder the strategic missteps of a company that owned the core of the digital revolution, but instead of leading it, was nearly destroyed by it.

That question is, "If an inflection point has made the business model inadequate for the future, what fundamentally must change, and how do we change it?"

Let's take the case of Mr. Richard J. Harrington, who became CEO of Thomson Corporation in 1997 and saw the looming reality of major industry changes. He detected a major shift in the correlation of forces. Harrington had joined the company in 1982 and became CEO in 1997. The firm dabbled in regional newspapers, professional publishing, and textbooks. In fact, the company seemed like a grab-bag of publishing ventures. Although the business he took over was doing quite well, with almost $9 billion in yearly revenue, Harrington looked over the horizon, and what he saw worried him. He saw the inevitability of change wrought by emerging technology. Harrington clearly grasped how the digital revolution was changing the business landscape, how the firm's business model would generate less and less revenue in a fast-approaching future. He determined that Thomson would not be left behind by the looming inflection point. In fact, he believed his firm could and should be a leader.

This was a bold move. You don't see this often in corporate America. It's quite rare that a company in a comfortable position actually engages with a time-horizon longer than the next fiscal year. In fact, far too often you see the exact opposite. Too much of the "ain't broke, don't fix it" mentality— dawdling, and excuse-making, and timidity.

Management guru Gary Hamel put it this way:

> Every business is successful until it's not. What's disconcerting, though, is how often top management is surprised when "not" happens. ... Denial follows a familiar pattern. Disquieting developments are at first dismissed as implausible or inconsequential ... then rationalized away as aberrant or irremediable ... then grudgingly mitigated through defensive action ... and then finally, though not always, honestly confronted.

But Harrington was willing to take the short-term hit in earnings and the costs of tooling up for the future demands of a radically new publishing model. Thomson would focus on electronic publishing in the professional field. They would build an integrated information enterprise and enter a market with established competitors such as McGraw-Hill and Reed Elsevier. It would take time, it would take patience, businesses would be sold, new businesses bought, new competencies acquired, it would take the guts to tolerate depressed earnings while the company restructured.

Thomson spent $7 billion over the next several years to buy more than 200 businesses and it shed more than 130 of its regional newspapers. In a business culture oriented toward short-term earnings, this was indeed a bold move. Within just five years, Thomson had transformed itself and was threatening Elsevier's number one position in the professional publishing field.

Richard Harrington had become Thomson CEO at a moment when the company wasn't in trouble. It was quite comfortable, in fact. But unlike

Kodak, Harrington looked over the horizon, and he saw an unfavorable correlation of forces. Forces that would transform the industry, create a strategic inflection point, and engulf Thomson.

Under Harrington, Thompson confronted reality, saw the coming inflection point, and responded superbly.

In sports, the strategic inflection point emerges periodically, most often in the form of rule changes that dictate changes in strategy. Sometimes the inflection point we can identify retrospectively was the result of a series of smaller changes.

A major and quite gradual example comes from chess. Until the 15th century, the queen in chess was a relatively weak piece. Through gradual changes in the game's rules and by contemporary convention, the queen emerged in 16th-century European chess as the most powerful piece on the board. From weakest piece to strongest piece by virtue of a rule change fits our definition of a strategic inflection point, and drastically different status of the queen required radical transformation of strategy and tactics of the game.

Major rule changes can cause major changes in how a game is played. These effects cascade into strategy. In one of America's most popular sports—professional football—seemingly minor changes in the rules have resulted in wholesale transformation of the game.

In 1978, for instance, a simple rule change that only affected a handful of players in a tiny portion of the playing field radically altered the strategies pursued. The five-yard bump rule changed how a defensive back could interact with a wide receiver on the snap of the ball.

After the change, a defender was only allowed to bump a receiver within five yards of the line of scrimmage on the snap. Beyond that and a flag would be thrown for continued aggressive interference with the receiver. This seems a simple enough rule change, but its effect was astounding—it gave receivers more leeway to display athleticism, and we saw the institution of wide open "pro-style" pass-heavy offenses that led to large numbers of 300-yard passing games.

266

It also led to subtle changes in the physical makeup of players in the cornerback position. This is the swift defensive back who plays pass protection on either side of the field. Until the five-yard bump rule, cornerbacks were big and strong to stop the run, and they were counted on to bump the receiver and rough him up on pass plays.

After the rule change, all-pro cornerback Eric Allen says that the position changed radically and that coaches began putting small and quick types into the position. Allen said that, "Guys who made their living on the bump-and-run can't do that anymore. And it's obvious now that receivers can do just about anything they want."

We can see that the changed regulatory environment led to radical changes in the game's strategy and even the types of players recruited to play the position affected by the new rules. One other rule change in 1994 was so subtle it might have gone unnoticed by the average fan, and yet had a tremendous impact on the game.

Eight inches. The rule change affected just eight inches on the field, and yet it has had a strategic impact on the game that continues today. The rule change affected the position of offensive linemen. Previously, all linemen had to line up even with the center's jersey. The rule change allowed them to line up eight inches farther back "even with the belt buckle of the center." This additional eight inches gives linemen a split-second more to pick up their blocks on hard-charging defensive linemen.

It allows them to form the pass protection pocket sooner, and for the first time, they can actually hear the signals in a noisy stadium. This affords greater protection for the quarterback, who, in turn, has more time to pass the ball. The receivers have a moment more to elude coverage and break free. It makes for better communication between quarterback and the line and leads to fewer penalties. It puts more pressure on the defense and leads to changes in both offensive and defensive strategy.

In short, this rule change redounds to the benefit of the entire offensive unit. The good effects cascade and effervesce throughout the game.

The strategic inflection point in this case exerted a dynamic change on the game. It meant dramatic changes in the way the game is played. It demands new skill sets and skills in different combinations than were required prior to the change. Perhaps most important, it requires the acumen to recognize the radical impact of small regulatory changes on strategy, on the whole character of the game.

Politics would seem an area fertile with strategic inflection points. The weight of regulation on political competition is quite heavy. And yet they are difficult to exploit, partly because phalanxes of political operatives play the game 24-7, regardless of our place in the election cycle.

One minor inflection point was the limitation of the president's term from unlimited successive terms to two consecutive terms. A vengeful Republican Congress enacted this legislation in the wake of Franklin Roosevelt's four consecutive election victories. Roosevelt's tenure had been an aberration, and the Congress intended to keep it so. And in one sense, the change merely codified what had been a tradition among American presidents since the time of Washington. But the change also forced presidents in their second term into lame duck status, since there was no longer any chance they might run for office again.

Consider also the process by which we nominate candidates from major parties. Consider how the power has shifted from the party conventions to the primaries, where delegates to the convention are won. And then, the jockeying of pride of position among states to schedule their primary ahead of others so as to garner more influence. Interacting with this is the individual candidate campaign, which must decide where to compete and how. It must raise scarce campaign dollars and decide how to spend them in a strategic marketing mix.

New technologies can present politicians with inflection points as well. In U.S. presidential politics, think of Franklin Delano Roosevelt's use of radio, Kennedy and Reagan on TV, and perhaps the Internet in Obama's campaign for the presidency in 2008. The lesson here is this: You may not see yourself as being in a technology sector, but that doesn't mean that you won't experience an inflection point based on new technology.

In military conflict, technology can yield a temporary competitive advantage to the side that most quickly recognizes and adapts most to the changes wrought.

A famous example is Western Christendom's launch in the year of the first of nine Crusades over the period 1095 to 1291. Knights and peasants repeatedly marched east to liberate the Holy Land from the domination of Islam. It is supremely relevant to our discussion today about strategic inflection points, in that a clash of cultures has historically entailed a dramatic change to which the people and organizations involved must adapt or perish. The Crusades represent the dramatic collision of two great cultures—broadly conceived, Western and Eastern. In the best of circumstances, cultures have difficulty meshing at first, as suspicion is the first response. And in this circumstance, these two great cultures touched in the most heated of circumstances—Holy War.

The Arabs and Turks of the Middle East first faced such an inflection point in 1095. This first Crusade was the most successful, as Jerusalem fell to the Crusaders. This owes at least in part to the surprise in military tactics and strategy utilized by the Frankish knights against the Saracens. But the surprise was mutual, as the technologies of two different types came into conflict for the first time on a grand scale.

It was superior European technology that presented the Arab armies with a strategic inflection point. Suddenly, the Muslim armies faced an enemy whose armor could resist their curved short swords and their light arrows, whose crossbows conferred fire superiority, whose horses were much larger and more powerful, whose combat tactics were aided by the use of saddles and stirrups, whose siege machines could conquer native forts, whose own castles were almost impregnable to Muslim attack, and whose crossbow gave the Europeans undoubted fire superiority.

The crossbow, in fact, was an extreme technological game-changer. While the longbow took years to master and great strength to use, a man could become proficient at the crossbow in mere hours. And the crossbow's heavy bolt could pierce plate armor.

The Muslims faced, for the first time, the holy orders of the Knights Templar and the Teutonic Knights. Historian Steven Kreis calls these warriors the most effective fighting forces in the Holy Land. These forces were armed with lances, and the charge of these immense knights in the open field was virtually unstoppable.

Another example finds the Europeans getting the short end—this time in the 13th century. When we think of European history, we don't usually think of Genghis Khan and his descendants Kublai Khan and Batu Khan. These were the Mongols that conquered much of the known world in the 13th century. Batu Khan's Mongol Horde conquered several Hungarian armies in Southern Europe in 1241 and was on the verge of sweeping into Austria when it challenged an army under King Béla of Hungary.

The Mongols under General Subutai and Batu Khan annihilated the Hungarians, a force that included Hungarian heavy cavalry, Knights Templar, nomadic light cavalry mercenaries, and Serbian valiants.

The Europeans never stopped the Mongol Horde. Only the death of the Great Khan Ogedai in December of 1241 broke the tempo of the Mongol invasion of Europe. The death of the Khan required the Princes of the Blood to lead the horde back to Mongolia for the selection process of a new Khan.

The Europeans slammed into their own strategic inflection point, the same kind of inflection point that gave them victory over the Saracens in the Holy Land 150 years earlier. This time, the Europeans faced a raft of new military techniques that led to their defeat.

The Mongols succeeded against the European-style knight and its military formations because of a new combination of tactics and combat style. They employed speed and unique supply techniques that gave them far greater mobility and maneuverability to project power. They utilized scouts and intelligence analysis far more than their counterparts and attempted to maneuver the enemy onto battlefields of Mongol choosing. They sent spies for almost 10 years into Europe, and they mapped the old Roman roads and determined the level of ability of each principality to resist invasion as well as who might ally with whom.

The European concept of courage placed great emphasis on personal valor, and so leaders were often exposed to danger and killed during a melee. By contrast, the Mongols protected their leaders, who posted themselves on high ground from where they could observe the battle and make tactical decisions as the events unfolded.

The cumulative effect of all of these novel tactics and superior techniques was to present Europe with an inflection point. One scholar has discovered in Chinese accounts of the Battle of Mohi in 1241 that it was the Mongols who introduced the use of gunpowder in combat into Europe. In the end, it was fortune and not Europe's adaptation that stopped the Horde from attacking Italy and Germany and from conquering perhaps all of Europe, just as it eventually conquered China and what is now Russia.

Business, sports, politics, and war—the strategic inflection point is a whimsical, surprising, deadly player in all of these realms. In our own lives, we have to be alert to the emergence of an inflection point. Andy Grove says that one of the biggest problems with the inflection point is telling them apart from garden variety changes—especially, as we have seen, when our disposition is to resist change. We want to do business as usual. We want to believe changes are minor. We react to changes, but we don't want to tear the business into pieces and reassemble them every time someone says boo. But we also don't want to be oblivious to the changes around us that may portend ill for us if we don't read them correctly and respond to the indicators— signals given us by a new boss, a changed spouse, a company whose policies change for seemingly no reason, changes in the rules of our lives we have set, both explicit and implicit.

So how do you recognize a strategic inflection point as distinguished from an historical hiccup? Andy Grove, who coined the term, had quite a bit of experience in dealing with inflection points in the high tech industry. His insights are valid across the spectrum of organizations and individuals dealing with sudden and sometimes radical change.

Andy gives us some warning signs. If the company or firm or entity you're dealing with gives signs of having "shifted," it means you may be experiencing an inflection point. If suddenly your attention is drawn away from your lifelong competitor or a single company that has had you captive, and now you're worried about someone or something new, then there may be an inflection point.

Grove has a final acid test. He asks himself a rhetorical question that he calls the "Silver Bullet" test: What if I had only one bullet? Where would you aim? If you have been aiming somewhere for most of your life, but suddenly you change the direction of your pistol, that's a key signal that you may be dealing with something more than a minor change in the competitive landscape.

Surprise! Perils and Power of Strategic Deception
Lecture 14

For aficionados of military history, surprise and deception can hardly be separated from strategy and tactics. Deception, in fact, is a routine part of life. If information is power, then disinformation and deception can confer upon us even more power. In sports and politics, business and war, it's a virtue to surprise your adversary.

Surprise and Deception in Conflict

- From the Trojan Horse, to Pearl Harbor, to MacArthur's landings at In'chŏn, to General Schwarzkopf's famous "left hook" during the first Gulf War in 1991, surprise and deception have played major roles in conflict.

- The stratagem—a trick for deceiving the enemy—is called upon in wartime not as an end in itself but as a means to achieve that much-sought goal in tactical warfare: the surprise. Probably no other principle of war can multiply combat power as effectively as a well-planned and well-executed surprise.

- The great commanders from Hannibal to Stonewall Jackson all incorporated stratagem into their battle planning, and they did so with the objective of achieving surprise.

- Until the rise of general staffs in the early 19th century, the source of surprise was the intuition and imagination of a great general. Then there came a period of time, from the start of the 20th century until World War II, when stratagem and surprise fell out of favor among leading generals.

- Among the exceptions to this rule was **T. E. Lawrence**, one of history's great strategic theorists and practitioners and a decidedly unconventional leader. He is better known as Lawrence of Arabia from his leadership of the Arab Revolt in 1916–1918.

- Another unconventional leader of the time was Winston Churchill, a deep thinker and aficionado of one of the most powerful techniques in strategy—the deception operation, otherwise known as the stratagem. Churchill was also fascinated by technological advances and their potential for epic turns in the tide of war.

The Distinction between Strategy and Tactics
- Both strategic and tactical surprise contain the same elements, but strategic surprise consists in attacking and successfully disrupting an enemy's mobilization, deployments, and grand strategy. Achieving surprise at the strategic level is much more difficult than at the tactical level, primarily because of the scale of operations, the multiplicity of variables, the time involved, and the greater chance of discovery.

- A failed strategic surprise can still retain value as a tactical surprise, although with considerably less impact. In fact, the difference in impact can change the course of conflict.

  o In 1916, the British had a superb opportunity to break the trench warfare stalemate on the Western Front with a strategic surprise: the mass introduction of the tank, a game changer that could have altered the outcome of World War I.

  o Lieutenant Colonel Ernest Swinton was the central champion of the tank and the tactics that would maximize its impact. He urged the use of tanks to break through enemy lines and strike quickly at the enemy's artillery. He also believed that "the fact of their existence should be kept as secret as possible...."

  o But the commanding generals were oblivious to the power of deception and surprise to multiply the force of an attack, and they ignored Swinton.

  o A paltry 32 tanks were used in an attack at the Battle of the Somme, and these were fed into the line across a broad front and piecemeal. The effect was to achieve technological surprise and a bit of local panic—a minor tactical success.

274

o   It's worth remembering that you have only one opportunity to use a powerful and novel weapon for the first time. This example of the tank demonstrates exactly how not to do it.

The Rich Possibilities of Surprise

- Surprise is the gap between what we expect will happen and what actually does happen. Strategic surprise is not merely the unusual or the unexpected. It is the gap in expectations that you or an opponent create and exploit quite deliberately.

- Uncertainty is already one of our greatest worries, whether in business, the military, or politics. How awful, then, to discover that our enemies are doing their best to increase our uncertainty. Worse still, our enemies will use deception to give us false certainty, to raise false expectations, or to divert our attention.

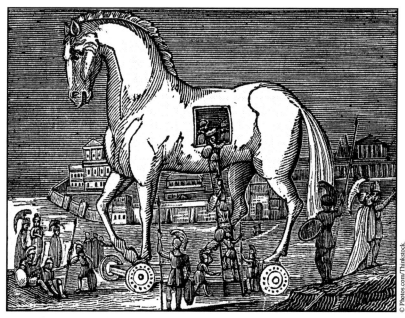

The hollow horse was just one part of the deception carried out at Troy; the Greeks also burned their camp to convince the Trojans that they were admitting defeat.

- The Trojan Horse represents one of history's most famous instances of surprise coupled with deception designed to gain a military advantage. We all know the story of the Greek soldiers hiding inside a magnificent gift to the city of Troy, but their larger deception—pretending to leave the scene of battle to create false expectations in the minds of the Trojans—was just as important as the ruse of the hollow horse.

- For many strategists, the notion of surprise now holds a place of honor as a circumstance to be greatly valued and highly sought. If you can surprise your opponent tactically, you reap rewards out of all proportion to the energy expended. At the strategic level, surprise is much more difficult to secure, but a successful strategic surprise has the potential to result in both short- and long-term wins.

- Each of the five types of surprise—intention, time, place, strength, and style—can be linked to deception that creates mistaken expectations. Other tactics can also help generate surprise, including stealth and ambiguity, but in general, deception is an amplifier of surprise.

Five Types of Surprise

- The first type of surprise involves intention. Does our enemy intend to strike us at all? This is a yes-or-no gateway decision that makes possible all of the following types of surprise.

- The second type of surprise is that of timing—striking when the enemy does not expect us.

  o The Japanese attack on Pearl Harbor stands as the classic example of successful strategic surprise, involving deception at both the strategic and tactical levels. At the very time that Japan's fleet was streaming toward Hawaii, the Japanese ambassador was seeking negotiations with Secretary of State Cordell Hull.

  o In the year 1307 in France, King Philip IV devised a surprise operation that led to the mass slaying of the Knights Templar, to whom Philip was deeply in debt. Philip had the knights arrested in a comprehensive surprise operation; they were then tortured into giving false confessions and burned at the stake.

- o A 20th-century example, just as violent, was the Night of the Long Knives, which took place in 1934 in Nazi Germany. This was Adolf Hitler's surprise purging of the leadership of his SA, which had become too much of a threat to his political power.

- o In politics, the term "October surprise" refers to a tactic of releasing news with the capacity to affect the presidential election shortly before it takes place, giving opponents as little time as possible to respond.

- While the timing of a surprise is obviously important, the place of a surprise can be equally so. Place here refers to the point of attack or the direction of attack, striking where the enemy does not expect us.

- o Prior to D-Day in 1944, the Allies carried out a deception campaign known as Operation Bodyguard to convince German intelligence that the expected invasion of France would be launched at the Pas-de-Calais, the shortest route across the English Channel. The result of the deception was to shape German expectations according to Allied designs.

- o More recently, in the first Gulf War in 1991, the threat of amphibious invasion by U.S. Marines pinned Saddam Hussein's forces in place in defensive positions. Meanwhile, General Norman Schwartzkopf conducted his now famous "left hook," a sweeping maneuver through the desert to cut the Iraqi lines of communication and supply.

- In some cases, we may know that an event will occur, but we are surprised by its magnitude or strength. Throughout history, armies have used the technique of masking the size of their forces to confound the enemy.

o   In the 13th century, the Mongols used this element of surprise often and effectively, exposing only a part of their forces in formations designed to convince an enemy to attack an apparently smaller opponent.

o   The Mongols were also adept at maneuvering enemies into position for the most advantageous attack. They would draw the enemy forward by disappearing into the woods or behind a hill. When the opposing forces advanced, Mongol troops would suddenly appear from the flanks or the rear.

o   In addition to making themselves appear fewer in number, Mongol troops also used deception to make themselves appear more numerous. They would light numerous campfires at night or drag foliage behind their horses to create large dust clouds.

•   The final type of surprise is one of style, that is, striking in a way that is unexpected. This is a catch-all category that encompasses a broad array of unexpected weapons and tactics.

o   Technological innovations of weaponry and innovations in tactics can yield a decisive advantage when coupled with their surprise use. We saw this in the example of the first use of the tank in World War I, and we've seen how the introduction of new tactics was decisive at the ancient battles of Cannae and Delium.

o   Although we most often think of surprise as connected to offensive operations, it's also possible to achieve a defensive surprise. Britain conducted one such operation in World War I in its withdrawal of troops from the Gallipoli Peninsula.

Surprise in Sports

•   Both individual and team sports offer opportunities to gain advantage from surprise. In fact, professional and college sports have reached such a level of sophistication that scouting, reconnaissance, film study, and statistical analysis are just as much a part of the game as practice or weight training.

- Analysts pore over the tendencies of opposing team behavior in every scenario imaginable, searching for weakness and a key to competitive advantage.

Summing Up Surprise
- Surprise and deception go hand-in-hand and can serve as powerful weapons. Surprise multiplies the effectiveness of our capabilities and can yield incredible short-term competitive advantage. Deception multiplies the effectiveness of surprise.

- At the same time, we must remember that surprise is a double-edged sword; it helps to be aware of the types of surprise in case they're used against us.

Name to Know

Lawrence, T. E. (1888–1935): Lawrence was an adventurer who found a battleground for his natural strategic talents in the deserts of the Middle East during World War I, leading the Arab revolt, and wove an epic of strategic thought and history, *The Seven Pillars of Wisdom*, that set forth timeless principles of small-unit tactics and guerilla warfare.

Suggested Reading

Erfurth, *Surprise*.

Grabo, *Anticipating Surprise*.

Luttwak, *Strategy: The Logic of War and Peace*.

Whaley, *Stratagem*.

Questions to Consider

1. The effectiveness of surprise speaks to the power of controlling information and using it to our benefit at the most propitious moment. Yet we can be oblivious to the power of the information we control and may not even be aware that we control it. What kinds of information do

you control exclusively, what is its quality, and would your results differ if you changed the way you handled it?

2. Whether or not you have previously thought of how to leverage information to your benefit by using timing and location to best advantage, do so now. Consider how the value of your information goes up or down depending on how you use it. Would you gain an advantage from the judicious incorporation of subtle surprise into your handling of information? If so, specifically how?

3. The effectiveness of a planned surprise can be enhanced by including as many of the surprise factors as possible—timing, intention, place, strength, and style. Building on the previous queries, consciously find ways to incorporate the five factors into your repertoire of strategic action. Specifically, how might the timing of an announcement in contravention of opponent expectations enhance your position?

4. You can use surprise defensively, as well as offensively. Power can arise simply from the changing of your routine. This is more than merely acting unpredictably; it means consciously altering your routine so as not to be taken advantage of. Have you become so predictable in the way you deal with others that your reactions are routine and easily countered by opponents? If so, choose a typical situation where your response has been perhaps too habitual and thwart expectations by doing the unexpected.

Surprise! Perils and Power of Strategic Deception
Lecture 14—Transcript

For aficionados of military history, surprise and deception can hardly be separated from strategy and tactics. Deception, in fact, is a routine part of life. If information is power, then disinformation and deception can confer upon us even more power. In sports and politics, business and war, it's a virtue to surprise your adversary.

From the Trojan Horse, to Pearl Harbor, to MacArthur's sudden landings at Inchon, to General Schwartzkopf's famous "Left Hook" during the first Gulf War in 1991, surprise and deception have played major roles—sometimes decisive roles—in conflict.

Stratagem and surprise have been a part of war since there have been wars. Surprise is a bedrock principle of war of every major military establishment in world, and rightly so.

The stratagem is called upon in wartime, not as an end in itself, but as a means to achieve that much-sought goal in tactical warfare—the surprise. Probably no other principle of war can multiply combat power as effectively as a surprise well-planned and well-executed. Every country does it, and every country has its own name for it. The Russians call it *dezinformatsiya*. The French call it *ruse de guerre*. The British and Americans call it stratagem. And it also goes by other names as well: diversion, demonstration.

The great commanders—Hannibal, Alexander, Caesar, Genghis Khan, Marshal de Saxe, Napoleon, Stonewall Jackson—all of them incorporated stratagem into their battle planning, and they did so with the objective of achieving surprise. Deception, in fact, has been called the bodyguard of surprise.

Until the rise of general staffs in the early 19th century, the source of surprise was the intuition and imagination of the great general. Stratagem and surprise were almost exclusively the province of great warrior minds. And then, there came a period of time when stratagem and surprise fell out of favor among the leading generals.

From the dawn of the 20th century until World War II, surprise and deception was simply not part of the repertoire of what generals did. The initiation of surprise and deception was the exception.

The leading generals of the day did not do surprise. The author of a great book on strategems, Barton Whaley, laments that "the commanders appointed to send the big battalions to glory—Joffre, Nivelle, Foch, the young Moltke, Falkenhayn, Robertson, Haig—neither used nor understood surprise, much less deception ... it was never part of what then passed for grand strategy."

There were, however, exceptions. Contemporaneous with these conventional World War I generals was T. E. Lawrence, one of history's great strategic theorists and practitioners and a decidedly unconventional leader. He is better-known as Lawrence of Arabia from his leadership of the Arab revolt in 1916–1918.

Lawrence knew that the generals of the time disdained surprise. For the ordinary general of the time, deception and the resulting surprise were not part of the repertoire of battle. Lawrence captured this air of disdain with a famous observation from his masterwork, *The Seven Pillars of Wisdom.* Said Lawrence: "For the ordinary general, deceptions were just witty hors d'oeuvres before battle."

Another unconventional leader of the time was Winston Churchill. Churchill is known for his bulldog countenance, his ever-present cigar, his steadfastness in the face of the Nazi onslaught in 1940 as Britain's wartime Prime Minister. But Winston Churchill also loved surprise. He was one of the few great practitioners of surprise in war in the first half of the 20th century.

Churchill was a deep thinker and an aficionado of one of the most powerful techniques in strategy—the deception operation, otherwise known as the strategem. He was fascinated by technological advances and their potential for epic turns in the tide of war—the tank, the artificial harbor Mulberry, Commando strikes, and Wizard warfare (deceiving the enemy by broadcasting deceptive radio traffic).

Let's take a moment to note our distinction between strategy and tactics. Both strategic and tactical surprise contain the same elements, but strategic surprise consists in attacking and successfully disrupting an enemy's mobilization, deployments, and grand strategy. But achieving surprise at the strategic level is much more difficult than at the tactical level, primarily because of the scale of operations, the multiplicity of variables, the time involved, and the greater chance of discovery.

A failed strategic surprise can still retain value as a tactical surprise, although with considerably less impact. In fact, the difference in impact can change the course of conflict. Here's an example. In 1916, the British had a superb opportunity to break the trench warfare stalemate on the Western Front with a strategic surprise, the mass introduction of a super-weapon—a game-changer that could have altered the outcome of World War I: the tank.

Lieutenant Colonel Ernest Swinton was the central champion of the tank and the tactics that would maximize its impact. He urged their use en masse to break through the enemy lines to strike quickly and deeply at the enemy's artillery. In his very words, "tanks should not be used in driblets." "The fact of their existence should be kept as secret as possible until the whole are ready to be launched, together with the infantry assault, in one great combined operation." But the opportunity for a strategic surprise was frittered away. The commanding generals were oblivious to the power of deception and surprise to multiply the force of an attack, and the generals ignored Swinton.

In fact, General Douglas Haig apparently had no sense of the incredible strategic significance of the tank coupled with its shock value. He demanded that the few tanks available be fed into the attack immediately on arrival, squandering any chance for them to be used en masse in a surprise to break the stalemate once and for all.

Instead, a paltry 32 tanks were used in a September 1916 attack at the Battle of the Somme. Tanks were fed into the line across a broad front and piecemeal, or in penny-packets, to use a term of the day. The effect was to achieve technological surprise and a bit of local panic as a minor tactical success.

Later, writing in his classic treatise on tank warfare *Achtung Panzer*, the armored warfare theorist Heinz Guderian was incredulous at the British blundering: Said Guderian, "A very large number of machines was available, and yet no attempt was made to use this force against a single objective."

For their own part, the Germans had blown their chances at a powerful surprise in 1915 when they had used poison gas for the first time. Now, with the tank, it was the British turn to squander an almost unassailable advantage. You have only one opportunity to use a powerful and novel new weapon for the first time, and this example of the tank demonstrates exactly how not to do it.

An angry Colonel Swinton had this to say: "With the example before us of the stupendous mistake of the Germans in first releasing gas over a short sector, we, sixteen months later, with our eyes open, committed a similar error. We threw away a surprise."

It was not until a year later that the British mustered a mass tank attack utilizing new tactics at Cambrai. With 324 tanks, they achieved a tactical surprise and breakthrough and gains that superseded in one day all that had been gained in the previous four months of the bloody Battle of Passchendaele. But the opportunity for a powerful strategic surprise had already been lost; the Germans had already developed countermeasures and were beginning to produce their own tanks.

The secret of the tank had been revealed to no good end and for a minor tactical purpose a year earlier. Surprise was forfeited, along with the opportunity to decisively alter the course of World War I.

Now, your dictionary of choice offers benign descriptions of "surprise": to encounter suddenly or unexpectedly; an unusual or unexpected event. But it's not that simple; within those mundane words lurks power. We should consider the rich possibilities offered by surprise in all situations of conflict or competition. Surprise is the gap between what we expect will happen and what actually does happen. We want to close that gap. Our enemies want to widen that gap. Or, conversely, we want to widen the gap for our surprise, and our enemy wants to close it. In short, mind the gap. Strategic surprise is not merely the unusual or the unexpected. It is the gap in expectations that you or an opponent create and exploit quite deliberately.

Uncertainty is already one of the greatest worries, whether in business, in the military, or in politics. How awful, then, to discover that our enemies are doing their very best to increase our uncertainty. Worse, still, our enemies will use deception to give us false certainty to raise our false expectations, to make us look in one direction, and then surprise us in the worst possible way from the opposite direction.

We're all familiar with this technique. In fact, I know you're already cognizant of one of history's most famous instances of surprise coupled with deception designed to gain a military advantage. The Trojan War occurred sometime in the 12th or 13th centuries B.C. in what is modern-day Turkey, and it was played out in Homer's *Iliad* and other ancient works of poetry. At the end of this 10-year-long struggle between the Greeks and the city of Troy, the Greeks appeared to admit defeat. They burned their camp, and left a magnificent wooden horse dedicated to the Goddess Athena with the inscription, "The Greeks dedicate this thank-offering to Athena for their return home."

The Trojans brought the horse into the city, and they celebrated their victory. But the horse was hollow and filled with soldiers, a *ruse de guerre* devised by the Greek warrior Odysseus. That night, the soldiers emerged from the horse, slew the guards, and opened the city gates to admit the army of Greeks that had returned in the night. The city was burned and its population massacred.

While everyone knows the story of the Trojan Horse, the larger deception is just as important as the ruse of the hollow horse. The Greeks engaged in a great and elaborate deception, pretending that they were leaving the scene of battle to create false expectations in the minds of the Trojans.

For many strategists, the notion of surprise now holds a place of honor as a circumstance to be greatly valued and highly sought. For some strategists, it holds almost mystical properties. If you can surprise your opponent tactically, you reap rewards all out of proportion to the energy expended. At the strategic level, surprise is much more difficult to secure, but the rewards of successful strategic surprise have potential to win not only the day, but for the longer-term as well.

Surprise performs a valuable function in strategy. It can rescue a seemingly lost position from defeat. It can act as a force multiplier. Surprise is really a combination of factors working in tandem with each other, synergistically. The gap between our expectations and what actually happens can be wide or narrow, depending on a number of discrete factors of the unexpected that yield five types of surprises. All five of the surprise types are linked to expectations: intention, time, place, strength, and style.

Each of these types of surprise can be linked to deception that creates the wrong expectations—in general, deception as an amplifier of surprise. Other tactics can also help generate a surprise for us, including stealth and ambiguity. But overwhelmingly, deception is the preeminent cause of surprises of place, time, and strength.

Let's look now at our five types of surprise and how deception has been used in history to create or amplify an advantage. The first element of surprise is intention. Does our enemy intend to strike us at all? This is a yes or no gateway decision that makes possible all of the following types of surprise. It's a precondition that undergirds the four other types of surprise. What is the enemy intention? Will the enemy attack?

The second type of surprise is that of timing—striking when the enemy does not expect us. Here is an example of strategic surprise that illustrates both. One of the most infamous examples of surprise in combat was the Japanese attack on Pearl Harbor on December 7, 1941. This attack on the Hawaiian Islands attempted to destroy the United States' naval striking power in the Pacific and brought the United States into the war on the side of the allies. The term "Pearl Harbor" has become synonymous with treachery.

Yet Pearl Harbor stands as the classic example of successful strategic surprise. It involved deception at both the strategic and tactical levels. At the very time that Japan's imperial fleet was steaming toward Hawaii, the

Japanese ambassador was seeking further negotiations in Washington with Secretary of State Cordell Hull.

The Japanese successfully deceived the United States, for instance, in believing that no attack was imminent. Japanese deception was evidenced by entries in the official war diary that "our deceptive diplomacy is steadily proceeding toward success." In other words, the deception was the cultivation of normalcy and continued peace negotiations. In fact, the Japanese deception extended to their own diplomats in Washington, Nomura and Kurusu, who continued negotiating in good faith.

But at home in Japan, the discussions at the Imperial Liaison Conference were cold and cynical and calculating. Here is what a member of the Imperial Liaison conference had to say:

> Our diplomats will have to be sacrificed. What we want is to carry on diplomacy in such a way that until the very last minute the United States will continue to think about the problem, we will ask questions, and our real plans will be kept secret.

Japanese timing was impeccable.

It came at a time of least preparedness for the defending forces at Pearl Harbor. The attack began shortly before 8:00 on a Sunday morning. The Japanese intentionally took advantage of the American custom of the weekend, when most ships were in port and most sailors were on liberty. While there had long been expectations of a conflict of some sort between Japan and the United States, when that conflict would occur was unknown. In this case, Japan seized the strategic initiative and struck at a propitious time. The attack achieved partial strategic surprise and total tactical surprise.

There are other sinister examples as well. In France of 1307, King Philip IV devised a surprise operation that led to the mass slaying of the Knights Templar. Philip was in deep debt to the Templars. His solution was to have all of them arrested in a comprehensive surprise operation. They were then tortured into giving false confessions and burned at the stake.

A 20th century example, just as violent, was the 1934 "Night of the long knives" in Nazi Germany. This was Adolf Hitler's surprise purging of the leadership of his SA Stormtroopers, which had become too much of a threat to his political power.

Sometimes, the timing of a surprise is such an important component of the surprise itself that it can even acquire a nickname. The timing of the surprise is so well-known that it becomes part of the description of it. So we find a paradox—the expectation of a surprise. In this case, the surprise is not the timing. The most prominent example of this is in American presidential politics. The event is called the "October Surprise."

This term entered the lexicon of American politics after a famous example of it in the 1972 presidential campaign between Richard Nixon and George McGovern. Twelve days before the election—in October of 1972—U.S. National Security Advisor Henry Kissinger announced in a White House Press conference that peace was at hand. He referred, of course, to the Vietnam War. The timing of the announcement just two weeks before the election was perceived as a political maneuver to enhance Nixon's already high chances at re-election. Since that time, the "October Surprise" is the expectation that news with the capacity of affecting the presidential election outcome will be released in October. The tactic is to provide as little time as possible for a competitor to respond.

While the timing of a surprise is obviously important, the place of a surprise can be equally so. This refers to the point of attack or the direction of attack. Striking where the enemy does not expect us. In mid-1944, the war in Europe had reached a pivot point. Everyone knew that an invasion of Nazi-occupied France was imminent. In the East, the Soviet Union was beginning a mighty push against Germany. And along the French coast facing the English Channel, the Germans prepared for an Allied invasion. Where would it come? And when? The Germans didn't know.

The allies wanted to achieve strategic surprise, which is difficult in an era of modern warfare. And so they helped the process along. The allies took active measures to create a set of false expectations in the minds of German intelligence. These measures took the form of a vast deception campaign called *Operation Bodyguard*. The point was to convince German intelligence that the invasion of France would be launched at the *Pas de Calais*, which was the shortest route across the channel.

In reality, the real target was Normandy, while in the deception Normandy was presented as a diversionary tactic. In addition, the deception also aimed to convince the Germans that the real invasion would arrive later than it actually did.

The result of the deception was to shape German expectations according to allied designs. And, just as importantly, to help the Germans believe what they wanted to believe. The allies successfully manipulated the German response in the most advantageous way.

More recently, in the first Gulf War in 1991, the allies used deception against Saddam Hussein's million-man army to pin them in their defensive positions. The deception fed into Iraqi fears of an amphibious invasion by 8000 U.S. Marines that never came. The warships *Missouri* and *Wisconsin* had shelled Failaka Island early during the war to reinforce the idea that there would be an amphibious assault attempt. This was supported by an early visible amphibious raid on the Kuwaiti coast and by actions to destroy Iraq's navy. The press unwittingly helped in this misdirection by reporting amphibious training, the build-up of troops just south of Kuwait, and then by anguishing over the prospect of World War I trench warfare.

The Marines waited on ships to land on the beaches of Kuwait City, to make it appear that the main attack would be launched into Kuwait from the sea and then directly into Iraqi defenses. The threat of invasion pinned the defenders in place, while General Norman Schwartzkopf conducted his now famous "Left Hook," a sweeping maneuver through the desert to cut the Iraqi lines of communication and supply.

Oftentimes we may know that an event will occur, and we may know where, but we are surprised by its magnitude, its strength, and its direction—striking in greater strength than is expected. Throughout history, armies have used the technique of masking the size of their forces to confound the enemy. The Mongols under the Khans in the 13th century used this element of surprise often and effectively. This consisted in exposing only a part of their forces in formations designed to convince an enemy to attack an apparently smaller force.

The Mongols were particularly adept at luring enemies into vulnerable positions by showing themselves from a hill or some predetermined location. They would then disappear into the woods or behind hills to draw an enemy forward. In essence, they were maneuvering the enemy into position for the most advantageous attack. Mongol troops strategically positioned would appear suddenly from the flanks or from their rear to complete the surprise of size and direction. Conversely, Mongol formations would sometime make themselves appear fewer in number.

More often, they used deception to make themselves appear more numerous. They would feed into the intelligence collection efforts of their enemy scouts and spies—they would light numerous campfires at night to make their force appear five times larger than it was. They would drag foliage behind their horses to create dust clouds characteristic of larger forces. And since each Mongol traveled with at least three to four horses, they would let prisoners and family members ride them so as to appear more numerous in the distance.

The fifth and final type of surprise is one of style. Striking in a way that is unexpected. This is a catch-all category that encompasses a broad array of unexpected weapons, products, and tactics. The style of an attack or defense can be the source of advantageous surprise. We surprise the enemy by using something new, or by doing something not expected of us.

Technological innovations of weaponry and innovations in tactics can yield a decisive advantage when coupled with their surprise use. We saw this in the previous example of the tank at the battle of Cambrai. And we have seen how the introduction of new tactics were decisive at the ancient battles of Cannae and Delium.

The most powerful example of this type of surprise is the use of the atomic bomb on August 6, 1945 against the Japanese city of Hiroshima. Now, while we most often think of surprise as connected to offensive operations—after all, we do call it the "surprise attack"—it's possible to achieve defensive surprise as well. The British conducted one such successful defensive operation in World War I in its war against Turkey.

In December 1915, the stalemate on the Gallipoli Peninsula had become intolerable for the British, and the difficult decision was reached to evacuate. This decision was taken with full knowledge that such a withdrawal under fire could lead to horrendous casualties as the troops would be almost defenseless during what is now called a "retrograde operation."

But a deception was planned, one of the few of the war. From December 8 to 20, more than 80,000 men and hundreds of big guns were evacuated onto ships over the course of many nights until only a few hundred men were left manning the trenches. Ironically, the Turks believed the indication of withdrawal was the actual deception. They refused to be deceived that the British were withdrawing!

I've talked extensively about surprise in combat, but sports offers opportunities to gain advantage from surprise as well. In fencing, in wrestling, in soccer, the feint has always been used at the individual level to surprise an opponent and to throw him off-guard. In team sports, deception plays a major role in strategy. Professional and college sports have reached such a level of sophistication that scouting, reconnaissance, film study, and statistical analysis are just as much a part of the game as the practice field and the weight room. Analysts pore over the tendencies of team behavior in every scenario imaginable, searching for weaknesses and a key to competitive advantage.

I witnessed an exciting example of this when I was in college, and it has stayed with me all my life. I was a young football fan at the University of North Carolina, and we were playing a surprisingly tough Miami of Ohio team in our season opener. The game wasn't going well for my hometown North Carolina squad. And things appeared to get worse. Our quarterback Bernie Menapace kept the ball on a run to the near sideline, right in front of us home fans. They forced him out of bounds, and he was slow to his feet. He gripped his side and limped back to the huddle. A collective sigh deflated the crowd, and we all sat back to await the next play, maybe a timeout for an injury. The officials set the ball on the near hash mark, near the home team fans.

What happened next, hardly anyone in the stands expected. Many of us missed it. Our team casually sauntered toward the line, not yet obviously lining up, our quarterback still nursing an apparent injury. Suddenly, the crowd gave a mighty roar. Something was happening; no one seemed to know what. Something down on the field. Inexplicable. There was chaotic and confused movement. And suddenly, as if by some divine intervention, North Carolina running back Mel Collins was streaking down the far sideline for a Carolina touchdown.

The Miami team was the victim of a trick play—the "swinging gate." In this play, the entire offensive line is on one side of the ball, while the quarterback and running back are on the other side. And in this case, the swinging gate formation had been combined with an additional element. It had been a masterpiece of deception and surprise set up earlier in the week. Officials on the field for the game had even been alerted, so they wouldn't inadvertently rule against a surprise that was legal.

Here's what had happened: In watching film of the upcoming opponent, the Carolina coaches had noticed an odd procedure of Miami's defense. The defensive huddle faced away from the ball, with only the defensive captain facing the opponent. This was a critical piece of information. The Miami tendency to huddle a certain way suddenly became a possible liability, and the feigned injury of the quarterback lulled the defensive captain into a false sense of security. Deception, a surprise of style, and flawless execution of a trick play created a maneuver that won the game.

Surprise and deception go hand-in-hand and can serve as powerful weapons. Surprise multiplies the effectiveness of our capabilities, and can yield incredible short-term competitive advantage. Surprises of intention, timing, place, strength, and style can sometimes win the day for us in one major surprise blow. Deception multiplies the effectiveness of surprise.

At the same time, we have to remember that surprise is a two-edged sword. We must be on-guard against those self-same types of surprise in case they're used against us. A knowledge of the types of surprise can help us prepare so that surprises are not used against us.

Deception and surprise are two of the most effective tools we can use as we continue honing our ability to think and act strategically to gain lasting competitive advantage in the challenges that we face.

The Sources and Uses of Reliable Intelligence
Lecture 15

The profession of spy is as old as history, and it is the spy that we most often think of when we consider the topic of intelligence. But information from spies is just one aspect of a complex process that can aid us in our quest to think strategically. This lecture explores the sources and uses of reliable intelligence and how it contributes to the crafting of prudent strategy, including the engine of any successful intelligence apparatus, the intelligence cycle.

A Crucial Mistake of the Death Star Commander

- At the end of the 1977 film *Star Wars*, Luke Skywalker leads the Rebel Alliance in an attack on the Empire's Death Star. In one subtle yet powerful scene, a military intelligence officer, armed with a report analyzing the rebels' attack, advises the Death Star commander to evacuate. But the commander rejects the advice, believing that the Empire is on the verge of triumph.

- In competition, we strive for knowledge, predictability, and the reduction of uncertainty, yet we sometimes reject reliable information if it conflicts with our own internally derived biases.

- In this lecture, we examine the role of intelligence collection and its crucial importance in the crafting of good strategy. We also learn how to harness the power of intelligence principles for both business and personal decision making in areas where we find ourselves in competition.

- Leonard Fuld, a leader in the field of competitive business intelligence and one of the country's top theorists and practitioners of intelligence, gives us this simple directive: "By actively seeking intelligence and learning how to use it, you can turn information into a powerful weapon to give you a competitive advantage."

Intelligence Defined

- Intelligence is not just information but *analyzed* information. The principles of intelligence collection, analysis, and dissemination are useful in the military, sports, politics, and business. They can also be applied in our daily lives.

- When we think of intelligence in its military or espionage contexts, we tend to think of spying, but this type of so-called human intelligence ("humint") is never more than one aspect of intelligence, which in turn, is only one aspect of strategy.

Intelligence Gathering in Sports and Politics

- Teams in the NFL invest millions of dollars in technology, staff, travel, and refined expertise in what they call scouting. They evaluate opposing players and the plays that are called by opposing coaches in a myriad of game situations. They ask scenario questions and develop tendency charts on other teams' intentions in certain situations in order to discern their probable courses of action during a game.

  o This type of scouting is perfectly legal as long as it taps into open sources and does not violate league rules. Occasionally, thought, teams can go too far. For instance, intercepting another team's signals and deciphering them is in violation of the NFL's regulations.

  o Sophisticated surveillance of an opponent's resources, capabilities, and intentions continues to play a crucial role in the outcome of football games. Millions of dollars are at stake in a successful season, and most NFL teams believe the investment is worthwhile.

- Both major U.S. political parties maintain departments of what is called "opposition research," where researchers unearth information on tax liens, divorce records, and lawsuits in the attempt to discredit opposing candidates or develop attack points. They also comb through voting records of targeted incumbents. Use of such intelligence is often timed to have maximum effect on election results.

Types of Intelligence Analysis

- Jan Herring, a former CIA analyst, has identified five types of intelligence analysis, categorized according to their uses: (1) prevention of surprises to the organization by providing early warning, (2) support of the decision-making process, (3) competitor assessment and monitoring, (4) planning and strategy development, and (5) support of the collection and reporting process.

- Intelligence is the final product of a conscious, intentional, targeted process designed to enlighten us about the resources, capabilities, and intentions of our friends and enemies—and ourselves. Those three elements—resources, capabilities, and intentions—are extremely important, especially in competitive situations. It's always useful to know how our competitors stand with regard to these factors.

- In football, for example, the resources available to an opponent include money, draft picks of future players, and contacts throughout the industry. The opponent's capabilities consist of developed resources, which appear as strengths and weaknesses in various aspects of the game. The opponent's intentions answer the question: How will these capabilities be used against us?

- Gathering information about these three elements is designed to reduce uncertainty.

The Intelligence Cycle

- The intelligence cycle consists of five steps: (1) planning and setting of priority intelligence requirements, (2) collection, (3) analysis, (4) dissemination, and (5) action. The cycle is a virtuous one in that the collection and analysis of information helps refine the target, focusing our efforts on the next spin of the cycle. The speed of the cycle depends on the criticality of the issues and the time demands of the situation.

- The first stage in the cycle is setting priority intelligence requirements. This phase determines what information you will collect and what information you will ignore. It gives direction to your efforts so that you don't collect information aimlessly or conduct never-ending research to put off the necessity of making tough choices.

- The second stage in the cycle is the systematic, three-dimensional process of collecting information. This stage involves tapping into multiple sources, such as databases; trade show materials; press releases; interviews of relevant people, such as a competitor's former employees; and even conversations that you might "overhear." It's important to discipline yourself to pursue comprehensive information collection; don't rely on the techniques or sources with which you feel most comfortable.

- The third stage, analysis, is believed by some to be more an art than a craft. We've already seen some of the tools that are used at this stage, such as PEST, value chain, five forces, and SWOT analyses. But there are many others, including competitor, political risk, and scenario analyses. Each of these tools has strengths and weaknesses; you should never rely on a single technique to inform your strategic decision making.

Figure 15.1

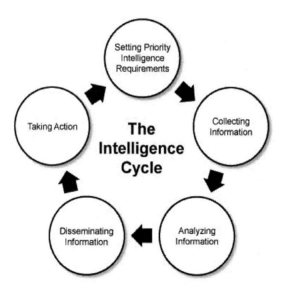

The five-step intelligence cycle is the engine that drives our vision of the future and, ideally, yields useful, actionable information.

- The fourth stage is dissemination, and it is here that many intelligence efforts fail. Some intelligence analysts make the mistake of simply presenting collected facts as intelligence with minimal analysis, minimal links to the current situation, and minimal relevance to what must be done strategically. Beware of the "nice-to-know" syndrome. Intelligence is a perishable product; it is meant to be disseminated and used.

- The fifth stage, action, requires courage. When you consider your findings, you must have the courage to say, "This means that our firm should..." or "This means that I should...."

The Cassandra Curse

- The ancient Greek story of Cassandra perfectly captures a common irrational response to intelligence: the irrationality of desiring to know information yet refusing to accept it when it's offered if it contradicts what you (or the higher-ups) believe.

- Cassandra was the beautiful daughter of King Priam of Troy. The god Apollo was taken with her beauty and gave her a great gift, the gift of prophecy. Even so, she spurned Apollo's romantic overtures, and he responded with a curse. He allowed Cassandra to keep her gift of prophecy, but she would never be believed and could never affect the course of events.

- Perhaps no one is better equipped to see into the future than the professional intelligence analyst, but the commander often ignores intelligence in favor of trusting his own instincts. Even we have trouble believing ourselves at times or knowing what to do with intelligence we uncover.

- The obstacle we must overcome here is the paradox of leadership: The very qualities that make for a strong leader at the most senior levels are the same qualities that cause those leaders to reject the informed advice of others. This paradox exists in both business and the military.

Pivot Points in History

- Small pivot points in history often add up to major differences in the eventual course of events, and intelligence is often key to those pivot points—the availability of intelligence and the courage and boldness to act on it.

- The Civil War was surely a major historical turning point for the United States. If the South had won the Civil War, world history would certainly have developed in radically different ways, and in fact, the South came very close to winning.

  o In September 1862, General Robert E. Lee was on the march into Maryland with his Army of Northern Virginia. His intent was to relieve the pressure on Virginia and to carry the war to the North. At the time, the commander of the Army of the Potomac, Major General George McClellan, was unaware of Lee's capabilities and intentions.

  o As Lee marched north, a Union private found a copy of a Confederate order that gave details about movements of Lee's army, including the splitting of his forces. When McClellan read the order, he realized that it gave him the opportunity to beat Lee and, perhaps, end the war, but he failed to fully exploit the strategic advantage of the intelligence.

  o Time was critical for McClellan, but he moved too slowly, perhaps overestimating the size and strength of Lee's forces. The result was the indecisive Battle of Antietam, the bloodiest day in U.S. military history. General Lee retreated to Virginia, and the Civil War lasted another two and a half years.

  o The incredible temporary advantage afforded by critical intelligence was squandered by McClellan in one of history's great pivot points. The lesson here is that when critical, high-quality intelligence is available, boldness is required to act decisively, correctly, and quickly.

- First-rate intelligence coupled with a strategic plan gives us an amazing ability to see and affect the future. Intelligence sheds new light that we ignore at our peril, and it is the lifeblood of strategic thinking.

Suggested Reading

Gudgin, *Military Intelligence.*

Hall and Citrenbaum, *Intelligence Analysis.*

Johnson, *Secret Agencies.*

Keegan, *Intelligence in War.*

Questions to Consider

1. The difference between being well-informed and being well-educated is similar to the difference between information and intelligence. The first is passive and routine, while the second is active and creative. Can you think of examples similar to those in the lecture that make use of analysis to explain a situation in your own experience?

2. The best way to understand the intelligence process and its value is to put it to use. Using the resources/capabilities/intentions framework outlined in the lecture, prepare a rough assessment of your toughest competitor. Are there differences between your competitor's stated aims and the resources and capabilities to achieve them?

3. The intelligence cycle is the engine of information analysis and prevents our drowning in a sea of white noise. Construct your own intelligence cycle to determine your priority intelligence requirements; then act to collect and analyze information and draw the necessary conclusions. By making this a routine activity, the quality of your intelligence improves over time and with multiple iterations of the cycle.

The Sources and Uses of Reliable Intelligence
Lecture 15—Transcript

The profession of spy is as old as recorded history, and it is the spy that we most often think of when we consider the topic of "intelligence." That is, the collection and evaluation of information about our enemies, opponents, competitors, and friends. But information from spies is only one aspect of a complex process in the creation of intelligence that can aid us in our quest to think strategically.

This lecture explores the sources and uses of reliable intelligence and how it contributes to the crafting of prudent strategy.

To get us started, the popular motion picture *Star Wars*, released in 1977, has a short scene that pierces to the very heart of the lesson in today's lecture. At the end of the film, Luke Skywalker leads the rebel alliance in an attack on the Empire's Death Star. The Death Star is a powerful weapon that is about to destroy the rebel planet. Wave upon wave of fighters attack the Death Star in seeming futility. Then, the scene switches to a scene inside the Death Star. At that point, a military intelligence officer approaches the Death Star Commander Grand Moff Tarkin, who is played by Peter Cushing. It is here that we are presented with the conundrum of intelligence in decision making. This is a powerfully subtle scene in the film. It is rich in meaning and highly instructive. In my opinion, it invests *Star Wars* with depth and legitimacy and realism and elevates it to a level far above mere space opera.

Perhaps you missed it? Here is the scene. Even as the rebels press their attack outside, the military intelligence officer approaches Grand Moff Tarkin with an intelligence report. He speaks these words: "We've analyzed their attack, sir ... and there is a danger. Shall I have your ship standing by?" The response of the commander is critical: "Evacuate? In our moment of triumph? I think you overestimate their chances."

This is the conundrum. When things appear to be going well, even at a crucial moment, commanders reject intelligence. Even when commanders are presented with reliable information, they reject it if it conflicts with their own internally derived biases. And yet, we continue to strive for knowledge;

we strive for predictability; we strive to reduce uncertainty. And good strategy depends on the reduction of uncertainty.

This lecture is about intelligence. In this lecture, we examine the role of intelligence collection and its crucial importance to the crafting of good strategy. First, we consider intelligence, what it is and what it isn't. And then we learn the role of competitor intelligence in helping us to craft strategy. Second, we reveal here the intelligence cycle to show how intelligence is produced. How you can produce intelligence, as distinct from mere information. Third, we learn the major obstacles that thwart our use of intelligence in practice.

Our objective here is to learn the fundamental principles of intelligence as it is practiced by intelligence agencies and utilized by world leaders. We learn how to harness the power of intelligence principles for our business firms and for our personal decision making in areas where we find ourselves in competition. Why should we do this? For competitive advantage, either sustained, or to seize fleeting advantages offered by brief pivot points afforded to us as windows of opportunity.

Leonard Fuld is a leader in the field of competitive business intelligence and one of the country's top theorists and practitioners of intelligence. He tells us this simple directive: "By actively seeking intelligence and learning how to use it, you can turn information into a powerful weapon to give you a competitive advantage."

What is intelligence? Well, there is a story—and it may be apocryphal—that an old French rulebook on the card game of bridge suggests as its rule number one: "Always try to see your opponent's cards." "Always try to see your opponent's cards" is, at bottom, the role of intelligence. In games of competition—whether in politics, or in sports, or in business, or in battle—we always want to see our opponent's cards. Intelligence, at bottom, is about seeing the other guy's cards.

Intelligence. We use it; we hear it used. It's ubiquitous. But what is it? Let's consider first what it is not: It is not spying; it is not a database; it is not a crystal ball. Intelligence is not the compilation of nice-to-know facts to store in a library. It is not just information; we have far too much information; we are drowning in information. It is none of those things. The most succinct definition of intelligence I have seen is these two words: "analyzed information."

When we think of intelligence in its military or espionage contexts, we tend to think of spying, of aerial reconnaissance, of clandestine surveillance, electronic warfare and signals interception. We think of the CIA and the National Security Agency and the Soviet Union's old KGB. We think of deception. We think of disinformation and operations security. We think of stroke and counterstroke, of an elaborate chess game played out on a chess board comprising the nations of the earth.

And this is all correct, but intelligence also is more subtle than this and has applications great and small outside the realm of world leaders and closer to home for you and for me. So-called human intelligence information from spies—or "Humint" as it is called by the intelligence establishment—is never more than one aspect of intelligence, which in turn is only one aspect of strategy. That said, the principles of intelligence collection, analysis, and dissemination and action are useful not only in the military, but in sports, politics, and business as well. And those principles are applicable to our daily lives, once we understand them.

Wait—daily lives? Sports? Yes. Think of American professional football. Teams in the national football league, the NFL, invest millions of dollars in technology, staff, travel, and refined expertise in what they call scouting. They engage in all sorts of activity off the field so that they can gain a competitive advantage on the field.

Teams evaluate opposing players, they evaluate the opposing coach's play-calling in a myriad of game situations. They ask scenario questions, such as: "What is the most frequent play called in a third-down-and-long situation at various locations on the field?" They do this so that they may develop tendency charts on the other team's intentions in certain situations. Then, when these situations occur on the field during a game, a team is better able to react to the enemy's probable course of action. This type of scouting is perfectly legal as long as it taps into open sources and does not violate league rules. Occasionally, teams can go too far. For instance, intercepting another team's cryptic signals and deciphering them in violation of the NFL's regulations.

Such interception of signals and code-breaking has been around for centuries. The British deciphered the French navy's semaphore code in 1808, which allowed them to read the signals passed between French ships and the shore and act accordingly to outmaneuver Napoleon's navy.

And so, we fast-forward to a modern instance of signals interception in the city of New York in 2007. It was the opening game of the NFL season, and the New England Patriots were caught filming the New York Jets' defensive signals in violation of NFL rules. As punishment, the Patriots were ordered to hand over all tapes of illegal filming to the league office, fined a total of $750,000, and made to forfeit a first-round draft pick. The Patriots' coach, Bill Belichick, was personally liable for a half-million dollars of the total fine.

But sophisticated surveillance of an opponent's resources, capabilities, and intentions continues to play a crucial role—if not a deciding role—in the outcome of professional football contests. Millions of dollars are at stake on a successful season and most NFL teams believe the investment worth it.

In politics, too, intelligence plays an increasingly influential role. Both major U.S. political parties maintain departments of what is called "opposition research." Political researchers unearth information on tax liens, divorce records, and lawsuits in their attempts to discredit candidates. They also comb through voting records of targeted incumbents. Operatives from both parties conduct expensive and labor-intensive research to ascertain the weak points of opponents and develop attack points. How the intelligence is used varies by situation and is usually utilized for maximum impact, especially timing.

For example, just prior to the 2000 presidential election, a news report surfaced revealing that Republican candidate George W. Bush had received a ticket for driving under the influence of alcohol in 1976. Republican strategist Karl Rove credits the Al Gore campaign for the timely report just five days before the presidential election. So we can see that the development of intelligence and its exploitation in competition has wide applicability.

Let's look now at the types of intelligence analysis available to us. Jan Herring is one of the creators of modern competitor intelligence. He is a former CIA analyst, and he launched the first major competitive intelligence function in a U.S. corporation back in 1986. Herring is considered one of the founders of the field of competitive intelligence and its application to business.

According to Herring, there are five types of intelligence analysis: preventing surprises to the organization by providing early warning; supporting the decision-making process; competitor assessment and monitoring; intelligence assessments for planning and strategy development; and analysis as a key part of the collection and reporting process.

Intelligence is the final product of a conscious, intentional, targeted process designed to enlighten us about the resources, capabilities, and intentions of our friends and enemies—and ourselves. Those three elements are extremely important—resources, capabilities, intentions—especially in competitive situations. We always have actual and potential competitors, and if we have any intention of prevailing against those competitors, it makes sense to know something about them. We must know what resources are available to them. We must know what capabilities they have. Can they utilize those resources? We must know what they intend to do with those capabilities, either for good or ill.

For an example of how this applies, say, in sports, we need look no further than our game of football. The resources available to an opponent consist of money, draft picks of future players, and contacts throughout the industry. The capabilities of an opponent consist of the developed resources— capabilities could be manifested in a powerful running game, mediocre passing game, and an outstanding linebacking corps on defense. In other words, the opponent's capabilities show up as strengths and weaknesses in various aspects of the game. The intentions of an opponent consist of his immediate and future decision making. How will our opponent use his capabilities against us?

As you can see, all of this is designed to reveal to us the future. We are striving to reduce uncertainty, striving to make life more predictable. Now the obvious question is, how do we obtain intelligence? Useful intelligence? Actionable intelligence? These natural questions bring us to the intelligence cycle. Usable, actionable intelligence doesn't just happen. It doesn't just serve itself up to us on demand. It's a product of conscious effort, planning, logic, lots of insight, and a little bit of luck. Superb intelligence is like a precious gold nugget. At the heart of our intelligence efforts is the intelligence cycle. This is the engine that drives our vision of the future. It's a five-step process that, ideally, yields actionable intelligence that our CEO or commander can use—intelligence that we can use.

The intelligence cycle consists of: 1) planning and setting priority intelligence requirements; 2) collection; 3) analysis; 4) dissemination; 5) action. And then the cycle goes around again. It is what we like to call a virtuous cycle. As we collect information, analyze it, and produce our intelligence product, it helps us refine our target; it helps us focus our efforts on the next spin of the intelligence cycle. The velocity of the cycle—how fast the cycle spins— depends on the criticality of the issues and the time demands of the situation.

Let's look briefly at each step in the cycle so that we can create our own virtuous cycle of intelligence. The first stage in the cycle is priority intelligence requirements, or PIR. This phase of the intelligence cycle determines what information you will collect and what information you will ignore. It gives direction to your efforts so that you don't flail around in a sea of information. It targets and focuses your efforts. Too many people collect information aimlessly. Young students have this problem, and so do many older folks, even businessmen who should know better. Instead of designing a plan of attack, determining what our goals are, we plunge into the morass of research. Research keeps us from having to choose; we can put off the necessity of making tough choices.

Now, research can be fun. Ask any novelist. But at some point, we have to select what is important, and this is much easier to do prior to information collection than after. We must determine our priority intelligence requirements beforehand to guide our collection efforts.

The second stage in the cycle is collection. This means that you begin to acquire information at different levels and from different sources. It is much, much more than doing a Google search. Collection is systematic and three-dimensional; it involves collecting information from multiple sources—from databases, to trade shows, to press releases, to interviews of relevant people, to "overhearing" conversations.

Here is where good judgment and determination come into play. We are naturally drawn to techniques and sources with which we feel comfortable. Bodybuilders are like that—they gravitate to certain exercises they do well, and they neglect exercises that are necessary, but painful. Likewise, we gravitate to the techniques that we do well—database searches, trade show attendance, searching press releases, interviewing our competitors' former employees. In this phase, we must discipline ourselves to pursue comprehensive information collection. We must ensure that our efforts have depth, so as to give us a full, three-dimensional picture that is not biased from the very start.

This brings us to the third stage, which is analysis. This is where the analyst earns his or her money. Some people believe that analysis is a kind of art rather than a mere craft. Certainly it is not routine work and successful analysts have certain characteristics—patience, persistence, insight, and broad intellectual context. The tools of analysis we can use at this stage are many, and entire books are devoted to their use. Some of the techniques we've already seen are SWOT analysis, value chain analysis, PEST analysis, and five forces industry analysis, But there are many others, including competitor analysis, political risk analysis, and scenario analysis. The important thing to remember is that each of these tools has strengths and weaknesses. We should never rely upon a single technique to inform our strategic decision making.

The fourth stage is dissemination, and it is here at this most critical of moments that many intelligence efforts fail. Some intelligence analysts make the mistake of simply presenting collected facts as intelligence with minimal analysis, with minimal conclusions, with minimal links to the here-and-now, with minimal relevance to what we must do strategically. Beware of the "nice-to-know" syndrome. Intelligence is a perishable product—unlike our gold nugget. Intelligence is meant to be used; it requires action on our part; it informs our decision making. The typical lack of analysis is what leads to the expression "actionable intelligence." But that's redundant. Real intelligence is always focused on present and future actions.

And this brings us to the fifth stage of action. When we present our findings or when we consider our findings for our own personal use, we must have courage. We must have the courage to utter the words: "For our firm, this means that we should do ..." or "For me, this means that I should take this action ...."

The result of all of this should be targeted, crisp reports that make clear what's going on. So why do so many firms seem to get it wrong? Why don't more firms incorporate intelligence? Why don't more firms act on intelligence?

There are many reasons for this seeming irrational response to intelligence. The irrationality of desiring to know the future and yet refusing to accept the information when it's proffered if it contradicts what the higher-ups believe already. And even despite our best efforts we are often faced with a phenomenon that can be called the Cassandra Curse. This name comes from Greek mythology. Greek mythology is so enduring for us because it speaks so much to the human condition, to the verities and to the foibles that touch human beings in every epoch.

Let's turn to the tale of Cassandra, because this minor Greek story captures the conundrum of intelligence perfectly. Cassandra was the beautiful daughter of King Priam of Troy. Apollo was taken with Cassandra. Apollo is perhaps best known as the god of the light and knowledge. He was taken with Cassandra's beauty, made romantic overtures to her, and he gave her a great gift—the gift of prophecy. Even so, she spurned him.

And Apollo responded with a curse. He allowed Cassandra to keep her gift of prophecy, her ability to see into the future. But she was cursed so that no one would believe her; nor could she change or even affect the course of events. She could not avoid disaster if she foresaw it. The Cassandra Curse.

Intelligence professionals feel that they are sometimes cursed like Cassandra. Consider this paradox for a moment. There is sometimes no one better equipped to see into the future, however imperfectly, than the professional intelligence analyst. But is the analyst believed? Does the commander believe the intelligence officer over his own instincts? Think of *Star Wars* again as the intelligence officer informs Grand Moff Tarkin of the danger in the rebel attack. Even we have trouble believing ourselves at times, of knowing what to do with the intelligence we uncover, to understand its implications. Exclusive knowledge can sometimes paralyze us. It can paralyze the leader. Courage is required.

There is a big obstacle to overcome here. And it's a paradox of leadership. This paradox exists in both business and in the military, it exists wherever big and irrevocable decisions must be made. The paradox of leadership is this: The very qualities that make for a strong leader at the most senior levels are the same qualities that cause those leaders to reject the informed advice of others, even if those others are intelligence professionals.

This is true in business; it's true in the military as well. Sometimes much of the character of intelligence discussion takes on the quality of the old saying, "For want of a nail, the shoe was lost. For want of a shoe, the horse was lost. For want of a horse, the rider was lost. For want of a rider, the battle was lost." And so on. There is a large kernel of truth in this view, that small pivot points in history add up to major differences in how things eventually turn out. And intelligence is often the key to these pivot points—the availability of intelligence and the courage and boldness to act upon it.

The Civil War was surely a major historical turning point for the United States. If the south had won the Civil War, world history would certainly have developed in ways so radically different that we cannot even fathom the repercussions. Given objective factor endowments that figure into the construction of a nation's engine of war, the South never should have come close to winning the Civil War. And yet the South came so very close to winning.

Let's talk about one of those pivot points here, one that relates directly to the role of intelligence in planning strategy. The year is 1862. It is September, and General Robert E. Lee is on the march into Maryland with his Army of Northern Virginia. His intent is to relieve the pressure on Virginia and to carry the war to the north, perhaps even bestir confederate sympathizers in Maryland.

The Northern commander of the Army of the Potomac, Major General George McClellan, is unaware of the capabilities and intentions of his opponent. But the winds of fortune soon change this. As Lee marches north, on September 13, history faced a pivot point that turned on intelligence and how it was handled. Union Private Barton Mitchell found a copy of General Lee's Special Order No. 191 in an envelope wrapped around several cigars. He found it in a field in Frederick County, Maryland, a field just vacated by a confederate rear-guard force. The orders gave details of the Army of Northern Virginia movements during the early days of its invasion, including the splitting of Lee's Army. The found orders were sent up the chain of command, where they reached the commander, Union Major General McClellan.

Here is an instance where a commander was blessed with a gift of critical intelligence, a clear statement of the intentions of his opponent. For a brief moment in 1862, the fog of war was lifted for General McClellan. He could see into the future. He had intelligence that could enable him to destroy Lee's army in detail and end the Civil War in September of 1862. When McClellan read the order, he stated, "Here is a paper with which if I cannot whip Bobbie Lee, I will be willing to go home." But one historian responds: "He couldn't whip Bobbie Lee … and he didn't." At the critical pivot point in history, McClellan hesitated.

Many military historians believe that McClellan failed to fully exploit the strategic advantage of the intelligence for two classic reasons: First, was the intelligence authentic, or was it the bait for a trap? This possibility gave McClellan pause. Second, the intelligence told McClellan Lee's intentions, but what were Lee's capabilities? How big was Lee's army? McClellan did not know. McClellan always seemed to think he was outnumbered, and this tendency fueled his hesitation. We know now that throughout his time as commander of the Army of the Potomac, General McClellan habitually overestimated the size and strength of Lee's army.

Time was critical for McClellan to be able to use the information given to him, and he moved too slowly. The result was the indecisive Battle of Antietam, the bloodiest day in U.S. military history, when more than 7000 soldiers lost their lives. General Lee retreated to Virginia, and the Civil War lasted another two and a half years. We speak of windows of opportunity that open and close; here is one such example. The incredible temporary advantage afforded by critical intelligence was squandered in one of history's great pivot points. So we can see that even when critical, high-quality intelligence is available, it requires boldness to act decisively, correctly, and quickly.

Let's sum up. intelligence is analyzed information, and the intelligence cycle that makes intelligence possible consists of priority setting, collection, and analysis, and dissemination. It's a virtuous cycle, as the information we analyze and disseminate also helps us refine our priorities and focus our efforts on the next spin of the intelligence cycle. But for the fruits of the cycle to count as intelligence, there must be a constant focus on the actions being considered. Intelligence is always about possible action. The Cassandra Curse refers to what can happen when first-rate intelligence is ignored or not put to use.

This is the conundrum. Remember those words from *Star Wars*: "We've analyzed their attack, sir … and there is a danger." We must understand what intelligence is, and what it is not. We must know how to set priorities, collect information, and analyze it to create intelligence of genuine value.

But we must know more—we must also, above all, have the courage to act on that intelligence decisively and prudently so as not to squander its value. First-rate intelligence coupled to a strategic plan gives us an amazing ability to see and affect the future—an ability that ancient Greeks familiar with the Cassandra story might have regarded as almost god-like. Intelligence sheds new light that we ignore at our peril, and it is the life blood of strategic thinking.

Move and Countermove—The Theory of Games
Lecture 16

W hen people interact with each other, they are playing games, whether lovers in a romantic game, drivers maneuvering in a traffic game, or politicians vying for votes in a political game. Game theory offers a mathematical approach to crafting strategy to win games involving two or more players. In this lecture, we look at a range of games to investigate how game theory works.

Let's Meet in New York!
- The game theorist **Thomas Schelling** devised a game in which two people are promised $1000 each if they can set a time and place to meet in New York City. The two people are unknown to each other, can't communicate, and must give an answer in 30 seconds.

- This game demonstrates the fact that in the absence of information, we are forced to use our powers of reason and logic. The overwhelming majority of people list the meeting place as Times Square, Grand Central Station, or the Empire State Building and the meeting time as noon.

- In a variation of this game, participants are given more time and more information. Interestingly, as the information supply goes up, the clarity of analytical thinking goes down. The range of times and places given in response to this challenge is far greater than in the absence of information.

The Game of Life
- Life is a series of games. When you drive in heavy traffic and jockey for position against anonymous competitors, you are playing a game. When you ask your boss for a raise, you are playing a negotiating game. When people interact in ways designed to achieve a goal, they are playing a game.

- Game theory demonstrates how rational people reason when presented with dilemmas that provide incomplete information. The theory

Rush hour is one of life's many games: a situation in which several goal-oriented decision makers interact.

contends that it can provide the best, most rational strategy for a host of games we play.

- Games can be defined as situations in which several goal-oriented decision makers interact with one another. The outcome of the interaction for a given player depends on the actions of the other players. Moreover, one player's actions are contingent on the others' responses.

The History of Game Theory

- Concentrated development of game theory began in the 1920s with John von Neumann's efforts to analyze the technique of bluffing in poker. Twenty years later, von Neumann and his collaborator claimed that game theory could form the basis for the science of economics.

- Game theorists create mathematical models consisting of variables and equations that represent a variety of games we encounter in the real

313

world. These equations purport to demonstrate the "best" strategy to pursue in the real-world situations they represent.

- Game theory makes assumptions about how the world works and how people behave. It assumes, for example, that each of us is a "rational actor," which means that we will behave rationally in interacting with others. In goal-directed interactions, we will seek to maximize utility, that is, to receive the highest payoff or minimize damage to ourselves. This is a cost-benefit analysis applied to the human mind.

- One of the major contributions of game theory to the world of strategy came during the Cold War and the nuclear standoff between the Soviet Union and the United States. Game theorists recognized that the nuclear arms race had all the characteristics of a two-person strategic game, specifically, one known as the Prisoner's Dilemma.

  o The Prisoner's Dilemma demonstrated how the nuclear arms race could lead to complete destruction through only a tiny misstep by either side.

  o This game involves two players in a situation where each does not know the move of the other, and they have the options to cooperate or defect from the game. Interviewed separately, each prisoner is given the option of implicating the other in a crime or of remaining silent. If both cooperate to protect each other, they both receive a beneficial payoff (a light sentence). If both defect to implicate the other, they each receive a longer sentence.

  o If one prisoner cooperates while the other defects, the cooperator gets the lighter sentence, but the defector goes free. In this situation, the dominant strategy is to defect because cooperation involves too much risk.

  o In the Cold War, game theory showed that the danger in the nuclear standoff was the dominant strategy of defection. The game gave the advantage to the state that launched a successful nuclear first strike.

Rational Irrationality

- Game theory prompts us to consider not just our own plans but the responses of others who have an interest in the outcome. Anticipating these responses should allow us to identify and select the strategy that maximizes our payoff.

- An opponent's response, however, can sometimes be irrational or unpredictable in our judgment. We can also misjudge the payoff of a game; that is, other people might be playing for higher or lower stakes. Thus, what appears irrational to us could very well be rational to our opponents.

- Opponents might also feign irrationality to achieve strategic results. In other words, a player may act irrationally because he or she believes that it is rational to do so. We must incorporate this concept of rational irrationality in our calculations.

- In a multiplayer game, one player may have the goal of "defeating" another, regardless of the personal cost. This type of rational irrationality is seen in an auction game for a $20 bill.

  o In this game, the winner must pay the highest bid for the $20 bill, while the person who comes in second must pay the losing bid. For example, if the winning bid is $4, the winner pays that amount to receive the $20 bill, and the person who came in second pays $3.

  o As the auction progresses, the payoff changes dramatically for the two final bidders. They are no longer bidding to win $20 but to minimize their losses.

- The assumption of rationality can also lead us to misidentify the payoffs for a particular game for another player. We may assume that everyone in the game is motivated by the same incentive, but in the world of work, for instance, some are motivated by money, some by recognition, some by the ability to exercise authority, and so on.

- One of the most prevalent forms of misperception is the fallacy of "mirror-imaging." We assume that an opponent or fellow worker shares the same values and incentive system as ours. We may be wrong, but our actions and the responses we anticipate are based on this assumption. We're then surprised by an "irrational" response.

- Former Defense Secretary Robert McNamara discovered this fallacy for himself during the Vietnam War. McNamara was playing a rational game of carrots and sticks in a limited war, and he assumed that the Vietnamese would recognize they could not win such a war against the United States. The Vietnamese, however, were playing a different game: a total war of national liberation.

The Tragedy of the Commons

- The Tragedy of the Commons is a dilemma that arises when individuals who pursue their own rational self-interest yield a group result that is suboptimal. The name refers to a situation described by ecological scientist Garrett Hardin, in which herders graze their cows on a common parcel of land. With no incentive to restrict grazing, the parcel of land is quickly made useless by overgrazing.

- The key to this dilemma is that the herder receives all the benefits from grazing his or her cows, while the damage is shared by the group. Thus, it's perfectly rational for each herder to graze as many cows as possible, even as this depletes the shared and limited resource. In fact, the rational herder concludes that the only sensible course to pursue is to keep adding animals to the herd.

- Hardin portrayed our national park system as a modern-day commons. The parks themselves are limited in extent, but our population seems to grow without limit. The values that visitors seek in the parks are, thus, steadily eroded.

- This pursuit of private gain and shared cost is a hidden dynamic that Hardin uncovered in the economic system of private enterprise. Game theory models it as the CC-PP game: commonize costs—privatize profits.

- Hardin claims that CC-PP captures much of the wealth-creation pattern in a free economic system. If, for example, a private industry dumps waste into a river in pursuit of its profit-making venture, this cost is shared by all, while the profits accrue to the business.

The Free Rider Problem

- The Free Rider Problem represents another familiar situation in economics. Here, a common resource is shared, whether individuals pay for it or not.

- College students recognize the phenomenon of the late-night keg run: The party is at its height, and the keg runs dry. The hat is passed for contributions to buy another keg. But the student who is thinking rationally realizes that whether or not he or she contributes, the keg will arrive soon and the benefits will be available to all who are still at the party. This is the free rider.

- In economics, the Free Rider Problem is called a "collective action" problem. How can you get people to work together to achieve a collective goal when individuals may be motivated by different incentives and may not be motivated at all by a group goal? One solution is to create incentives to get people to respond in accordance with your goals.

Lessons Learned from Game Theory

- Game theory offers us insight into how people reason and forces us to consider the notion of a payoff. It compels us to consider the stakes of a game and whether all participants view the stakes and the payoff in the same way.

- We can also recognize the weaknesses of game theory as applied in the world of daily living. The artificial notion of rationality expressed in behavior could cause problems for us if we expect people to act in accordance with it.

- Still, game theory provides a structured way to understand cooperative alternatives to pure conflict, in some cases, allowing outcomes to be maximized for all sides.

Name to Know

Schelling, Thomas (1921–): A political scientist, strategist, game theorist, and arms control advocate, Schelling exerted powerful influence on strategic thinking in the nuclear era and in explaining the dynamics of racial segregation in the United States through the use of relatively simple modeling.

Suggested Reading

Binmore, *Game Theory*.

Schelling, *The Strategy of Conflict*.

Von Neumann and Morgenstern, *Theory of Games and Economic Behavior*.

Questions to Consider

1. One benefit of game theory is that it concentrates our minds on the dynamic of our interactions with others and helps us to quantify the various payoffs available. This is particularly helpful when we play numerous iterations of a particular game. Do you interact in a game-like situation with people at work or with competitors? If so, think about how the concepts in this lecture clarify what is actually going on in the game.

2. Can you quantify the payoffs in the various games you play? After identifying several ongoing games in which you participate, identify the payoff structure and determine whether you are a winner or a loser most of the time.

3. Now that you understand the structure of the game you play, consider actions you can take to either change the payout for different decisions or to structure the game differently so that you can improve your strategic position.

Move and Countermove—The Theory of Games
Lecture 16—Transcript

When people interact with each other, they are playing games—whether lovers in a romantic game, drivers maneuvering in a traffic game, sports teams playing an overt game with clearly defined rules, or politicians vying for votes in a political game. Game theory offers a mathematical approach to crafting strategy to win games involving two or more players. Whether game theory is actually useful in practical matters depends on whom you ask. Game theorists are adamant that their theory of games is not only useful to crafting strategy, but many believe that game theory is strategy. As with any theory, game theory has positives and negatives, and it can illustrate and predict outcomes when people do act rationally, and even find ways to cooperate.

Here's an example of how the average person, without much information at all, can find ways to cooperate with other people so everyone wins. It's a game that I call "Let's meet in New York!" It demonstrates how, with almost no information, we can coordinate with other people for mutual gain. In fact, this absence of information provides us with our most creative and analytical opportunities. Without information, we're compelled to focus and to use our powers of reason and logic.

This example comes from Thomas Schelling. Schelling was a game theorist who penned a powerful work of game theory and nuclear strategy in 1960 called *The Strategy of Conflict*. Let's play the game. Suppose I promise to give you and another person a thousand dollars apiece for just telling me where you plan to meet each other in New York City. You don't know this person, and you can't communicate with this person. This seems a relatively easy task until the rules are spelled out. I give you only two pieces of information—New York City and a specific date. Now you give me the time and place of your meeting in thirty seconds. That's it.

I play this game with students in my classes to demonstrate the power of analysis over mere information. In the absence of information, we are forced to think. It's as if our minds are forced off the familiar track we normally traverse. We are forced by necessity beyond the usual modes of thought and into unfamiliar territory.

The answers come in, and they are surprisingly the same every time I conduct this exercise. Ninety percent of people list the place of meeting as Times Square or Grand Central Station or, in a tip of the hat to the classic film *An Affair to Remember*, the Empire State Building. The overwhelming majority list the time as noon.

But there's more to this experiment. What happens if I give the same task to a group of students but with this changed condition: I provide with a five-page "tip-sheet" full of facts about the city and the unknown person you are expected to meet. And you get a full three minutes to come up with an answer. That's 600 percent more time and approximately 2000 percent more information.

Are the results better? Is there more correct coordination? Is there more of a consensus as to where and when the meeting will take place? No, of course not. The clarity of analytical thinking is dulled in the glut of information. As the information supply goes up, the clarity of analytical thinking goes down. The range of different times and places that students answer is far greater than in the absence of information. Why is that?

This is the world of the intelligence analyst, whose occupation is making sense of the world both without information and with information overload. The intelligence analyst tries to anticipate the actions of a few select adversaries in the presence of overwhelming information, the vast majority of which is useless or even misleading. This is not the normal state of affairs for most of us.

Ordinarily, we make arrangements with information we have, or we do something else. Only on occasion are we forced into situations where we must take into account another person's actions in situations when we cannot communicate, and yet we very much desire a specific outcome. For instance, the common happenstance of a husband and wife getting separated in a busy mall at Christmastime. The two of them will find each other—not through gathering of information, but through logical analysis.

Life is a series of games. When you drive in heavy traffic and you jockey for position against anonymous competitors, you are playing a game. When you go talk to your boss to ask for a raise, you are playing a negotiating game. When people interact in ways designed to achieve a goal, they are playing a game.

Game theory can demonstrate how rational people reason when presented with dilemmas with incomplete information. Game theory contends that it can provide the best, rational strategy for a host of games that we play—games that can be mathematically modeled. Here, we learn how game theory contributes to our understanding of how people reason about problems and how to utilize this contribution to help us pursue the best strategy in our own games more often.

Games are situations in which there are several goal-oriented decision makers interacting with each other. The outcome of the interaction depends not on your actions alone, but on the actions of the other player. Moreover, your actions are contingent on each other's responses. And so, in playing the "game" we must take into account what the other person might do. This is what makes the game strategic. Game theory looks at this type of situation mathematically. It attempts to bring mathematical precision to human decision making in game-type situations.

Concentrated development of game theory began in the 1920s. Innocently enough, it involved one man's efforts to analyze a tactic in the game of poker—the technique of bluffing. John von Neumann wanted to understand the process and discover if there might be a mechanism for it. Almost 20 years later, in 1944, von Neumann and his collaborator Oskar Morgenstern, were claiming that game theory could form the basis for the science of economics.

So we can understand what von Neumann and Morgenstern were talking about, let's go back to poker. Unlike other games, in which the pieces or arguments are clearly visible to every player, poker incorporates an element of mystery. You can't see the other players' cards. And those players can misrepresent what they have in their hands through facial expression, body language, and by actions in the game. Even a series of actions throughout a series of hands can be a strategic ploy intended to create a false pattern, to lull an opponent into a false sense of knowledge.

Leading an opposing player to misapprehend what you have in your own hand and to mistake your intentions is called a bluff. Von Neumann elected to study this game to determine if there might be a scientific, or mathematical, way of modeling the situation in poker and determining the best way to bluff.

Game theorists create mathematical models consisting of variables and equations that represent a variety of games we encounter in the real world. These equations purport to demonstrate the best strategy to pursue in the real-world situations they represent.

This all sounds like a good idea. Is it? Like all good theories, this one comes with assumptions about how the world works and how people behave in that world. One assumption is that of economic rationality. Game theory assumes that each of us is a "rational actor," which means that we will act rationally in interacting with others. Rational behavior means that in goal-directed interaction with others, we seek to maximize our utility.

This means we act to receive the highest payoff of the options available to us. Or we seek to minimize the damage that is done to us. It's business-type cost–benefit analysis applied to the human mind. It is this assumption of rationality that vexes game theory and its ability to actually predict human behavior.

One of the major contributions of game theory to the world of strategy came during the period 1950–1991, a time of nuclear standoff between the Soviet Union and the United States. Game theorists recognized that the nuclear arms race had all of the characteristics of a two-person strategic game. In fact, the nuclear game closely resembled the dynamic at work in a game called the Prisoner's Dilemma, which is one of the most widely known games utilized by game theorists.

There is a reason that it is the most widely known game. It captured the dynamic in arms races, and, as such, had applicability for the foreign policy establishment. Most precisely, the Prisoner's Dilemma highlighted the dangers involved during the nuclear arms race in during the Cold War. The game theory folks thought that they might be able to contribute to the nuclear debate by ascertaining what the best possible strategy in such a dangerous game might be. Prisoner's Dilemma demonstrated how the nuclear game—as it was structured—would lead to complete nuclear destruction if only there was a tiny misstep by either side.

Briefly, here is the Prisoner's Dilemma. The game is structured with two players in a situation where each does not know the move of the other, and they have the options to cooperate with each other or to defect from the game. Interviewed separately, the prisoners are given the option of implicating the other prisoner in a crime, or of remaining silent. If both cooperate to protect each other, they both receive a beneficial payoff of a light one-month sentence. If they both defect to implicate the other, they both receive a payoff of a three-month sentence.

The interesting part of the game is when the prisoners' decisions differ. If one cooperates while the other defects, the cooperator gets the sucker's payoff of a one-year sentence, while the defector goes free. In this situation, the dominant strategy is to defect; there is just too much risk attached to cooperation. And this is the dynamic we saw during the Cold War arms race. Game theory showed that the incredible danger in the nuclear standoff was the dominant strategy of defection. The game gave the advantage to the state that launched a successful nuclear first strike.

Game theory contributes to our thinking in a number of ways. It gets us to consider not just our own plans, but the responses of others who have an interest in the outcome. The responses from other players can have a tremendous impact on the situation we're dealing with, changing it radically. So we must anticipate responses, and then understand and select the best, winning strategy that maximizes our payoff.

That's the way it's supposed to work. But our opponent's response can sometimes be irrational or unpredictable in our judgment. We can sometimes misjudge the payoff of a game—other people might be playing for different stakes, or higher or lower stakes.

So what appears irrational could very well be rational to our opponent. Moreover, an opponent might feign his own irrationality to achieve a strategic result. Another way of putting it is that a player acts irrationally, because he believes that it is rational for him to do so.

We must incorporate this concept of rational irrationality in our calculations. In a multi-player game, it sometimes becomes the goal of one player to defeat another by preventing him from winning, regardless of the cost to himself. This type of rational irrationality is on display in my classes every semester as I have my students play an auction game. When I teach international economics, I introduce the subject to my students with an auction. This is an auction game created by Max Bazerman.

The auction game works this way. I tell them I am auctioning a $20 bill. Bidding starts at $1 and proceeds in $1 increments. There are only two rules: First, is that the winner pays the winning bid to receive the $20 bill. Second, the person who came in second in the auction must pay the losing bid. So, for instance, if the winning bid is $4, the winner pays his $4 to receive the $20 bill, and the person who came in second pays $3.

This seems like an easy way to make $20. But people tend to believe what they want to believe. People assume they know the rules of an auction, and they ignore the rules of this one. This is partly because we have mindsets that assimilate new information only with difficulty.

As the auction progresses, the bidding is brisk until it reaches $9 or $10. At that point, students quickly drop out until only two are left. These two students suddenly find themselves playing in a game entirely different from the one they thought they were playing. The bidding usually escalates well beyond $20. And the flurry of bidding activity is amusing to the rest of the class. Instead of an open auction with many participants and a chance to steal 20 bucks from the absent-minded professor, they find themselves in a two-person game, locked in a bidding war—feverishly bidding. The pay-off for the game has dramatically changed. The bidding is no longer to win $20 on the cheap. It's to minimize losses. The players will often go well beyond the original $20 to limit their losses. And the bidding has a ratchet effect as the stakes get higher and higher with no retreat possible.

I've run this auction with students outside the U.S. as well with similar results. In pursuit of the elusive $20 bill, students appear ready to spend as much as it takes to keep from "losing." Who knows what drives the dynamic—ego, the excitement of the crowd egging them on, an internal calculus that operates differently than for those of us who merely observe the proceedings. Regardless, the exercise demonstrates that quite often we are not rational in our decision making, even in the realm where we would expect to find the most rational decision making of all: our personal economics.

Our assumption of rationality can lead us to mis-specify the payoffs for a particular game for another player. We may assume that everyone in the game is motivated by the same incentive. In work for instance, some are motivated by money, some by free time, others by awards and recognition from the crowd, still others from quiet recognition from a superior, and others simply by the permission to exercise authority within a particular sphere of activity. This is a form of misperception. One of its most prevalent forms is the fallacy of "mirror-imaging." We assume that an opponent or fellow worker shares the same values and incentive system as ours. We may be wrong, but we base our actions on this assumption and we anticipate a response based on this assumption. Only to be surprised by an "irrational" response.

Former Defense Secretary Robert McNamara discovered this fallacy for himself in a way that cost the United States dearly in blood and treasure during the Vietnam War in the 1960s. McNamara was playing a coolly rational game of carrots and sticks in a limited war. He assumed that the Vietnamese would recognize they could not win such a war against the United States. The Vietnamese were, however, playing a different game. A total war of "National Liberation."

In retrospect, McNamara recognized that "Rationality will not save us." Long after the war, McNamara acknowledged his mistakes in playing the wrong game. He said this:

> We viewed the people and leaders of South Vietnam in terms of our own experience. … We totally misjudged the political forces within the country. … We underestimated the power of nationalism to

motivate a people ... to fight and die for their beliefs and values. ...
Our misjudgments of friend and foe, alike, reflected our profound
ignorance of the history, culture, and politics of the people in the
area, and the personalities and habits of their leaders.

Closer to home, let's look at a game that all of us play at one time or
another—a game in which our rational independent actions in our own self-
interest can lead to an undesirable result in the long-run. This game that
illuminates economic issues for us is derived from a famous allegory called
the Tragedy of the Commons.

The Tragedy of the Commons is a dilemma that arises when individuals who
pursue their own rational self-interest yield a group result that is suboptimal.
The name refers to a situation described by ecological scientist Garrett
Hardin in a famous 1968 essay called "The Tragedy of the Commons." In
the scenario, herdsmen graze their cows on a common parcel of land. Since
there is no individual incentive to restrict grazing—and, in fact, there is great
incentive to graze as many cows as much as possible—the parcel of land is
quickly damaged and made useless by overgrazing.

The key to the dilemma is that the herder receives all the benefits from
grazing his cows, while the damage is shared by the group. So it's perfectly
rational for each farmer to graze his cows as much as possible, even as this
depletes the shared and limited resource. Let me quote Hardin:

> The rational herdsman concludes that the only sensible course for
> him to pursue is to add another animal to his herd. And another.
> ... But this is the conclusion reached by each and every rational
> herdsman sharing a commons. ... Each man is locked into a system
> that compels him to increase his herd without limit—in a world
> that is limited. Ruin is the destination toward which all men rush,
> each pursuing his own best interest in a society that believes in the
> freedom of the commons.

Hardin portrayed our national park system as a modern-day commons.
The parks themselves are limited in extent; for instance, there is only one

Yosemite Valley. But our population seems to grow without limit. The values that visitors seek in the parks are steadily eroded.

This pursuit of private gain and shared cost is a hidden dynamic that Hardin uncovered in the economic system we know as private enterprise—or capitalism. This is a game companies play, and it has a name. Game theory models this as the CC-PP game. Commonize Costs–Privatize Profits. Hardin developed this game and he claims, with some justification, that it captures much of the wealth creation pattern in a free economic system.

The businessman devises a "silent way" to commonize his costs while privatizing his profits. He claimed that many fortunes have been built in this way. If private industry pursues its profit-making venture and, say, dumps waste into a river or pollutes the air, this is a cost shared by all, while the profits accrue to the business. Commonly, this is called an externality, or an "external cost." Hardin claimed that this is a sleight of hand that masks the actual CC-PP game.

Another similar situation is a common problem in economics, which is called the Free Rider problem. It can affect all of us, and it probably has affected all of us at some point. It can be infuriating. With the free-rider problem, a common resource is shared, whether individuals pay for it or not. In the macro economy, we find examples everywhere—national defense, or clean air—but we also find examples in our daily lives.

Many of my students are familiar with the phenomenon of the late-night keg run. The party is at its height, and the keg runs dry. The hat is passed for contributions to buy another keg. Here is where the rational person gives pause. "Do I contribute? Or not? Regardless of whether I contribute, the keg will arrive soon, and I can enjoy its benefits without having contributed." This is the free rider.

And yet, somehow money is collected from people, and the keg arrives. What distinguishes the contributors from the free riders? What does this do to our assumption of rationality? Ironically, it's probably rational for everyone to have made their respective decision. It all depends on where you stop in the chain of reasoning. Some contribute because they believe everyone else will contribute. Some don't contribute because they believe everyone else will contribute. This is the problem with rationality and rational choice theory, and ultimately game theory.

Jon Elster is a brilliant scholar who has grappled with rational choice and game theory for many years. Elster attempted to construct a game theoretical foundation for Marxism based on rational choice theory, the economic notion that people act based on the expected benefits and the choices others are likely to make. Jon Elster would eventually cease striving, having lost faith in rational choice. He made the most obvious observation: "Do real people act on the calculations that make up many pages of mathematical appendixes in leading journals? I do not think so. ... There is no general nonintentional mechanism that can simulate or mimic rationality."

This leads us to calculating how other people actually do behave. If we understand that rational calculation might lead to different sorts of behavior, perhaps we can construct new "rules" of the game that will take these differences into account.

The free rider problem illustrated by the keg party example is an enduring problem in economics called a "collective action" problem. How can you get people to work together to achieve a collective goal when individuals may be motivated by different incentives, and may be motivated not at all by a group goal? In a modern, diverse workplace, personnel are often motivated in different ways—some by money, some by holidays, some by private praise, some by public acknowledgement, some by group rewards. The late economist Mancur Olson suggested one solution to the collective action problem. He suggested the creation of selective incentives to get people to respond properly—that is, to respond the way you want them to.

When group incentives are not sufficient to get people to contribute, then a different incentive with an individual payoff might work. I used this principle of selective incentives in a real-world situation, and I can say it does work. My problem was simple enough. How could I get people to wear nametags over the entire two-week period of a conference? You know as well as I do that most people stop wearing their nametag after the first day. Experience told me that my exhortations to wear nametags for the vague goal of increasing goodwill among the participants would be futile. They would not wear nametags to please me, nor would they wear nametags for the group goal of goodwill. The payoff simply was not high enough for each participant to wear a nametag all two weeks.

The task was to create an individual incentive for each person to wear his nametag every day, all day. They would wear nametags in their own self-interest, not the group interest. The solution? Specially created nametags became their ticket to all of their meals. Not wearing a nametag—no food.

"But I'm not wearing my nametag because you want me to," said one young man who was philosophically inclined. "I know," I answered. "But that's irrelevant. That's the beauty of selective incentives designed to achieve collective goals." In this game, I altered the pay-off structure so that it modified the behavior of the participants in accord with a larger objective, but which satisfied their individual needs.

So, what can we conclude about game theory? Like so many other theories, it offers us insight into how people reason. It forces us to consider the notion of a "payoff" and what that payoff is. It compels us to consider the stakes of a game and whether all participants view the stakes and payoff in the same way. We also recognize the weaknesses of game theory as applied in the world of daily living. We can see that the artificial notion of rationality expressed in behavior could cause problems for us if we expect people to act in accord with it.

Even if we could conclude that people are rational in some universal sense—and we cannot—this rationality is not always expressed in behavior. As we have seen, sometimes a rational person may act irrationally because it is rational for him to do so to achieve his goal.

The uncertainty principle tells us that the presence of an observer changes the behavior of what is being observed. That is a characteristic of any theory. Once the theory's precepts and predictions of behavior become part of the information available, this knowledge then alters the behavior as players incorporate the theory into their strategic calculations. It should be obvious why this reduces the usefulness of the theory.

As we've seen, game theory is not a panacea and cannot reveal the future. People oftentimes do not act rationally, and rationality is the basic assumption that must be fulfilled for game theory to function. There may be deception, and the participants may not agree on which "game" is being played, even if there is no deception, and even if both sides are acting rationally.

But game theory does offer us insight into understanding human interaction, especially when people do act rationally. It also offers a structured way to understand cooperative alternatives to pure conflict. What's attractive is that sometimes, unnecessary destruction can be avoided and outcomes can be maximized for all sides.

The Evolution of Cooperation
Lecture 17

We often link strategic thinking and strategy to conflict, but strategic thinking can also help us develop cooperative solutions to problems. Empirical evidence demonstrates that order can evolve out of chaos, even with individuals pursuing their own self-interest. In fact, an entire body of theory has emerged that posits collaborative strategies that can be followed to yield fruitful results without the destructive behavior we associate with conflict.

Christmas 1914: A Spontaneous Truce

- World War I presented us with the spectacle of mainly Christian nations fighting each other—Britain, France, and Russia on one side and Germany and Austria-Hungary on the other. On the first Christmas of the war, soldiers on both sides saw no reason not to call their own truce and celebrate Christmas Eve with the enemy.

- The truce began spontaneously, with Germans positioning small Christmas trees on the parapets of their trenches. As the trees were lit, soldiers on both sides of the line offered one another greetings.

- At dawn, the first tentative movements out of the trenches began, ostensibly to bury the dead left in no man's land. The truce quickly spread, and Germans and English met and mingled freely in many places along the line.

- Despite the best efforts of both high commands to maintain hostilities, the truce continued throughout the day and, in some places, for several days beyond Christmas. It broke down inevitably, but additional examples of cooperation during the conflict continued.

- Research has since shown that the unique characteristics of trench warfare—small combat units faced off against each other for extended periods of time—led to this instance of communication and cooperation.

Cooperation Theory

- Robert Axelrod led the way in crafting cooperation theory with an important book in 1984 called *The Evolution of Cooperation*. In it, he sought to identify the conditions necessary for cooperation to emerge and discover what actions could be taken to create those conditions. Axelrod examined not only trench warfare in World War I but also a slightly less contentious forum: the U.S. Senate.

- Axelrod saw that in spite of the self-interest of senators serving their own constituents—and conflicting with other senators—many opportunities presented themselves for these legislators to work with one another and to exhibit reciprocity.

- This principle is nowhere better illustrated than in the relationship between Republican Senator Orrin Hatch and the late Senator Edward Kennedy. Beholden to opposing political parties and ideologically opposed as well, these two powerful senators found ways to cooperate and compromise to mutual benefit.

The Prisoner's Dilemma Revisited

- The decision to cooperate always involves some risk. What if the other side defects? Does the payoff justify the risk? This conundrum returns us to the Prisoner's Dilemma.

- This "game" serves as a model to capture the dynamic in interactions of all kinds, specifically, the tension between decisions for short-term self-interest or long-term cooperative benefit.

- Axelrod notes that the Prisoner's Dilemma allows scholars from many different fields to talk to one another about strategy. It also allows us to understand why it may be difficult to cooperate in our own interactions or to trust others.

- As you recall, each player in the Prisoner's Dilemma has two choices: to cooperate or to defect. Each makes the choice without knowing what the other will do. In this example, the payoff is $1 for each if both defect,

$3 for each if both cooperate, and $5 for the defector and nothing for the cooperator if they choose different options.

- No matter what the other player does, defection yields a higher payoff than cooperation. If you think the other player will cooperate, you should defect, but if you think the other player will defect, it still pays for you to defect. Thus, defection is the dominant strategy, and cooperation seems impossible.

- We can escape this dilemma by playing the game more than once with the same opponent. In this situation, Axelrod's work showed that one very simple strategy, tit for tat, can solve the dilemma. This is a strategy of simple reciprocity, which cooperates on the first move and then does whatever the other player did on the previous move.

- This strategy works best under five conditions: (1) avoid unnecessary conflict by cooperating as long as the other player does, (2) respond quickly in the face of an uncalled-for defection, (3) show forgiveness after responding to a provocation, (4) show clarity of behavior to enable the other player to recognize patterns of action, and (5) expect an indefinite number of interactions.

- By pursuing these conditions, you can create an environment of accepted norms, fertile for cooperation.

- The strategy of reciprocity succeeds by eliciting cooperation from others, not by defeating them. In many situations, mutual cooperation can be better for both sides than mutual defection. This strategy is particularly useful in conducting business abroad, in countries where detailed contracts are not commonly used.

- Armed with the cooperative dynamic, in which the horizon of interaction stretches out, we can craft strategies apropos to the moment to maximize our long-term gains.

Cooperation in the Military

- We've already seen how soldiers on opposing sides cooperated at Christmas during World War I, but cooperation with enemies can be orchestrated from the top of military hierarchies, as well. When the dangers and costs of miscommunication become greater than any benefit derived from no cooperation, the groundwork is laid for mutually recognized and orchestrated cooperation.

- A familiar example is the "hotline" between Washington, DC, and Moscow. This direct, secure communication link between the United States and Russia was established in 1963 as a direct result of the Cuban missile crisis.

- Apart from the hotline, military establishments are concerned with the problems of unintended escalation and nuclear missteps resulting from a miscommunication. Indeed, during the latter stages of the Cold War, the U.S. and Soviet militaries found several ways to cooperate on some of the most dangerous issues threatening both nations.

- Military exercises and weapons testing are sometimes used to communicate strength, resolve, and readiness to a nation's adversaries. The downside to such signaling is that it can be misinterpreted as the real thing.

- Complicating the issue is the fact that military exercises are sometimes used to mask an actual intent to invade. The Soviets used this ruse in August 1968 when they crushed the liberal reforms of the Prague Spring in Czechoslovakia with an invasion.

- To forestall the possibility that military exercises might be interpreted as a prelude to invasion, the United States and the Soviet Union agreed to a regime of confidence and security-building measures that included mutual inspections of military exercises. This form of cooperation between enemies broke new ground.

- Another extreme example of cooperation between enemies is represented by the demilitarized zone between North and South Korea. This is a strip of land more than 150 miles long and 2.5 miles wide, and it's the most fortified border on Earth. A cease-fire, not a peace treaty, is in force here.

  o Cooperation under these conditions is extremely difficult, especially given that more than 50 Americans and 1000 South Koreans have died in policing this border.

  o Still, both sides have found it useful to cooperate with each other in accepted and routinized ways. As we discussed earlier, the combatants established a joint security area in the area of P'anmunjŏm.

The Theory of Spontaneous Order

- According to the second law of thermodynamics, systems of order will tend toward disorder and chaos, but the theory of spontaneous order suggests the exact opposite: that out of chaos, social order can emerge among self-interested individuals who are not intentionally trying to create a system.

- A simple example of this theory at work is a dirt path across a meadow. It's likely that no one person chooses to "build" a path in a particular place and direction. Many people chose to walk that route for their own purposes, and as a result, a structure emerged through the principle of spontaneous order.

- The self-regulating market economy is another example of spontaneous order. The market economy is a system animated by people pursuing their economic self-interest in creating value and conducting commerce. This system of economic exchange regulates itself through prices.

Cooperation in Business

- In business, competing firms sometimes find it necessary to cooperate rather than compete. In fact, cartels and price-fixing would be far more common were they not illegal in many wealthy countries. But even without explicit collusion, firms often refrain from unilateral action in order to avoid unpleasant responses from competitors.

- Price wars illustrate what can happen when tacit cooperation breaks down. Price wars benefit consumers, of course, but for the firms involved, shrinking profit margins can make the difference between survival and collapse.

- One instance in which businesses cooperate is the strategic alliance, a form of cooperation in which two or more firms align and harmonize their strategic actions. They do this because the benefits of cooperation are greater than those achieved by unfettered competition.

- In such an arrangement, companies seek synergy, a situation in which the whole result is greater than the sum of its parts. At times, strategic cooperation makes sense because other avenues to synergy are closed.

  o This was the case in 2011, when the Justice Department refused to allow the communications giant AT&T to acquire the cellular carrier T-Mobile.

  o Ultimately, AT&T and T-Mobile pursued a cooperative arrangement that allowed AT&T access to T-Mobile's cellular airwaves and enabled T-Mobile to expand its national coverage.

Cooperation Theory in Action
- As the general in charge of the KGB, Alexei Kondaurov once had the responsibility of controlling dissidents, yet he achieved a shaky accommodation with the dissident community during the era of *glasnost* and *perestroika*.

- In an effort to avoid brutalizing demonstrators, Kondaurov managed to communicate that crossing a certain line in a protest would provoke a police response, and the demonstrators attempted to respect that line. In essence, the two opposing sides in the Soviet Union achieved a live-and-let-live rapprochement.

- The problem of cooperation presents us with conundrums that, at first pass, may seem irresolvable. But cooperation theory shows us that where people of goodwill wish to better their lives, they will find ways to exist to one another's mutual benefit.

Suggested Reading

Axelrod, *The Evolution of Cooperation.*

Weintraub, *Silent Night.*

Questions to Consider

1. Think of your most intractable opponent and consider whether the two of you might find ways to achieve cooperation. The cooperation doesn't have to be overt; as mentioned in the lecture, "peaceful coexistence" between the Soviet Union and United States was this form of conflict mitigation. Develop a tit-for-tat exercise based on Axelrod's theory and then try it out.

2. This lecture contends that the longer the shadow of the future, the better the chances of cooperating with a competitor. Thus, the obvious lesson is to extend the shadow of the future with predictable iterations so that cooperation can "evolve." Can you think of a practical way to extend the shadow of the future so that the risks of an opponent's defection become less acute?

3. In your opinion, what were the main factors that enabled enemy soldiers from two different camps during World War I to mingle amiably and freely without being ordered to do so?

The Evolution of Cooperation
Lecture 17—Transcript

We often link strategic thinking and strategy to conflict, but strategic thinking can also help us develop cooperative solutions to problems. Empirical evidence demonstrates that order can evolve out of chaos through individuals pursuing their own self-interest, and an entire body of theory has evolved that posits collaborative strategies that firms and individuals can follow that will yield fruitful results without the destructive behavior we associate with conflict. Cooperation theory suggests ways that we can cooperate with others for mutual benefit, even with competitors, even with enemies.

It was Christmas, 1914, just four months into what would become one of the bloodiest conflicts in history—World War I. Trench lines stretched from the Belgian coast south to the Swiss frontier, and the war was in stalemate. Most of the bloodshed was in the future. The nasty trench warfare with its blinding mustard gas attacks, the suicidal over-the-top charges into machine-gun fire—all of this was still beyond even the most morose imagination to conceive. On this Christmas occurred something that every general fears, and every general works desperately to prevent: mass collaboration with the enemy.

We most often link strategic thinking and strategy to conflict, but strategic thinking can also help us develop cooperative solutions to problems. This lecture suggests ways that we can cooperate with others for mutual benefit. Even with a fierce competitor.

So much of life is competitive. And perhaps this is natural in a world of economic scarcity. Political philosophy tells us to expect conflict. From Thucydides in the 5th century B.C., to Thomas Hobbes in the 17th century, to Karl Marx in the 19th century, philosophers of all persuasions have suggested that conflict is endemic to the human condition. According to Thomas Hobbes, the only remedy for these inevitable conflicts was a strong central government, since he believed that cooperation could not develop without a strong state. Incidentally, this was the underlying belief, deeply ingrained, that animated the Soviet Union and has re-appeared even in post-Soviet Russia: that only a guiding central authority can possibly ward off chaos. But history shows us that cooperation can emerge, even in the most conflictual of situations—even during war.

World War I presented us with the spectacle of mainly Christian nations fighting each other—Britain, France, and Russia on one side and Germany and Austria-Hungary on the other. The religion of the combatants was relevant here: Christmas was a holy day and shared holiday for the combatants on both sides. On this first Christmas of the war, in 1914, soldiers on both sides saw no reason not to call their own truce, and celebrate Christmas Eve with the enemy.

The truce began in true spontaneous fashion. Germans received small Christmas trees from home in the mail. They positioned them on the parapets of their trenches Christmas Eve and lit them with candles. In the majority of areas, it was Germans facing English. Up and down the line, both sides began calling to each other, offering Christmas greetings, singing Christmas carols.

At dawn, the first tentative movements out of the trenches began, ostensibly to bury the dead left in the no man's land between the trenches. The truce quickly spread, and Germans and English met and mingled freely in many places along the line, exchanging gifts and addresses. In at least one place, a soccer match was held. Despite the best efforts of both high commands to maintain hostilities, the truce continued throughout the day and, in some places, for several days beyond Christmas. It broke down inevitably, as new soldiers moved into the line on both sides as replacements. But additional examples of cooperation during the conflict continued.

In the summer of 1915, in many places along the line, neither side would shell the other side's supply trains, because neither side wanted to do without rations. Even personal time was respected in one section of the line— between 8:00 and 9:00 am soldiers would conduct their private business in latrine areas marked by flags that were out of bounds for snipers on both sides.

So how was this possible, this spontaneous truce? This spontaneous cooperation in the midst of a deadly conflict situation? Research on the question shows that the unique characteristic of trench warfare led to first communication and then cooperation. The same small combat units were faced off against each other for extended periods of time. The soldiers of these opposing small units acted against orders from their own high commands to cooperate with each other in a literal "live and let live" system. So even in these unlikely situations, cooperation can get a foothold, it can evolve, and it can even remain stable in situations which otherwise appear unpromising. Friendship isn't necessary for the development of cooperation.

Today, many scholars believe that there is a way to cooperate when it makes sense strategically, even under conditions of potential conflict. Robert Axelrod led the way in crafting cooperation theory with an important book in 1984 called *The Evolution of Cooperation*. Axelrod wanted to identify the conditions necessary for cooperation to emerge, and then discover what actions could be taken to create those conditions. He examined not only trench warfare in World War I, but also an only slightly less contentious forum: The United States Senate.

Axelrod saw that in spite of the self-interest of senators serving their own constituents, and conflicting with other senators, many opportunities presented themselves for these legislators to work with each other, or to exhibit reciprocity.

This principal is nowhere better illustrated than the relationship between Republican Senator Orrin Hatch and the late Senator Edward Kennedy. Beholden to opposing political parties and ideologically opposed as well, these two powerful senators found ways to cooperate and compromise to mutual benefit.

The senate has developed an elaborate set of norms, or folkways. Among the most important of these is the norm of reciprocity—a folkway which involves helping out a colleague and getting repaid in kind. It includes vote trading but extends to so many types of mutually rewarding behavior.

Senator Hatch described the relationship this way:

> We did not agree on much, and more often than not, I was trying
> to derail whatever big government scheme he had just concocted.
> ... We did manage to forge partnerships on key legislation, such as
> the Ryan White AIDS Care Act, State Children's Health Insurance
> Program, and most recently, the Edward M. Kennedy Serve
> America Act. Ted was a lion among liberals, but he was also a
> constructive and shrewd lawmaker. He never lost sight of the big
> picture and was willing to compromise on certain provisions in
> order to move forward on issues he believed important. ... When
> our carefully balanced compromise legislation came to the Senate
> floor, Ted often had to lead the opposition to amendments offered
> by Democratic colleagues that he would rather have supported. But,
> he took the integrity of our agreement seriously and protected the
> negotiated package.

From No Man's land in Belgium to the United States Senate, the decision to
cooperate always involves some risk. What if the other side defects? Does
the payoff justify the risk? This is a conundrum. And this conundrum of
cooperation brings us to my own dilemma in lecturing on cooperation. When
we talk about cooperation, we often default to talking about what game
theorists call the Prisoner's Dilemma. Prisoner's Dilemma was invented in
1950 by a pair of Rand Corporation researchers. We discussed in the last
lecture how the Prisoner's Dilemma has been used to understand the nuclear
arms race in during the Cold War. But we didn't really discuss why.

Now, mention of the Prisoner's Dilemma often elicits both groans of half-
familiarity and raised eyebrows of surprise. This is partly because many have
heard of the game, and partly because many have not. But for both groups,
the same question often arises: Why do we talk so much, even reverentially,
about the Prisoner's Dilemma? What's so special about it?

Just this. This single model captures the dynamic in interactions of all kinds,
even, for example, repeated interactions between foraging stickleback fish.
Experiments show that these small fish—which get their name from the

spines on their back—achieve cooperation using a reciprocity strategy that resembles repeated rounds of the Prisoner's Dilemma game.

This model isn't totally accurate; no model is. But it captures a fundamental dynamic inherent in many interactions—the tension between decisions for short-term self-interest or for long-term cooperative benefit. Like any good model, it is simple and yet it explains much, in everything from evolutionary biology to networked computer systems.

Robert Axelrod notes that the Prisoner's Dilemma model allows scholars from many different fields to talk to each other about strategy across the disciplines—political scientists, economists, sociologists, philosophers, mathematicians, computer scientists, evolutionary biologists. It also allows us to understand why it may be difficult to cooperate in our own interactions, or begin to even trust someone else. As Axelrod notes, understanding the Prisoner's Dilemma can even aid in divorce negotiations.

Let's do a quick review of Prisoner's Dilemma. There are two players. Each player has two choices: to cooperate or to defect. We call it Prisoner's Dilemma because its original form gave us two prisoners who face the choice of informing on each other or remaining silent. Each makes his choice without knowing what the other will do.

Here is a typical payoff to illustrate the game. If both players defect, both players get \$1. If both players cooperate, both players get \$3. If one player defects while the other player cooperates, the defector gets \$5 and the cooperator gets zero. No matter what the other player does, defection yields a higher payoff than cooperation. If you think the other player will cooperate, you should defect. On the other hand, if you think the other player will defect, it still pays for you to defect). Therefore the temptation for both is to defect—this is what we call the dominant strategy. So it seems that cooperation is impossible.

How do we escape this dilemma? We play the game more than once with the same opponent. If we play the game more than once, Robert Axelrod's pioneering work in the 1980s and 1990s shows us that one very simple strategy works to get us out of the dilemma: tit-for-tat.

This is a strategy of simple reciprocity, which cooperates on the first move and then does whatever the other player did on the previous move. Axelrod determined this as the best strategy by means of a computer tournament in which he solicited the best minds in the country to submit computer programs to run iterations of the Prisoner's Dilemma. In the initial research, two rounds of a tournament were held, and the strategy of tit-for-tat won both.

This strategy works best under these five conditions: First, we should avoid unnecessary conflict by cooperating as long as the other player does. Second, we respond quickly in the face of an uncalled-for defection by the other. It is important to respond sooner, rather than later. If you wait to respond to uncalled-for defections, there is a risk of sending the wrong signal—one of weakness. Third, we show forgiveness after responding to a provocation; immediately return to tit-for-tat reciprocity rather than start an escalation. Fourth, we show clarity of behavior so that the other player can recognize and adapt to our pattern of action. Finally, we have to have an expectation that we'll continue the interaction for a long and indefinite period of time. An indefinite number of these interactions is necessary for cooperation to emerge. For cooperation to prove stable, the future must have a sufficiently large shadow. In the lingo of cooperation theory, we must have a lengthy shadow of the future. By pursuing these conditions, we can create an environment of accepted norms, fertile for cooperation.

Many institutions have developed stable patterns of cooperation based upon such similar norms. Diamond markets, for example. Their members exchange millions of dollars worth of goods with only a verbal pledge and a handshake. The key factor is that the participants know they will be dealing with each other again and again. Therefore any attempt to exploit the situation will simply not pay.

There is a lesson here. The strategy of reciprocity succeeds by eliciting cooperation from others, not by defeating them. In many situations, mutual cooperation can be better for both sides than mutual defection. Suppose you want to conduct business abroad, in a country with little or no tradition of contract law. What do you do? Do you draw up detailed contracts listing specific penalties for non-performance of specific tasks? You can ask yourself what good such a detailed contract would be, if broken. What would you gain if you tried to enforce it?

I can speak from experience conducting business abroad in India and Russia. I can conduct business on nothing more than a handshake and an email. I need not be friends with my international partner, nor need we trust each other. And I need not bother with detailed contracts, especially in countries with no tradition of contract law. And so I rely upon reciprocity. I look forward to a long future of cooperation. If the other side defects for a short-term gain, I respond quickly by signaling a clear defection of my own. If cooperation resumes, I ignore the previous defection. If defection persists, both sides forgo future benefits.

In point of fact, I apply Robert Axelrod's theory to my own actions, because, as he says: "The shadow of the future provides the basis for cooperation, even among egoists."

Armed with the cooperative dynamic in mind where the horizon of the future stretches out, we can craft strategies apropos to the moment to maximize our long-term gains. In military affairs, we saw at the beginning of the lecture how the lowliest soldiers on opposing sides began to cooperate with each other to survive, and to ease the daily hardships of life in the trenches. No one directed the cooperation; it emerged on its own in response to individual and mutual needs. And it arose between two sides facing each other for a long period of time with a long shadow of the future: World War I had not ended quickly, and soldiers in Christmas 1914 had no idea how long it might last.

But cooperation with enemies can also be orchestrated from the top of military hierarchies as well. When the dangers and costs of miscommunication become greater than any benefit derived from no cooperation, it lays the groundwork for mutually recognized and orchestrated cooperation.

A familiar example is the "Hot Line" between Washington, D.C., and Moscow. The hotline is a direct secure communication link between the U.S. and Russia that was established in 1963 and directly resulted from the near-catastrophic Cuban Missile Crisis. In that crisis, miscommunication and delays took both countries to the brink of nuclear war—definitely a less than optimal result for both countries.

Over subsequent years, the phone itself has been used a handful of times when elements in the national command structure deemed it necessary that direct superpower communication was necessary.

Apart from the hotline, military establishments are concerned with the problems of unintended escalation and nuclear missteps resulting from a miscommunication. Indeed, during the latter stages of the Cold War, the U.S. and Soviet militaries found several ways to cooperate on some of the most dangerous issues threatening both nations.

The U.S. and Russia were implacable enemies who fought each other politically around the world and, through their proxy countries, fought each other militarily. Yet, both saw the benefit of cooperation in carefully circumscribed areas. Neither side wanted the game they were playing to spiral out of control. They did not want it to leave the agreed-upon board of play nor tempt the other side to violate the rules.

The final cost—nuclear Armageddon—was one neither nation was willing to pay. And so they reached accommodations, particularly in the area of military exercises. Nation states have always used their military forces to communicate to their potential adversaries. From military parades, to military exercises, to nuclear weapons testing, states try to communicate strength, resolve, commitment, readiness. The United States and the Soviet Union engaged in this brinksmanship for decades. India and Pakistan trade intimidating behavior. North and South Korea continually play dangerous war games. The downside to all of this military signaling is that it can be misinterpreted as the real thing. It can have an entirely unanticipated result. What might appear to the signaling side as a clear message can be easily misinterpreted by the side receiving the message. This is particularly true of military exercises.

Complicating the issue is that sometimes military exercises are used to mask an actual intent to invade. The Soviets did this very thing in August of 1968 when they crushed the liberal reforms of Prague Spring in Czechoslovakia with an invasion. Prior to the Soviet invasion of Czechoslovakia in 1968, the Soviets hastily scheduled and held military exercises that served as cover for an actual invasion. NEMEN was a large Soviet mobilization exercise that looked indistinguishable from an actual mobilization for war. Quite suddenly, invading forces from the Soviet Union, Poland, East Germany, Hungary, and Bulgaria quickly occupied Czechoslovakia.

What might prevent the Soviets from another such deception against the West, masking an invasion of West Germany by "exercises?" For that reason, aggressive military exercises might reasonably be interpreted as the prelude to invasion, thus also sparking a preemptive strike by the threatened state. To forestall this possibility, the United States and the Soviets agreed to a regime of mutual inspections of military exercises called Confidence and Security-Building Measures, or CSBMs. This was a form of cooperation between enemies that broke new ground. It incorporated military on-site inspections for the first time, and it was a trial run to test the feasibility of on-site inspections for nuclear weapons. I was a participant who received the Soviet inspectors for their very first inspection of American military exercises in 1987. It was a tense affair. Reciprocity was only just being established. But it laid the groundwork for numerous inspections to come and the development of a regime of military cooperation that lasted throughout the 1990s.

Another extreme example of cooperation between enemies is the designated truce zone on the Demilitarized Zone between North and South Korea. This is a strip of land over 150 miles long and 2.5 miles wide, and it's the most fortified border on Earth, with more than a million soldiers facing each other in a technical state of war that has existed since a cease-fire was agreed-to in 1953. A cease-fire, not a peace treaty, is in force.

Cooperation under these conditions is extremely difficult, especially given that more than 50 Americans and 1000 South Koreans have died in hostilities along this border, just policing it. And yet even under these conditions of mutual deadly hostility, both sides have found it useful to cooperate with each other in accepted and routinized ways. The combatants established a joint security area in the village of Panmunjom on the DMZ, a place we've discussed before.

Discussions between North and South are held in blue buildings that straddle the Military Demarcation Line. This Joint Security Area is a circular area roughly a half-mile in diameter. It serves as a neutral area, where free movement of both sides anywhere within the JSA boundaries. There are several powder-blue, one-story buildings where officials from the two sides meet when necessary. A conference table covered with green velvet sits directly over the border line, and a microphone cable runs down the middle of the table and is recognized as the international border.

Cooperation can emerge elsewhere as well, in less contentious surroundings. Nineteenth-century science reminds us not to count too much on the durability of the systems we create. The Second Law of Thermodynamics explains how systems of order will tend toward disorder and chaos in a process of entropy. But clearly this is not always the case.

Another theory describes a different outcome. In fact the theory of spontaneous order suggests the exact opposite—that out of chaos, social order can emerge spontaneously. This is at the heart of a theoretical notion that regimes of cooperation are possible, if we pursue them.

Theory. When I talk about theory to my students, I sometimes see the eyes begin to glaze over. But a good theory should not just explain, it should predict; it should be useful; it should always link to the real world.

The idea of spontaneous order is one such theory. The theory of spontaneous order describes the emergence of social order from combinations of self-interested individuals who are not intentionally trying to create a system. People even build structures when they're not consciously trying to do so. It suggests that even structures can emerge "spontaneously" through the independent actions of individuals acting in their own interest.

A simple example of this is the dirt path across a meadow. It's likely that no one person chooses to build a path across the meadow in this particular place and direction. Hundreds, perhaps thousands, of people chose to walk that route for their own purposes. As a result, the path—a "structure"—was constructed through this principle of spontaneous order.

The self-regulating market economy is another example of spontaneous order. The market economy is a system animated by people pursuing their economic self-interest in creating value and conducting commerce. The father of modern economics, Adam Smith, called this process "the invisible hand" in his famous work on economics—*The Wealth of Nations*.

In the pursuit of individual self-interest thousands of individuals create a system of economic exchange that regulates itself through prices. Prices inform us of the relative supply and demand of thousands of goods and services. This, of course, stands in contradistinction to Thomas Hobbes's prediction that a world without planned structure would be a war of all against all, where life is "solitary, poor, nasty, brutish, and short." Surely Hobbes's world would be the result in a world without a planned economic allocation method? Given that resources are scarce and humanity's seeming proclivity toward violence would all but guarantee that conflict and bloodshed would occur.

But often as not, peaceful means of exchange are routinized over time as participants recognize the rational self-interest of pursuing cooperative strategies. In business, competing firms sometimes find it necessary to cooperate rather than compete. In fact, cartels and price-fixing would be far more common were they not illegal in many wealthy countries. But even without explicit collusion, firms often refrain from unilateral action in order to avoid unpleasant responses from competitors.

Price wars are an example of what can happen when tacit cooperation breaks down. Price wars benefit consumers, of course, and from that point of view we all enjoy the benefits of competition. But for the firms involved, shrinking profit margins can also make the difference between survival and collapse.

One instance in which businesses cooperate is the "strategic alliance." This is a form of cooperation in which two or more firms align and harmonize their strategic actions. They do this because the benefits of cooperation are greater than that achieved by unfettered competition.

In such an arrangement, companies seek synergy, where the whole result becomes greater than the sum of its parts. At times, strategic cooperation makes sense because other avenues to synergy are closed. For instance, in 2011, the communications giant AT&T ran afoul of the U.S. Justice Department and the Federal Communications Commission when it sought to acquire cellular carrier T-Mobile. The Justice Department thwarted the deal, citing concerns about the effect such a merger might have on consumers.

After retreating, AT&T and T-Mobile pursued instead a cooperative arrangement. AT&T sought access to T-Mobile's cellular airwaves to relieve its own congested network. For its part, T-Mobile, with its small share of the market, sought survival in an industry where scale offers important advantages.

The companies agreed to a seven-year roaming agreement to expand T-Mobile's national coverage. This isn't the optimum solution that the competing companies sought, but it still serves the purpose of a strategic alliance—to obtain synergies unavailable to either company in isolation.

One final surprising example of cooperation in the midst of conflict, even when the conflict is institutionalized in a rigid system. I met and interviewed Alexei Kondaurov in 2005 while working on a project in Moscow, and I find him to be not only an interesting man, but a living example of cooperation theory in action. Until the early 2000s, Alexei worked for Yukos Oil Company as head analyst, after which he became a member of the Duma, the Russian Congress. But Alexei is famous—or infamous—for another former occupation earlier in his career. Alexei Kondaurov served as a KGB general. In fact, Alexei was the general who headed the infamous Fifth Directorate of the KGB, which was responsible for dissident control. It was created in 1967 by KGB head Yuri Andropov. Alexei held the position under Gorbachev until the KGB was restructured and became the FSB. Alexei's job was to crack down on dissidents, to disrupt their protests, to sometimes arrest and detain them.

But Alexei was respected by the dissident community, for Alexei is a pragmatic man. He had a job to do, and he recognized that dissidents have a "job" to do as well—to dissent. Alexei served during the era of Glasnost and Perestroika, and he did not want to brutalize demonstrators nor crack down on them as had been done by his predecessors. They achieved a shaky accommodation. There was an understood line that, if crossed, would provoke a police response. That line varied from protest to protest, but was understood and observed for the most part during the last several Gorbachev years. In essence, this was a mutual survival game, a live-and-let-live rapprochement, a strange and surprising example of cooperation. Yet, this is typical of the kind of game we play when we are faced with repeated interactions with an opponent over time. Especially when our own personal interests may conflict with the larger interests of an organization we may serve.

The problem of cooperation presents us with conundrums that, at first pass, may seem irresolvable. But cooperation theory shows us—and economics confirms—that where people of goodwill wish to better their lives, they always find a way to trade, to exchange, to exist to each other's mutual benefit. They find ways to cooperate in strategies that maximize everybody's welfare.

When Strategy Breaks Down
Lecture 18

W hy do good generals falter at the crucial moment? Why do smart companies do stupid things? Most of us like to believe in the notion of common sense, yet we see numerous examples of suboptimal outcomes in the world of business and elsewhere. In this lecture, we explore some of the systemic obstacles we face when crafting and executing strategy that can lead to these outcomes.

Case Study: Kodak

- Thanks to a strategy of focused research and development, Kodak dominated film manufacturing throughout much of the 20th century. The firm even secured a patent on the first digital camera in 1975 but chose not to develop this technology. Why?

- Part of the explanation lies in the fact that Kodak had spent its entire existence in a relatively slow-moving industry, and it had a set of nondigital core competencies. Shifting itself to compete with consumer electronics firms would have required drastic changes.

With the advent of digital technology, threats to film and camera manufacturers should have been clear.

- Kodak sensed this and began acquiring a variety of firms in digital sectors, though never in a way that contributed to an overall change in strategic focus. Kodak also had a long history of supporting cheap cameras. When disposable, single-use cameras appeared in the late 1980s, they made it hard for Kodak executives to see anything other than film as the bedrock of their profits. Thus, Kodak continued to rely on chemical film as its cash cow.

- Was there a way for Kodak to use some of its existing competitive advantage yet also profit from the shift to digital photography? Perhaps the company could have moved far more aggressively to a leadership position on the output side of the digital photography industry, in finished prints.

- Kodak faced a strategic inflection point and chose to stay its longstanding course, even in the face of overwhelming evidence that the firm's mainstay product line was on the cusp of extinction.

Strategic Masquerade
- The path to crafting good strategy requires closing off some options when we decide to take action. Kodak, for example, was never going to dominate all aspects of digital photography the way it had dominated chemical photography. The company needed to make a strategic choice about what to pursue and what to forgo.

- A strategic masquerade is the phenomenon of substituting something else, such as slogans or operational techniques, in place of the real-world choices of strategy. Some familiar operational techniques include total quality management, benchmarking, best practices, and so on.

- Strip away these trendy programs and you come to the heart of strategic management: the ability to make tradeoffs, to decide to do some things and not others. Making these decisions is an awesome responsibility, and it paralyzes some leaders who are unready for the rigors of setting strategic direction.

- Benchmarking, best practices, and other operational techniques can move the efficiency frontier of an industry forward, but they do not achieve competitive advantage, and they do not constitute strategy.

- As we've said, strategy is about doing things differently, assembling your firm's activities in ways that other firms cannot copy. It's not about the most popular efficiency or cost-cutting program of the moment.

- In our personal lives, too, we sometimes substitute technique for strategy. We fool ourselves into thinking that we are acting strategically or progressing along some path when we are actually absorbing ourselves in minor tasks. Procrastination and routinization of our lives are common manifestations of the strategic masquerade on a personal level.

- It's easy to become absorbed in addressing the demands of today such that we forget the choices of tomorrow. When tomorrow finally comes, we find ourselves unprepared to meet its challenges or grasp the opportunities it presents. Part of this problem comes with the desire to keep all options open.

Strategic Misalignment
- A second way that strategy can be derailed is through misalignment. In any complex organization that has a mission, the working parts must mesh. In strategy, we sometimes find internal, external, or incremental misalignment.

- Internal misalignment can occur among the working parts that constitute the engine of the firm—resources, capabilities, and intentions—or among the organization's structure, operations, and the strategy itself.

  o In our personal lives, the same principle is at work. We develop a strategy—or we think we do—only to find ourselves thwarted repeatedly by systemic obstacles within ourselves. This internal misalignment means we have not addressed the coordination of our resources, capabilities, and intentions.

  o Strategy is much more than setting worthy goals and then striving mightily to achieve them. It means evaluating our resources in light of our strategy and acquiring more resources if necessary. It means developing capabilities as the instrument by which we achieve those goals. And it means, of course, being honest with ourselves with regard to our resources and capabilities.

- External misalignment can occur without warning, over time. It can slip up on us because there is no dramatic change or metaphorical explosion. Slow changes in the external environment can sabotage our strategy. As change occurs, we need to examine its impact and alter our strategy accordingly. If we don't, we can find ourselves out of sync with reality.

  o Military examples we've already considered demonstrate how continued pursuit of internal consistency can result in external misalignment.

  o Generals are often accused of "fighting the last war," and there is more than a little truth to this. The periods between wars are usually times of strategic stagnation for military organizations. Strategists tend to look backward, evaluating what has already happened. They rarely incorporate the future into their deliberations, especially with respect to changes in technology.

  o As we've seen, by the time of the Civil War, the rifle had largely replaced the musket, and ammunition had changed, too, with the adoption of the minié ball. These changes in technology rendered the frontal assault almost suicidal, yet armies on both sides continued using this attack.

  o Fifty-five years later, Europeans made the same mistake in World War I, with even more disastrous results.

- External misalignment, also known as strategy creep, strategic dilution, or strategic erosion, can result from attempting to stay abreast of current changes without any strategic focus.

  o Current resources and personnel are gradually given additional assignments until they are stretched too thin, perhaps to the breaking point.

- At the individual level, we may find ourselves given additional and diverse responsibility at work. Such add-ons may be increasingly far afield from the firm's mission; they leech our time and sap our strength. We are swept along in a kind of chaotic current rather than aboard a ship with a distinct destination.

Conspirators against Strategy

- The elements that conspire against sound strategy include groupthink, bureaucratic politics, overconfidence, loss of focus, and "great idea" people with a "can-do" attitude.

- The term "groupthink" refers to a kind of quasi-philosophy that holds to the principle that group values are right, good, and sought after. This can be a powerful force in organizations that compel groups of executives to think alike and not diverge from the party line. Groupthink destroys the leeway to disagree and allows bad ideas to thrive.

- While groupthink is a pathology of excessive agreement within a group, a second conspirator against good strategy is insufficient agreement as a result of bureaucratic politics.

  - Rather than rational, calculated decision making that yields an optimal strategic result, an organization's actions may be the result of politicking and negotiation by its top leaders.

  - Even if leaders share an overall goal, they inevitably differ in how to achieve it. This leads to bargaining for power. The overall direction that results—the company's "output"—is suboptimal.

  - This kind of internal politics helps clarify what happened at Digital Equipment Corporation (DEC) beginning in 1992. At the time, DEC was faced with the strategic decision of where to direct its focus. The CEO required a consensus decision on this issue from his senior leadership, but after hard bargaining, agreement could not be reached. The result was the announcement of a non-strategy and, ultimately, the faltering of the company.

- A third conspirator against good strategy is overconfidence, the tendency to overestimate our own judgment and knowledge about a situation. When we receive new information, we tend to believe that we understand it without much analysis.

- All these causes of strategic erosion lead to a loss of focus, which is simultaneously a cause and a symptom of strategic erosion. Paradoxically, strategic erosion can also occur as a result of success. Proposed changes in direction are framed as "building on our success" and come clothed in the trendy slogans of the day.

  o A warning sign of this kind of pathology is the news that someone has been brought into a company to "shake things up." This is particularly insidious because it sounds so reasonable, but in fact, its premise is completely false.

  o To borrow a phrase from marketing, "brand equity" cannot be "extended"; it can only be diluted. Coca-Cola has tried numerous times to extend its brand equity, only to find that its brand means "soft drink" and nothing else.

  o Loss of focus may occur when "strategic-sounding" language is used to give a sense of legitimacy to bad ideas or when we fail to learn the lessons of business history.

Strategy Erosion at Walmart
- In April of 2005, Walmart hired a new head of marketing, presumably to "shake things up." By August, Walmart was buying ad space in *Vogue* at a cost of almost $1 million per issue. This placement violated everything the Walmart brand stands for.

- On the heels of this blunder, Walmart continued to experiment, creating supercenters, remodeling, decluttering its shelves, going organic—in short, unfocusing its brand to attract more affluent consumers. And as it made these changes to capitalize on a slowing economy, Walmart also raised prices.

- The simple explanation for why an otherwise smart company made these moves is that Walmart succumbed to overconfidence and mission creep. It lost focus on its core strategic value: "saving people money so they can live better."

Avoiding Strategic Pathologies
- The strategic pathologies we've discussed in this lecture—groupthink, politics, overconfidence, and loss of focus—can all give impetus to decisions that, viewed from the outside, are obviously misguided.

- To avoid these pathologies, we must steer a bold course and maintain our focus against the internal and external forces that threaten it, keeping our eyes on our strategic goal.

Suggested Reading

De Bono, *Think! Before It's Too Late.*

Feinberg and Tarrant, *Why Smart People Do Dumb Things.*

Hughes-Wilson, *Military Intelligence Blunders.*

Mintzberg, Ahlstrand, and Lampel, *Strategy Bites Back.*

Rumelt, *Good Strategy, Bad Strategy.*

Questions to Consider

1. You doubtless know people who are tactically and technically proficient, but who, for some reason, never rise above the mundane or routine. One reason for this may be the substitution of task-oriented technique for actual strategic thinking. Examine your own approach to your plans and assess whether you absorb yourself in detailed execution in the absence of genuine strategic thinking; if so, act to correct that now.

2. Total quality management and Six Sigma are identified in the lecture as fine management tools but not actual strategies. Consider whether management tools in your own firm have substituted for actual strategy; distinguish these techniques and then identify your firm's actual strategy.

3. Real strategy requires tradeoffs and the boldness to assume risk; technique provides a comfortable substitute, in both our personal lives and the world of commerce. Choosing what to do also means choosing what not to do, so that resources are not squandered in trying to be all things to all people. What difficult conscious tradeoffs have you made in your personal strategic plan? If you find that you've made none, then it may be time to reexamine your approach.

When Strategy Breaks Down
Lecture 18—Transcript

Why do good generals falter at the crucial moment? Why do smart companies do stupid things? You know what I'm referring to. You see it all the time. You read in the newspapers about a company launching a new product, or taking a new initiative, or announcing a new acquisition—real head-scratchers. And you wonder to yourself, "Do they know something that I don't?"

The answer is usually, no, they don't know something that you don't. In fact, your first impression is probably the correct impression. We know that even the best-laid plans can go awry. There is, in fact, a folk-law that dictates this. We call it Murphy's Law—anything that can go wrong, will go wrong. But this also can serve as an excuse for constructing and executing bad strategy, even in the face of overwhelming evidence that the chosen course is folly.

In this lecture we explore some systemic obstacles we face when crafting and executing strategy, both within organizations, and in our own personal decision making. For our first example, let's return to the case of Kodak. Smart company, right? At one time, a powerful multinational; dominated not only black-and-white film throughout much of the 20th century, but also color film, starting in the early 1960s, thanks to a strategy of focused research and development; even secured a patent on the first digital camera in 1975. But, unlike with color film, Kodak chose not to develop digital camera technology.

But why? Did Kodak think it was making the best available choice? The warning signs had started early: Sony announced a digital camera in 1981 that would allow printing of images onto paper. But Kodak had spent its entire existence in a relatively slow-moving industry, at least compared to consumer electronics firms like Sony. Kodak had a set of non-digital core competencies, and shifting itself to compete with consumer electronics firms like Sony would have required especially drastic changes. Kodak even sensed this, and began acquiring a variety of firms in digital sectors, though never in a way that contributed to an overall change in strategic focus.

Moreover, Kodak had a long history, going all the way back to 1900, of supporting cheap cameras, and sometimes even giving them away, in order to get more and more customers hooked on using chemical film. When disposable, single-use cameras appeared in the late 1980s, those throw-away cameras again made it hard for Kodak executives to see anything other than film as the bedrock for their profits. So Kodak continued to rely upon its cash cow—chemical film—which had served the company well for more than 100 years.

But the threats should have been clear. Now, what about the opportunities? What might Kodak have done? Was there a way for Kodak to use some of its existing competitive advantage, yet also profit from the shift to digital photography? Well, even digital photos are printed, and Kodak had traditionally been the leader in finished prints. Maybe Kodak could have moved far more aggressively to lead in finished prints of all kinds. The "Kodak Moment" might have been re-positioned as a brand on the final output side of the vast new digital photography industry. Maybe so. However, Kodak's actual strategy appeared to be: Stay the course, even in the face of overwhelming evidence that the firm's mainstay product line was on the cusp of extinction.

Do you need me to tell you that this was a bad decision? No, you could tell me beforehand that this was a bonehead decision. Digital photography was not a "nice to have," whose pursuit might dilute the company's focus. No, digital photography was a strategic inflection point that put the company's very survival at risk—this was a bad strategic move.

So why do smart companies do strategically stupid things? And why do smart people sometimes do strategically stupid things? Why do we seem so susceptible to gaffes and bonehead decisions in business, in politics, in military conflict, and in sports?

In this lecture, we learn the ways that our environment can deceive and pressure us. We learn how our own psychological limitations can skew our judgment with regard to crafting and executing prudent strategy. We learn how things go wrong strategically and why, in the face of overwhelming evidence, we pursue a futile strategy.

We pursue three main points: First, we look at what I call the strategic masquerade. Second, we look at how strategy can be derailed because of misalignment of various types. And third, we learn to beware the disease of incrementalism, or what has been variously called call strategy creep or strategic dilution or strategic erosion. This is how a good strategy can eventually, almost inevitably, go bad. Here we learn how to recognize the various imposters that masquerade as strategy so we can avoid the traps and pitfalls of faux strategic thinking.

First, the strategic masquerade. In business, the path to crafting good strategy is not an easy road. It requires courage and sacrifice. It requires tradeoffs. When we decide to actually take action, it means that we close off our other options. We can't do all of the other things that tempt us. It's like choosing a college. Having all of our options open is great, and receiving acceptances to our top three choices is great as well. But eventually, we must choose a college—one college—and forsake the others.

Strategy is like that. We have to choose not to do certain things. To trek down a chosen path, we choose not to take the many other paths open to us. Kodak was never going to dominate all aspects of digital photography the way it had dominated chemical photography, not even if it made acquisitions across a bunch of different technologies. Kodak needed to make a strategic choice about what to pursue and what to forego.

Moreover, we often find that leaders play a strategic masquerade. They substitute something else in place of the real-world choices of strategy. They substitute slogans, or they substitute an operational technique, and they call it strategy. You've probably heard of at least some of these operational techniques: TQM, benchmarking, The Search for Excellence, best practices, Six Sigma, reengineering, business process management.

Strip away these slogans and trendy programs for doing the same old thing, just a little more or a little better, and you come to the heart of strategic management—the ability to make tradeoffs, to decide to do some things and not others, to sacrifice all other options in favor of the option that you select. It is an awesome responsibility, and it paralyzes some leaders who are unready for the rigors of setting strategic direction.

For some, especially if times are good, substituting techniques or jargon for strategy is common. Benchmarking, best practices, TQM, and such like. These are superb techniques, but they do not constitute strategy. They move the efficiency frontier of an industry outward, but they do not achieve competitive advantage. These techniques are great, but that's all they are—techniques. They are techniques that any company can and probably should adopt. They can reduce costs and add to the bottom line. But they aren't strategy, and they certainly are not the source of lasting competitive advantage. When all the competitors in our industry adopt the programs I just mentioned, then the entire industry grows more efficient, but no one has more than a momentary advantage.

Strategy is about doing things differently. It's about assembling your firm's activities in ways that other firms cannot copy. It's not about the efficiency or cost-cutting program du jour. And it's about the courage to act, not just conduct a masquerade. In our personal lives, too, we sometimes substitute technique for strategy. We fool ourselves into thinking that we act strategically or progress along some path when actually we absorb ourselves in minor tasks. We spin on the treadmill of procedures. We dabble in the peripherally significant instead of tackling the centrally important.

One example of this pathology is procrastination. It's the most common manifestation of the strategic masquerade on a personal level. Another example is the day-to-day plodding and routinization of our personal lives. Activity is mistaken for action, and movement is mistaken for progress. Perhaps you know people of this sort—people unable to transition from ideas to action, people who believe that meeting and discussing a subject is tantamount to addressing it and executing a plan. There is nothing wrong with this type of behavior—nothing at all—if you are satisfied with short-term thinking. It is a life of tactics, where the tactics are unconnected with each other in a grand scheme.

We can become absorbed in addressing the demands of the day such that we forget the choices for tomorrow. And when tomorrow finally comes, we find ourselves unprepared to meet the challenge or to seize the moment or to grasp the opportunity. And part of this problem comes with the desire to keep all options open. Every leader has this problem, and every person who wants to think strategically has this problem. For once a strategic decision is made, all other options are foreclosed, and this can be a painful thing to accept. Think of the choice of college major, or choice of career, or even the choice of a vacation destination. Think of deciding between job offers. Remember the truism that what we want to be five years from now should inform what we do today.

Now, let's look at the second way strategy can be derailed. This can result because of misalignment of various types. What do I mean by misalignment? In business or in sports or in any complex organization that has a mission, its working parts have to mesh; they have to "fit together." They must fit together snugly for the firm to run smoothly. It's very much like a complex machine; all the bolts must be tightened and all the parts must be appropriate to the machine. The machine's activities must be appropriate to its purpose. All of the elements must align with each other.

For a more exciting analog, think of a team of oarsmen, pulling in unison to move a boat as rapidly as possible across the water. Pulling in unison, in alignment—that's key. If even one oarsman "misaligns," the oars tangle; the ship falters.

In strategy, we can have internal misalignment, external misalignment, and incremental misalignment. Internal misalignment can occur among the working parts that constitute the engine of our firm—resources, capabilities, and intentions. "Capabilities" can mean the organizations' structure and operations—the way it gets things done. Misalignment among the organization structure, operations, and the strategy itself, can occur. We must have internal consistency. For instance, we know intuitively that Google is a much different company that the Mexican cement conglomerate CEMEX. We sense that the operations are different and that the type of person working for each company differs dramatically by company. We anticipate that the operations and structure of Google would be misaligned to implement the strategy of CEMEX, and vice versa.

In our personal lives, the same principle is at work. We develop a strategy—or we think we do—only to find ourselves thwarted repeatedly by systemic obstacles within ourselves. That's internal misalignment. This internal misalignment means we have not addressed the coordination of our resources, our capabilities, and our intentions. You see, strategy is much more than setting worthy goals and then striving mightily to achieve them. It means evaluating our resources in light of our strategy—and acquiring more resources if necessary. It means developing capabilities as the instrument by which we achieve those goals. And it means, of course, being honest with ourselves with regard to all of this. Beware of internal misalignment—ensure than your resources, capabilities, and intentions fit together.

Now, external misalignment. External misalignment can occur without warning, over time. It can slip up on us because there is no dramatic change or metaphorical explosion. There is no signpost to tell us "warning—misalignment ahead!" Slow changes in our external environment can sabotage our strategy, even if we are internally consistent, even if we are doing the current things right.

This type of misalignment occurs when there is some change in the external environment that radically impacts us personally, or impacts our firm or our industry. As change occurs, we have to examine the impact of the change and alter our strategy accordingly. If we don't, we can find ourselves out of sync with reality. We can find ourselves misaligned with the external environment. This is what happened to Kodak.

Military examples we've already considered demonstrate perhaps even more clearly how continued pursuit of internal consistency can result in external misalignment. Generals are often accused of "fighting the last war," and there is more than a little truth to this. The periods between wars are usually times of strategic stagnation for military organizations. Even while some in the military always strive to learn the lessons of the last war, in practice, most analysis stops when the last bullet is fired. Perhaps only those losers from the last war who are certain they want a rematch will be really motivated to look ahead to how the next war might be different. For the most part, strategists look backward, evaluating what has already happened. They rarely incorporate the horizon of the future into their deliberations, especially with respect to changes in technology. As a result, strategic misalignment can occur as militaries execute their internally consistent strategies against each other, with devastating results. This, as we've seen, is what happened both in the American Civil War and in the First World War.

In 1861, Napoleonic principles of war, as presented by the great military theorist Jomini, still held sway in the United States, both in the North and South. But the technology of war had changed, with the rifle replacing the musket in large quantities for the first time. Ammunition, too, had changed, with the adoption of the Minié ball, named for Claude-Étienne Minié. This ammunition allowed soldiers to reload their rifled muskets faster and fire them more accurately, and this meant that the rate of fire against advancing infantry was increased, as was the distance at which they could be engaged.

This change in technology rendered the preferred method of frontal assault in closely packed ranks almost suicidal. And yet armies on both sides continued their frontal assaults. Fifty-five years later, Europeans who ignored United States Civil War made the same mistake in World War I, only with even more murderous results.

If anything, the European strategies of the time were even more focused on frontal assaults, executed using technology made even more outdated by the arrival of magazine-loading, small-bore rifles, quick-firing artillery, and machine guns.

We know what happened in World War I: the squandering of an entire generation by the infantry charge into the teeth of machine gun fire, with the resulting millions of lives lost in four years of European War. But we often fail to learn the lesson from that catastrophe for our own projects and pursuits: Beware of misalignment between your strategy and the external environment presented by new technology.

This brings us to a third type of strategic misalignment—one that can result from attempting (but without any strategic focus) to stay abreast of current changes. Instead of a clever course correction, the result can be a creeping incremental misalignment. Beware the disease of incrementalism, or what has been variously called strategy creep or strategic dilution or strategic erosion. This is how a good strategy can eventually, almost inevitably, go bad. The culprits are the folks who add-on to the mission of the organization.

The military calls it "mission creep." This happens when current forces in-place are given additional assignments one-by-one—nothing too onerous or too far afield.

These can be tricky. Starbucks deciding to broaden the menu of things to eat with its coffee—maybe that's a good way to deepen its advantage as a third destination, after home and work. So how about sandwiches and coffee? And how about a range of deli meats?

And yet, *in toto*, we suddenly find resources and personnel for the original mission stretched, maybe to the breaking point, unable to perform the mission they were originally assigned and originally designed for. At a more individual level, we find ourselves given additional and diverse responsibility at work, increasingly far afield from the offices' mission. Add-ons that leech our time, sap our strength. We lose focus on our particular mission and we endure a relentless expansion of busywork. We find ourselves swept along in a kind of chaotic current rather than aboard a ship with a distinct destination.

These are the conspirators against us: groupthink, bureaucratic politics, overconfidence, loss of focus, "great idea" people with the "can-do" attitude. The first conspirator against good strategy is groupthink. Four years after George Orwell wrote his dystopian novel entitled *1984*, the Orwellian term "Groupthink" first appeared in a 1952 article published in Fortune magazine. Coined in 1952 by an organizational theorist named William Whyte, this doesn't refer to the instinctive conformity in each of us, the yearning to belong to some group. Groupthink refers to a kind of quasi-philosophy, which holds that group values are right, good, and sought after.

Groupthink is a powerful force in organizations that compels groups of executives to think alike and not diverge from a party line. Divergence from that party line is derided as "negative" or "counterproductive." While there is some merit to the notion that upbeat, positive attitudes are desirable in a firm, there comes a point where honesty trumps optimism. But groupthink destroys the leeway to disagree, and it brands those who do disagree as mavericks or troublemakers. Bad ideas can thrive in such an atmosphere, and strategy is a vulnerable target.

While groupthink is a pathology of excessive agreement within a group, a second conspirator against good strategy is insufficient agreement, due to in-group politics, what is sometimes called bureaucratic politics. This is an organizational behavior concept borrowed from political science, and it refers to a failure to reach productive agreement at all in support of a strategic direction.

If we think of an organization as a black box that receives inputs and then delivers outputs, so-called bureaucratic politics explains what goes on inside the box in a particular way. Rather than rational, calculating decision making that yields an optimum strategic result, bureaucratic politics says that we can understand an organization's actions as the result of politicking and negotiation by its top leaders. As you well-know, any organization has different departments that compete with each other for budget dollars, for new programs, and for primacy.

Even if leaders share an overall goal, they inevitably differ in how to achieve it. This leads to bargaining for power. The overall direction that results—the company's "output"—is sub-optimal. This kind of internal politics helps clarify what happened at Digital Equipment Corporation.

In 1992, Digital Equipment Corporation was faced with a strategic decision of great import. It could select a direction to take, but only one. The three options were to focus on computer hardware manufacture, consulting IT solutions for clients, or semi-conductor chips. The CEO at the time, Ken Olsen, made a pivotal decision to require a consensus direction from his senior leadership to proceed. After hard bargaining among the proponents, they could not achieve consensus. The resulting non-strategy announced by DEC was a travesty: "DEC is committed to providing high-quality products and services and being a leader in data processing." This, of course, is no strategy at all. Bureaucratic politics had yielded a suboptimal decision and substituted a slogan for actual strategy. The company faltered and in 1998 was acquired by Compaq, which then was acquired by Hewlett-Packard.

A third conspirator against good strategy is overconfidence. High spirits and optimism often characterize the C-Suite, or executive suite. They also characterize much of what we do in our daily lives, especially when harnessed to a goal we truly want to achieve. As a result, we tend to overestimate our own judgment and knowledge about a situation. When we receive new information, we tend to slot this new information into the grooves meant for old facts. We then tend to believe that we understand the new situation without much analysis. We are overconfident, and we do not give pause for healthy circumspection.

In an article called "Cocksure," Malcolm Gladwell put it this way:

> As novices, we don't trust our judgment. Then we have some success, and begin to feel a little surer of ourselves. Finally, we get to the top of our game and succumb to the trap of thinking that there's nothing we can't master. As we get older and more experienced, we overestimate the accuracy of our judgments, especially when the task before us is difficult and when we're involved with something of great personal importance.

A fourth conspirator against good strategy is loss of focus. All of the foregoing causes of strategic erosion lead to a loss of focus, which is simultaneously a cause of strategic erosion, even as it is one of its symptoms. Paradoxically, strategic erosion can occur as a result of success. Proposed changes in direction are framed as "building on our success," and they come clothed in the trendy slogans of the day.

"Change agents" tell us we must "change with the times." Sometimes we forget that the change agent's job is to get us to change, regardless of circumstances. Marketing people invariably utilize the destructive phrase "Extend our brand equity" to justify strategic changes that inevitably erode a particular brand.

A warning sign for this kind of pathology is the use of a phrase we're all familiar with: "Shake things up." When you hear that someone has been brought into a company to "shake things up," watch for that company to start losing focus.

This is particularly insidious, because it sounds so reasonable. But, in fact, its premise is completely false. Brand equity cannot be "extended." It can only be diluted. Coca-Cola has tried numerous times to "extend" its brand equity. One such "brand extension" left retailers saddled with millions of dollars in inventory of Coca-Cola–branded clothing. Coke found that its brand means "soft drink" and nothing else.

Because strategy is generally misunderstood, incredibly bad actions can often get through the screen of common sense because it's couched in strategic-sounding language. Jargon can give a sense of legitimacy to bad ideas. Loss of focus occurs because many otherwise bright people are generally ignorant of business history. Bad ideas often resurface every 10 to 15 years, dressed in new clothing and carrying a new phrase or trendy slogan. We are, in fact, so bereft of history that we seem doomed to repeat not only the errors of the past, but to implement entire failed programs of the past. Such ignorance leaves us vulnerable to satin slogans that sound reasonable but actually have been tried, and which have failed.

Let's look at a stupendous example of strategy erosion in one of America's great companies. Think of Wal-Mart—one of the most-hated, or most-loved companies, depending on your point of view. Regardless of that point of view, we must acknowledge that Wal-Mart is, indeed, a great success story. It's the world's largest company and it employs more than 2 million people. Surely, the company that Sam Walton founded in 1962 is doing something right. And yet, Wal-Mart sometimes gets things spectacularly wrong, particularly where strategy is concerned.

Let's revisit Wal-Mart's bizarre activity in 2005. In April of that year, the company hired a new head of marketing, presumably to "shake things up." As you might expect, by August, Wal-Mart was buying ad space in *Vogue* magazine at a cost of almost $1 million per issue. Yes, *Vogue* magazine. When I tell this to even my most inexperienced students, they immediately recognize it as foolhardy. It makes no sense. It violated everything the Wal-Mart brand stands for. "Everyday Low Prices."

On the heels of this blunder Wal-Mart continued to experiment, hiring a change agent to "get the blood flowing," as *Advertising Age* put it. Eleven months later, the change agent was fired. Wal-Mart continued its experimentation, creating supercenters, remodeling, decluttering shelves by reformulating its brand mix, going organic, unfocusing its brand to attract more-affluent consumers. But as Wal-Mart moved to attract well-heeled customers in order to capitalize on a slowing economy, it raised prices.

Why would a "smart" company act this way? Any first-year marketing student could have told you it was unwise. Most any person on the street could have told you it was unwise. You could have told them it was unwise. Wal-Mart had succumbed to overconfidence and mission creep. Wal-Mart's CEO during 2000 to 2009, H. Lee Scott Jr., wanted the clothing in the company's stores to sell as well as basic goods. And so a 19-year executive from Target was promoted to the position of chief marketing officer to make Wal-Mart clothes appealing to a wider audience. But in the process, Wal-Mart forgot about its core customers. No longer could Wal-Mart's core customers count on a low-price guarantee on every item. Wal-Mart lost focus on its core strategic value: "saving people money so they can live better." Only in 2011 did Wal-Mart acknowledge its mistakes as it began restoring the shopping experience that made the retailer great.

In this lecture, we have seen how strategy can break down. How obstacles to good strategy can be significant. We've seen how on occasion, smart companies can sometimes do strategically stupid things, and how smart people sometimes do strategically stupid things as well. Groupthink, in-group politics, overconfidence, and sheer loss of focus can all give an impetus to decisions that look hopelessly misguided from the outside. We are all susceptible to gaffes and bonehead decisions. We have to be on-guard against the many ways that our environment can deceive and pressure us. How it can erode our strategy. We must always steer a bold course and maintain our focus against all of the malignant external forces that threaten it, keeping our eyes on our strategic goal, and securing our strategy itself against the forces that would sabotage it.

Leverage Cognitive Psychology for Better Strategy
Lecture 19

The mind is complex, and understanding how it reaches decisions is the subject of entire fields of science and social science. In this lecture, we explore some of the theories and their practical applications that can help us cultivate the skills to improve our decisions and to avoid some of the pitfalls of irrational decision making.

Thinking about Thinking
- Most of us think of ourselves as rational people when it comes to making decisions. We investigate a bit, strive to be objective, and come to a conclusion, but the fact is that we don't think very much about thinking. We remain unaware of the brain's functions even as it yields results to us.

- How we perceive, what we remember, how we call upon memory, and how we combine it with new information—these functions occur independently of any conscious direction on our part. All we know for certain are the results of our thought processes.

A Model of Thinking
- An early model of how we think posited that we are rational beings who seek to maximize our utility. We consider a range of likely options and make the best choice. The social scientist Herbert Simon modified this assumption with his notion of "bounded rationality."

- Simon's fundamental insight was that the world is too complex to allow us to consider all the information at our disposal. Instead, we decide in an environment of bounded rationality, meaning rationality with limits—limits of information, cognition, and time.

- Research confirms that before our minds ever begin to grapple with rational decision making, the brain automatically filters incoming information to make it more manageable. It reduces the choices for us on the basis of experience, education, cultural values, and so on.

- For this reason, our mental models don't always match up well with reality, particularly in high-stress, high-stakes situations. The mind simply can't cope with the vast sea of incoming information, so it constructs a simplified mental model of reality, and that's what we work with. Within the boundaries of this model, we act rationally.

Groupthink

- CIA veteran Richards Heuer writes, "An experienced specialist may be among the last to see what is really happening when events take a new and unexpected turn. When faced with a major paradigm shift, analysts who know the most about a subject have the most to unlearn."

- In 1989–1990, CIA specialists were slow to see and understand the implications of the Soviet withdrawal from Eastern Europe on East and West Germany or realize how quickly the reunification of Germany would take place. In this case, generalists in the agency could see and accept what the specialists were missing.

- A mindset is a collection of assumptions or methods held and used by one or more people or groups of people. It can become so ingrained that it creates and perpetuates a powerful conformity of approaches, tools, and assumptions. We speak of "groupthink" whenever the mindset of a group of people becomes especially entrenched.

- One of the most well-known examples of groupthink is the Cold War mindset that led to myopia on the part of the U.S. foreign policy establishment. Our nation allied itself with unsavory regimes in the 1950s–1970s to counter what was perceived as Soviet aggression in the Middle East, Africa, and elsewhere.

Barriers to Clear Perception

- Accurate analysis is made difficult by a number of strong barriers to perception, including these three: (1) Mindsets tend to be quick to form but resistant to change; (2) we tend to perceive what we expect to perceive; and (3) new information is assimilated to existing images.

- We form mindsets quickly, but they are resistant to change. Once we achieve a certain mindset or accept a certain paradigm, we become locked in to it analytically.

    o A common experiment that illustrates a mind rut involves a graphic with several figures in a row, each more distorted from the original than the last. The gradual transitions can make it difficult to notice that the final image is actually a different subject than the original, not just a distorted version of it.

    o The mind rut suggests what makes sense and ought to be there, but it also suggests what we should ignore. Our earliest experiences have already and mistakenly determined that these new developments are just distortions of a pattern we already know, preventing us from noticing new patterns.

- As our analytical mindsets become rooted, we begin to take shortcuts in our decision making, which means that we tend to perceive what we expect to perceive. Our thinking is based on what we already "know" about a situation, and as a result, we have trouble processing truly new information. Our expectations influence our perceptions.

    o This barrier to perception was evident in World War II, when the head of the Luftwaffe refused to believe that the Allies had developed a long-range fighter plane even after the Germans had shot one down.

    o When Germany attacked the Soviet Union in June of 1941, Stalin's belief in the paradigm of Soviet-German nonaggression was so strong that he refused to believe reports of the attacks from his own units.

    o The errors in the phrases shown in the box illustrate the idea that we have been conditioned to see what we expect to see and to overlook what we don't expect.

Figure 19.1

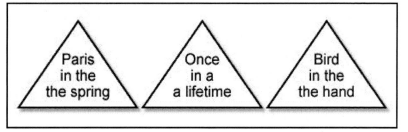

The business of perception is more complicated than most of us realize.

- As we receive information and begin to process it, we also tend to assimilate new information to existing images. In other words, new information is not treated independently but in relation to thought processes already underway.

  o This incremental receipt of information can lead to false conclusions, as occurred before the 1973 Arab-Israeli war, a potential conflict that U.S. intelligence had not anticipated.

- o Analysts were proceeding on the basis of each day's intelligence, assimilating it with the narrative already constructed from the previous day. This gave rise to an ongoing "assembly line" narrative, rather than a coherent understanding of the big picture.

Pathologies in Group Decision Making

- In group decision making and problem solving, the variables multiply with every additional person, complicating what is already a complex process.

- Political considerations enter into the deliberations, along with tendencies of groups to take on dynamics of their own. As we know, people behave differently in groups and in group decision making. They reinforce one another's inclinations, and those who disagree tend to be forced out.

- In his investigation, psychologist **Irving Janis** found that concern for group solidarity and consensus seeking could degrade the quality of strategic decision making. Janis offered as examples the Bay of Pigs invasion decision by Kennedy's team and, later, the cover-up of the Watergate burglary by Nixon and his circle of advisors.

- Eight symptoms of groupthink cluster around three categories: (1) overestimations of the group's power and morality, (2) a tendency toward close-mindedness, and (3) pressures to conform and achieve consensus. When these factors are in play in group dynamics, suboptimal decisions result.

- These suboptimal decisions may be based on an incomplete survey of alternatives or objectives, failure to examine risks of the preferred choice, failure to reevaluate previously rejected alternatives, poor information search, selection bias in collecting information, and failure to work out contingency plans.

Symptoms of Groupthink

- Illusions of invulnerability that create excessive optimism and encourage risk taking

- Unquestioned belief in the morality of the group that causes members to ignore the consequences of their actions

- Rationalization of warnings that might challenge the group's assumptions

- Stereotyping of those who are opposed to the group as weak, evil, biased, spiteful, impotent, or stupid

- Self-censorship of ideas that deviate from the apparent group consensus

- Illusions of unanimity among group members

- Direct pressure to conform placed on any member who questions the group, couched in terms of "disloyalty"

- The existence of "mind guards"—self-appointed members who shield the group from dissenting information

An Analytical Process Model

- Several techniques can be linked together to form an analytical method that helps us think strategically and develop greater insight into any issue that challenges us. These techniques include situational logic, the application of theory, comparison with historical situations, and data immersion.

- The first step in the analytical process model is to define the problem. Here, it's important to articulate the problem in such a way that the answers yielded will make a difference.

- Next, we suspend judgment and identify all the plausible hypotheses that should be considered; then, we trim the list to a workable number of hypotheses for more detailed analysis.

- The next step is to collect information to evaluate all the reasonable hypotheses. Exploring information that supports alternatives you have not yet seriously considered can generate creative thought and new possibilities.

- Next, argue against the hypotheses. You may find that much of the evidence supports your expectation of the most likely hypotheses, but that same evidence may also be consistent with different hypotheses. Proceed by trying to reject hypotheses rather than confirm them.

- Finally, it's important to monitor your analysis for surprises. Our world changes rapidly, and our analytical conclusions are always tentative. Specify critical nodes to monitor for changes that might significantly alter the probabilities.

- When we generate hypotheses, we find ourselves susceptible to coming up with explanations that comport with our store of information, dictated in a fashion by our mindset. Use these techniques to break out of the mind rut:

  o The use of situational logic is an inductive approach that begins with consideration of concrete elements of the current situation rather than generalizations involving similar cases. We regard the situation as unique rather than as a class of events.

  o Application of theory is a deductive approach that reasons from the general to the specific case. It suggests that when a given set of conditions arises, certain other results ought to follow with some degree of probability.

  o Comparison with historical situations is, essentially, the case study method. Historical cases are dissected to understand events and how actors arrived at their decisions, whether good or bad.

o Finally, data immersion involves immersing yourself in data while consciously suppressing any preconceptions. The idea here is that patterns that emerge from the data can then be tested.

Cognitive Psychology Applied to Strategy
- The field of cognitive psychology is always pursuing new research into how the mind works. For strategy, it's especially important to understand both outside distortions that can interfere with analytical clarity and ways that our internal cognitive processes can also distort our perceptions of the outside world.

- Refining our practical understanding of the perplexing world of human behavior takes time, but on that basis, we can learn to craft strategy—and behave strategically—in ways that have a greater chance of success.

Name to Know

Janis, Irving (1918–1990): Few group dynamic theorists can match the impact of Janis in his recognition and study of groupthink as a powerful negative influence on competent decision making. Janis highlighted the dangers of consensus building as a substitute for rational analysis.

Suggested Reading

Allison, *Essence of Decision.*

Halperin, *Bureaucratic Politics and Foreign Policy.*

Heuer, *Psychology of Intelligence Analysis.*

Janis, *Groupthink.*

Jervis, *Perception and Misperception in International Politics.*

Schafer and Crichlow, *Groupthink versus High-Quality Decision Making in International Relations.*

1. Groupthink can plague any level of an organization and often does in the form of a faux consensus about the "facts." One difficult public policy question concerns the American view of Russian President Vladimir Putin. In your view, is there a consensus groupthink at work with respect to views of the Russian president that lingers from the time of Cold War?

2. Does groupthink affect you in any way in your team interactions, and do you feel pressure to conform to groupthink ideas? If so, from where does this pressure arise, and who decides the central notions around which groupthink clusters?

3. Correct analysis is impossible when the original problem is defined incorrectly, and this misspecification is at the heart of much incorrect analysis. From the start, we must ask, "What's going on here?" with a rational, open mind that ensures we do not define the problem so that the answers we search for are what we intend to find beforehand. How do you select and define your main challenges in your group interactions, and is the problem definition usually aligned with your group's mission?

4. The pathologies that inhibit good decision making are many, and it is the rare person who is not affected by at least one or two. After watching the lecture, you probably have a good idea of which are problems for you and which are not. In an honest self-assessment, consider which of the cognitive problems discussed here affect you most and identify how to guard against these tendencies.

Leverage Cognitive Psychology for Better Strategy
Lecture 19—Transcript

Almost everyone would like to be a strategic genius, especially if it required no special investment of time or effort. But the mind is complex, and understanding how it reaches important decisions is the subject of entire fields of science and social science. In this lecture, we step back to explore some of the theories and practical applications of those theories. Our goals are to cultivate skills that can further improve our strategic decision making, as well as avoid some of the pitfalls of irrational decision making.

We also learn what psychology teaches us about how the mind actually functions when making decisions and how to identify and resist outside pressures that can distort our own cognitive processes. We can become better strategic analysts simply by avoiding psychological pitfalls that make us bad analysts.

A strategic personality is more adept than the norm at developing powerful and effective strategy, and we can identify those characteristics and cultivate them. The good news is that keen analysis—which is so central to strategic thinking—can be cultivated. There are cognitive decision-making processes that all people share to a degree. These processes, once understood, can be adjusted to yield advantageous decisions more often than before. We can also learn to avoid the thinking traps that tend to lead us astray.

In turn, we can learn to craft strategy that has a greater chance of success by adapting our strategy to the difficult waters that make up the perplexing world of human behavior. The analytical process can help us discover what it is we do and why. This is where the mind clashes with a confusing outside world and attempts to make sense of it. We learn the barriers to perception and the weaknesses and biases in thinking processes, and why accurate analysis is so, so very tough. We become familiar with the group dynamics that yield suboptimal outcomes. Finally, we learn analytical tools and techniques designed to reveal and to overcome the distortions created by the various pathologies that affect our analysis.

Intelligence analysts think and analyze for a living. They do this perhaps even more intensely and rigorously than many scientists in a laboratory—the stakes can be much higher, the time crunch even greater, and the sources of information and its sheer volume overwhelming. Most important, they are attempting to divine the capabilities and intentions of a moving target—other human beings acting in complex situations. Analysts examine large amounts of data, combing them for clues, patterns, linkages according to a set of priority intelligence requirements. Cognitive psychology has much to say about how we process data and analyze it, especially when we're searching for particular intelligence that either corroborates or disconfirms our hypotheses. The analyst usually works with incomplete and often contradictory data. There are gaps in the information, and what information we do have may be ambiguous. To fill these gaps, the analyst uses what we call judgment. We use this word "judgment" often, but the ultimate nature of judgment remains a mystery.

One dictionary definition of judgment is "the process of forming an opinion, evaluation, estimate, notion, or conclusion by discerning and comparing—as from circumstances presented to the mind." Analysts fill gaps in their knowledge with their judgment. This is a quality built up over time from experience, knowledge, consultation. Judgment necessarily means going beyond the available information. Richards Heuer notes that "it always involves an analytical leap, from the known into the uncertain."

Most of us fancy ourselves cool and rational people when it comes to making decisions. Sure, we'll make snap judgments on trivial issues, but where the big issues of the day are concerned, we believe we're spot-on.

And so we investigate a bit, accept the inputs as they come in, we strive to be objective about the issue at hand, we affect a cool, rational attitude, we come to a conclusion based on the facts and make a decision or recommend a course of action. But the fact is, we don't think about thinking. We don't think anywhere near enough about thinking. This is a basic finding of cognitive psychology. We remain unaware of the brain's functions even as it yields results to us. We get our "mind-product" without knowing its provenance. We don't understand how the human mind does what it does as it copes with an incredibly complex world.

Much of what we know about decision making comes from researchers who study human behavior in decision-making scenarios, both as individuals and in groups. Research has demonstrated, above all, our ignorance of how we think. How we perceive, what we remember, how we call upon that memory, and how we combine it with new information—these functions occur independently of any conscious direction on our part. All we know for certain are the results of our thought processes.

One prominent cognitive psychologist, Reinhard Selten, put it this way: "We may decide what to think about, but not what to think. The results of thinking become conscious, but most of the procedure of thinking remains unconscious and not even accessible to introspection."

We've tried to crack this nut of thinking about thinking. One model of how we think is that we are rational beings who seek to maximize our utility. We consider a range of likely options and we make the best choice. For a long time, this was a fundamental assumption of much economic theory. But it's not really practicable or even true, and most of us know this. But the influential social scientist Herbert Simon modified this assumption and introduced us in 1957 to something he called "bounded rationality."

Thanks to Herbert Simon, we have a way to articulate the fact that we don't make purely rational decisions. Simon's fundamental insight was that we don't consider all information at our disposal. The world is too complex for that. Instead, we decide in an environment of what he called "bounded rationality." This means that our "rationality" has limits. These limits can be information, the cognitive limits of our minds in handling large amounts of data, and the limited time available to us to make decisions.

Simon contended—and subsequent research has confirmed—that before our minds ever begin to grapple with rational decision making, the brain automatically filters the incoming information to make it more manageable. It reduces the choices for us. It does so on the basis of past experience, education, cultural values, role requirements, and organizational norms, as well as by the specifics of the information received. Our mental models don't always match-up well to what's actually out there, particularly in high-stress, high-stakes situations.

The mind simply can't cope with the vast sea of information cascading onto it. And so, the mind constructs a simplified mental model of that reality, and that's what we work with. Within the boundaries of this simplified model of reality, we act rationally. This view of the mind as filter and autonomous model-maker is widely accepted. One of the most influential experts on intelligence analysis is Richards Heuer. He put it this way:

> People construct their own version of "reality" on the basis of information provided by the senses, but this sensory input is mediated by complex mental processes that determine which information is attended to, how it is organized, and the meaning attributed to it.

Ironically, the folks who study a subject most intently and become experts are usually the most susceptible to falling into a reified mindset. This mindset can color and control our perceptions. "An experienced specialist may be among the last to see what is really happening when events take a new and unexpected turn. When faced with a major paradigm shift, analysts who know the most about a subject have the most to unlearn."

An example of this occurred within the CIA during the period of upheaval in Europe in 1989 and 1990 known as the Velvet Revolutions. As the Soviet Union voluntarily withdrew from Eastern Europe, the reunification of Germany was suddenly on the international agenda. Specialists on the former East and West Germany were slow to see and understand the implications of what was happening in Eastern Europe and how fast it would happen. In this case, generalists in the agency could see and accept what the specialists were missing. The encrusted mindset of the specialists had not encompassed the possibility of rapid change of this sort.

Such a mindset is just one of the problems blocking our clear understanding of what is happening in the world around us, particularly the issues we focus on as most important. A mindset is a set of assumptions or methods held and used by one or more people or groups of people. A mindset can become so ingrained that it creates and perpetuates a powerful conformity of approaches, tools, and unquestioned assumptions for analysis. We can speak of "groupthink" whenever the mindset of a group of people becomes especially locked in on itself. In one sense, any mindset eliminates certain possibilities and hypotheses; it squelches them before they can even emerge to be considered.

One of the most well-known is the Cold War mindset that led to myopia on the part of the U.S. foreign policy establishment. This myopia led to a framing focused almost exclusively on the U.S.-Soviet Superpower rivalry. This two-actor rivalry colored conflict around the world. Because of this, anti-colonial and nationalist movements were automatically assumed to be part of the Soviet architecture for world revolution. It fostered reliance upon two-player game theory to explain what was going on, but which actually obscured what was going on in what was then commonly called the Third World. The Cold War mindset led the U.S. to ally itself with certain unsavory regimes in the 1950s, 1960s, and 1970s to counter what were perceived as aggressive Soviet moves in the Middle East, Africa, and Central and South America.

This doesn't mean that mindset is inherently bad. In fact, for any aspiring strategic thinker, the point is to cultivate a strategic mindset—that is, a set of methods and assumptions most conducive to effective strategy. But there exist a number of strong barriers to perception, and this is why accurate analysis is so tough. Generally speaking, decision makers face major challenges with respect to uncertainty. The human brain has trouble dealing with the natural "fog of conflict." On top of that, the brain has to parse out the artificial uncertainty that opponents generate to deceive us. Finally, even as we grapple with this welter of uncertainties, our own natural biases and cognitive limitations impinge on our perception of these issues.

As you can see, we have several issues that can interfere with accurate perception. This business of perception is really more complicated than most of us realize. Barriers to clear perception can warp our analyses, cause us to stumble, and lead us unknowingly astray. Group decision-making dynamics make our task even more demanding.

Here are just three of the barriers to our understanding. First, mind-sets tend to be quick to form but resistant to change. Second, we tend to perceive what we expect to perceive. Third, new information is assimilated to existing images.

Our mindset—we form mind-sets quickly, but they are resistant to change. Once we achieve a certain mindset or we accept a certain paradigm with regard to a group of issues, it locks us in analytically. It can become a mind -rut. It's difficult to crowbar ourselves out of that mindset, even when we become aware of inaccuracies in that mindset.

A common experiment that illustrates a mind-rut is a graphic with several figures in a row, each more distorted from the original than the last. The sequence is carefully prepared so that the concluding image is actually an entirely different subject than the original. For example, when subjects begin with the first figure they might see image of a man's face, but looking at each in turn, at some point, the figure of a woman may begin to be seen. The gradual transitions can make it quite difficult to notice that the final image is actually a quite different image, not just a distorted version of the original. By contrast, subjects who are shown a single image recognize the "changed" image as a man or woman sooner than those who view the image in a context of prior expectations.

The mind-rut suggests what makes sense and ought to be there, but it also suggests what we should ignore. In this way, our earliest experiences have already and mistakenly determined that these new developments are mere warts and distortions on a pattern we already know, and preventing us from noticing new patterns that we ought to be noticing.

We tend to perceive what we expect to perceive. As our analytical mind-sets become rooted, we begin to take shortcuts in our decision making. We think in repertoires, routines, and standard operating procedures. We think based on what we already "know" about a situation and as a result, we have trouble processing truly new information. We interpret it and assimilate it with what we think we already know. Our expectations influence our perceptions. In short, you see what you expect to see, and you don't see what you expect not to see. Politicians, scientists, analysts, and businessmen retain these types of pre-existing images and beliefs, even in the face of discrepant information. We become vested in our mindsets.

Famous examples come to us from conflict. In World War II, the Germans shot down an allied fighter over Aachen. This indicated that the allies had developed a long-range fighter plane to escort their bombers over Germany. But when informed of this information, the head of the German Luftwaffe said: "I'm an experienced fighter pilot myself. I know what is possible [and] what isn't. ... I officially assert that American fighter planes did not reach Aachen. ... I herewith give you an official order that they weren't there."

When Germany attacked the Soviet Union in June of 1941, Joseph Stalin refused to believe the reports from his own units under attack. He had been warned by the U.S., British, and his own intelligence sources that an attack was imminent. He ignored them. Belief in the paradigm of Soviet-German nonaggression was so strong as to overrule actual reports of the attack. Soviet units that reported the German attacks were not believed, and they were ordered not to respond to "provocation" by firing back. It took two full weeks for Stalin to process the dissonant information that had challenged his mindset with regard to Germany. In that period, it's reported that he suffered a short-lived nervous breakdown.

As you see, expectations can be very strong. We develop our expectations from many different sources, such as past experience, professional training, and cultural and organizational norms. And sometimes just habit.

Look at these diagrams, each with a well-known phrase. Now look again. Did you notice the additional word? It's more than likely that you didn't. Because we have been conditioned to see what we expect to see and overlook that which we do not expect.

We tend to assimilate new information to existing images. The order in which we received information can affect how it's used. We receive information and we begin to process and build our story. Additional information is then added to the story and substantiates it. In this way, subsequent information is treated not independently, but in relation to thought processes and theories already underway. When we receive information this way, in small increments, we tend to assimilate it into our existing worldview. This incrementalism can lead us to false conclusions. This happened to the U.S.

intelligence community prior to the 1973 Arab-Israeli war, a possible conflict that U.S. intelligence had not anticipated.

Analysts were proceeding on the basis of the day's intelligence received, rapidly assimilating it with the narrative already constructed from the previous day. This gave rise to an ongoing "assembly line" intel narrative rather than a coherent understanding of the big picture derived from systematic consideration of an accumulated body of integrated evidence.

Finally, the group dynamic that yields suboptimal outcomes is revealed. What about group decision making and problem-solving? Several pathologies afflict decision making in groups. The variables go up with every additional person, complicating what is already a very complex process.

Political considerations enter into the deliberations along with tendencies of groups to take on dynamics of their own. In other words, a group is much more than the sum of the individuals who comprise them. People behave differently in groups and in group decision making. They reinforce each others' inclinations. Those who disagree tend to be forced out and replaced with "team players."

Irving Janis investigated the effects of group dynamics on decision making and found that concern for group solidarity and consensus-seeking could degrade the quality of strategic decision making. Janis offered as examples the Bay of Pigs invasion decision by President John F. Kennedy's team in 1961 and, later, the cover-up of the Watergate burglary in 1973 and 1974 by President Richard Nixon and his circle of advisors. Both political crises exhibited symptoms of groupthink that led to a series of poor decisions resulting in disasters in both cases.

These eight symptoms cluster around the overestimations of the group's power and morality, a tendency toward close-mindedness, and pressures to conform and achieve consensus: illusions of invulnerability that create excessive optimism and encourage risk taking; unquestioned belief in the morality of the group that causes members to ignore the consequences of their actions; rationalizing warnings that might challenge the group's assumptions; stereotyping those who are opposed to the group as weak, evil, biased, spiteful, impotent, or stupid; self-censorship of ideas that deviate from the apparent group consensus; illusions of unanimity among group members, silence is viewed as agreement; direct pressure to conform placed on any member who questions the group, couched in terms of "disloyalty"; mind guards—self-appointed members who shield the group from dissenting information.

When the above factors are in play in group dynamics, suboptimal decisions result. These include: incomplete survey of alternatives; incomplete survey of objectives; failure to examine risks of the preferred choice; failure to re-evaluate previously rejected alternatives; poor information search; selection bias in collecting information; failure to work out contingency plans.

One typical pathological result of groupthink is to settle on the first available alternative instead of identifying the best available alternative.

We see that how decision-making groups are structured and perform have a powerful effect on the policies that come out of them. Leaders can move groups, such as committees, toward either greater successes or greater losses, depending on how the group is composed and how it takes in information, evaluates options, and arrives at a decision. When members of a group know how to avoid groupthink, the group can come to a much better decision for the group itself, as well as those whom the group represents.

We've seen many of the internal cognitive obstacles that obscure reality, hinder our understanding, and block clear analysis. Analytical skill can be acquired with practice and the use of tools and techniques to overcome these challenges. Here, first, is an analytical process model that aids our decision making and ensures that various courses of action are considered. I follow this model with several specific tactics that can generate hypotheses that may be outside your usual comfort area.

We use these analytical techniques to enhance our generation of plausible hypotheses and to correct cognitive distortions. These include: situational logic, the application of theory, comparison with historical situations, and data immersion. Moreover, the various techniques can be linked together to form an analytical method that helps us think strategically and delve deeper into any issue we grapple with.

Defining the problem—this is where we ask, what's going on here? What is actually going on? Are we defining the problem so that the answers yielded will make a difference? Of course, this can often be the toughest part of the challenge. That's why we have other techniques.

Generating hypotheses—suspend judgment and identify all the plausible hypotheses that should be considered. Brainstorm, and then trim the list to a workable number of hypotheses for more detailed analysis. Don't screen out reasonable hypotheses only because there is no ready evidence to support them.

Collecting information—collect information to evaluate all the reasonable hypotheses, not just the one you already have in mind, the one that seems likely. When you explore information supporting alternatives that have not been seriously considered before, it can generate creative thought and new possibilities.

Argument against the hypotheses. You'll probably find that much of your evidence supports your expectation of which is the most likely hypothesis. But that same evidence may be consistent with different hypotheses as well. Here is where you develop arguments against each hypothesis rather than looking for reasons to confirm them.

Hypothesis selection is not a popularity contest. Proceed by trying to reject hypotheses rather than confirm them. The most likely hypothesis is usually the one with the least evidence against it, not the one with the most evidence for it.

Monitor for surprises. When we commit something to paper or our computer screen, it tends to take on a fixed character. Remember that we don't deal in a static situation. Rather, our world is rapidly changing, and our analytical conclusions are always tentative. The situation can change or it may remain unchanged, but you receive new information that alters your understanding of it. Specify critical nodes to monitor for changes that might significantly alter the probabilities. Pay particular attention to any feeling of surprise when new information does not fit your prior understanding. Remain poised to be proven wrong. When we generate hypotheses, we find ourselves susceptible to coming up with explanations that comport with our store of information, dictated in a fashion by our mindset. Here are some ways to break out of the mind-rut.

Situational logic—this is an inductive approach that begins with consideration of concrete elements of the current situation, rather than with generalizations involving similar cases. We regard the situation as one-of-a-kind rather than as a class of events. This has the virtue of enhancing details that make the case unique.

Application of theory—this is a textbook-style, deductive approach that reasons from the general to the specific case. It suggests to us that when a given set of conditions arises, certain other results ought to follow with some degree of probability.

Comparison with historical situations—we can compare our current situation with earlier historical examples. An entire method of instruction in higher education is built on this technique. It's called the case study method. Historical cases are dissected to understand the event and how actors arrived at their decisions, whether good or bad. We seek understanding of current events by comparing them with historical precedents in the same country, or with similar events in other countries. We can then fill in the gaps of our current knowledge by looking at the historical analog. This has a danger when we apply an historical analogy indiscriminately. For instance, after Neville Chamberlain's debacle at Munich in 1938, the "appeasement" analogy was used for decades as a negative example that eliminated certain diplomatic options in foreign affairs. No one wanted to be accused of "appeasement" in dealing with other nations.

Finally—data immersion. One method of analysis, if used judiciously, can aid the clarification process. The analyst immerses himself in the data while consciously suppressing any preconceptions. The idea is that patterns emerge from the data that can then be tested. This method has problems in that data, numbers, "facts" never speak for themselves. But as a means of jump-starting original thinking, it can be useful if other techniques are overused.

The world of cognitive psychology is always changing and pursuing new research agendas into how the mind works. There's always more to learn about how the mind functions when working on a problem. For strategy, it's especially important to recognize and resist both outside distortions that can interfere with analytical clarity, and ways that our internal cognitive processes can also distort our perception of the outside world.

We've seen how we can be more conscious of how we perceive the world, reduce the degree to which we misperceive it, and in the process, develop a more fully strategic personality. Refining our practical understanding of the perplexing world of human behavior takes time, but on that basis, we can learn to craft strategy—and behave strategically—in ways that have a greater chance of success.

Strategic Intuition and Creative Insight
Lecture 20

The flash of brilliance that inspires great triumphs always startles us by how obvious it is—in hindsight. This moment of insight comes to great leaders in business, the military, sports, science, and politics. It is what separates the merely good strategists from the great. And in this lecture, you'll learn how you can cultivate your own strategic intuition as an adjunct to analysis.

Coup d'oeil, the Flash of Insight

- Carl von Clausewitz called the flash of insight behind a great strategic idea *coup d'oeil*, "stroke of the eye." As we've seen, such insights operate in the business world, in the military, in science, and elsewhere.

- Whether this strategic glance can be cultivated or trained is a question that has long been debated. We used to think of analysis and intuition as two distinctly different processes, but now scientists believe that there is a single mode of thought that combines the two. This new model is called "intelligent memory."

- The latest research suggests that we can cultivate our own abilities to achieve insight in certain circumstances. We can certainly evaluate the circumstances that lead to the flash of insight and strive to create those conditions for ourselves.

Decision-Making Models

- Most decision-making models focus on a four-step process: (1) analyze the problem, (2) list available options, (3) evaluate the options against common criteria and weight the criteria according to importance, and (4) add up the results to reach a decision.

- This process permeates decision making in business, but according to strategic theorist William Duggan, "Decision-makers only use this four-step method if they have to—if official procedures make them do it. When left to their own devices, they use strategic intuition."

- Researchers in military strategy have divided decision making into two separate modes, analytical and intuitive. The analytical approach serves well when time is available to examine all facets of the problem and its solution. Intuitive decision making is appropriate when time is short, but it doesn't work well when the situation includes inexperienced leaders, complex situations, or competing courses of action.

- According to research psychologist Gary Klein, expert decision makers do not generate multiple options and then pick one. Instead, they study a situation, and the problem and solution come to them at the same time. They think through the implications to arrive at a course of action and they commit to it, or they reject it if it they think it will not work.

- Duggan tells us that strategic intuition consists in the "selective projection of past elements into the future in a new combination as a course of action that might or might not fit your previous goals, with the personal commitment to follow through and work out the details along the way." This definition fits closely with Porter's definition of strategy as "doing things differently."

Strategy as Best Practice?
- Let's consider the principles of strategy as the equivalent of acquiring best practices in business. If everyone observes best practices, then the efficiency frontier is pushed out, and no one achieves sustained competitive advantage.

- If everyone has read the book of strategy, how, then, do you obtain even fleeting competitive advantage? The answer comes down to which leaders apply strategic intuition. The Civil War comes very close to being a controlled experiment to test this notion of strategic intuition versus strategy as a checklist.

  o The two sides in this war were staffed with officers who were classmates at the same military academy, were taught the same theories by the same instructors, and had served with one another in a previous major conflict.

o   Under these circumstances, we might expect that objective factors would win the day. For instance, the North possessed overwhelming superiority in almost every category used to measure military power: population, territory, armories, industrial production, and so on.

o   The reasonable conclusion is that a war with the South would end quickly, in the North's favor, but the war lasted four years, and for much of that time, the outcome was in doubt. Strategy and strategic thinking, specifically the factor of strategic insight, can help explain this counterintuitive result.

o   In May of 1863, near Chancellorsville, Virginia, Robert E. Lee's Army of Northern Virginia faced a Union army twice its size, commanded by Major General Joseph Hooker. Both Lee and Hooker had attended West Point and served in the Mexican-American War.

o   Hooker commanded the superior force, was entrenched on superb terrain, and was better supplied. In this situation, surely the superior force would easily defeat the inferior opponent. Yet in the most lopsided contest of the entire Civil War, Lee won by violating a bedrock of conventional wisdom: Never divide your army in the face of a superior foe.

o   Lee held Hooker's army in check all day with just two divisions of troops. Meanwhile, Stonewall Jackson marched around the Union right flank and caught the Northerners completely by surprise.

Intuitive Decision Making
- In his studies of firefighters, Gary Klein has learned that experienced first responders don't consider two options or even one before they take action; they simply act. For Klein, this discovery was the equivalent of stumbling onto "the phenomenon of intuition."

- In the world of first responders, Klein views intuition as the gradual amalgamation of large repertoires of patterns that are acquired over many years of practice—actions and responses that train the mind to understand a multitude of experiences and quickly yield the correct answer in similar situations in the future.

- Without these patterns, without this experience base, decision makers would be paralyzed. Formal analyses can be valuable to supplement intuition, but they can't substitute for intuition in many areas of decision making.

- Klein has successfully moved our perception of intuition from the extremes of the inexplicable and the skeptical to a reasonable recognition of its value. He suggests that we combine intuition and analysis, allowing intuition to help us recognize situations and decide our actions, while using analysis to verify our intuitions.

Developing Intuitive Insight

- A seven-step process will help you begin to develop and use your intuitive insights to tackle problems.

- First, recognize that the first option you think of is probably the best. Record this option and hold it for consideration. Evaluate your first impulse in the context of your experience, by imagining how your decision would be carried out and what could go wrong.

- Next, make sure you understand the problem. You can deliberate all day, but if you don't understand what's going on, your choice of action will likely be wrong.

- Third, override your intuitions when they mislead you. Intuition without reflection can lead to fixation. To break free of inaccurate beliefs, ask yourself whether there is any evidence that would make you change your mind. If not, then you've built a cocoon around your beliefs.

- Use your intuition to think ahead of the curve. The world is too complex to think ahead using careful analysis of situations; rely on your intuition to help you connect the dots, flag inconsistencies, and warn you of potential problems.

- Accept a degree of uncertainty. You will never have perfect information. The key is knowing when you have enough information, then having the courage to act.

- Use the right decision-making strategy. If the issues are complicated and no one has good intuitions about the overall situation, analysis makes more sense than relying on gut feelings.

- Finally, watch out for the naysayers—managers who don't value the experience of key employees, who expect employees to follow directions without clarification, who are intolerant of uncertainty, and so on.

- The good news to take from this lecture is that brilliant insights are not necessarily the stuff of genius, and creativity is not a mysterious force. The ability to assemble and reassemble data in new and innovative ways is not limited to people like Napoleon or Steve Jobs; all of us can access it and develop it.

Suggested Reading

Duggan, *Napoleon's Glance.*

———, *Strategic Intuition.*

Klein, *The Power of Intuition.*

Kuhn, *The Structure of Scientific Revolutions.*

Questions to Consider

1. Do you dismiss intuition as somehow unworthy of consideration in the process of sober analytical decision making? If so, think how you might begin to listen to your voice of experience rather than to attack a problem with the same habitual set of tools.

2. First responders don't weigh and analyze alternatives; they react to the situation based on a vast trove of experience stored up from similar situations that informs their conscious actions instantaneously. Are there situations in which you simply "know" the answer to complex challenges that fall within the range of your particular skills and experience? How might the concepts in the lecture, especially the notion of *coup d'oeil*, aid you in listening to your professional intuition and making decisions that spring from your own flashes of insight?

3. Understanding the strengths and limitations of the two types of decision making can aid in choosing wisely at crucial moments, as Lee did at Chancellorsville. Compare and contrast the advantages and disadvantages of the two types of decision making: analytical and intuitive.

Strategic Intuition and Creative Insight
Lecture 20—Transcript

"Why didn't I think of that?" The world is full of examples of instances when this lament strikes us. Whether it's a piece of corrugated cardboard to wrap around our paper coffee cup, or a plain stone called a "pet rock," or the insight that informs a scholar that the earth is truly not the center of the universe, or the intuition that causes a great general to violate every textbook prescription and attack at the proper moment when the enemy least expects. It may be counterintuitive, it may go against what everyone else knows is conventional wisdom. This flash of insight operates in the business world, in the military, in sports, in science, and in politics. It is what separates the merely good strategists from the great.

It's rare, and yet it's prevalent enough to have garnered a name. Perhaps showing his admiration for Napoleon, Carl von Clausewitz called this quality of strategic insight *coup d'oeil*. This is a French phrase that means "stroke of the eye." *Coup d'oeil* is the flash of insight that propels us to launch a strategic idea. This *coup d'oeil* goes by other names, too—intuition, instinct, sixth sense.

Whether this strategic glance can be cultivated or trained over time is a question that has been debated for centuries. Is it a form of genius or is it a skill that can be learned? Traditionally, this notion of the flash of insight at the proper time and place has been thought mysterious, even a form of extrasensory perception, and perhaps unfathomable. But this idea that intuition is inaccessible has undergone a radical reassessment in recent years. We used to think of analysis and intuition as two distinctly different processes, but now scientists believe that there is a single mode of thought that combines analysis and intuition. Scientists call this new model "intelligent memory," and it operates as creative insight, in which the brain assembles existing pieces of information and combines them in novel ways. This, of course, is the very essence of business strategy as defined by Harvard Business Professor Michael Porter.

In science, Thomas Kuhn, the great philosopher of science, contended that the scientific method starts with a profound respect for past achievements that the scientist then combines in a flash of insight. We have these commonalities across disciplines. In chess, it is the quality shared by all great masters—the flash of insight that leads to beautiful and elegant combinations for victory; patterns of interaction that elude the majority of us, but once shown to us, we see them so clearly.

What is new—and what concerns us here and now—is the idea of intuition as a quality that can be cultivated. Can strategic insight be cultivated? Can we develop *coup d'oeil*? Perhaps we can. The latest research suggests just that, under certain conditions, we can cultivate our own abilities to achieve insight in certain circumstances. We can certainly evaluate the circumstances that lead to the flash of insight. And then we can strive to create those conditions ourselves.

Let's first look at how the experts tell us to make decisions. Second, we look at several examples of *coup d'oeil* in action. Third, we review what the latest research says. And finally, we learn some easy steps to cultivate our propensity to receive that blinding insight at the moment we need it most.

We have several models of decision making that have been developed by bright minds with the best of intentions. Decision-making models can be illustrated with flow-charts, decision-points, and arrows, all giving the process a kind of scientific precision. We all like to think of ourselves as smart, rational people, and the idea of our thinking processes being scientific—well, that's good for the ego.

The process usually goes something like this: We analyze the problem, list our different options, evaluate all of our options against common criteria and weight the criteria as to importance, then add it all up. Voila! The decision is made for us. For lots of folks, this is desirable. As one academic has said, "Who wouldn't want to be thorough, systematic, rational, and scientific?" This four-step process, or one much like it, permeates decision making in business. But this model of decision making is more honored in the breach than in the observance. Procedures can take on a life of their own and they persist, even when experience shows them to be lacking.

Strategic theorist William Duggan teaches at Columbia University's business school and advises the U.S. military on decision-making theory. He points out the gap.

> Decision-makers only use this four-step method if they have to—if official procedures make them do it. When left to their own devices, they use strategic intuition. And the more complex or unfamiliar a situation, the more they must do so. Yet there seems to be something sacred in the world of planning about this four-step method, and about the second step especially ... generate multiple solutions.

Here again, some of our finest analysis comes from the military, which first recognized the importance of strategic intuition and gave it equal prominence with analytical decision making. It divided decision making into two separate modes and cited two different situations where the two types of thought are appropriate.

First, the analytical approach. This approach serves well when time is available to analyze all facets affecting the problem and its solution. However, analytical decision making consumes time and does not work well in all situations—especially during execution, when circumstances often require immediate decisions.

Second, intuitive decision making. This is appropriate when we don't have time. It speeds up decision making. Intuitive decision making doesn't work well when the situation includes inexperienced leaders, complex or unfamiliar situations, or competing courses of action.

Until the 21st century, this was the official military view. These two separate processes. But the latest research shows us a quite different reality. As Gary Klein shows us, expert decision makers do not generate multiple options and then pick one; they do something very different. Expert decision makers study a situation (step A) and the problem and solution come to them at the same time (step B). They think through the implications to arrive at a course of action (step C) and then they commit to it, or they reject it if it they think it will not work (step D).

This type of decision making has been ridiculed by many folks enamored of the more scientific model, calling it "flying by the seat of one's pants." But in an earlier century, it was the subject of a more elegant phrase: the stroke of the eye—*coup d'oeil.*

Carl von Clausewitz was ahead of his time in many ways with much of his thought on conflict between nations. His thoughts on what he called "military genius" appear as fresh today as when he first penned them more than 170 years ago. Clausewitz tried to explain exactly how the greatest military commanders made their most brilliant decisions during the hottest of battles, where nothing is certain. "[Conflict] is the realm of chance," said Clausewitz. "No other human activity gives it greater scope: no other has such incessant and varied dealings with this intruder. Chance makes everything uncertain and interferes with the whole course of events."

So, rising to the challenge is the quality of military genius, which consists of two equal parts. "[A]n intellect that, even in the darkest hour, retains some glimmerings of the inner light which leads to truth and second, the courage to follow this faint light wherever it may lead."

Coup d'oeil is a French word, and it may create an unnecessary halo effect over the quality itself. So let's talk about strategic intuition in more straightforward terms so that we can better come to grips with it. According to William Duggan, strategic intuition consists in the "selective projection of past elements into the future in a new combination as a course of action that might or might not fit your previous goals, with the personal commitment to follow through and work out the details along the way." It's no coincidence that this definition fits very closely with Porter's definition of strategy as "doing things differently"—the assembly of resources in new and imaginative ways to achieve a competitive advantage.

We have so many advanced methods of analysis and decision making today, that we sometimes forget they are aids to problem solving, not the problem solvers themselves. Human beings are the problem solvers.

Let's consider the principles of strategy for a moment as the equivalent of acquiring what we call in business "best practices." If everyone observes best practices, then the efficiency frontier is pushed out, and no one achieves sustained competitive advantage. Everyone achieves competitive parity in the longer run as knowledge is diffused. We can even call it a form of arbitrage. But in the short run, even temporary competitive advantage can be a powerful tonic. It can be enough to win a battle or two or three. In war, in business, in politics, in sports, it can sometimes be enough.

So the question remains, how do you obtain even fleeting competitive advantage when everyone has read the book of strategy? If, for instance, every general practices the art of war as drawn from a well-known body of strategic theory, then on what axel does the wheel of victory turn? Does the outcome then become a simple mathematical calculation? It becomes a matter to which leaders apply strategic intuition.

So what happens when both sides of a conflict are both steeped in the military strategy of the time, when officers are schooled in the latest theory and opposing each other on the field of battle, applying those theories against each other? Do we have such a case? As a matter of fact, we do: the American Civil War.

The Civil War is a superb example of a case that comes close to being a controlled experiment to test our notion of strategic intuition versus strategy as a checklist. Few times in history will two sides in a conflict be staffed with officers schooled as classmates at the same military academy, taught the same theories by the same instructors, and having served with each other in a previous major conflict—and with the battles fought over ground increasingly familiar to both sides.

The Civil War offers a four-year skein of battles, great and small, in which the theories of strategy of the day were tested and tested again. In such a conflict, we might expect that, with so many things "being equal," that objective factors would win the day. We might be able to simply tote up the objective factor endowments of each side and predetermine a victor. In the Civil War, for instance, the North was possessed of overwhelming superiority in almost every category that we use to measure military power. It was a conflict between a modern industrial society versus an agrarian economy. The North possessed tremendous advantages in population, territory, armories, industrial production, naval power, and railroad mileage. In such a conflict, a reasonable person might conclude that the outcome should not be in doubt. Moreover, such a conflict ought to end quickly. Most observers at the time thought it would end quickly, in the North's favor.

But it did not end quickly. It lasted four years and took more than 600,000 lives. For much of the conflict, its outcome was in doubt. In fact, at times a Southern victory appeared within reach. We can look to strategy and strategic thinking to explain this counterintuitive result. We look, specifically, to the factor of strategic insight—or *coup d'oeil*—to explain the unexplainable. This insight has both tactical and strategic applications. It is the insight of when, at the crucial moment in battle, to strike at a particular position, or to fall back to a new position. Such insight has a strategic element in planning, an instinctual foresight granted by experience and, some say, providence. It offers a lightning strike of insight of when to diverge from strategic doctrine as commonly practiced, of when to break the rules in ways unimagined by lesser leaders—those animated "by the rules."

Napoleon, perhaps the embodiment of everything we imagine when we envision *coup d'oeil*, observed that

> The art of war consists, with an inferior army, of always having more forces than your enemy at the point where you attack, or at the point which is attacked; but this art cannot be learned either from books or from practice. It is a feeling of command which properly constitutes the genius for war.

Let's look at our example from the Civil War, the Battle of Chancellorsville. The time was May of 1863. The South was in the ascendance following a string of victories in the Eastern Theater by the Army of Northern Virginia over the Union Army of the Potomac. General Robert E. Lee's Army of Northern Virginia is considered by some historians to be the greatest fighting force of the 19th century—cohesive, well-trained, well-led, loyal, and motivated by chivalric values.

This Confederate States Army, was confronted by a northern army twice its size near Chancellorsville, Virginia, under the command of Union Major

General Joseph Hooker. Again, we are presented with the conundrum of objective factors versus strategy versus high-concept strategic insight.

Think of it—Lee versus Hooker. Both schooled at West Point Military Academy. Both served in the Mexican-American War of the late 1840s, and they fought together at the Battle of Chapultepec in the Mexican-American War in 1847. The Virginia terrain was familiar to both men. They both learned at the figurative feet of the Swiss-born French strategist Antoine Jomini, whose principles were taught in West Point classrooms.

Hooker commanded the superior force; he was entrenched on superb terrain, better supplied and greater numerically by two-to-one—133,000 union soldiers versus only 60,000 southern troops. In this situation, surely the superior force would easily defeat the inferior opponent using Jominian principles of planning and maneuver. And yet in the most lopsided contest of the entire Civil War, Lee won. It's been called his perfect battle. Lee violated one of the most bedrock pieces of conventional wisdom. Never divide your army in the face of a superior foe. Yet this is exactly what Lee did. Hooker played by the book and Lee broke the rules. It was the human qualities of intuitive audacity versus analytic timidity.

What happened? Hooker had concentrated his army in a formidable position, which he had carefully and skillfully fortified. Lee went into bivouac to confer with his top lieutenant General Stonewall Jackson, During the night Lee's engineers reconnoitered the Federal front and pronounced a direct attack impracticable.

Something in the lay of the land, the descriptions of his engineers, something in his experience told Lee what to do. It was then that Lee said to Jackson, "We must attack from our left," and Jackson was prepared. According to Lee's own account, he, quote, "stated to General Jackson, we must attack on our left as soon as practicable, and the necessary movement of the troops began immediately." While Jackson moved surreptitiously in a forced march around the Union flank, Lee confronted and attempted to hold in place the great mass of Hooker's army with just two divisions of troops, just 13,000 men against 70,000. The dense forest on the front prevented Hooker from detecting the small confederate numbers.

For their part, on the other side, the Confederates made fierce feint attacks with infantry and artillery against Hooker's front. They kept up almost continuous fire. This deceived Hooker and made him hesitate to advance from his entrenchments to find out the actual situation. This way, Lee held him all day in check, while Jackson swiftly marched around the Union right flank.

Jackson attacked at 5:00 pm after a forced march and caught the federals completely by surprise. They were cooking their dinner when Jackson's troops charged the Union camp and swept everything before them. It was only the approaching darkness that halted the Confederate attack and prevented a complete rout of the entire Army of the Potomac. The decision to split his army in the face of 2:-1 odds may have seemed like madness to junior officers or even veterans. It was something that Hooker did not expect. It was a decision born of necessity. It was no strategic checklist that led Lee to make his decision. It was strategic insight—Lee's intuition, his knowledge of the terrain, his knowledge of Hooker's timidity, his faith in the indomitable Stonewall Jackson, in his cavalry commander, Jeb Stuart. All of this came together in the mind of Lee in some unknown calculus. The result was a decision to go against what he and Hooker had learned in school at West Point from Jomini.

Seventy years later another general from another country recognized what Lee accomplished at Chancellorsville and what it meant for generals in all places and in all times. German General Waldemar Erfurth penned a classic on warfare called *Surprise*. In it, he urged a balance between the mundane checklist view of strategy and an overreliance upon instinct. But above all, he urged the daring necessary to strike when an opponent has left himself vulnerable.

> The military leader must indeed be able to rid himself from traditional precepts, yet in doing so, he should never forget that heterodoxy has it limits beyond which it is no longer effective ... but becomes dangerous. Above all, the soldier must learn to recognize the mistakes of the enemy and to exploit them, though this may sometimes require departure from accepted military rules.

In our own time, folks who study intuition recognize that there is much more to strategic intuition than magic, or a hunch, or instinct. Gary Klein has become one of this country's foremost experts on intuitive decision making. Gary studies firefighters to see how they make their fast decisions under extreme time pressure and stress. He already knew that in the literal heat of a fire, an experienced firefighter doesn't make decisions according to the standard analytical model—comparing the many ways to, say, put out a fire. Gary thought that they'd come up with maybe two options, and then act. He was wrong.

Most firefighters, especially ones with more experience, usually just considered a single option. They would just act. The most common statement he heard from firefighters was, "We don't make decisions." These firefighters would simply respond to the situation. Gary was amazed. "I had stumbled onto the phenomenon of intuition, although I didn't realize it at the time. Although I wasn't looking for intuition, intuition had found me." It turns out that these firefighters, and nurses, and doctors, and military officers—early responders of all types share a common skill: "intuitive decision making."

In business, the idea of intuition in decision making is not all that readily accepted. It still carries the whiff of magical incantation. But in the military— for instance, the United States Marine Corps, intuitive decision making is part of the training process. The term "intuitive decision making" appears in their manual on command and control, and it's compared favorably with analytical decision making.

In this case, Gary Klein views intuition as the gradual amalgamation of large repertoires of patterns that are acquired over many years of practice—actions and responses that train the mind to understand a multitude of experiences and then quickly yield the correct answer in similar situations in the future. Without these patterns, without this experience base, decision makers would be paralyzed. Formal analyses can be valuable to supplement intuition, but they can't substitute for intuition when it comes to business decisions or career decisions or political decisions.

Gary Klein has successfully moved our perception of intuition to a reasonable recognition of its value. Two extreme views predominated—the realm of the magical, where intuition was inexplicable; and the realm of the skeptical, where intuition was ridiculed. He suggests that we combine the approaches of intuition and analysis. Let's build on the strengths of each, recognizing their weaknesses as well. A good synthesis of the two that seems most effective is when we allow intuition to lead the way so that it directs our analysis. This way, intuition helps us recognize situations and helps us decide our actions. Analysis then verifies our intuitions to make sure they aren't misleading us. In this way, we can come up with a method of cultivating our own intuition and of relying on it—learning to trust it under the right circumstances.

Here is a seven-step general guide to help you to begin developing and utilizing your intuitive insights as you tackle problems.

1) Recognize that the first option you think of is probably the best. This is not always true, but it tends to be correct and it is substantiated by research. So recognize your first impulse before you erode it with too much analysis. Record it and hold it for consideration. Analyze it as part of your decision-making process. Evaluate your first impulse in the context of your experience—by imagining how your decision would be carried out, and what could go wrong. Do your own personal scenario-planning.

2) Ensure that you understand "what's going on here." You can deliberate all day, but if you don't understand what is going on, your choice of action will likely be wrong.

3) Override your intuitions when they mislead you. It's dangerous to use intuition without reflection because it can lead to fixation. We may think we understand a situation even if we don't, and then we make matters worse by catering to our bias and explaining away all contrary evidence. To break free of inaccurate beliefs, ask yourself if there is any evidence that would make you change your mind. If not, then you've built a cocoon around your beliefs.

4) Think ahead. Intuition can help us think ahead of the curve by creating expectations, by connecting the dots, by flagging inconsistencies, or by warning us of problems. The world is too complex to think ahead using

careful analysis of situations. We have to rely on our intuition instead. But to rely on it, we have to give intuition a chance.

5) Uncertainty is a natural component of intuitive decision making. Too many people become frustrated, even fearful, with uncertainty. Uncertainty can paralyze them or send them chasing for information that will arrive too late, and still won't be enough to answer all the questions. You never have perfect information to make a certain decision, until you've been overcome by events. They key is knowing when there is enough information to act and then having the courage to act. Here, it's helpful to remember Clausewitz's recipe for military genius: "[A]n intellect that, even in the darkest hour, retains some glimmerings of the inner light which leads to truth' and second, the courage to follow this faint light wherever it may lead."

6) Use the right decision-making strategy. You can rely on intuition, sure, but at times it's best to evaluate all of the factors that impinge on your decision. If the issues are complicated and no one has good intuitions about the overall situation, analysis makes more sense than relying on gut feelings.

7) Watch out for the naysayers. Here are the signs: Management doesn't value the experience of key employees. Superiors expect employees to follow directions without being given the chance to have them clarified. Management is intolerant of uncertainty and relies on massive amounts of data collection as a cure for uncertainty. Systems encourage everyone to manage by using simple numerical goals to make things clear. Management starts looking for ways to substitute computer systems for human expertise.

There is, of course, a lot more than these seven tips, but they're a start, and they can get you on your way to becoming a more intuitive thinker, a more effective strategic thinker.

Through all of this, let's remember the good news—brilliant insights are not necessarily the stuff of genius and creativity is no longer a mysterious force. The ability to assemble and reassemble data in new and innovative ways is not limited to the Napoleons or the Steve Jobs of the world; it's accessible to you and to me, and it can be developed. With the right approach and right techniques, creative insight can be cultivated.

From Systemic Problems to Systemic Solutions
Lecture 21

A problem that crops up repeatedly, in your work or personal life, is likely a systemic problem. Strategic thinking enables us to recognize the symptoms of what Peter Drucker called the "recurring crisis," to unwind the problem, and to tackle the underlying systemic issue. In this way, we can often construct our own conscious systems to solve the pathology of systemic problems.

Systems and Systemic Problems

- John Foster Dulles, President Eisenhower's secretary of state, offers us a succinct formulation of the plague of the systemic problem: "The measure of success is not whether you have a tough problem to deal with, but whether it is the same problem you had last year."

- The notion of systems can be quite flexible, but for our purposes, a good definition of a system is a collection of people, processes, and things that interact with one another and form an integrated whole. Systems have structure, behavior, and interdependence, and most of them generate results or output.

- Systems interconnect and depend on one another to function. Consider the systems that support us: garbage collection, food distribution, public transportation, fuel for automobiles, electrical grids, police protection, manufacturing assembly lines, the legal system, cell phones, water recycling and purification, and so on.

- Everything in our world happens in the context of a system. One action in one part of a system cascades throughout the system. We create systems, either consciously or unconsciously. We tap into existing systems. We link our systems together, and we often use them without even seeing them.

- In fact, too often, we don't see systems; we simply have expectations. We expect the bus to be on time; we expect water to flow from the tap every time we turn the handle. This is fine most of the time, but it pays to think about our systems, to consider our most important systems and how they might be hurting us.

Essential Components of Systems
- **John A. Warden III**, a former general and one of the U.S. military's premier strategic thinkers, gives us a systems approach that recognizes the essential sameness of all systems.

- In Warden's view, every system has five essential components, and he suggests thinking of these as concentric circles. Moving outward from the center, these components are: (1) a leader; (2) a conversion process that provides food or energy to keep the system going; (3) infrastructure, such as blood vessels, roads, or transmission lines; (4) the entire population; and (5) the action units, which could be anything from antibodies, to police officers, to maintenance workers.

Figure 21.1

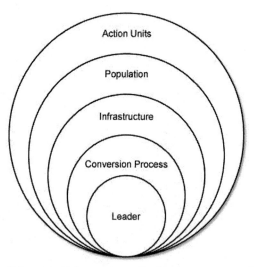

Warden's essential components are present in diverse systems—a living body, an industrialized state, even a drug cartel.

- This approach gives us a great way to categorize information and compare seemingly disparate systems. What is the purpose of the system? What is the desired end result? Does the system deliver that result?

Case Study: IBM
- Systemic problems can afflict even the biggest, smartest companies; the case of IBM provides us with an example.

- In 1999, the chairman of IBM, Lou Gerstner, was confronted with a perplexing situation. The company was strong, but its growth was slowing, and it seemed to be missing business opportunities. This was odd because from 1993 to 1999, IBM won more patents than any other American company. For some reason, IBM wasn't leveraging those patents into new businesses.

- Gerstner suspected that the wrong incentives might be in place, and he directed a task force to investigate the problem. The findings of the task force were painful: IBM's sharp focus on achieving short-term profitability had engendered strategic myopia throughout the firm. Managers simply weren't incentivized to spot emerging growth opportunities.

- Further, top management had created a climate of fear with its demands for "fact-based analysis and detailed financial forecasts." All but the most reckless managers would shun the uncertainty and risk of investing in a new business.

- Top management wanted investment in new businesses, but the system it fed was not equipped to deliver that output. The system was designed to deliver something else: stability and sobriety. This was an archetypal systemic problem.

- If an executive finally did launch a new business, the start-up was burdened with the same expectations for near-term earnings as IBM's billion-dollar legacy businesses. New business programs had to promise impossibly ambitious financial returns. The targets, of course, were never met, and the start-ups budget would be quickly slashed.

411

- Gerstner recognized that the system would have to change for the problem to be solved. Over the course of five years, IBM developed a new management program called Emerging Business Opportunities to change the incentive structure. In the first five years of the program, IBM launched 22 successful new businesses.

- The case of IBM gives us a powerful lesson: To tackle a systemic problem, you must understand its deep roots. Without understanding the systemic nature of the problem, any solution will be misdirected.

Case Study: Best Buy
- As a vice president in advertising at Best Buy, Jeff Severts recognized that his reputation was linked to an internal system of monthly sales performance measured against the firm's financial forecasting. Sometimes the forecast was met and sometimes not; to Severts, the results seemed capricious.

- Severts looked hard at the forecast system and saw that the forecasts weren't very good. Further analysis revealed that Best Buy's forecasting was entwined with many key management systems, including budgeting, performance measurement, compensation, and purchasing—each with an agenda that yielded forecasts wide of the mark.

- Severts experimented with an idea he had learned from business columnist James Surowiecki: When it comes to predicting events that are driven by confusing variables, a diverse group of nominally informed individuals often has an advantage over a few "experts." Severts saw that a group of Best Buy employees would be immune to the systematic biases that skewed the company's internal forecasts.

- Severts initially solicited forecast estimates from 190 employees across his business, and he found that their estimate was off by less than 0.5 percent. A later test with more employees yielded results that were 99.9 percent accurate.

- In this case, Severts identified the systemic problem as the method of forecasting, which yielded bad results. He discovered that incentives within the system guaranteed that the forecasts would be skewed in ways having nothing to do with actual sales performance.

Case Studies from India

- Examples from India shows how imagination and business acumen can solve systemic problems in ways that not only earn a company profits but can save lives and improve the standard of living for hundreds of thousands of people.

- In Sujala, a small village in India, the Byrraju Foundation targeted disease control not by staffing the small dispensary with doctors or outfitting it with medicines but by focusing on a systemic problem: impure drinking water. Byrraju installed a simple and effective water purification system for the village, and disease among the villagers plummeted.

- Hindustan Unilever, a subsidiary of the world's second-largest household products company, has leveraged soap and salt to build market share and help solve endemic social problems in its home country.

  o Unilever's decision to market a lower-priced soap resulted in a campaign to teach rural populations about the importance of hand washing to reduce the spread of germs.

  o Unilever also discovered a more resilient type of iodine that could be used to enrich salt, to counter the iodine deficiency in the diets of most Indians.

Sources of Systemic Problems

- In the Indian case studies, the systemic problem affected health. In the case of Best Buy, the systemic problem involved information, and at IBM, the problem was with incentives. Another possible source of systemic problems is morale.

- A good test for determining whether you've identified a truly systemic problem is to ask yourself "Why?" at least five times. Such a series of questions forces you to keep going until you reach the truly systemic cause. Once you've identified the problem, the next task is to look for creative ways to solve it or avoid it.

Warden, John A., III (1943–): Controversial, impatient, and contrarian, Warden is the quintessential strategic thinker and visionary who revolutionized American thinking about air power in the late 20th century. One biography notes, "to this day his name inspires both warm affection and cold contempt in the defense establishment."

Suggested Reading

Burlton, *Business Process Management.*

Hamel and Breen, *The Future of Management.*

Questions to Consider

1. To avoid systemic problems before they surface, it pays to evaluate the systems in our lives and ask whether they actually produce the results that we think that they do. Do you have systems in place, such as the nail by the door to hold your keys, that yield optimal outcomes... or not?

2. List the systems you depend upon simply to survive.

3. Does your company have a recurring crisis, euphemistically called "crunch time" or "all hands on deck"? If so, consider whether this might actually be a systemic problem that can be remedied by implementing a new system.

From Systemic Problems to Systemic Solutions
Lecture 21—Transcript

If we face the same problems daily, in our work or in our personal lives, it's a good indication that there is a system in place that is causing that problem repeatedly. Strategic thinking enables us to recognize what Peter Drucker called the symptoms of the recurring crisis. We can unwind the problem, and we can tackle the underlying systemic issue that vexes us. We can even construct our own conscious systems to solve the systemic problem that leads to the recurring crisis. This method has applications across a range of fields, from business to the military—anywhere recurring patterns of behavior can be identified.

When introducing the notion of a systemic problem in my classes, I pose this question: "Who has experienced the problem of finding misplaced car keys in the morning when you're about to leave for work or school?" Almost everyone raises a hand in recognizing this universal malady. "And you solve the problem by finding your keys after a 10-minute search."

If we are truly rational human beings, who value our time and who don't enjoy looking for car keys every morning, this problem should happen only once. But for my students, it happens repeatedly.

So I ask my class to think to the moment they unlock their apartment door and step over the threshold. "Ask yourself this question: Do my keys have to go into this disaster area called an apartment where they are bound to get lost? Do my keys perform any valuable function for me at all in this apartment?" If the answer is no—and it should be no—then those keys should stay there, right beside the door. So, let's drive a nail in the wall about eye-level, and every day we hang our keys beside the door when we come home. We have just created an orderly, logical system that has solved the "problem" of lost keys. We just replaced a dysfunctional system with a functional system. We have just solved a systemic problem.

It was a famous American statesman from more than five decades ago who described this phenomenon of the nail by the door. John Foster Dulles was President Eisenhower's Secretary of State, famous for much, much more than the remark I cite here. But there is perhaps no better and more succinct formulation of the plague of the systemic problem—the chronic pain that surfaces again and again. The key, or your glasses, or a valuable piece of information that you've misplaced—lost once again.

Dulles said this: "The measure of success is not whether you have a tough problem to deal with, but whether it is the same problem you had last year." Or the same problem you have every morning.

A systemic problem is a problem that arises repeatedly because of the interactions or processes or the system in place. The system may even have been designed to do something else. It may have been designed to produce an outcome different than what we're looking for.

Now, let's remember that everyone does not think alike. Not all people attack problems the same way. Many people never talk about "systems." Instead, some people see the world holistically, as an interconnected organism. Some people see the world in spiritual terms. Others see it as an atomistic collection of rational choice actors. An artist looks at a landscape and frames the scene for painting, noting the colors both lush and subtle. A biologist sees that same landscape as a complex ecosystem. A soldier sees cover and concealment and avenues of approach. A developer sees possibilities for urban expansion.

Frankly, it can take a long time to understand that there are many different ways of viewing a situation, and this largely depends upon your personal experience, your education, your history, your intellectual makeup, and whether or not you have been exposed to any or many problem-solving methods. What to one person seems obvious, to another person seems alien.

But the notion of systems can be quite flexible. It can be adapted to many points of view, large and small. Let's break down exactly what we mean by "system," especially in the sense of strategic analysis, then we can look at some examples of systemic dysfunction. Systemic dysfunction happens when we expect certain outcomes from a system that's designed to yield a different outcome.

416

When we find ourselves in such a fix, we should focus on the system, not on the bad result. A system is a collection—it's a collection of people, processes, and things that interact with each other. They form an integrated whole. Systems have structure, behavior, and interdependence, and most of them generate results or outputs.

Think of the solar system of its planets, asteroids, and central star. Think of the complex pattern of traffic lights in a huge metropolis like New York. Our world is comprised of systems, both involving us and external to us. Systems interconnect and they depend on each other to function. Consider the systems around us that support us: garbage collection, food distribution, public transportation, fuel for automobiles, electrical grids, police protection, manufacturing assembly lines, the legal system, cell phones, water recycling and purification. Think of nature's systems: the ecosystem around you. Even popular movies pay homage to the notion of the system—think of *The Lion King's* Circle of Life.

Everything in our world happens in the context of a system. One action in one part of a system cascades throughout the system. We create systems, either consciously or unconsciously. We tap into existing systems. We link our systems together and utilize them without even seeing them.

But too often, we don't see systems; we simply have expectations. We expect the bus to be on time; we expect water to flow from the tap every time we twist it; we expect bread to be on the shelves when we visit the store. This is fine most of the time. But it pays to think of our systems. It pays to consider our most important systems and how they might be hurting us.

The nail where we hang our keys is an example of replacing an inappropriate system that delivers bad outcomes with an efficient system that delivers for you the desired outcome. And if you happen to be someone who "loses" keys often, the new system is incredibly valuable. It can give back to you between one and two hours per week, not to mention the reduction in stress.

One of the most innovative thinkers about strategy and systems is John A. Warden III, a former air force general and architect of the highly successful air war against Iraq in the first Gulf War. Some consider Warden one of the premier strategic thinkers of the last century in the realm of air power. Much of Warden's focus was on systems—how to develop them and how to attack enemy systems successfully.

Well, we're not interested in attacking anyone else's systems right now. We're concerned with understanding our own and how to improve them. Warden shows us a way. Warden recognized the essential sameness of all systems. His systems approach is applicable regardless of the type of system, because the great thing about systems is they all exhibit system characteristics. Whether a living body, an industrialized state, a drug cartel, or an electric company, every system follows the same organizational scheme.

In Warden's view, every system has five essential components, and he suggests thinking of those as concentric circles: At the center is a leader. Next to that is a conversion process that provides food or energy or fuel to keep the system going. Next, moving outward is infrastructure, such as blood vessels, roads, or transmission lines. In the next ring comes the entire population. Finally, the outer layer surrounding all the others are the action units, which could be anything from antibodies in biology, to police officers, or to maintenance and repair workers. John Warden showed imaginatively how each of these seemingly dissimilar areas could be regarded as systems that share important commonalities.

This approach gives us a great way to categorize information and compare seemingly disparate systems with each other. What is the purpose of the system that you're considering? What is the end result we strive for? Does our system deliver that result? Or is our system delivering something else, totally unexpected and unacceptable.

Now, we often look for answers not at the systemic level but inside the system at its components, and we may find that the components of the system are superb and functioning exactly as they are expected to. But the systemic result—the overall result—is useless.

So think, now, of our systems—the ones that impact us, the systems we control. Define the system's scope and extent, identify the components, ask yourself what the system is supposed to provide—I mean really provide.

Examine the incentive drivers throughout the system. Evaluate whether they truly incentivize people to do what you want them to do. Recognize that you'll find systems that sometimes yield bad outcomes. Resources are squandered solving the same problem repeatedly; the symptoms are addressed each time they arise. Sometimes a problem isn't even recognized as such. Instead, it's viewed as a normal state of affairs, as if things couldn't get any better. Sometimes the systemic problem is created by something that is mistakenly regarded as beneficial.

Here's an example. I am a business presentations coach. I coach teams of MBA students who compete against other teams in analyzing a business case, and the then present their results. I see lots of presentations. Ever wonder why so many presentations, lectures, and after-dinner speeches are so bad? There's often a systemic reason for it—a systemic problem. For example, I am asked to speak on occasions, and sometimes the organization wants a lot of control over my talk, including how I give it and what handouts are distributed and when. In fact, "steering committees" often try to turn my talk into their notion of what constitutes a good presentation by giving me strong suggestions that they believe are quite good, but which actually violate fundamental speaking precepts. As a result, they turn every talk into an imitation of every other talk. They channel speakers into the same dull routine. They do this with the idea that they add value to the process. But in reality, the steering committee perpetuates bad presentations under the guise of improving them—a systemic problem.

Systemic problems can afflict even the biggest, smartest companies—even a smart company like IBM; especially big companies like IBM. In 1999, the chairman of IBM was Lou Gerstner, and he was confronted with a perplexing situation. He guided the world's largest information technology company, with more than 320,000 employees and revenues of more than $91 billion and he had just brought the company out of a difficult period. After six years of cost-cutting and retooling, the company was strong. But its growth was slowing, and it was missing business opportunities right and left—from life sciences to computing, to the explosive growth in open source software, to the development of handheld and mobile computing devices. The IT world seemed to be passing the aging giant.

This was quite odd, because from 1993 to 1999, IBM won more patents than any other American company: an astounding 12,773. But leveraging these patents into new businesses? Almost nonexistent. IBM had the finest minds, the strongest financial position, a superb brand, leading market share across a range of products and services, but new business ventures were absent. In fact, Gerstner discovered that internal new business ventures that he had engineered at startup were canceled by unknown forces so as to meet quarterly earnings goals.

Gerstner suspected that the wrong incentives might be in place. So Gerstner directed a task force that investigated for three months and found the root of the problem. The task force met with Gerstner in December of 1999. The results were painful. So painful that Mike Giersch, vice president of corporate strategy said that "We had to admit that we had screwed things up." IBM's sharp focus on achieving short-term profitability had engendered strategic myopia throughout the firm. Managers simply weren't incentivized to spot emerging growth opportunities.

Top management also created a climate of fear, with its demands for "fact-based analysis and detailed financial forecasts." All but the most reckless managers would shun the uncertainty and risk of investing in a new business.

This was the heart of the problem. The system penalized new ventures; disincentives kept anyone from participating in them. Top management wanted investment in new businesses, but the system it fed was not equipped to deliver that output. The system was designed to deliver something else— stability and sobriety. Here was an archetypal systemic problem.

If an executive finally did plunge in to launch a new business, the start-up was burdened with the same expectations for near-term earnings as were IBM's billion-dollar legacy businesses. New business programs had to promise impossibly ambitious financial returns. The targets, of course, were never met, and the start-ups budget would be quickly slashed. Moreover, the task force found the obvious—top flight talent wanted nothing to do with these new business boondoggles. Most aspiring managers avoided the risk of new business ventures in favor of building careers within the IBM mainstream. Who could blame them?

Gerstner and his deputies wondered what could be done to help new business teams intercept fast-moving opportunities—without disrupting IBM's smooth-running profit machine. Gerstner could have tried a classic "top down" authoritarian "solution." He could have opted for a quick fix. In a show of machismo, he could have ordered a change in results without diagnosing the problem, without recognizing that the system of incentives was at fault. But he did the smartest and toughest thing a CEO can do. He showed guts.

Gerstner recognized that the system would have to be changed for the problem to be solved. And IBM accepted the challenge of inventing an entirely new and far-reaching management process. It took five years. IBM developed a new management program called the Emerging Business Opportunities process to change the incentive structure. It launched in 2000. In the program's first five years, IBM launched 22 successful new businesses with a total of $15 billion in annual revenues by the end of 2005. Systemic problem solved.

And from this example, we take a powerful lesson: To tackle a systemic problem, you must understand its deep roots. Without understanding the systemic nature of the problem, any solution will be misdirected. Thinking back to our lost key example at the beginning of our lecture, we could easily misdirect our efforts to supposedly more efficient ways of searching for our keys. We might even allot 15 additional flex minutes in the morning to search for the keys, which we inevitably "lose." But these high-cost repetitive "solutions" can be obviated by attacking the systemic nature of the problem and solving that.

Here's another example. Consider the case of Jeff Severts, a vice president at Best Buy, a leading consumer electronics retailer. As a vice president in advertising, Severts recognized that his reputation was linked to an internal system of monthly sales performance measured against the firm's financial forecasting. Sometimes they met the forecast, and sometimes not. It seemed capricious, and Severts was stung by the criticism when they "fell short."

But fell short of what? Severts looked hard at the forecast system and saw that the forecasts weren't very good. In fact, they were awful, and many people knew it. Instead of giving up at that point, Severts examined the system components: how the company assembled its sales forecast. He discovered that expert merchant teams would err by as much as 10 percent—even when looking out just 30 days. Severts found that many factors degraded Best Buy's forecasts—the forecasting was entwined with many key management systems, including budgeting, performance measurement, compensation, and purchasing—each with an agenda that yielded forecasts wide of the mark.

So what to do? Severts realized that he couldn't take on senior management and a host of clerk-types invested in the current system. But he could work within his own bailiwick, which was the gift card business within Best Buy. The answer came to him while hearing a talk by James Surowiecki, the *New Yorker* business columnist whose book, *The Wisdom of Crowds*, was a bestseller. Surowiecki argued that large groups of people "are often smarter than the smartest people in them." When it comes to predicting events that are driven by confusing variables, a diverse group of nominally informed individuals often has an advantage over a few "experts." A crowd has access to the usual sorts of corporate reporting data. But it can also leverage information that never shows up in a formal report. And a crowd is immune to the systematic biases that skewed Best Buy's internal forecasts.

In early 2005, Severts tested his idea in his own department of Best Buy's billion dollar gift-card business. He called for emailed forecast estimates from 190 employees across his business. The only incentive to participate was the chance to win a $50 gift certificate, which he paid for personally. His own small official team's projections were usually off by five percent. In the test, the gift-card sales were audited and finalized, and Severts found that the team's estimate was indeed off by the usual five percent.

And what of the crowd's average estimate? It was off by less than one-half of 1 percent. The crowd's forecast was 10 times more accurate than that of the experts. Severts had managed to tap into information inside the organization and set up a system that yielded better results than the formalized company system. You might think that this revelation was greeted with applause. Of course not; entrenched interests never go quietly when it's their time to go.

So Severts set up another test, this time against Best Buy's vaunted merchant teams. It was the rabble versus the oracles. More than 350 people submitted estimates of holiday sales for Thanksgiving 2005. The final audit results showed that the official merchants' preseason forecast was 93 percent accurate. The crowd's forecast, on the other hand, which had also been made four months prior to the holiday season, was 99.9 percent accurate. This finally got senior management attention in a positive way, and Severts was given the go-ahead to conduct more "crowd wisdom" experiments company-wide.

In this case, Severts discovered the systemic problem was the method of forecasting, which yielded bad results. He discovered that the incentives within the system guaranteed that the forecasts would be skewed in ways having nothing to do with the actual sales performance, but having much to do with individual careers. Severts's solution bypassed this dysfunctional system. It tapped into more objective information provided by people with little personal stake in the forecast.

Here's another trio of examples, each of which happens to come from abroad. They show how imagination and business acumen can solve systemic problems in ways that not only earn a company profits, but can save lives and improve the standard of living for hundreds of thousands of people.

In India, many problems faced by this dynamic developing nation are systemic in nature. These problems can be grouped into clusters. The problems belonging to each cluster can be traced to a single malady that, if corrected, would solve all of the subsidiary problems in the cluster at once. So these are systemic problems involving disease and malnutrition. Disease and malnutrition afflict most of rural India. I visited one Indian village outside of the south central city of Hyderabad. The Byrraju Foundation targeted disease control in this small village of Sujala, not by staffing the small dispensary with full-time doctors or with mass deliveries of medicines and antibiotics. Byrraju focused, instead, on the systemic problem—impure drinking water that carried disease-causing microbes. Byrraju installed a simple and effective water purification system for the village, and disease among the villagers and its manifestations plummeted. Instead of treating each villager with hard-to-obtain medicine for a range of illnesses, the water purification plant offered a systemic solution.

Our next two examples also come from India. Unilever is the world's number two household products company behind Procter and Gamble. Its Indian subsidiary Hindustan Unilever has shown itself to be a shrewd competitor in this developing nation of one billion people. It is also innovative in helping to solve endemic social problems and in building market share among the poorest segments of Indian society. Two products that Unilever has leveraged are soap and salt.

First, soap. As with the example of water purification, sometimes we can identify a problem cluster around a single phenomenon or type of behavior. In this case, Unilever had several problems to tackle. First, how can you differentiate soap? Unilever decided to market a lower-priced soap to the poorer segments of society and do so as a health issue. In support of this marketing effort, Unilever sent teams of educators into hundreds of rural villages to teach the local population about the spread of germs causing disease. That washing hands with soap and water could reduce the spread of disease in the villages.

Unilever's other campaign was the marketing of their special brand of salt. Iodine is an element required by humans for healthy thyroid gland function. But the diets of most Indians are iodine-deficient. The company discovered in the early 2000s that the processing of salt and traditional Indian cooking methods purged up to 50 percent of Iodine from salt. So, Unilever sought and found a more resilient type of iodine that could withstand these cooking techniques and began to market this enriched salt throughout the country. The company positioned its salt as a health enhancement.

We can see that Unilever not only chose to fulfill needs of consumers in India, but did so in a way that helped to address social problems and to make available necessary products to what has commonly been called the "bottom of the pyramid." This is the strata of poor people whose cumulative buying power is nonetheless a powerful untapped source of economic development. In all three of these cases, the systemic problem affected health.

But in the Best Buy case, by contrast, the systemic problem involved information. At IBM, the systemic problem was the incentives. For college students who keep losing their keys, the systemic problem is probably lack of skills (they've never learned to hang up their keys), though they might see it as a lack of resources (for example, don't have a hammer).

Another possible source of systemic problems is morale. Morale is often a symptom of one of the other kinds of systemic problems we've already discussed. But sometimes it might be an underlying cause.

Here is what British Defense Doctrine has to say:

> Success in war often depends more on moral than on physical qualities. Numbers, armaments, and resources cannot compensate for lack of courage, energy, determination, skill, and the bold offensive spirit that springs from a national determination to succeed. The development and subsequent maintenance of the qualities of morale are, therefore, essential to success in war.

Good coaches also understand the importance of assessing systemic problems. Powerful strategy is obtained not merely by analyzing what went wrong in just the previous game. Instead, powerful strategy depends on looking for systemic problems that appear across multiple games.

How do you know when you've identified a truly systemic problem? You can ask yourself "Why?" over and over—five times is a common number—to get to a root cause. To take the IBM example, the chain of questions could have started like this: Why don't we commercialize any of our new technologies? Because engineers are preoccupied with current projects. Why are engineers preoccupied with short-term projects? Because that's what managers tell them to do. Why do managers tell engineers to focus on short-term projects? Because that's how incentives are set up.

A series of "why" questions can force you to keep going until you reach a truly systemic cause of the problem. And once you've identified a systemic problem, you can look for creative ways to avoid the problem, like Jeff Severts did when he created an alternative way to gather data at Best Buy.

Or you can look for creative ways to simplify the problem, like Byrraju Foundation did in India when it turned problems involving many diseases into a problem of water quality.

Systems. Our world is a complex mesh of interconnected and interdependent systems that sometime vex us, but which we cannot do without. Systems deliver our milk and bread, pick up our trash, and clothe us. They shelter us, protect us, and educate us. Systems offer us tremendous advantages in achieving our goals, but sometimes, systems can yield outputs that can hurt us in ways unintended. By recognizing the role of systems in our lives, we can more easily identify the root cause of problems that may seem inexplicable, intractable, and repetitive. And we can more quickly reach decisions that make sense and attack the actual dilemma.

Even cursory analysis of systems great and small can help us in improve our efficiency, sharpen our decision making, and tackle problems in ways that ensure that they won't be visiting us again tomorrow, or next week, or even next year.

Seize the Future with Scenario Analysis
Lecture 22

The future presents us with a paradox in our decision making: to make sound decisions, we must know the future, yet the future is unknowable. One powerful tool that can help us resolve this conundrum is scenario analysis, the process of repeatedly asking "What if?" and assembling our answers into plausible stories about the future.

The President's Daily Brief

- A crucial part of U.S. foreign policy is the President's Daily Brief (PDB), which contains the intelligence community's best estimate of what will happen in the world in the next 24 hours. The objective of the PDB is to reduce uncertainty so that critical decisions can be made with as much surety as possible.

- We'd all like to extend our vision as far as possible into the future, yet simultaneously, the horizon of the future always gets closer. In spite of a vast amount of information, our ability to see into the future seems more limited than ever.

Uncertainty = Risk

- In the business world, uncertainty means risk, and risk costs money. Businesses seek to reduce uncertainty in order to reduce risk and the costs of doing business.

- The question of what the future holds is often the most important question for a CEO and for various levels of the corporate hierarchy. It's often an important question in our personal lives, too. Anyone who faces competitive situations has a desire to know the future.

- In the highly charged and competitive business world, knowing as much as possible about the future of the business, the industry, competitors, and the market is a necessity.

Like a grandmaster in chess, a CEO faces a mind-boggling number of possibilities almost immediately in trying to predict the future.

Seeing into the Future?

- A game of chess is a circumscribed and fully comprehensible activity, yet predicting just one move into the future means knowing 1600 possible positions. Predicting two moves involves 2.5 million possible positions.

- CEOs and other business leaders are confronted with variables beyond even the number in a chess game every day. How can we possibly construct a process to address the multiplicity of questions they face in reaching a decision?

- One tool that provides a midrange solution is scenario analysis, used by both military and business establishments for decades. In this process, a menu of alternative futures is assembled.

- These scenarios are not blind guesses; they are the product of asking "What if?" with respect to key drivers that affect us or our organization.

This technique requires us to assemble the information we gather as part of our investigation process into plausible stories about the future.

A Rehearsal for the Future

- Most of us are already familiar with the idea of scenario planning. We may call it by a different name—training, rehearsal, standard operating procedure, contingency plan—but many of us have actually engaged in it at some point. In essence, the construction of scenarios allows us to rehearse the future.

- Organizations tasked with critical missions, such as the military or police, continually rehearse the future, as do sports teams.

- One of the most important aspects of effective scenario analysis is that the response is rehearsed under conditions that closely resemble the actual projected event. Football players practice scenario responses under game-like conditions. Elite commandos train under hyper-realistic conditions, including the use of live ammunition in exercises. Tactical evaluation exercises take place over a period of days and involve putting units under extreme stress.

- In business, war games are used to simulate crisis decision making in likely scenarios involving competitors. These exercises have the advantage of moving senior management out of the structured corporate board meeting, where certain options might be taboo for discussion.

Origins of Scenario Planning

- The idea of scenario planning arose from the early work of nuclear strategy theorist **Herman Kahn**. Kahn became famous for developing scenarios about nuclear war when he worked for the RAND Corporation in the 1950s.

- In the late 1960s, scenario planning was introduced at Royal Dutch Shell by **Pierre Wack**. His premise was that it is necessary to assume the predictability of some factors. If the future is 100 percent unknowable, then planning is useless.

- The task as Wack saw it was to separate what is predictable from what is fundamentally uncertain. The predictable elements were called "predetermineds," and these would appear in each scenario in the same way. The uncertainties, however, would interact and play out in different ways as the horizon of the future extended.

Objectives of Scenario Planning
- The first objective of scenario planning is to generate projects and decisions that are robust under a variety of different futures.

  o The notion of "robust" projects and decisions is truly elegant. Rather than measure a proposal against the best possible scenario, it's measured against all the scenarios that emerge from the process.

  o Projects are crafted to perform to minimum expectations under all scenarios. A scenario-based culture is suffused throughout the organization so that projects and decisions are weighed against several possible futures, instead of the future that is preferred.

- The second objective is to improve the quality of thinking about the future. Rather than a one-dimensional, linear thought process that yields a single "official future," scenario planning stretches our minds. It forces us to consider possibilities that we might otherwise dismiss.

- The third objective is to deepen and enrich the way people interpret the information around them, which becomes notably and qualitatively different than the thinking of others.

Basic Process for Scenario Planning
- The basic process for scenario planning involves asking and answering a series of questions.

- First, identify the focal issue or decision. What is it that you already do and why? What is it you want to do? This issue is generated by the mission of the firm and the objectives that arise from striving to accomplish that mission.

- Second, what are the key factors in the local environment? What do you consider your success indicators? What are your assumptions about key factors, such as customers, suppliers, competitors, and other identifiable stakeholders?

- Third, what are the driving forces in the macro-environment that influence the key factors you identified earlier? In this step, include such issues as demographic shifts, industry growth, technology progress and pace, activity of competitors, and so on.

- Next, rank the factors and forces by impact and uncertainty, looking for critical uncertainties. Examples of two forces might be the uncertainty surrounding the default of the United States on its debt and the volatility of public opinion over a particular initiative.

- Select the scenario logics. This means that you operationalize environmental drivers. You develop these factors on two axes, both measured as high and low. You plot a two-by-two matrix of impact (high or low) and uncertainty (high or low). This matrix yields four possibilities involving the major uncertainties identified in step 4.

- The sixth step is to flesh out the scenarios and weave the pieces into a narrative. You are telling a story about the future.

- Next, you determine the implications of each scenario on your original focal issue. In other words, evaluate how the decision plays out in each of the four possibilities in the matrix.

- Finally, identify and select leading indicators that alert you to the actual direction history is taking.

- It's helpful to give each scenario a name that captures its spirit and dynamic, such as Crisis Mode or Open-Market Dynamic.

The Power of Scenario Analysis
- The power of scenario analysis was demonstrated at Royal Dutch Shell soon after its adoption.

- Up until 1965, corporate planning at Shell was based on a technique called "predict and control." This involved the development of a single-line forecast of the future based on clear questions. At Shell, this course was modified to include several scenarios, but each scenario was given a probability of occurrence.

- The new scenario-planning process concentrated on the development of equally plausible scenarios with a focus on causality, not probability. The idea here was to stretch the thinking of executives.

- The first major test of Shell's scenario planning process came in the early 1970s. The question to be considered was the price of oil. The company developed six scenarios initially, one of which, the Crisis Scenario, was counterintuitive at the time.

- As it turned out, the Crisis Scenario predicted the 1973 oil shock and embargo that took everyone else by surprise. Shell was more prepared than any other company to deal with the crisis, having already thought through its implications beforehand.

- Subsequently, Shell correctly forecast the overcapacity in the tanker business and Europe's petrochemicals and recognized the denouement of these predictions earlier than its competitors.

Personal Scenario Planning
- Ways to apply scenarios in our own lives are obvious most of the time, but many of us rarely take advantage of the process. Young people entering the workforce, for example, would benefit tremendously from rehearsing their job interviews in advance.

- Your scenarios can be as simple as asking yourself a series of "What if?" questions based on your judgment of the different ways that certain situations might play out. You then rehearse the options you identify.

- One of the tasks for which scenario planning can be quite useful is delivering a speech. This activity carries predetermineds (the speech itself, the venue) and uncertainties (the question-and-answer period, environmental factors, equipment issues). You can respond to these uncertainties by practicing your speech and answering questions from a friend.

- At times, uncertainties can be almost impossible to predict, in which case, you can craft standardized responses that will serve you in almost any situation.

Combining Intelligence and Planning

- The President's Daily Brief may be the closest anyone will ever get to having a crystal ball to foretell the future, but even it has limitations. The PDB offers analyzed information that suggests general directions for future events, but it's only when such intelligence is combined with scenario planning that it becomes fully actionable.

- The future confounds CEOs, presidents, generals, and us. But we can dissipate some of the fog by planning for multiple futures. With scenario analysis, we can progress confidently, knowing that our projects and decisions can withstand the worst possibilities we can conceive.

Names to Know

Kahn, Herman (1922–1983): Kahn was the man whom *The New Yorker* once called the "heavyweight of the Megadeath Intellectuals" and who was a prescient futurist focusing on the strategy of nuclear war. He also was one of the first to predict the rise of Japan as a world-class economic power.

Wack, Pierre (1922–1997): Wack persevered against internal inertia at Royal Dutch Shell to pioneer development of what has become sophisticated scenario analysis, realistic forecasting of likely courses that history may take.

Suggested Reading

Gilad, *Business War Games*.

———, *Early Warning*.

Schwartz, *The Art of the Long View*.

1. A natural inclination is to assume that history progresses in linear fashion, that there is only one future, even as we are explicitly aware of the many choices we make on which our futures depend. As an exercise, select a major decision point for your company or for you personally, and consciously visualize how alternative futures might unspool.

2. Given two or more paths resulting from different decisions, one way to cobble together realistic scenarios is to assess the probable reactions of the major players to different stimuli. Ask, "If I do this, what will the other player do?" Pick a recent situation that required a major decision from you. How did you decide?

3. At a macro level, it is difficult to sort through the multitude of external factors that affect us. "What's the future?" is the eternal question that baffles leaders from all professions. An answerable version of that question is: "What are the likely three futures?" From there, we then prepare a response that is robust under each of several likely scenarios. Consider three likely futures for yourself or someone close to you, and identify what robust responses to each might be.

Seize the Future with Scenario Analysis
Lecture 22—Transcript

A crucial element of United States foreign policy is the PDB. But you may never have heard of the PDB. The PDB is the President's Daily Brief. Every morning, the President of the United States is greeted in the Oval Office by his Director of National Intelligence. The Director hands the president a slender leather binder. In this binder is a wealth of information. In fact, it may be as close as anyone ever gets to having a crystal ball to forecast the future. The PDB contains the distillation of an $80 billion annual budget of intelligence collection focused on the previous 24 hours. This intelligence is analyzed into crystalline form for the President's thoughtful consideration.

The Presidential Daily Brief is the nation's best estimate of what will happen in the next 24 hours, in the next week. The President uses this information for the crafting of prudent foreign policy. The objective of the PDB is to reduce uncertainty, so that critical decisions can be taken with as much surety as possible. Is it really a crystal ball? Is it infallible? Of course not, but it serves a valuable function. It is surely better than the alternative of no reasonable assessments of the resources, capabilities, and intentions of our friends and enemies.

Wouldn't it be great to have a PDB for our own use every day? Wouldn't it be great if a CEO had at least a weekly brief on all of his competitors? A professional assessment of likely courses of action? We constantly try to extend the horizon of what we know. The sooner we know it, the better. The better we know it, the sooner we can react. We all want to know the future for our own decision making, and yet the future is unknowable.

This is the topic of today's lecture—the mystery of the future and how it affects our thinking and decision making in conditions of competition. How the mystery of the future affects our strategy making. We want to push out our view of the future, extend our vision as far as possible. Yet simultaneously, the horizon of the future gets closer every day. In spite of a cascade of information, our ability to see into the future seems more limited than ever.

We are awash in information, but we have less and less time to react to unexpected events. And so the future presents us with a paradox—we search in vain for the certain decision under conditions of uncertainty. Is there any way we can resolve this conundrum to our advantage?

This lecture explores the horizon of the future and discusses ways that the military and select corporations extend their view over that horizon. In the process, we learn how our own future-oriented thinking can clarify the options available to us and help us select the appropriate action.

Let's begin with business. Uncertainty in the business world means risk. Political risk, credit risk, economic risk, and all of the permutations and subsidiary issues that go with risk. And risk—uncertainty—costs money. Businesses have to mitigate the perceived risks with insurance and a host of other risk-mitigation techniques. Businesses want to reduce uncertainty so as to reduce risk and the costs of doing business.

So here's the CEO's most important question: What's the future? In fact, this is often the most important question at various levels of the corporate hierarchy. And it's often the most important question in our personal lives, too.

Anyone who faces competitive situations has an insatiable desire to know the future. We want to know what's going to happen. It's more than idle curiosity. We believe that the more we know, the better our decision making, and this is more than likely correct. Even parents can think this way, as they try to help their children meet the challenges of a competitive world.

But the future eludes us—just out of our reach, shrouded in an impenetrable fog. Everyone in leadership positions—and everyone faced with competitive challenges—longs for knowledge of what will happen. We hunger for knowledge about the future, even if only a sliver of truth that can afford us a fleeting competitive advantage. In a highly charged and competitive business world, knowing as much as possible about the future of our business, our industry, our competitors, our market is a necessity.

Insider trading, at bottom, is acting on exclusive information about the future so as to profit by trading on that information. In this case, exclusive information about the future provides a carefully circumscribed temporary advantage. It should be clear how exclusive information in this case renders a decision clearer, more certain. But this is a finite case, sometimes dealing with a single datum of information about a single future scenario. Moreover, the action to be taken is clear—to buy or not to buy.

In a broader context, we want to know what decisions to take and we want to know how our competitors will respond to those decisions—move and countermove with two, three, four, sometimes five or more competitors moving against us. Simultaneously, we want to know how the market will respond to our actions, and we want to know if our firm, or our army, or we ourselves have the capability to confront the unknown challenges. It's the quest for the certain decision in conditions of uncertainty.

This concept, the future, is slippery. Some folks may believe it's easy to see into the future, if only for a short distance in time. This type of confidence is born of arrogance and the ignoring of context; it is a view that perceives the "future" as linear, as on a singular path and is "obvious." This type of shallow consideration founders on the rocks of incorrect assumptions. Or it founders on assumptions about reality that have changed since they were first adopted. In reality, seeing into the future is a difficult, almost impossible exercise, even for the $80 billion per year intelligence establishment of the United States.

How difficult is it to see into the future? Let's take a simplified version of the future and see how people regularly attempt to predict it. Take the game of chess. The chess game is a circumscribed and fully comprehensible activity. Each player commands eight pieces and eight pawns. The game is played on a square board divided into light and dark squares, 64 in total. One player moves a piece and then the opposing player moves. In this game, we sometimes ascribe mystical powers to the best players in the world—the international grandmasters of the game. We attribute to them the ability to "see ahead" several moves in the game. How else can these players assemble elegant and complex combinations leading to victory? So how far into the future does a grandmaster see? 10 moves? 8 moves? 6 moves? How about just 4 moves?

Surely it's not outlandish to assume that an international grandmaster such as Garry Kasparov can see just four moves into the future? But the future is not that easy. There are 40 possible variations in a chess game's first move. Seeing one full move ahead means knowing 1600 positions. Seeing just two moves into the future involves 2.5 million possible positions. Three moves, four billion possibilities. And for the fourth move? The possibilities available run to 318,979,564,000 different variations. That's about 319 billion possibilities. It should be quite obvious that the chessmaster doesn't see very far into the future at all. In fact, after just two moves, he is confronted with a sheer cliff of 2.5 million possibilities, impossible to scale.

Now back to the reality that you and I face each day. Back to the reality of the business leader confronted with problems of complexity that defy description. Think of our CEO confronted with such a multiplicity of variables as to make a chess player weep. Our CEO butts against that sheer wall of possibilities almost immediately as he begins to think of the future. How can we even begin to grasp the reality, the complexity of it all? When does the CEO decide on an action? Too soon, and all could be lost; too late, and all could be lost. At what point do we heed the cliché that we mustn't let the perfect become the enemy of the good? The paradox is that we all want perfect information in situations whose conditions guarantee we will never have it. But at some point we must declare the case closed; we must assert that no new information will be admitted into the decision process. So how can we possibly construct a process to get through this briar patch of obfuscation?

Fortunately, there is a tool available to us that provides a mid-range solution: scenario analysis. Military establishments have used a version of scenario analysis for decades. War is probably the ultimate competitive activity, and military intelligence has found it a helpful way to understand and predict enemy actions. In business, scenario analysis is a competitive analysis tool first used by Royal Dutch Shell in the 1960s. In both business and the military, the concept of scenario analysis is to assemble a menu of alternative futures. Think of these alternative futures as stories about the future. The word itself, scenario, comes from the theater—scenario, which is an outline of the plot of a dramatic or literary work and which includes information about its characters and scenes. Likewise, analysis is a tool that is, in essence, a story with a plot and with characters.

These scenarios are not blind guesses; they are the product of a venerable tradition of counterfactual history. It's a technique of asking "What if?" with respect to key drivers that impact us or our organization. One way of thinking about scenario analysis is to consider a movie that was made based on the classic board game Clue. Clue is a murder mystery board game that was created in England in 1948 (it was first sold in the U.S. by Parker Bros, under the name of Clue, in 1949). Players attempt to solve the mystery of who killed Mr. Boddy. The game was made into a 1985 comedic motion picture. In an unusual twist, three versions of the film with three different endings were made and shown in different theaters around the country.

And that's the point: The film had three equally plausible endings. Each of the endings—or scenarios—incorporated the same elements or "clues," but yielded different results. And this is what we do in scenario analysis. Scenario analysis requires us to consider the elements we develop as part of our investigation process and to assemble them into equally plausible stories about the future.

In the original method of scenario analysis, theories about the future would be generated by keen-minded experts. Again, not just one future, but several futures; it's really "scenarios" analysis. Scenarios are, indeed, stories about the future, and these stories help to clarify for us the choices available. Peter Schwartz is a futurist who did his early work in scenario analysis at Stanford Research Institute (SRI) in the 1970s. He then became a scenario analyst for Royal Dutch Shell Corporation in the 1980s. Schwartz said this about the utility of scenarios:

> They form a method for articulating the different pathways that might exist for you tomorrow, and finding your appropriate movements down each of those possible paths. Scenario planning is about making choices today with an understanding of how they might turn out.

Most of us are already familiar with idea of scenario planning. We may actually have engaged in it at some point. We may know it by a different name—training, rehearsal, standard operating procedure, contingency plan. In essence, the construction of scenarios allows us to rehearse the future. Many organizations rehearse the future, particularly those organizations tasked with critical missions: the army, navy, and air force, the police, fire departments, early responders of every stripe—all of them rehearse the future. Military basic training is the application of scenario rehearsal. The nation's more elite troops constantly rehearse various likely scenarios, some of them highly unlikely. Delta Force, the United States' anti-terrorist response unit and the Navy's Seal Team Six (DEVGRU) do nothing but rehearse for the future in every scenario imaginable.

In sports, too, teams rehearse the future. In fact, football is a complex laboratory for scenario analysis. Players are taught to "read" opposing formations and react to them within seconds. Teams relentlessly practice situational responses. If Situation A arises, then my opponent has certain options open to it. Consequently, my team practices Responses X, Y, and Z.

One of the most important aspects of effective scenario analysis is that the response is rehearsed under conditions that closely resemble the actual projected event. Sports teams practice scenario responses under game-like conditions. Elite commandos train under hyper-realistic conditions, including the use of live ammunition in exercises.

My own experience with scenario analysis, planning, and response was with NATO during the Cold War in NATO tactical evaluation exercises. These exercises were conducted under conditions as realistic and severe as training limits would allow. These could be considered rehearsals of the future. Rehearsing the possibilities of a massive Soviet attack across the German border.

Several NATO countries provided officers as referees (Germans, Belgians, British). Our unit—a hawk missile battalion—would inaugurate an exercise, deploying as it would during a Soviet attack. The sites and scenarios would vary, but the procedures were invariably the same as we responded to the various scripts given to us over a period of days. Action and then response, action and then response, putting stress on the unit, imposing casualties, pushing it hard, harder, until eventually the unit fails.

In business, too, war games are used to simulate crisis decision making in likely scenarios involving competitors. These exercises have the advantage of moving senior management out of the structured "corporate board meeting," where certain options might be taboo for discussion. Those options can be surfaced in the war games. This is where conventional thinking and the official "party line" can be safely challenged.

In all of these examples, the linking thread is rehearsal. Said Peter Schwartz: "You run through the simulated events as if you were already living them. You train yourself to recognize which drama is unfolding. That helps you avoid unpleasant surprises, and know how to act."

Royal Dutch Shell pioneered and led the use of scenario planning in the business world. At the time, this was quite bold and unconventional. But the origins of this approach arose from the early work of nuclear strategy theorist Herman Kahn. Herman Kahn can be called the father of scenario analysis. Kahn became famous in developing his scenarios about nuclear war when he worked for the RAND Corporation in the 1950s—thinking about the unthinkable. At the time, he was roundly criticized for actually thinking logically about a future in which nuclear weapons could be used.

Kahn served as an uncooperative model for the title character in the Stanley Kubrick movie *Dr. Strangelove*. His only transgression, if you call it that, was not ducking the issue of nuclear war. Instead, he thought long and hard about how various futures might play out.

At Shell in the late 1960s, scenario planning emerged for a very specific reason. Pierre Wack introduced scenario planning into Shell. His premise was that some things are predictable. It is necessary to assume that some things are predictable. If the future is 100 percent unknowable, then planning was useless. So scenarios were introduced as a way to plan without having to predict things that everyone knew were unpredictable. It was a midrange solution.

The task as Wack saw it was to separate what is predictable from what is fundamentally uncertain. The predictable elements are called "predetermineds." The predetermineds would appear in each scenario in the same predictable way. The uncertainties, however, would interact and play out in different ways as the horizon of the future extended. With this as the groundwork, let's look at the objectives of scenario planning and then at one example of the step-by-step process.

Scenario planning has three basic objectives. The first objective is to generate projects and decisions that are more robust under a variety of different futures. The notion of more "robust" projects and decisions is truly elegant. Rather than measure a proposal against the best possible scenario, it's measured against all the scenarios that emerge from the process. Projects are crafted to perform to minimum expectations under all scenarios. A scenario-based culture is suffused throughout an organization so that projects and decisions are weighed against several possible futures, instead of the future that is preferred.

The second objective is to improve the quality of our thinking about the future. Rather than a uni-dimensional, linear thought-process that yields a single "official future," scenario planning stretches our minds. It forces us to consider possibilities otherwise dismissed—perhaps dismissed prematurely.

The third objective is to deepen and enrich the way people interpret the information around them, which becomes notably and qualitatively different than the thinking of others. One Shell executive summarizes it this way:

> [At Shell, scenarios] are designed to "think the unthinkable" and to challenge conventional wisdom. If one looks at the early scenarios developed at Shell, one can clearly see that they not only told stories about the future, but that they also identified risks, established milestones or indicators to monitor, and in the end sometimes led to actual management action.

Obviously, an organization like Shell devotes tremendous resources to its scenarios. It's a complex process. But we can make use of a similar process in our personal decision making.

Here is the basic process for scenario planning. It involves asking and answering a series of questions. First, identify the focal issue or decision. What is it that you already do and why? What is it you want to do? This issue is generated by the mission of the firm and the objectives that arise from the striving to accomplish that mission.

Second, what are the key factors in the local environment? What do you consider your success indicators? What are your assumptions about key factors such as customers, suppliers, competitors, and other identifiable stakeholders? Identify the players in the scenario, the actors in the play.

Third, what are the driving forces in the macro-environment that influence the key factors you identified earlier? In this step, we include issues such as demographic shifts, industry growth, technology progress and pace, activity of competitors, and such like.

Fourth, rank the factors and forces by impact and uncertainty. Here you look for critical uncertainties. The scenarios cannot differ over predetermineds since these are the same in every alternative scenario. Examples of two forces might be the uncertainty surrounding default of the United States on its debt and the volatility of public opinion over a particular initiative.

Fifth, select your scenario logics. This means you operationalize your environmental drivers. You develop these factors on two axes both measured as high and low. You plot a 2-by-2 matrix of impact (high or low) and uncertainty (high or low). And this matrix yields four possibilities involving the major uncertainties identified in Step Four.

The sixth step is to flesh out the scenarios and weave the pieces into a narrative. You are telling a story about the future.

Seventh, you determine the implications of each scenario on your original focal issue. Here is where you rehearse the future. In other words, evaluate how your decision plays out in each scenario—in each of the four possibilities in your 2-by-2 matrix.

Eighth, we identify and select leading indicators that alert us to the actual direction that history is taking.

It is helpful to name each scenario, a descriptive terminology that captures the spirit and dynamic of what is going on (Crisis Mode, Open Market Dynamic, Cup Runneth Over).

Scenario analysis is a powerful tool, and this was demonstrated at Royal Dutch Shell soon after its adoption. Up until 1965, corporate planning was based on a technique called "predict and control." This was the development of a single line forecast of the future based on clear questions. At Shell, this course was modified to include several scenarios, but each scenario was given a probability of occurrence. This was not an advance over the old method. At that point, Shell instituted its current scenario planning process— the development of equally plausible scenarios with a focus on causality, not probability. The notion was to stretch the thinking of its executives. It was to move them out of linear thought processes that yielded an "obvious" future, and get them to consider possibilities less probable, but catastrophic if realized.

The first major test of Shell's scenario planning process came in the early 1970s. The question to be considered was the price of oil. Logical, given Shell's business. The company developed six scenarios initially, one of which was counterintuitive at the time. This became known as the "Crisis Scenario," in which the oil producing countries would cease producing oil at a rate that was unprofitable to those controlling the supply. This scenario predicted the 1973 oil shock and Arab embargo when everyone else was surprised. As a result, Shell was more prepared than any other company to deal with the crisis, having already thought through its implications beforehand.

Subsequently, Shell consistently bettered other oil companies. It correctly forecast the overcapacity in the tanker business and Europe's petrochemicals and recognized the denouement of these predictions earlier than its competitors.

Big organizations such as Shell and the United States military can utilize scenario planning, but we can engage in it as well. We can utilize the concept of "rehearsing for the future" in our personal lives in many ways.

Once you think about it, ways to apply scenarios in our own lives are obvious most of the time. But many of us rarely take advantage of the process. Young people entering the work force would benefit tremendously from rehearsing their job interviews in advance. To arm themselves with the skills necessary to answering questions deftly. But aside from the mock interview procedures enacted by some business schools, young people rarely take advantage of this. Even when we know we're entering into a stressful situation whose parameters are known, we rarely "rehearse for the future" in such a way that accurately duplicates the activity itself.

You needn't construct an elaborate schema of scenarios. Your scenarios can be as simple as asking yourself a series of "what if?" questions based on your judgment of the different ways that things might play out. And then you rehearse the options you identify.

One of the most useful scenario-related activities is our response to the task of delivering a speech. The crafting of a speech and a rehearsal for a public speaking engagement offers a wonderful opportunity to engage in scenario planning. This activity carries the same basic elements of the Shell scenario-planning process—it has predetermineds and it carries uncertainties. The predetermined aspect is the speech itself, the venue, the time, and all of the logistical arrangements that you can count on. The uncertainties relate mainly to the give-and-take of the question-and-answer period afterward. Other negative uncertainties that may impact the event are environmental factors such as bad weather, audio-visual equipment failure, heating or cooling problems, and such like.

How do you respond to these eventualities? One solution is to game out what you will do in advance. With respect to your speech, practice in the room where you deliver it. Answer tough questions from a friend designed to prepare you for that eventuality. Even if you aren't asked any of the same questions, you have benefit of the pressure beforehand. And practice these eventualities exactly as you will perform them, not with starting and stopping and fidgeting.

At times, the uncertainties are almost impossible to predict, in which case it is best to craft standardized "robust" responses that will serve you in almost any situation. My own responses are conditioned from my experience in such situations. For instance, there can be a tremendous difference in preparing to deliver a speech in the United States and delivering one in a foreign country. I learned this difference the hard way as I arrived to deliver a talk at a political headquarters in the city of Izhevsk, Russia, several years ago.

Every expectation I had of the event was destroyed in succession, including the language spoken. I expected a small, private round-table discussion in English but I arrived to find something entirely different. I arrived to find a televised press conference entirely in Russian. I was introduced not as a visiting professor, but as a political organizer visiting from the United States to provide advice to the local political party.

In 2003, I was introduced to a college audience in the city of Ufa, Bashkortostan, not as a visiting professor, but as a former CIA agent who was calling for war with Iraq. Could even the best scenario planning have predicted either of the above occurrences? Maybe. When planning a presentation to an unfamiliar audience, scenario planning would mean anticipating a full range of possible expectations and reactions from the audience. And that's the lesson here; that's what real scenario planning is all about. With experience, we can learn how to prepare robust responses— responses so robust, in fact, that they can handle a very wide variety of situations.

To bring us full circle, we close with a revisit of the President's Daily Brief. It's as close as we'll probably come to a crystal ball to foretell the future, but even the PDB has its limitations. Take the PDB of August 6, 2001, which was entitled "Bin Ladin Determined to Strike in U.S." Many have pointed to this memorandum as some kind of smoking gun to hold the presidential administration somehow culpable in ignoring warnings. But armchair analysts are always bold in hindsight and see a "clear warning" where none is really present. The PDB offers analyzed information that suggests general directions for future events. But it's only when such intelligence is combined with scenario planning that it becomes more fully and immediately actionable.

This is a lesson for all of us. These days, you can have web sites and paid analysts sending you electronic streams of high-quality intelligence day or night, 24/7, But your ability to use that intelligence will vastly improve—and may ultimately depend—on the scenarios that you create and rehearse.

The future remains an enigma for us. And it probably always will. It confounds CEOs, presidents, and generals leading armies of thousands. And it confounds us. But in this lecture we learned that we can dissipate some of the fog that befuddles us. We can improve our thinking and sharpen our decision-making processes by considering more than one scenario. We can't know the future. But we can plan for multiple futures. In fact, with the use of scenario analysis, we need not fear the unknown. We can march forward quite confident, knowing that our projects and our decisions can withstand even the worst of the possibilities that strike.

The Correlation of Forces, Luck, and Culture
Lecture 23

"Correlation of forces" is a deceptively simple phrase that captures the combination of external forces that seem to buffet us without rhyme or reason. How we deal with those forces can mean the success or failure of our strategic plans. One powerful current in the correlation of forces is culture; in this lecture, we look at the dimensions of culture to see how this force may affect strategic planning in business.

Correlation of Forces

- During the Cold War, the Russians used the term "correlation of forces" to refer to a method of calculating and evaluating world power. The Soviet method took into account military, political, economic, social, moral, revolutionary, and other factors. It was simultaneously a philosophical construct, a measuring method, and a guide to action.

- The Soviets studied the correlation and adjusted their behavior to take advantage of the large, impersonal forces at their disposal. Where possible, they also worked to tilt those forces in their favor. This strategic approach allowed the backward economy and society of the Soviet Union to achievable notable successes against the far more advanced U.S. economy.

- For us, the correlation of forces is a powerful concept that captures the environmental factors that affect a conflict situation over a long period. It accurately describes the chaotic and confusing factors that act on us constantly, for good or ill.

- It's important to note that we are not at the mercy of these powerful, impersonal forces. We can place ourselves in an advantageous position with respect to these forces and turn them to our advantage, much as practitioners of aikidō do in redirecting the force of an attack.

- In an earlier lecture, we talked about conducting an environmental scan. The correlation of forces suggests the possibility of looking at various external environmental scans as a whole. It offers us a holistic, long-term view of cultural, political, economic, and technological factors.

- Looking at the correlation of forces allows us to contemplate our response to environmental "curve balls" in advance and react in ways that maximize our goals, rather than being self-destructive.

Luck

- Some people seem to win in life far more often than they fail. We call this luck, but in fact, it's the result of recognizing larger tendencies in the environment and using them to achieve positive outcomes.

- What we call "good luck" and "bad luck" is actually a type of response to the correlation of forces. We can conceive of the "luck" we experience as the result of a consistent behavior pattern over time as we interact with the environment around us.

- If we shape our behavior to ride with the correlation of forces, our luck is more likely to be good than bad. If we ignore the correlation of forces and try to use force, whether intellectual or brute, we will likely find that our luck is bad more often than not.

- Writer Max Gunther identified five basic behaviors exhibited by lucky people and almost nonexistent in the unlucky.

    o Lucky people are those who form many friendly contacts with others. Today, we call this behavior "networking."

    o Attending to hunches is another lucky behavior. Think of a hunch as a conclusion based on real data, that is, facts you have accumulated and assessed, either consciously or unconsciously.

    o The next behavior is acting boldly. Gunther calls this the *audentes fortuna juvat* ("fortune favors the bold") phenomenon. Bold people are ready to accept lucky opportunities, know the difference between boldness and rashness, and don't insist on certainty.

o Lucky people also exhibit the ratchet effect, the ability to get out of bad situations quickly. As one of Gunther's subjects notes, "If you are losing a tug-of-war with a tiger, give him the rope before he gets to your arm. You can always buy another rope."

o Gunther classifies the fifth lucky behavior as the pessimism paradox, by which he means acknowledging Murphy's law and Mitchell's law ("Life is as slippery as a piece of soap, and if you think you have a good grip on it, you're wrong"). Lucky people have a clear-eyed appreciation for a range of outcomes; thus, they are never surprised by the worst-case result.

• These five behaviors have been found to improve the outcomes in the lives of people who practice them. They are strategic behaviors that seek to tilt the intangibles in favor of us reaching our goals.

• If we think of the correlation of forces as constituting the environmental terrain, then the five behaviors may be seen as a kind of positioning according to principle. Smart positioning does not guarantee victory, but it increases the odds of a positive outcome.

The Cultural Environment

• A major part of the correlation of forces is the cultural environment. Cultural forces are deep-rooted and greatly affect how people behave. One tool we can use to understand and predict culturally based behavior is the idea of dimensions of culture, created by Dutch researcher Geert Hofstede in the early 1970s.

• Knowing the culture scores of a country can help us understand derivative aspects of that country, such as its political processes, social relations, and economic organization. It can help us understand why people act the way they do, why things work the way they do, and why institutions have certain structures.

- In an increasingly globalized world, this type of knowledge is extremely valuable, especially as we guard against judging others according to stereotypes or projecting our own cultural expectations onto those from other cultures ("mirror-imaging").

- Hofstede defines culture as "the collective programming of the mind that distinguishes the members of one group or category of people from another." For Hofstede, culture gives rise to whole systems of values.

- Visual manifestations of culture—the practices of culture—fall into three categories: symbols, heroes, and rituals. Culture provides the interpretive matrix that allows us to decode culturally inspired practices and repertoires.

- Although we rarely think about them in our own culture, such practices and repertoires make life predictable and social systems possible. They become noticeable only when we must deal with someone within the framework of an entirely different cultural paradigm.

- Cultural behavior is predictable based on identifiable cultural factors that are measured along the four dimensions posited by Hofstede: power distance, uncertainty avoidance, individualism, and masculinity. This model has proven resilient in its predictive power over decades and can be applied in politics, sports, economics, sociology, and religion.

Dimensions of Culture
- Let's look at each of the four dimensions of culture to see how they can influence the structure of businesses and how people behave in those organizations.

- The power distance index measures how human inequality is handled in a culture with regard to prestige, wealth, and power. It conditions the shape and character of organizations with regard to how hierarchies are structured and staffed, how rigidly the levels of hierarchy are maintained, and the decision-making processes within the hierarchy.

Cultural characteristics can influence the structure of organizations and how people behave in these organizations.

○ The power distance score captures how individuals in a society perceive authority and how they react to it. A high score means that superiors and subordinates view each other in entrenched roles. There is no hope for upward mobility.

○ Russia has a power distance score of 93, while the score for the United States is 40.

• The uncertainty avoidance index measures a society's sensitivity to the unknown. It captures how people react to unknown situations, and it affects the structure of institutions and the types of operational repertoires developed to conduct transactions. It is the extent to which people feel threatened by uncertain or unknown situations.

○ Generally speaking, the higher the uncertainty avoidance score, the more rule driven a society is, with repertoires and standard operating procedures in organizations and institutions clearly spelled out.

- o Greece has one of the highest scores here at 112, while the United Kingdom has a score of only 35.

- The individualism index captures how the concept of the individual is handled in society, which affects how people live and work together and in what kinds of institutions. The opposite of individualism is collectivism.

  - o Among other things, this score indicates whether people are motivated more by group or individual rewards.

  - o A country with a high individualism score is Australia, at 90. Guatemala has one of the lowest scores in the world, 6.

- The last dimension looks at aggressive versus nurturing behavior. This dimension captures the proclivity of a society toward one of two types of goal-directed behavior: ego goals (masculine) or social goals (feminine). A country with a high ego goals score is Slovakia, at 110. One of the highest-scoring cultures in the world for social goals is Sweden, at 5.

- No single dimension has a deciding impact on individual behavior or group organization. These dimensions indicate tendencies in societies and the strength of those tendencies relative to other societies. The four dimensions work in tandem in various combinations to yield different patterns of expectations with regard to culturally based behavior.

- Businesses tend to dispense with culture because it's difficult to define, quantify, and assess. But understanding the dimensions of culture presents us with a chance to seize significant competitive advantage.

Three Powerful Concepts
- The correlation of forces is a phrase from an earlier time, but it captures the combination of external forces that seem to buffet us without rhyme or reason. Although we can rarely affect the correlation of forces directly, we can certainly recognize its main currents and adjust our personal actions to ride those currents to our own benefit.

- The correlation of forces, the notion of luck, and the dimensions of culture are three powerful concepts that you can immediately harness to your needs to gain analytical power and dramatically increase your chances of achieving strategic success.

Suggested Reading

Gunther, *The Luck Factor*.

Hofstede, *Culture's Consequences*.

Riggio, *The Charisma Quotient*.

Questions to Consider

1. The lecture points out that the correlation of forces affecting us is sometimes an amorphous thing to comprehend. There is no one-size-fits-all correlation; the forces that exert pressure on you might not affect others at all. Consequently, it's up to each of us to prepare our own "correlation map" to evaluate the macro-forces at play that affect us directly and indirectly. This is true for your firm, and it's true for you personally. At both the firm and individual professional levels, prepare correlation-of-forces maps to identify the macro-forces that exert steady pressure for good or ill in your life.

2. Few things in life offer us the opportunity to change radically our circumstances like simply vowing to be lucky. We have seen that "luck" is no more than the collection of positive behaviors that people choose to enact. After reviewing the lecture, identify two or three luck-producing behaviors that you can adopt right now and consciously enact them as a change in behavioral habit.

3. Culture is a complex phenomenon, but investing time in understanding the cultures with which we deal gives us a competitive advantage over those who engage in the simplistic exercise of mirror-imaging, especially where business is concerned. Consider how your expectations and, hence, your actions might differ with respect to conducting business in Puerto Rico, Russia, and Malaysia.

The Correlation of Forces, Luck, and Culture
Lecture 23—Transcript

During the Cold War, the Russians used a term called the correlation of forces. To the Western ear, it sounded ominous, and it was probably meant to be. The correlation of forces—or *sootnosheniye sil*—referred to a Soviet method to calculate and evaluate world power. It began as a broad-based concept that attempts to capture the sweep of history.

The correlation of forces is multidimensional. In the Soviet method, it consisted of military, political, economic, social, moral, and revolutionary factors as well as intangible factors such as the strength of various international movements. It was simultaneously a philosophical construct, a measuring method, and a guide to action. It was this complex notion the Soviets assessed to gauge their progress in the struggle against the democratic capitalist nations of the West for more than 40 years. The Soviets studied the correlation and they adjusted their behavior so to take advantage of the large, impersonal forces at their disposal. Where possible, they also worked simultaneously to tilt those forces in their own favor. It was this strategic approach that allowed the backward economy and society of the Soviet Union to achievable notable successes against the far more wealthy and more advanced economy of the United States.

We can find utility in this correlation of forces. It's a powerful concept that captures the environmental factors that impact a conflict situation over a long period. While the term has its origins in a particular era of international rivalry, the correlation of forces accurately describes the chaotic and confusing environmental factors that act upon us constantly, for good or ill. But this does not mean that we are at the mercy of these powerful forces, not at all. A good sailor is never at the mercy of the sea. A good sailor is friends with the sea and has struck an accommodation. In fact, he understands that the same correlation of forces that buffet others can be at his disposal. A good sailor can adapt his behavior. A good sailor can place himself in the most advantageous position with respect to these forces and his eventual destination. These are impersonal forces, and we can confront them or we can befriend them and turn them to our advantage.

Think of the Japanese martial art of *Aikido*. *Aikido* is a system of self-defense that relies upon redirecting the force of an attack rather than opposing it head-on. An opponent may attack suddenly, quickly, from any side. Instead of meeting the attack with a force of our own, we use the attacker's energy against him and for our own benefit. We redirect the force rather than oppose it, rather than expending energy to overcome it.

In like fashion, the environment in which we dwell pulses with energy and many forces are at play. This energy and these forces are oblivious to our existence. They are impersonal, objective, and powerful—cultural forces, economic forces. A correlation of forces. They are much like the winds and currents of a mighty ocean and we are in a sailing vessel. We can consider ourselves sailors—canny and shrewd, or callow and naive. As canny and shrewd sailors on this sea of uncertainty, we can either fight these powerful forces, or we can turn this environmental energy into our own.

There are tendencies and patterns in our society and world that affect us for good or ill, and the effect often depends on whether we recognize those patterns and on how we respond to them. These powerful external forces are neither for us nor against us, they are simply what we make of them. In a sense, it is up to us whether our luck is good or bad, whether opportunities elude us, or whether they make themselves available. We can influence the correlation of forces around us.

We've talked about conducting an environmental scan in earlier lectures. The correlation of forces suggests the possibility of looking at the various external environment scans together as a whole; it offers us a different prism. It's a holistic way of viewing things; it's a method that takes a long-term view. These forces are cultural, political, economic, and technological. But of course, they can encompass other forces as well—forces that may be particular to your own circumstances. The central idea of our response to these factors is to craft a mode of behavior that yields dividends regardless of the environmental curve balls thrown our way. In other words, we contemplate our response in advance; when the unexpected happens, we react in ways that maximize our goals rather than in ways that may be momentarily satisfying but self-destructive in the longer run.

456

Let's now explore how to recognize larger patterns and tendencies in personal lives, in our workspace, in our own society, and in foreign societies so that we may utilize techniques that put larger cultural forces on our side. Let's look at how to engage in positive patterns of behavior to ride with the main currents of life where opportunities multiply and where collateral possibilities make themselves known. I don't know what forces will affect me today, tomorrow, or next year. I do know that I can control my own responses to those forces. I study their tendencies and I take advantage of them by positioning myself by engaging in behavior that ensures the best chance for a positive outcome, regardless of what my goal might be. And more often than not, I achieve a positive outcome. You've seen folks like this, folks who seem to win in life far more often than fail. It's mysterious, because what they do is relatively invisible. To the observer, someone's ability to recognize larger tendencies and to use them to personal profit can appear mysterious.

If all of this seems a bit abstract, let's bring it down to earth. We have a name for it: We call it luck. What is luck? Random House offers this definition: "The force that seems to operate for good or ill in a person's life, as in shaping circumstances, events, or opportunities." Is luck really something that just "happens" to people? Is it random? Or is it more complex than that? Is what we call "good luck" and "bad luck" actually a type of response to the correlation of forces? In other words, we can conceive of the "luck" we experience as simply the results of our consistent behavior pattern over time, interacting with the environment around us.

For instance, if we shape our behavior to ride the correlation of forces, our luck is more likely to be good than bad. And the converse, if we ignore the correlation of forces and try to use force, whether intellectual or brute, we will likely find our luck is bad more often than not.

We have research to substantiate this. Writer Max Gunther wrote a classic in 1977, later reprinted in 2010, called *The Luck Factor*. Over a 20-year period, Gunther evaluated more than 1000 subjects on the question: "What do lucky people do that unlucky people don't do?" The results of his work appear in this book, in which he identifies the five basic behaviors exhibited by lucky folks. These behaviors are almost nonexistent in the unlucky. He gives them provocative names.

Here they are: The Spiderweb structure is the result of the first type of luck-generating behavior. The luckiest people are those who have formed a great many friendly contacts with other people. Today, we call it networking. Max Gunther put it this way, rather poetically:

> You cannot know what thunderbolt of good fortune is being prepared for you now by some distant engine of fate. You cannot know what complex interconnection of human relationships will guide the thunderbolt in your direction. But you *can* know ... with certainty ... that the probability of your getting hit is directly proportional to the number of people who know your name.

How many people know your name? Opportunities will not seek you out in your apartment or in your ranch house on the cul-de-sac. This means that you put yourself into the mainstream of interaction. That is where the opportunities lie.

The next behavior is the hunching skill. Gunther tells us that "A hunch is a piece of mind stuff that feels something like knowledge, but doesn't feel perfectly trustworthy." A hunch is sometimes called instinct. It's a conclusion that is based on real data, on facts that you have accumulated and have assessed either consciously or unconsciously. The hunch itself arrives unbidden, and it's based on facts that have not quite reached the surface so that you are aware of them. In sum, it's the ability to know something without being quite able to explain how you know it. This ability dwells substantially in the realm of feelings. We should not ignore these unsettling messages that may, at times, conflict with the surface "facts." We should give room for the seeds of a good hunch to grow and sprout, to bear fruit. Context is a large part of the soil from which hunches grow, and we ought to broaden our own intellectual context. This context provides the backdrop against which new facts are processed. This means pursuing eclectic education. We should cultivate in ourselves a broad-based knowledge to improve the quality of our "hunches."

The next behavior is the *audentes fortuna juvat* phenomenon. *Audentes fortuna juvat* is a Latin phrase, which means, "fortune favors the bold." Gunther notes that it "sounds like some Roman general trying to rally unenthusiastic legionnaires for the next day's battle." But more than a cliché, it carries a measure of truth. Research shows that lucky people tend to be bold people—that is, people who act boldly. The most timid men and women tend to be, without fail, the unluckiest. Boldness means acting in ways that can increase luck.

Here are three rules to play by as newly emboldened people: 1) be ready to inspect lucky opportunities when they come your way; 2) know the difference between boldness and rashness—it's easy to talk yourself out of meeting a challenge by calling it "rash"; 3) don't insist on having total advance knowledge of any situation you are about to enter; if you insist on certainty, you paralyze yourself.

The next behavior is the ratchet effect. A ratchet is a device that preserves gains. It allows a wheel to turn forward but prevents it from slipping back. Likewise, where luck is concerned, if the wheel turns the wrong way, lucky people get out. "They have the capacity to get out of deteriorating situations quickly." Gunther tells the story of a Swiss banker who explained his fabulous financial success this way: "If you are losing a tug-of-war with a tiger, give him the rope before he gets to your arm. You can always buy another rope." The vivid metaphor captures the spirit of prudence and cold calculation necessary to quit at the right moment. To lock the ratchet at the appropriate time.

The fifth and final behavior is the pessimism paradox, which is guided by two laws that interlock. The first law is that of Mr. Murphy—anything that can go wrong will go wrong. It doesn't mean you expect it to go wrong, no, it means that you have identified and assessed the risks of the worst possible outcome rather than ignored it. The second law is called Mitchell's Law and it can be loosely stated as, "Life is slippery like a bar piece of soap, and if you think you have a good grip on it, you are wrong." No life is ever totally under the control of its owner, and lucky people are those who adapt to this environment of uncertainty. "They ready themselves for the opportunities, and they guard themselves against its hazards." Does this mean lucky people are pessimistic? Of course not. It means that they have a clear-eyed appreciation for the range of outcomes so that they are never surprised by the worst-case result.

These five behaviors have been found to improve the outcomes in the lives of people who practice them. It is strategic behavior that seeks to tilt the intangibles in favor of us reaching our goals. It's a positioning game and looks to the longer term. If we think of the correlation of forces as constituting the environmental terrain, then the five behaviors may be seen as a kind of positioning according to principle. It does not guarantee victory, but smart positioning increases the odds of a positive outcome. These principles of behavior, if followed assiduously, greatly enhance the odds of fulfilling our strategic plan.

A major part of the correlation of forces consists in the cultural environment. Cultural forces are deep-rooted and greatly affect how people behave. Regardless of how people may dress or how they may superficially act in controlled situations, it is their culture that charts the general path of their behavior, both individually and in groups. So what if you could understand those broad cultural tendencies? What if you could get beyond surface stereotypes and gain an appreciation for what motivates the actions of those around you. What if you could predict their behavior more often than not in crucial situations?

We have a tool to do just that. It's called the dimensions of culture. It was created by Dutch researcher Geert Hofstede in the early 1970s. After decades of use and revalidation, it remains one of our surest guides to understanding and predicting culturally based behavior. It can tell us why things happen the way they do when strong cultural factors are at work.

Here's why this kind of knowledge is so valuable: If we know the culture scores of a country, it can help us understand derivative aspects of that country, such as its political processes, its social relations, and its economic organization. It can help us understand why people act the way they do, why things work the way they do, and why institutions have a certain structure. In short, knowledge about a culture of a country can inform us as to the types of behavior we can expect to find in people from that country. Not always, but much of the time, it informs us about tendencies and influences, whether they are strong or weak.

In an increasingly globalized world, this type of knowledge is extremely valuable, especially as we guard against judging others according to stereotypes. Or, even worse, projecting our own cultural expectations onto those from cultures different than our own. Sometimes, we project our own characteristics onto folks from other societies. We create a set of expectations based on those same assumptions. Oftentimes, these projections are invisible to us, because our own cultural biases are for the most part invisible to us. They are embedded in our psyches as unexamined assumptions.

By explicitly investigating the cultural bases of institutional activity of a nation, we can filter out "mirror-imaging," the projection of our own characteristics onto other societies. We avoid inadvertently inserting our own cultural bias in our perspective. It's far more constructive to set aside those cultural biases when we try to make sense of people of other nationalities.

Geert Hofstede defines culture as "the collective programming of the mind that distinguishes the members of one group or category of people from another." It is a kind of "software" of the mind. For Hofstede, culture gives rise to whole systems of values. There are the "core elements" of culture. Values are not pertinent unless manifested, and the visual manifestations of culture are covered by the terms symbols, heroes, and rituals. These constitute the practices of culture, which are really subject to accurate interpretation only by cultural "insiders." Culture provides the interpretive matrix that allows us to decode culturally inspired practices and repertoires. These repertoires of human interaction are parts of daily life we rarely think about. Repertoires make life predictable and social systems possible. Our modes of conducting business or of performing simple tasks can become so routinized and habitual that they become invisible to us. They acquire this mantle of ritual or custom. For example, take business customs, such as the shaking of hands or perfunctory greetings.

Such customs are rooted in habit and necessity and convenience. While we sometimes think of customs as somehow quaint or ceremonial, they can serve essential functions. But our own customs tend to be invisible to us. Or if not invisible, we don't call them customs. Rather, it's just the "way we do things here." Customs are not things we think about consciously, at least not until we're prodded by having them pointed out. They become noticeable only when we must deal with someone who conducts business within the framework of an entirely different cultural paradigm. Hofstede put it this way:

> It is as though we—or the people of any other society—grow up perceiving the world through glasses with distorting lenses. The things, events, and relationships we assume to be "out there" are in fact filtered through this perceptual screen.

Customs make life predictable. And based on our expectations of human behavior, we daily make such predictions. "Our predictions may sometimes not prove true," says Hofstede, "But the more accurately we know a person's mental programming and the situation, the more sure our prediction will be."

I think you see where this is going. Culture is a tremendous part of that array of forces that comprise the correlation of forces. We want to understand these forces and direct their power to support our strategic plan. The dimensions of culture makes this possible. Cultural behavior is not random. It is predictable based on identifiable cultural factors that we measure along four "dimensions"—power distance, uncertainty avoidance, individualism, and masculinity. These four factors have proven durable for decades in assessing culture's impact in the international business world. They have proved reliable in explaining behavior—otherwise chaotic and confusing behavior.

Now, all this may be interesting in an abstract sense, but it is also quite useful in a practical sense in our pursuit of clear, strategic thinking. The Hofstede model has proven resilient in its predictive power over decades. It has application in any area where cultural differences may divide people. The dimensions of culture can be used in politics, in sports, in economics, in sociology, in religion. The model can help us answer the question: "Are cultural factors at work in my situation that make certain individual and organizational behavioral outcomes more likely than others?" This is a perfectly reasonable question.

462

Hofstede's model is built on the notion that different nations possess identifiable cultural characteristics. They can influence the structure of business firms, their behavior, and how the people behave in those organizations. If we know the predominant cultural traits of a state, then we may be able to chart the general direction of cultural forces at work. Cultural differences can indicate problem areas that may arise if, say, a business attempts to organize itself outside the bounds of what is generally accepted within a culture.

Let's look at each of the four dimensions of culture to get an idea how to use this tool. There are four dimensions of culture differences among nations: power distance, uncertainty avoidance, individualism, masculinity. First, the power distance index measures how human inequality is handled in a culture with regard to prestige, wealth, and power. It conditions the shape and character of organizations with regard to how hierarchies are structured and staffed, how rigidly the levels of hierarchy are maintained, and the decision-making processes within the hierarchy.

Power distance captures how individuals in a society perceive authority and how they react to it. A high power distance score means that superiors and subordinates view each other in entrenched roles. There is no hope for upward mobility. An example of a nation with a high power distance score is Russia, at 93. A country with a low power distance score is the United States, at 40.

The uncertainty avoidance index measures a society's sensitivity to the unknown. It captures how people react to unknown situations, and it affects the structure of institutions and the types of operational repertoires developed to conduct transactions. It is the extent to which people feel threatened by uncertain or unknown situations. Generally speaking, the higher this uncertainty avoidance score, the more rule-driven a society is, with repertoires and standard operating procedures in organizations and institutions clearly spelled out. Greece has one of the highest scores at 112, while the United Kingdom has a score of only 35.

The individualism index captures how the concept of the individual is handled in society. It affects how people live and work together, in what kinds of relationships, and in what kinds of institutions. The polar opposite of individualism is collectivism. The index measures the degree of individualism or collectivism in a society. Among other things, this score indicates whether people are motivated more by group rewards or by individual rewards. A country with a high individualism score is Australia, at 90. Guatemala has one of the lowest scores in the world at 6.

Finally, aggressive versus nurturing behavior. This cultural dimension captures the proclivity of a society toward one of two types of goal-directed behavior—ego goals or social goals. According to Hofstede, these two poles can also be thought of as masculinity and femininity, with masculine as assertive, tough, and focused on ego goals of material success. Femininity stands for a society in which social gender roles are supposed to be modest, tender, and concerned with the quality of life. As you might imagine, the gender-based way of framing this particular index has come under fire, and yet the contrast between aggressive ego goals and nurturing social goals remains durable. A country with a high ego-goals score is Slovakia, at 110. One of the highest-scoring cultures in the world for social goals is Sweden at 5.

No single dimension has a deciding impact on individual behavior or on group organization. These dimensions indicate tendencies in societies and the strength of those tendencies relative to other societies. These four dimensions work in tandem in various combinations to yield several different patterns of expectations with regard to culturally based behavior.

I think you can see the connection to the correlation of forces. Suddenly a great deal of what seemed inexplicable is now much clearer than it was. It takes no great leap of faith to understand how a Slovak and a Swede might react differently to the same set of facts. This factor of culture has traditionally been given meager consideration in the business world. Business dispenses with culture, because it's difficult to define, difficult to quantify, and difficult to assess how it impacts the bottom line. Chief Executive Officers, who are numbers-oriented, are slow to get their minds around the factor of culture because it doesn't show up on the balance sheet. Few people outside of business and psychology are even aware of the power embedded within the dimensions of culture. As such, this presents the opportunistic among us with a chance to seize significant competitive advantage. For if we gain more understanding of the correlation of forces that toss us about, we are better armed to steer a clear course through to achieve our strategic goals.

The correlation of forces is a phrase from an earlier time, but it captures the combination of external forces that seem to buffet us without rhyme or reason. Some of these forces are intangible and others we overlook. While we can rarely affect this correlation of forces directly, we can certainly recognize its main currents and adjust our personal actions in ways to ride those currents to our own benefit. How we deal with those forces can mean the difference between failure and success. We increase our chances of receiving what is usually called "good luck."

The correlation of forces is a holistic view that combines information from our environmental scan, with information from the dimensions of culture. The correlation of forces, the notion of luck, and the dimensions of culture—these are three powerful concepts that you can harness to your needs right this second. They give you potent analytical power and dramatically increase your chances of achieving strategic success.

Strategic Thinking as a Way of Life
Lecture 24

Nature dictates that the future remains closed to us, but a multitude of techniques can reduce the ambiguity in our lives. Seeing what's next requires knowing what's past, learning what's here, and arming ourselves with the tools to meet a broad range of challenges. In this lecture, history's great strategic thinkers show us that we can prepare ourselves for almost any challenge with techniques and logical thinking to craft strategies to suit our needs.

The Certainty of Uncertainty
- Uncertainty is everywhere, in both our personal and our professional lives, and as much as we'd like to be able to predict the future, we know we can't. However, as we've seen throughout these lectures, the measure of our success is not whether we can predict the future but how prudently we prepare for it.

- By adopting various combinations of strategic thinking techniques and tools of analysis and by seizing a substantial role in developing our circumstances, we can improve our chances of succeeding at the tasks we set for ourselves. In other words, we can successfully alter the conditions that affect the future that concerns us.

Benjamin Franklin
- One early American who practiced the art of strategic thinking on a level that has rarely been matched was **Benjamin Franklin**. He was able to both visualize the future and craft it, acting in ways to maximize a productive relationship to his environment.

- It was Franklin's vision, coupled with an equally determined drive, that led him to press forward throughout his life. In fact, this idea of pressing forward characterizes many great people. Franklin both seized opportunities and created them.

- Franklin also exhibited the strategic personality's thirst for knowledge and ideas. When he was only 21, he created a group to discuss scientific and political ideas that later evolved into the American Philosophical Society. He and his associates founded the first public library in America, and he was instrumental in founding what would later become the University of Pennsylvania.

- In short, Franklin shared with most strategic thinkers curiosity combined with a lust for life. He was always powerfully engaged with his environment and left us legacies in multiple fields—science, politics, education, literature, military affairs, and business and finance.

- Franklin lived by a set of principles designed to maximize his natural gifts. These 13 principles constitute a blueprint for a robust and future-oriented existence. Four of the principles—order, resolution, frugality, and industry—suggest that one key to tackling uncertainty is to establish an island of certitude.

Winston Churchill

- Another man with a fabulously strategic mind was Sir Winston Churchill, perhaps best known for his role as Britain's prime minister during the darkest days of World War II. His personal courage, his resolve, and his powerful rhetoric inspired the resistance of the nation.

- Churchill had the knack for being on the scene of great events, the result of a personal drive that moved him constantly from the periphery into the mainstream of life. Many of us would do well to engage with life as he did.

© iStockphoto/Thinkstock.

The extraordinary exploits of Winston Churchill were born of a highly focused strategic intent.

- Churchill believed that he would die at a young age, as his father had. Thus, he operated with a sense of urgency, moving quickly to establish his legacy. At age 21, he became a war correspondent and then served in the British military, always seeking the riskiest assignments. At one point, he was captured by the Boers, but he escaped from prison camp and rejoined the British army.

- When he returned to Britain, Churchill became first lord of the Admiralty, but his political star fell after Britain's failure to seize control of the Dardanelles during World War I. In the wake of that catastrophe, Churchill learned what he called the "five distinct truths" governing decisions about military operations. These principles can be applied to strategic decision making in almost any enterprise.

    o Churchill's five principles are as follows: (1) One must have full authority; (2) there is a reasonable prospect of success; (3) greater interests are not compromised; (4) all possible care and forethought are exercised in the preparation; and (5) all vigor and determination are shown in the execution.

    o The first dictum was the lesson he clung to most fervently; he rebelled against accepting responsibilities without the necessary power of effective action to achieve the desired results.

- Lessons in hand, Churchill returned briefly to the military, then took on various posts in government. Throughout the 1930s, he engaged at the periphery of politics to prepare for an eventual comeback. On May 10, 1940, he became prime minister and guided Britain through four years of war. In that time, he earned a reputation as a crafty leader, enamored of surprise and deception.

- Throughout his life, Churchill sought adventure, and he shared with Ben Franklin a passion for study. He especially valued history, the wisdom of the ages as an indispensible guide for the future. This embrace of the past as prologue is what catalyzed Churchill's decision making.

- Learning and accumulated experience served as the platform from which Churchill confronted reality and launched grand notions. He recognized that simply having a good idea isn't good enough. Carrying out one's plans requires boldness, decisiveness, and relentless follow-through.

- We are all capable of shaping destinies in like fashion—perhaps not the destinies of nations but our own destinies and, perhaps, the destiny of our business.

Steve Jobs
- **Steve Jobs**—entrepreneur, media mogul, techno-artist, public relations master—demonstrated the characteristics of a man who possessed coup d'oeil and exercised it with relentless effectiveness.

- Like only a handful of persons in history, Jobs transformed the world. His vision, determination, and strategic execution revolutionized six industries: personal computers, animated movies, music, phones, tablet computing, and digital publishing. He changed the way we live and communicate and inspired us to think strategically.

- Perhaps Jobs's most famous ad campaign was the exhortation for us to "Think Different." That's like a mission statement for any strategy. Jobs not only conjured visions of how we might do things differently, but he solidified those visions into strategic intent and he executed tactics to bring those visions into being.

- Jobs's career resembled that of Winston Churchill. He clashed often with his contemporaries and saw his fortunes wax and wane several times. In 1985, he was forced out of Apple, the company he had founded, but he then purchased a small film animation and computer company, Pixar, as well as a not-so-successful computer platform development company, NeXT.

- In the late 1990s, Jobs was brought back to Apple and soon took over its leadership. In a dramatic demonstration of *coup d'oeil*, he redirected Apple's strategy in a single meeting, simplifying and riveting the focus of the company. He tasked his engineers to create four products, desktop and portable computers for consumer and professional markets.

- In the wake of the iPod, Jobs launched an even larger strategy: Apple would become, in the words of Jobs biographer Walter Isaacson, "the hub for an astounding array of new gadgets." What followed included the iPod, iTunes, the iPhone, and the iPad. Apple has since enjoyed a phenomenal run of innovation and prosperity.

- Throughout his career, Jobs exhibited traits of the master strategist: focus, strategic intent, relentless determination and drive, brilliant insight at the crucial moment, carefully coordinated use of surprise, precise execution of strategy, and detailed follow-through.

Oprah Winfrey
- The media personality and producer **Oprah Winfrey** has forged a vivid personal brand and self-improvement mission. Her seemingly endless curiosity and her ability to convert even minor details from her personal life into an enduring brand remind us of author and publisher Benjamin Franklin.

- Winfrey has relentlessly voiced strategic intent in the mainstream of life's everyday battles. She has inspired millions, perhaps allowing a comparison with Winston Churchill.

- And just as Steve Jobs influenced tastes and preferences in technology for perhaps a generation to come, Winfrey has often shaped and influenced the American national dialogue on everything from books to entertainment, from politics to personal health care.

- You might regard these comparisons as exaggerated, but a strategic personality can thrive in virtually any field—politics, technology, science, entertainment, and so on. Moreover, consider this: The distance between us and the greatest strategic minds is rarely as vast as we suppose. Those persons who are bold enough always have new realms for strategic endeavor.

The Attitude of a Strategic Thinker

- Writer and minister Robert J. Hastings wrote: "It isn't the burdens of today that drive men mad, but rather regret over yesterday and the fear of tomorrow. Regret and fear are twin thieves who would rob us of today." This quote reminds us that it's our attitude toward events that shapes how we deal with them.

- Becoming a strategic thinker means shedding doubts and uncertainty. It means mining the past for insight on the present in order to embrace the future. What we want to be five years from now informs what we do today. It tells us how to move our pieces on the great chessboard of life.

- The gifts of strategic thinking include a life without fear of the future; a life that is eager and prepared for challenge; a posture of welcome toward uncertainty and a determination to bend uncertainty to our own advantage; recognition that each of us has choices; and determination to never be buffeted by events but to influence events with our own will, imagination, analysis, planning, and execution.

- Thinking strategically helps us to impose a bit of order onto a reality that remains stubbornly disorderly. It empowers us to lay down a rudder, to harness the wind, and to propel ourselves in our desired direction. The benefits of strategic thinking are many: increased productivity and work satisfaction, less stress, and the achievement of goals more often than not. Although our journey is never free from chance and uncertainty, thinking strategically surely makes the ride more enjoyable.

Names to Know

Churchill, Winston (1874–1965): A cigar-smoking, gravel-voiced adventurer who learned from his mistakes and consistently put himself in the mainstream of life, Prime Minister Churchill inspired his nation at its most critical time in modern history—and prevailed. Journalist, officer, cavalryman, politician, historian, Cold War warrior—Churchill's career spanned more than six decades of the most turbulent times, and few men can claim to have singlehandedly influenced the path of world history as greatly as Churchill.

Franklin, Benjamin (1706–1790): The 18th-century embodiment of the Enlightenment man, Franklin lived a life of seized opportunities and realized dreams in the fields of science, politics, diplomacy, and business. He also contributed to America's store of wit in dozens of famous sayings, including "In this world nothing can be said to be certain, except death and taxes."

Jobs, Steve (1955–2011): The most iconic and perhaps irascible business executive of the last 50 years, Jobs both created and revolutionized a series of industries, including personal computers, music, digital communications, and animated films. His relentless drive, his impatience with others less gifted with vision, and his clarity of thought serve as the archetype of the successful entrepreneur.

Winfrey, Oprah (1954–): One of America's premier strategists in the field of entertainment, Winfrey offers a textbook example of how to plan, marshal resources, and execute a well-conceived strategy. She was criticized for creating or popularizing the "confession culture" that permeates popular media in the 21st century, but in actuality, she has made and remade herself and her approach several times.

Suggested Reading

Bossidy and Charan, *Confronting Reality*.

Christensen, Anthony, and Roth, *Seeing What's Next*.

Franklin, *The Autobiography of Benjamin Franklin*.

Handy, *The Age of Paradox*.

Hayward, *Churchill on Leadership*.

Isaacson, *Steve Jobs*.

1. Consider the major strategic thinkers in this lecture—Benjamin Franklin, Winston Churchill, Steve Jobs, and Oprah Winfrey—and identify key strategic similarities they share with other public figures you may admire, such as General George Patton, Jack Welch, Madonna, Lady Gaga, President Bill Clinton, Tim Tebow, or Meg Whitman. What *are* those key characteristics?

2. Evaluate your own thinking in light of the 24 lectures in this series. If what you've heard sounds flat or unintelligible, then you have work to do to hone your strategic thinking skills. Choose and focus on one lecture per week to absorb the message presented and vigorously enact the principle in scenarios of your choosing.

3. Strategic thinking means envisioning a future and working actively to make that future come to pass by using the finest analytical tools developed across the spectrum of disciplines. Where do you want to be a year from now? Five years from now? As a supremely important exercise, sketch this out, use the strategic planning process to broad-brush your midrange objectives and strategy, then identify the most effective tools and tactics from this course to begin *immediate* implementation.

Strategic Thinking as a Way of Life
Lecture 24—Transcript

History's great strategic thinkers show us that we can prepare ourselves for most any challenge. But first, we begin with a famous caveat: In the year 1789, Benjamin Franklin wrote the following in a letter: "Our new Constitution is now established, and has an appearance that promises permanency; but in this world nothing can be said to be certain, except death and taxes." Given everything we now know about strategy, from Sun Tzu to Clausewitz to how our brains work, let's add one more thing to Franklin's very short list, nothing can be said to be certain, except death, taxes, and uncertainty.

Uncertainty plagues us. It's everywhere, in our professional lives and in our personal lives. It's tough to read the signals coming in, whether from other persons in close relationships to our coworkers, to our seniors and subordinates, to our competitors in other firms, on other teams. Throughout these lectures, we have emphasized this battle with uncertainty about the future and how to deal with it. But the measure of our success is not whether we can predict the future, it's how prudently we prepare for it. It's how we coolly disaggregate the churning morass of possibilities that cascade on us and make us want to throw up our hands in frustration.

We cannot predict the future, not even our own future, but we've seen that we really don't need to. By adopting various combinations of strategic thinking techniques and tools of analysis, and by seizing a substantial role in developing our circumstances, we can improve our chances of succeeding at the tasks we set for ourselves. We can successfully alter the conditions that affect the future that concerns us, in our personal lives as well as in the professional realm.

I tell my students that strategy is a plan of where we want to go based on an analysis of where we've been, where we are, and what resources we'll need to make the trip. On a personal level, it's a plan based on what's in here and what's out there. Of course, it's much more than that, but that simple trope keeps us focused on the essentials. It's enough to get our heads up out of the mundane daily tasks that absorb us.

In these lectures, we've discussed a full range of strategic thinking skills valuable for any strategic thinker. Now, let's look at how a few exemplary human beings have lived strategic lives, creating opportunities, seizing them, charting a course that is not free from failure, but with a trajectory that is ever upward. This final lecture offers several strategic thinkers who exemplify how to live a life informed by strategy, informed by principle, forward-looking thinkers who were also steeped in the past, who possessed what we might call a strategic imagination.

One early American who practiced the art of strategic thinking on a superior level that has rarely been matched was Benjamin Franklin. Visualizing the future and crafting that future, shaping it, manipulating it, acting in ways to maximize a productive relationship to his environment. Franklin was, of course, a man of extreme talent. He was an autodidact, self-educated. Living his life completely within the 18th century, he was a man greatly influenced by the Enlightenment. He counted Voltaire among his acquaintances. And this made him a man for all times, speaking with a voice armed with principles.

It was Franklin's vision coupled with an equally determined drive that led him to press forward his entire life. It's this pressing forward that characterizes so many great personages. He grew, he prospered, he adapted to his environment, seizing opportunities and creating them as well. When he wanted to get started in the Philadelphia printing business, he convinced the governor of Pennsylvania to send him to London to study printing technology. In return, he offered to provide the governor with better printed documents as a result of his study trip.

This adaptability served him throughout his life, and he lived that life in the most strategic manner conceivable. His personal entrepreneurial philosophy was typical of the great strategic thinkers of history. It was captured in this famous epigram: "If you would not be forgotten, as soon as you are dead and rotten, either write things worth reading, or do things worth the writing."

Franklin exhibited the strategic personality's thirst for knowledge and ideas. When he was only 21, he created a group to discuss scientific and political ideas—which later evolved into the American Philosophical Society. Franklin and his associates founded the first public library in

America in 1731. In 1749, he launched an initiative to found what would become later the University of Pennsylvania. He contributed to the text of the Declaration of Independence, and during the Revolutionary War years, he served as leader of a commission to seek support from France. He was the toast of Europe, and carefully managed a personal brand that established the stereotype of American rustic genius. We've noted how important the game of chess is as a training device for strategic thinking; Franklin was a chess-player. In fact, he was the first person in America that we know by name as a chess player. He was such a great admirer of this elegant game that he even wrote an article called the "Morals of Chess."

In short, Franklin shared with most strategic thinkers a curiosity combined with a lust for life. He put himself into the mainstream. He was always powerfully engaged with his environment, never on the metaphorical sidelines. He left us legacies in a half-dozen fields, any one of which would be enough to ensure his place in history—in science, in politics, in education, in literature, in military affairs, in business, and in finance.

The good news for us today is that the secret of his success was no secret at all. Franklin lived his life by a set of principles that maximized his natural gifts. Franklin developed his own strategic plan, a list of 13 principles. These were not merely notions of how to "live the good life" but a blueprint for a robust and future-oriented existence, the seizing of opportunities and the creation of others. The test of his principles is their continued applicability in the present. While all 13 of these virtues are surely worthy of consideration—and of your own pursuit, if only for historical interest—four of them immediately yearn for our attention:

> Order—Let all your things have their places; let each part of your business have its time.

> Resolution—Resolve to perform what you ought; perform without fail what you resolve.

> Frugality—Make no expense but to do good to others or yourself; waste nothing.

And finally:

> Industry—Lose no time; be always employed in something useful; cut off all unnecessary actions.

These four guiding principles suggest to us that one key to tackling the uncertainty that surrounds us is to establish an island of certitude in the midst of uncertainty. The world may be uncertain, but that is no need for us to share in that uncertainty. Indeed, the very nation and Constitution that Benjamin Franklin did so much to help establish depended vitally on strategic thinking skills that Franklin (and others) had cultivated across an entire lifetime.

Another man with a fabulously strategic mind, who strode the first half of the 20th century like a giant, was Sir Winston Churchill. Churchill is best known for his role as Britain's Prime Minister during the darkest days of World War II, when England stood alone against Nazi Germany. His personal courage, his resolve, and his powerful rhetoric inspired the resistance of the nation. But this was just one chapter in the life of one of the most extraordinary strategic minds of any century. For Churchill lived life as large as anyone in history, and had the knack of being on the scene of great events. This knack was the result of his personal drive that moved him constantly from the periphery into the mainstream of life, where great things happen. This alone is a lesson to the rest of us. The lesson is to engage, to move into the mainstream, where access to collateral possibilities make themselves known to us.

Churchill lived a rich life, outstripping that of any epic fictional character. Churchill's extraordinary exploits began much earlier and were born of an incredible drive. His father died at the young age of 45, and Churchill believed that he, too, would die young. He would have to move fast to establish a legacy worth leaving. It was perhaps this sense of urgency, above all else, that drove Churchill his entire life. This urgency is evident in his thirst for battle, for courage-testing trials, for confrontation. In 1895, Churchill became a war correspondent and travelled to Cuba to observe the Spanish fight the Cuban guerrillas and to write about the conflict for the *Daily Graphic*. It's there that he cultivated a life-long penchant for Cuban cigars at age 21.

He obtained a commission in the army and immediately did what any good strategist ought to: He put himself into the mainstream, albeit an extremely dangerous version of the mainstream. He sought the riskiest assignments—he served in British India, the Sudan and the Second Boer War. While in the Sudan serving as a cavalryman with the 21st Lancers, he participated in the last great British cavalry charge, at the Battle of Omdurman in September 1898. Then, it was off to South Africa. He sought assignment in South Africa in October 1899, where the British were fighting the Boers, and in the space of just eight months Churchill lived larger than most people live in a lifetime. As a correspondent, he accompanied a scouting expedition in an armored train, which led to his capture by the Boers. But he escaped from his prison camp located in Pretoria. He immediately rejoined the British army and as a commissioned officer in the South African Light Horse, he helped to relieve the British at the Siege of Ladysmith and then capture the city of Pretoria.

Churchill returned to Britain, and his political star rose until he reached the lofty post of First Lord of the Admiralty in 1911, three years before the start of World War I. Churchill crafted a strategy to relieve the pressure on the Western Front that was stalemated in trench warfare. He pushed hard for the 1915 invasion of the Turkish Gallipoli peninsula to seize control of the Dardanelles Strait. He envisioned it as a quick surprise stroke, but bungling execution of the plan led to a disaster. It seemed that Churchill was the only one who understood the importance of strategic surprise. The invasion and subsequent six months of trench warfare ended in an ignominious British withdrawal in late 1915. The Dardanelles became synonymous with fiasco and recklessness. It scarred Churchill's reputation, and he was cashiered from his position in the admiralty. He was shuffled off to a ceremonial job.

A lesser man might have been content to settle. But Churchill's relentless drive—his strategic intent—led him to begin his own reconstruction. It required a major change, a 90-degree turn from his political course. He emerged from the Dardanelles catastrophe with his lesson learned, what he called "the five distinct truths" governing decisions about military operations. These principles can be applied to strategic decision making in most any enterprise:

These five principles are: 1) one must have full authority; 2) there is a reasonable prospect of success; 3) greater interests are not compromised; 4) all possible care and forethought are exercised in the preparation; 5) all vigor and determination are shown in the execution. The first dictum was the lesson he clung to most fervently—he absolutely rebelled against accepting responsibilities without the necessary power of effective action to achieve the desired results.

Lessons in hand, he knew that he had to refurbish his reputation if he expected to continue making his mark in public affairs, so he did the one thing that was in character for him. It would also bring him back from political exile. In early 1916, Churchill sought to join the battle on the Western Front. He became a Battalion Commander of the 6th Battalion of the Royal Scots Fusiliers. His time at the front was brief, but he earned the respect of his officers and men.

Churchill returned to government in various administrative posts—as Minister of Munitions, Secretary of State for War, and Secretary of State for Air. After the War, Churchill served as Chancellor of the Exchequer in the Conservative government of 1924–1929. Then, with that uncanny knack for being on the scene of great events, he traveled to the United States on a speaking tour at a critical time in history. He took his one and only trip to Wall Street to visit the New York Stock Exchange. He was in the gallery on the morning of Thursday, October 24, 1929, when the New York stock market went into freefall. He had come to see how his American investments were faring. Not very well, it seems.

Through the 1930s, Winston thought, and he wrote, and he engaged at the periphery of politics so as to prepare for an eventual comeback. Until, on May 10, 1940, he became Prime Minister, even as France teetered on the brink of defeat and the Battle of Britain was soon to commence. He guided Britain through four years of war. In that time, he earned a reputation as a crafty leader, enamored of surprise and deception. He relished that he was privy to the most secret transmissions of the German enemy through the magic of the Ultra Secret, the decoding of secret enemy radio traffic.

In the end, he gave Britain victory, and he was rewarded—with election defeat. The British people thought that their wartime leader wasn't the man to lead them in the subsequent peace. It seemed, finally, the end to an amazing political, military, administrative, and journalistic career that had spanned five decades. For most larger-than-life characters, guiding his country through the greatest crisis in its history would have been more than enough. But there seemed no end to Sir Winston's resilience; he again became Prime Minister in 1951. It seemed that he would leave politics on his own terms. He ultimately did, when he retired in 1955.

Throughout his life, Winston Churchill sought adventure. A more sober way of looking at it was his desire to place himself in the main stream of events, where adventures are launched, where opportunities abound, where there is more to life than simple mundane things that just happen to you. He never settled for the tributaries of life, where every day is like every other. It's no coincidence that he shared with Benjamin Franklin a passion for study— Churchill absorbed information voraciously, he deliberated intensely. He especially valued history—the wisdom of the ages as an indispensible guide for the future. In Churchill's words, "The longer you look back, the farther you can look forward."

Churchill's universal embrace of the past as prologue is what catalyzed his decision-making. The British historian Sir John H. Plumb characterized Churchill's historical imagination this way: "History, for Churchill, was not a subject like geography or mathematics, it was a part of his temperament ... it permeated everything he touched, and it was the mainspring of his politics and the secret of his immense mastery."

History, learning, accumulated experience—all served as the expanding platform from which thinkers like Franklin and Churchill would launch their grand notions. It allowed them to confront reality.

Confronting reality is a Churchillian way of doing business. He recognized that simply having a good idea isn't good enough, not by any stretch. It takes imagination, sure, but it also takes boldness, decisiveness, and relentless follow-through. Don't think that the opposition rolled over for Winston

Churchill, just because he was Churchill. Churchill himself offered blood, toil, sweat, and tears in all of his ventures.

During the World War I period, he wrote:

> Most great exploits have to be conducted under conditions of peculiar difficulty and discouragement. ... How easy to do nothing. ... How hard to achieve anything. ... There are plenty of good ideas if only they can be backed with power and brought into reality.

These were extraordinary people who lived during interesting times. These were men who chose to be great by their thinking, their actions. We read about them because they were strategic thinkers who confronted reality, wrestled with it, and if not always victorious, came out on top more often than not.

We all are capable of shaping destinies in like fashion—perhaps not the destinies of nations, but surely our own, and perhaps the destiny of our own company. How do we do this? By seeing, and by thinking, and by planning—boldness, decisiveness, and relentless follow-through. There's a pattern here, and the great strategic thinkers of history anticipate this pattern. Think of Churchill's remark about how difficult it is to get things done: "How easy to do nothing ... How hard to achieve anything."

One person who understood this perhaps better than anyone in business in the early 21st century is Steve Jobs. We think of Steve Jobs in many ways: entrepreneur, media mogul, shrewd businessman, techno-artist, public relations master, presentation expert, family man, authoritarian, maniacally focused, opinionated. And Steve Jobs demonstrated characteristics of a great strategist, a man who possessed *coup d' oeil*—the blinding flash of insight at the crucial moment—and who exercised it with aplomb and relentless effectiveness. Like Churchill, Steve Jobs had reinvented himself again and again. His triumphant return to lead Apple in 1997, in fact, was not unlike Churchill's return as Prime Minister of England in 1951.

Like only a handful of persons in history, Steve Jobs transformed the world. His vision, his determination, and his strategic execution revolutionized six industries: personal computers, animated movies, music, phones, tablet computing, and digital publishing. Steve transformed the way we entertain ourselves, the way we communicate, the way we think about how we live our lives. He transformed our expectations about life. And he inspired us to think strategically.

Perhaps his most famous ad campaign was the exhortation for us to "Think Different." That's like a mission statement for any strategy. Think differently. Steve Jobs was a strategic thinker of the first rank. He not only conjured visions of how we might do things differently, he solidified those visions into strategic intent—an obsession with winning—and he executed tactics brilliantly to bring those visions into being, time and again. That's what made him such a success as a serial entrepreneur.

Steve Jobs' career resembled that of Winston Churchill. He clashed often with his contemporaries. He saw his fortunes wax, then wane, and wax again. In fact, he could have faded away after any one of several professional disasters that would have left a lesser personality devastated. In 1985, he was forced out of Apple, the company he had co-founded. But he then quickly purchased a small film animation and computer company from filmmaker George Lucas for $5 million, and he invested an additional $5 million of his own money. He became chairman and CEO of the company. The company was renamed Pixar, and Jobs began repositioning the company. Simultaneous with the Pixar deal, Steve continued his computer ventures by founding another computer platform development company called NeXT. NeXT had only mixed success. But both NeXT and Pixar anchored Steve in the high technology field. They served as important platforms for his continued interactions with major corporations, such as IBM, Microsoft, and Walt Disney.

Then, the mid-1990s saw what appeared as the re-emergence of Steve Jobs—even his reincarnation. Under Jobs, Pixar had transformed itself from a high-end computer maker to a creator of feature length animated films, and in 1995, it released its first blockbuster—*Toy Story*—which grossed more than $350 million worldwide. In 1996, Apple Computer bought NeXT, and it brought Steve back to the company he had co-founded 20 years earlier.

Apple had declined in the intervening years. In fact, it was a company adrift. It produced a bewildering welter of computer models for no good reason that Steve could figure out. So he asserted himself and managed to oust CEO Gil Amelio. He immediately recharted Apple's strategic course. He cut the payroll, and he got Apple out of the printer and server businesses. He slashed the number of different Apple computers by 70 percent. As Jobs would later say, "Deciding what not to do is as important as deciding what to do. ... That's true for companies, and it's true for products." He brought focus and excitement back to the company. After one meeting in 1997, Jobs said this: "I came out of the meeting with people who had just gotten their products canceled and they were three feet off the ground with excitement because they finally understood where in the heck we were going."

In a dramatic demonstration of *coup d'oeil*, Steve redirected Apple's strategy in a single meeting, simplifying and riveting the focus of the company. On a whiteboard, he drew a diagram, a matrix with four quadrants. The columns were labeled Consumer and Pro. The rows were labeled Desktop and Portable. The engineers' task was to create four products, one for each quadrant. Former Apple employee Phil Schiller says that the effect of this simplified strategy was electrifying. "The result was that the Apple engineers and managers suddenly became sharply focused on just four areas."

Interestingly, the board of Apple never voted on whether to approve the new strategy. Steve just forged ahead. The resulting products were the Power Macintosh G3, the Power Book G3, the iMac, and the iBook. The Pro users got the Power Macintosh and Power Book; consumers got "i" brand products, which started with the iMac and the iBook. And at the same time, he laid plans to transform Apple into something new and different. So he set his engineers in search of "The Next Big Thing." That next big thing, which arrived in stores two years later, turned out to be the iPod, the device that transformed the music industry.

And the larger strategy was even more breath-taking. Biographer Walter Isaacson put it this way:

> Jobs launched a new grand strategy that would transform Apple— and with it the entire technology industry. ... Apple would no longer

be just a computer company—indeed it would drop that word from its name—but the Macintosh would be reinvigorated by becoming the hub for an astounding array of new gadgets.

These new gadgets included the iPod and iTunes in 2001, the iPhone in 2007, and the iPad in 2010. And the new gadgets worked seamlessly with one another creating a ratchet effect; each new Apple product could stand on the shoulders of previous Apple products.

The strategy worked. And the business result was that Apple turned around completely and began a phenomenal run of innovation and prosperity. In May 2000 Apple's market value was one-twentieth that of Microsoft. Ten years later, Apple surpassed Microsoft as the world's most valuable technology company, and by late 2011 it exceeded Microsoft's value by more than 70 percent.

In all of this, Steve Jobs exhibited traits of the master strategist. Focus, strategic intent, relentless determination and drive, brilliant insight at the crucial moment, carefully coordinated use of surprise at the launch of a new product, use of and precise execution of his strategy, and detailed follow-through. He is an iconic figure and his impact, like our other exemplars of strategy, will likely continue for decades.

Benjamin Franklin, Napoleon, Winston Churchill, John Kennedy, Vince Lombardi, Martin Luther King, Steve Jobs—these strategic thinkers serve as exemplars across the professions. They demonstrate the power of a great strategy, well-executed in the face of titanic challenges.

In the end, what does it mean to be a strategic thinker? It means extending the shadow of the future; it means pushing our horizon out. To broaden our sense of what that can mean, let's briefly consider one more figure, someone whose career suggests additional features about strategic living—features that may play an even larger role in the future. Born just a year before Steve Jobs, the media personality and producer Oprah Winfrey has forged a vivid personal brand and self-improvement mission that are even more omnivorous than those of the other figures we've considered.

Oprah Winfrey's seemingly endless curiosity, and her ability to convert even minor details from her personal life into an enduring brand remind us of author and publisher Benjamin Franklin. Oprah Winfrey has relentlessly voiced strategic intent in the mainstream of life's everyday battles. She has inspired millions, perhaps allowing a comparison or contrast with Winston Churchill. And just as Steve Jobs influenced tastes and preferences in technology for perhaps a generation to come, Oprah Winfrey has often shaped and influenced the American national dialogue on everything from books to entertainment, from politics to personal health care.

You might regard these particular comparisons as exaggerated, but a strategic personality can thrive in virtually any field—politics, technology, science, entertainment, and so on. Moreover, consider this: The distance between us, in our everyday lives, and the greatest strategic minds is rarely as vast as we suppose. Those persons who are bold enough always have new realms for strategic endeavor.

There is a quote from a famous poem that I like to recall in my own life as I grapple with the same variables that nettle us all: "It isn't the burdens of today that drive men mad, but rather regret over yesterday and the fear of tomorrow. Regret and fear are twin thieves who would rob us of today." This quote from Robert J. Hastings reminds us that it's our attitude toward events that shapes how we deal with them. Strategic thinking skills cultivate an attitude capable of meeting those events.

Becoming a strategic thinker means shedding the doubts, the uncertainty. It means mining the past for insight on the present so that we can embrace the future. What we want to be five years from now, ten years from now, informs what we do today. It tells us how to move our pieces on the great chessboard of life. These are the gifts of strategic thinking: A life without fear of the future; a life that is eager for and prepared for challenge; a posture of welcome toward the uncertainty that we all face and a determination to bend that uncertainty to our own advantage; recognition that each of us has choices; determination to never be buffeted by events, but to influence events with our own will, our imagination, analysis, planning, and execution.

Thinking strategically helps us to impose a bit of order onto a reality that remains stubbornly disorderly. It empowers us to lay down a rudder, to harness the wind, and to propel ourselves in our desired direction. The benefits of strategic thinking are many—increased productivity, work satisfaction, more predictability, less stress, greater efficiency, perhaps more victories than otherwise, and the achievement of our goals more often than not. And while our journey is never free from the caprice of chance and uncertainty, thinking strategically surely makes the ride more enjoyable.

Timeline

c. 475–400 B.C. .... *The Art of War*, traditionally
credited to Sun Tzu

431– 411 B.C. .... Thucydides, *History of the
Peloponnesian War*

424 B.C. .... Pagondas defeats Athenians
at the Battle of Delium

216 B.C. .... Hannibal defeats Romans at
the Battle of Cannae

c. 389 .... Treatise by Vegetius on *Military
Institutions of the Romans*

6th century .... Game of chess originates in India,
arriving in Europe by the 10th century

1500s–1800s .... Tactics for fencing with a light
sword developed after gunpowder
made armor obsolete

1513 .... Niccolò Machiavelli, *The Prince*

1521 .... Niccolò Machiavelli, *The Art of War*

1732 .... Maurice de Saxe, *My Reveries
on the Art of War*, published
posthumously in 1756–1757

1747 .... *Instruction from Frederick the
Great to His Generals*

1757	Benjamin Franklin's "The Way to Wealth" published as a preface to the final edition of *Poor Richard's Almanac*
1799–1804	Napoleon Bonaparte installs himself as first consul
1804–1814/15	Napoleon Bonaparte proclaimed emperor
1805	Antoine Jomini, *Treatise on Grand Military Operations*
1815 (June)	Battle of Waterloo
1827	*War Maxims of Napoleon* published
1832	Carl von Clausewitz, *On War*
1838	Antoine Jomini, *Summary of the Art of War*
1854	Charge of the Light Brigade (Battle of Balaklava)
1861–1865	American Civil War
1861 (July)	First Battle of Bull Run
1862 (Sept.)	Battle of Antietam, where Lee's first invasion of the North was stopped by an intelligence coup
1863 (April)	Battle of Camerone (Mexico), where the French Foreign Legion forged its founding myth in a heroic stand against overwhelming odds

Timeline

1940–1945, 1951–1955 .... Winston Churchill serves as prime minister of England

1940 .... Battle for France

1941 (Dec.) .... Pearl Harbor attack

1942 .... Dieppe raid by Britain fails

1943 (July/Aug.) .... Russian defeat of the German offensive in the Battle of Kursk

1944 (June) .... D-Day (Operation Overlord)

1944 (Sept.) .... Operation Market Garden

1944–1945 (Dec./Jan.) .... Battle of the Bulge marks the defeat of the German effort to break out in Western Europe

1946 .... George Kennan, Long Telegram; enunciates U.S. containment policy

1950 .... Prisoner's Dilemma named and interpreted by mathematician Albert W. Tucker

1950–1953 .... Korean War

1953 .... John von Neumann and Oskar Morgenstern, *Theory of Games and Economic Behavior*

1954 .... Peter Drucker's *The Practice of Management* spreads the idea of "management by objectives"

1969.. Barton Whaley, *Stratagem*

1969.. George A. Steiner, *Strategic Planning: What Every Manager Must Know*

1973.. Bain & Co. founded by former partners and managers from Boston Consulting Group

1979.. Igor Ansoff, *Strategic Management*

1980.. Michael Porter, *Competitive Strategy: Techniques for Analyzing Industries and Competitors*

1984.. Robert Axelrod, *The Evolution of Cooperation*

1989.. Gary Hamel and C. K. Prahalad, "Strategic Intent"

1990.. Gary Hamel and C. K. Prahalad, "The Core Competence of the Corporation"

1991.. Desert Storm invasion of Iraq led by General Norman Schwarzkopf

1994.. Henry Mintzberg's *The Rise and Fall of Strategic Planning*

1994.. Gary Hamel and C. K. Prahalad, *Competing for the Future*

1995.. Michael Porter, *The Competitive Advantage: Creating and Sustaining Superior Performance*

Biographical Notes

Bonaparte, Napoleon (1769–1821): Once master of continental Europe, Napoleon is best remembered for a departure from his normally crisp execution of strategy when he failed to mask his flank and rear at the battle whose name is synonymous with defeat—Waterloo. Yet his legacy also extends to this day in the realms of the civil law tradition, modern civil government bureaucracies, and military theory and practice.

Churchill, Winston (1874–1965): A cigar-smoking, gravel-voiced adventurer who learned from his mistakes and consistently put himself in the mainstream of life, Prime Minister Churchill inspired his nation at its most critical time in modern history—and prevailed. Journalist, officer, cavalryman, politician, historian, Cold War warrior—Churchill's career spanned more than six decades of the most turbulent times, and few men can claim to have singlehandedly influenced the path of world history as greatly as Churchill.

Clausewitz, Carl von (1780–1831): The way we think about war and strategy cannot be divorced from this 19th-century officer and theorist, who revolutionized strategy in the same way that Adam Smith revolutionized economics. He fought in the Napoleonic Wars for both the Prussians and the Russians and participated in the battles of Waterloo and Borodino. He died in 1831, and it was left to his widow, Marie, to prepare his manuscript *On War* for posthumous publication.

Franklin, Benjamin (1706–1790): The 18th-century embodiment of the Enlightenment man, Franklin lived a life of seized opportunities and realized dreams in the fields of science, politics, diplomacy, and business. He also contributed to America's store of wit in dozens of famous sayings, including "In this world nothing can be said to be certain, except death and taxes."

Genghis Khan (1162–1227): Genghis Khan forged an empire as great as any in world history and, in the process, revolutionized warfare of the 13th century, conquering all of Asia and part of Europe. Despite his deserved reputation for ruthlessness, somewhat paradoxically, he introduced the notion of religious tolerance throughout his empire.

Guderian, Heinz (1888–1954): A great theorist and practitioner of the art of swift tank warfare, Guderian's *elan* and mastery of the battlefield were rivaled only by the great Erwin Rommel.

Hamel, Gary (1954–): *Fortune* magazine has called Hamel "the world's leading expert on business strategy," and *Forbes* has ranked Hamel as one of the world's top 10 most influential theorists on business, competition, management, and strategy.

Hannibal (247 B.C.–183–181 B.C.): Son of a famous general and sworn to eternal hostility against Rome from a young age, Hannibal Barca's name will always be associated with one of the greatest victories in all of history: his defeat of the Romans at Cannae.

Jackson, Thomas Jonathan (**Stonewall**; 1824–1863): Ahead of his time with regard to battlefield tactics, General Jackson's motto during the American Civil War was to "mystify, mislead, and surprise" the enemy.

Janis, Irving (1918–1990): Few group dynamic theorists can match the impact of Janis in his recognition and study of groupthink as a powerful negative influence on competent decision making. Janis highlighted the dangers of consensus building as a substitute for rational analysis.

Jobs, Steve (1955–2011): The most iconic and perhaps irascible business executive of the last 50 years, Jobs both created and revolutionized a series of industries, including personal computers, music, digital communications, and animated films. His relentless drive, his impatience with others less gifted with vision, and his clarity of thought serve as the archetype of the successful entrepreneur.

Jomini, Antoine (1779–1869): Theorist and general, Jomini authored the bible of 19th-century military strategy and influenced the world's militaries of that era more than any other individual theorist. He is distinguished by his effort to apply geometrical concepts to the battlefield.

Kahn, Herman (1922–1983): Kahn was the man whom *The New Yorker* once called the "heavyweight of the Megadeath Intellectuals" and who was a prescient futurist focusing on the strategy of nuclear war. He also was one of the first to predict the rise of Japan as a world-class economic power.

Kennan, George (1904–2005): Few people can claim to have set the foreign policy course for an entire nation for 40 years, but as a young embassy official in the Soviet Union in the 1940s, Kennan did exactly that when he crafted what would become the U.S. policy of containment with regard to the Soviets.

Kennedy, John F. (1917–1963): Few presidents can claim the kind of strategic vision that Kennedy possessed, founding the Peace Corps, laying the groundwork for the U.S. Special Forces, and charting a course for eventually reaching the moon.

King, Martin Luther, Jr. (1929–1968): America's great civil rights leader carried a passion for justice along with a strategic vision and the proper tactics to see that vision through to completion.

Lawrence, T. E. (1888–1935): Lawrence was an adventurer who found a battleground for his natural strategic talents in the deserts of the Middle East during World War I, leading the Arab revolt, and wove an epic of strategic thought and history, *The Seven Pillars of Wisdom*, that set forth timeless principles of small-unit tactics and guerilla warfare.

Lee, Robert E. (1807–1870): Offered command of the Northern army at the outset of the American Civil War, Lee instead sided with his home state of Virginia and created a legend in the subsequent four years as one of the greatest battlefield generals in American history.

Liddell Hart, Basil (1895–1970): Fighting in the Great War imbued this great military thinker with a revulsion toward static attritional warfare and led to his theorizing on the great potential of the armored tank. Liddell Hart extended his strategic theorizing into other realms and penned a work called *The Lawn Tennis Masters Unveiled.*

Lombardi, Vince (1913–1970): One of the great motivators and leaders that sports has ever produced, Lombardi's teams won the first two Super Bowls, and his aphorisms on leadership have since entered the lexicon as classics.

MacArthur, Douglas (1880–1964): MacArthur's personal magnetism, larger-than-life personality, and extravagant ego led him to incredible success in war for a decade and to ultimate political ruin shortly after his masterstroke at Inch'ŏn during the Korean War.

Machiavelli, Niccolò (1469–1527): A humanely educated man who is most remembered for his tract on political power, Machiavelli also offered his take on conflict in his treatise *The Art of War*. Literally a Renaissance man, Machiavelli collaborated on military projects with both Leonardo da Vinci and Michelangelo.

Mackinder, Sir Halford (1861–1947): A geographer by trade, Mackinder is forever linked to efforts to create a social science of geopolitics by dint of his famous formula for achieving world domination that appeared in a pivotal article in 1904.

Mintzberg, Henry (1939–): Mintzberg is a noted business professor and theorist whose sometimes contrarian notions frustrate his contemporaries through their brilliant insights and counterintuitive propositions. He appeared at number 30 on the 2009 Forbes biennial global ranking of management thinkers.

Pagondas (fl. 5th century B.C.): This obscure Theban general is credited with inventing the science of battlefield tactics, demonstrating a radical new approach to warfare of the time by his innovations at the Battle of Delium (424 B.C.) during the Peloponnesian War.

Porter, Michael (1947–): Possibly the most influential scholar on business strategy in the last 30 years, Porter became one of Harvard University's youngest tenured professors at age 26. His work in the field of corporate competition and strategy formulation transformed business education worldwide, and he commands speaking fees of more than $70,000 per lecture.

Prahalad, C. K. (1941–2010): Prahalad teamed with Gary Hamel in one of the great scholarly collaborations in business history, developing pathbreaking theoretical and practical notions that guide multinational corporate thinking today. Prahalad is most remembered for his last works, focused on market solutions to alleviate poverty at the "bottom of the pyramid."

Rumelt, Richard (1942–): Rumelt is a rousing scholar and consultant whose direct and concise writing on strategy is powerful in its simplicity and elegance, cutting through the static that permeates strategic thinking. Beginning his career in the field of electrical engineering, he slowly developed a reputation as a management guru and advocated that there are only two ways for companies to succeed for the long-term: They must either invent their way to it, or they must exploit some change in their environment.

Schelling, Thomas (1921–): A political scientist, strategist, game theorist, and arms control advocate, Schelling exerted powerful influence on strategic thinking in the nuclear era and in explaining the dynamics of racial segregation in the United States through the use of relatively simple modeling.

Spykman, Nicholas (1893–1943): Spykman is known in some quarters as the godfather of containment, the strategy that guided the United States in its rivalry with the Soviets for 40 years after World War II. Attacked as America's geopolitician during the war for daring to envision a postwar world based on raw power considerations, Spykman's predictions were substantiated in subsequent years after his early passing.

Sun Tzu (fl. 5th century B.C.): One of a handful of almost universally known strategists, the impact of Sun Tzu on strategy and the way we think about strategy has suffused thinking not only in present-day military circles but in business and political realms, as well. Descriptions of warfare in *The Art of War*, traditionally credited to Sun Tzu, suggest that the work was composed early in the Warring States period (475–221 B.C.). Famous generals who utilized Sun Tzu's principles were Chinese communist Mao Zedong, Vietnamese general Vo Nguyen Giap, and American generals Norman Schwarzkopf and Colin Powell in the First Gulf War of 1991.

Thucydides (460 B.C. or earlier–after 404 B.C.): This ancient Greek historian is the founding father of the modern political science school of realism, which sees the international system as resulting from configurations of state power. Carrying the rank of *strategos* in the Athenian military, he both fought in the Peloponnesian War and wrote about it.

Vegetius (fl. 4th century A.D.): The avatar of adequate training and preparation of military forces, Vegetius preached the necessity of proper development of superior military capability prior to battle. He wrote his treatise *Epitoma rei militaris* at the request of Emperor Valentinian, divining how the "ancient Romans" organized and utilized their legions so that Rome's military prowess might be resuscitated.

Wack, Pierre (1922–1997): Wack persevered against internal inertia at Royal Dutch Shell to pioneer development of what has become sophisticated scenario analysis, realistic forecasting of likely courses that history may take.

Warden, John A., III (1943–): Controversial, impatient, and contrarian, Warden is the quintessential strategic thinker and visionary who revolutionized American thinking about air power in the late 20th century. One biography notes, "to this day his name inspires both warm affection and cold contempt in the defense establishment."

Winfrey, Oprah (1954–): One of America's premier strategists in the field of entertainment, Winfrey offers a textbook example of how to plan, marshal resources, and execute a well-conceived strategy. She was criticized for creating or popularizing the "confession culture" that permeates popular media in the 21st century, but in actuality, she has made and remade herself and her approach several times.

Bibliography

To acquire a firm grounding in the most universally applicable strategic concepts in the shortest possible time, I recommend a handful of books and two articles as essential reading. Without attributing any importance to the order, they are: *Learning to Think Strategically* by Julia Sloan; *Strategy*, a sweeping survey of military strategy by B. H. Liddell Hart; the biography *Steve Jobs* by Walter Isaacson; *Blue Ocean Strategy*, a guide to creating new market segments by Kim and Mauborgne; *Good Strategy, Bad Strategy* by Richard Rumelt; *Makers of Modern Strategy*, a superb collection of the most important military strategy writers, edited by Peter Paret; and the classic *Harvard Business Review* articles "What Is Strategy?" (1996) by Michael Porter and "Strategic Intent" (1989) by G. Hamel and C. K. Prahalad.

Abrahams, Jeffrey. *101 Mission Statements from Top Companies: Plus Guidelines for Writing Your Own Mission Statement*. Berkeley, CA: Ten Speed Press, 2007. A superb resource for anyone interested in comparing and contrasting mission statement effectiveness, this collection of powerful and not-so-powerful mission statements provides fodder for crafting your own clear, concise, focused mission statement.

Alger, John I. *The Quest for Victory: The History of the Principles of War*. Westport, CT: Greenwood Press, 1982. This history of the development of the principles of war gets at the roots of how we have arrived at modern conceptions of battlefield performance.

Allison, Graham. *Essence of Decision: Explaining the Cuban Missile Crisis*. New York: Harper Collins, 1971. This first-rate scholar broke new analytical ground with this classic work on how bureaucratic interplay can affect group decision making.

Bibliography

500

Ansoff, Igor. *Strategic Management*. New York: Palgrave Macmillan, 1979, 2007. Sometimes called the father of strategic management, Ansoff brought a focus to the study of strategy in business that had been missing; he clashed with academic rival Henry Mintzberg over the efficacy of planning in the development of strategy.

Axelrod, Robert. *The Evolution of Cooperation*. New York: Basic Books, 1984. This classic work on cooperation theory has influenced a generation of social scientists and been cited in more than 500 books and 4000 articles.

Beckwith, Harry, and Christina Clifford Beckwith. *You, Inc.: The Art of Selling Yourself*. New York: Warner Business Books, 2006. The authors provide a wealth of techniques designed to help a person assemble the factors of success particular to the individual and the project that combine in the most effective manner.

Bensoussan, Babette E., and Craig S. Fleisher. *Analysis without Paralysis: 10 Tools to Make Better Strategic Decisions*. Upper Saddle River, NJ: FT Press, 2008. A superb introduction to analytical tools that are useful in a variety of business and non-business situations.

Binmore, Ken. *Game Theory: A Very Short Introduction*. Oxford: Oxford University Press, 2007. Game theory is complex, and although no short volume can do it justice, this guide offers the basics so that the average person can appropriate the major concepts and put them to use.

Bossidy, Larry, and Ram Charan. *Confronting Reality: Doing What Matters to Get Things Right*. New York: Crown Business Books, 2004. A rapidly changing and unpredictable business world leaves no wiggle room for indecision; it requires a sure grasp of reality and the confidence to face it with élan and practicality.

Braden, Kathleen E., and Fred M. Shelley. *Engaging Geopolitics*. Essex: Pearson Education, 2000. This primer on modern geopolitical concepts provides a superb introduction to the interplay among territory, power, and location and how this interplay influences conflict between nation-states.

Power can arise from location, and this volume shows how leaders deal with this synergistic relationship.

Brzezinski, Zbigniew. *The Grand Chessboard: American Primacy and Its Geostrategic Imperatives*. New York: Basic Books, 1997. Academic and former National Security Advisor Brzezinski is one of the 20th century's most influential political thinkers, and he is largely responsible for reintroducing powerful and enduring geopolitical concepts into the national dialogue about international conflict and cooperation. This volume anchors political prediction in the enduring geostrategic imperatives that have guided states for centuries.

Burlton, Roger. *Business Process Management: Profiting from Process*. Indianapolis: SAMS Publishing, 2001. A pioneering effort in the field of evaluating and managing business processes and ensuring that they achieve fit throughout complex enterprises comprising many systems.

Buskirk, Richard. *Frontal Attack, Divide and Conquer, the Fait Accompli, and 118 Other Tactics Managers Must Know*. New York: John Wiley & Sons, 1989. This is a basic primer for those wishing to plunge into the byzantine world of office politics and come out winners. Authored by a business school professor and written in accessible language, the book is useful and rich in examples.

————. *Modern Management and Machiavelli*. Boston: Cahners Books, 1974. Produced by a member of a university marketing faculty, this masterful exegesis of Machiavelli's *The Prince* is methodical in its application to the professional life of the modern businessperson and is rich in insight, effortlessly transporting the unchanging lessons of human nature and power from the 16th to the 21st centuries.

Campbell, Joseph. *The Hero with a Thousand Faces*. Princeton, NJ: Princeton University Press, 1949, 1968. This classic by America's greatest scholar of mythology chronicles the universal story that appears in every epoch in every corner of the world and provides the archetype for strategic intent.

Chandler, David. *The Military Maxims of Napoleon.* New York: Macmillan Publishing Company, 1987. Napoleon Bonaparte is called the greatest European soldier, and this compendium of Napoleon's military wisdom demonstrates why. The original 1901 annotations by Cairnes and those of Chandler in 1987 make this a useful guide to anyone involved in conflict.

Charan, Ram, and Larry Bossidy. *Execution: The Discipline of Getting Things Done.* New York: Crown Business Books, 2002. A Harvard academic and a former General Electric executive team up in this superb effort on execution, showing how, as the leader's most important yet neglected job, execution is often "the missing link between aspirations and results."

Christensen, Clayton. *The Innovator's Dilemma: The Revolutionary Book That Will Change the Way You Do Business.* Boston: Harvard Business School Press, 1997. On the cusp of change and innovation, who do you listen to and what do you do? This Harvard B-school professor has answers.

Christensen, Clayton, Scott D. Anthony, and Erik A. Roth. *Seeing What's Next: Using Theories of Innovation to Predict Industry Change.* Boston: Harvard Business School Press, 2004. Christensen and his partners offer a method whereby proven theories can be used to develop powerful insights into how the future will unfold in a given industry, which provides a basis for crafting prudent strategy based on those insights.

Clausewitz, Carl von. *On War.* Oxford: Oxford World's Classics, 2007. Clausewitz is considered the first of the modern strategists; he systematized the study of war while recognizing its place in the larger context of a nation's foreign policy tools. His influence began to be felt in the Franco-Prussian and Boer wars.

De Bono, Edward. *Think! Before It's Too Late.* London: Vermilion, 2009. The creator of the technique of "lateral thinking" offers a substantial contribution to the improvement of our thinking processes. Says the author: "This book is about why human thinking is so poor. It also suggests what we can do about it."

Dixit, Avinash K., and Barry J. Nalebuff. *Thinking Strategically: The Competitive Edge in Business, Politics, and Everyday Life*. New York: W. W. Norton & Company, 1991. This practical guide to strategic action distills much high-concept thinking into a handful of tactics usable in daily challenges presented by those with whom we interact at all levels. It provides examples that demonstrate winning tactics in action with both friends and rivals in situations of both cooperation and conflict.

Drucker, Peter. *The Effective Executive*. New York: Harper & Row, 1966. One of the most powerful treatises on business effectiveness, by the creator of modern American management, this volume offers timeless principles to improve any executive's personal performance, regardless of field of action.

Duggan, William. *Napoleon's Glance: The Secret of Strategy*. New York: Thunder's Mouth Press, 2002. Duggan teaches strategy at Columbia University and has examined closely the phenomenon of coup d'oeil in its various manifestations across business, political, and social activities, sharing his insights in this interesting volume.

———. *Strategic Intuition: The Creative Spark in Human Achievement*. New York: Columbia University Press, 2007. Professor Duggan expands on his work with the strategic glance and contends that the "strategic idea" as a result of flashes of insight has been left out of the strategic literature. He aims to reinsert it in a place of prominence.

Earle, Edward Meade, ed. *Makers of Modern Strategy: Military Thought from Machiavelli to Hitler*. Princeton: Princeton University Press, 1941. This is the first edition of the classic compendium of powerful essays on the world's greatest strategists. This edition contains a chapter on the German geopoliticians that was, surprisingly, omitted from later editions under Peter Paret (also recommended in this bibliography).

Erfurth, Waldemar. *Surprise*, in *Roots of Strategy*, Book 3. Harrisburg, PA: Stackpole Books, 1943, 1991. General Erfurth, in combination with brilliant translator and annotator Stefan Possony, offers a comprehensive analysis of the utility of surprise in conflict that is both historical and forward-looking.

Feinberg, Mortimer, and John J. Tarrant. *Why Smart People Do Dumb Things*. New York: Simon and Schuster, 1995. Even the most intelligent among us can commit folly on a grand scale and in spite of our best efforts. The authors explore the capacity for human error in the keenest of minds and offer a schema for avoiding the mind traps that threaten us at every turn.

Fleisher, Craig S., and Babette E. Bensoussan, *Business and Competitive Analysis: Effective Application of New and Classic Methods*. Upper Saddle River, NJ: FT Press, 2007. A comprehensive and deep presentation of many of the most effective tools of analysis used in business.

Foch, Ferdinand. *Principles of War*. 1901. Reprint, Whitefish, MT: Kessinger Publishing, 2007. An original and influential theoretical treatise on war principles by a great general. Foch observed, "The art of war, like every other art, possesses its theory, its principles; otherwise it would not be an art."

Franklin, Benjamin. *The Autobiography of Benjamin Franklin*. Washington, DC: Regnery History, 2007. This influential work is available in many editions, including free electronic versions. Its continued relevance and application testify to the enduring principles of behavior offered by the author. Franklin's advice on interacting with others, particularly in contentious situations, is strategic thinking at its finest.

Fuller, John Frederick Charles. *The Foundations of the Science of War*. Fort Leavenworth, KS: U.S. Army Command and General Staff College Press, 1993. http://nara-wayback-001.us.archive.org/peth04/20041016211236/http://www.cgsc.army.mil/carl/resources/csi/fuller2/fuller2.asp#220. For an example of primary-source thinking on war principles, Fuller offers a snapshot of strategic evolution in progress. In Fuller's compendium of principles, we see the exposition of military thinking that evolved in the early 20th century and the establishment of the bases of the principles of war eventually adopted by the United States.

Gilad, Ben. *Business War Games*. Franklin Lakes, NJ: Career Press, 2009. Rehearsing the future is one way of looking at war games. Military units do it all the time, and this book shows how war games can aid businesses, as well, priming them for the unpredictable moves of competitors.

———. *Early Warning*. New York: American Management Association, 2004. Ben Gilad is one of the triumvirate of founders of the modern competitive intelligence business field, and this volume is a primer on how early warning based on observed trends can help businesses avoid commercial disaster.

Grabo, Cynthia M. *Anticipating Surprise: Analysis for Strategic Warning*. Lanham, MD: University Press of America, 2004, 1974. This once-classified volume, called *A Handbook of Warning Intelligence*, was mandatory reading for intelligence analysts tasked with forecasting threats to the United States for two decades and provides guidance today for anyone wishing to sharpen analytical skills.

Gray, Colin. *Modern Strategy*. Oxford: Oxford University Press, 1999. The author is a career strategist and practitioner, whose service to the United States spanned 20 years during the Cold War. This work is majestic in its scope and reach and lengthens our horizon on strategy.

Grove, Andy. *Only the Paranoid Survive: How to Exploit the Crisis Points That Challenge Every Company*. New York: Currency, Doubleday, 1996. A classic book on dealing with innovation and rapidly changing technology from a top executive who not only survived the innovation wars but thrived.

Guderian, Heinz. *Achtung-Panzer!* London: Cassell & Co., 1992, 1937. One of the most important and seminal books on mobile warfare published in the first half of the 20th century, Guderian's work influenced the course of world history by introducing the German military establishment to the theories of Liddell Hart, combined with Guderian's own contributions to the development of tank tactics. Guderian went on to become perhaps Germany's greatest armored commander of World War II, rivaled only by Erwin Rommel.

Gudgin, Peter. *Military Intelligence: A History*. Phoenix Mill, Great Britain: Sutton Publishing, 1999. This sweeping narrative begins with early efforts at rudimentary military intelligence and takes us up to today's sophisticated intelligence agencies, looking candidly at British intelligence, the CIA, the Israeli Mossad, and other organizations.

Gunther, Max. *The Luck Factor: The Four Essential Principles.* New York: Macmillan Publishing Co., 1977. Gunther's conclusions in this pioneering study of luck have withstood the tests of time and trial and show us tangible ways to increase our chances of success.

Hall, Wayne Michael, and Gary Citrenbaum. *Intelligence Analysis: How to Think in Complex Environments.* Santa Barbara, CA: Praeger Security International, 2010. The authors—an academic and a former military intelligence officer—offer 14 powerful advanced analytical tools for use in any environment that requires the collection and accurate analysis of information, including tendency analysis, synthesis, cultural analysis, pattern analysis, and critical thinking.

Halperin, Morton. *Bureaucratic Politics and Foreign Policy.* Washington, DC: Brookings Institution, 1974. Halperin's analysis and explanation of the processes of bureaucracy-in-action are applicable to decision-making organizations of every size and character.

Hamel, Gary, and Bill Breen. *The Future of Management.* Boston: Harvard Business School Press, 2007. Gary Hamel is one of management's most brilliant thinkers, and this work demonstrates why as he presages some of the conundrums we can expect to face in coming years because of the growing systemic complexity and speed of globalized business.

Hamel, G., and C. K. Prahalad. "Strategic Intent." *Harvard Business Review* (1989): 63–76. http://www3.uma.pt/filipejmsousa/ge/Hamel%20 and%20Prahalad,%201989.pdf. Hamel and Prahalad combined to conceive and publish some of the most powerful concepts of the modern business pantheon, and this enduring work informs and instructs us on the necessary core of any competent strategy.

———. *Strategic Intent.* Cambridge: Harvard Business Review Press, 2010. Hamel and Prahalad's business classic extends far beyond the world of commerce and instructs us on the power and potential of a laser-focused strategic vision. The 2010 book is a short collection centered on the authors' 1989 article of the same name.

Handy, Charles. *The Age of Paradox*. Boston: Harvard Business Review Press, 1994. The great thing about Handy is his knack for writing timelessly, and this influential work has proven sturdy over more than a decade, particularly his identification of the sigmoid curve as an enduring template for development.

Hansen, Lars Bo. *Foundations of Chess Strategy*. London: Gambit Publications, 2005. Many have used chess as a training vehicle for businesses, but this volume takes the novel opposite approach to discover whether the vast research and modeling techniques developed for business strategy can be applied to the game of chess. In the process, much is revealed about the process of emergent strategy that is applicable to both the classic game and to the world of commerce.

Hanson, Victor Davis. *Ripples of Battle: How Wars of the Past Still Determine How We Fight, How We Live, and How We Think*. New York: Anchor Books, 2003. Echoes of particular battles can reverberate throughout history, their effects cascading from their original brief violence to affect how we live and think, even today.

Harvard Business School Press. *Executing Strategy for Business Results*. Boston: Harvard Business Press, 2007. A compendium of articles on strategy execution across the value chain and in a variety of circumstances.

———. *Thinking Strategically*. Boston: Harvard Business Review Press, 2010. A basic how-to volume to aid in the development of fundamental thinking skills to be used in a business environment.

Hayward, Steven. *Churchill on Leadership: Executive Success in the Face of Adversity*. New York: Three Rivers Press, 1997, 1998. A concise compendium of the rich and varied strategic life lived large by the most famous of all of Britain's prime ministers. Churchill's shrewd decision making and forward-looking calculation were hallmarks of an adventurer, and this work explicates the inner workings and outward results of Churchill's fabulous operational mind.

Heuer, Richards. *Psychology of Intelligence Analysis*. Washington, DC: Center for the Study of Intelligence, 1999. This volume, by one of the CIA's top analysts and thinkers-about-thinking, is still used to train CIA analysts in their craft.

Hofstede, Geert. *Culture's Consequences: Comparing Values, Behaviors, Institutions and Organizations across Nations*, 2nd ed. Thousand Oaks, CA: Sage Publications, 2001. Hofstede is one of the most-cited researchers in the world, thanks to his pathbreaking study on how to measure culture and its many consequences.

Hughes-Wilson, John. *Military Intelligence Blunders and Cover-ups*. New York: Carol & Graf Publishers, 1999. A powerful testament to the essential contribution of intelligence capability in war, this compendium of cases demonstrates that the tendency to misuse intelligence is prevalent and that even the finest organizations can fall prey to incompetence, hubris, and carelessness.

Hugo, Victor. *Les Misérables*. New York: Modern Library, 2009. This classic work by one of the great writers of history provides a gloriously stirring account of the carnage of battle and the redemption that courage and boldness offer to warriors engaged in what has been called the final argument of kings. Hugo's account of the sunken road of Ohain provides an abject lesson to those who would act rashly and in the absence of accurate intelligence of the battlefield.

Isaacson, Walter. *Steve Jobs*. New York: Simon & Schuster, 2011. Steve Jobs has been called the greatest business executive of the modern era, but perhaps his most enduring legacy is that of master strategist. Jobs lived possibly the purest strategic life of the modern era, unencumbered by the circumspection that robs so many others of greatness. This work reveals the scope and majesty of what the strategic imagination can do if given primacy.

Janis, Irving. *Groupthink: Psychological Studies of Policy Decisions and Fiascoes*. Boston: Cengage Learning, 1982. Janis was a pioneer in uncovering the insidious effects of groupthink on decision making in American foreign policy, and his insights have applicability to any group that makes collective decisions, whether business, church, school, little league, or other organization.

Jay, Antony. *Management and Machiavelli*. New York: Holt, Rinehart and Winston, 1967. A sophisticated yet highly readable Machiavellian analysis of the modern corporation, which in organization resembles nothing so much as the feudal state. Applicable behavioral insights abound.

Jervis, Robert. *Perception and Misperception in International Politics*. Princeton, NJ: Princeton University Press, 1976. Robert Jervis helps us examine the perceptual lenses that can distort the information we receive from others, leading to misallocation of resources and suboptimal outcomes in our own endeavors.

Johnson, Loch K. *Secret Agencies*. New Haven: Yale University Press, 1996. The U.S. security apparatus is the most sophisticated in the world, and the author takes us inside the secret agencies that make up this secret web to examine the three functions of modern intelligence: espionage, counterintelligence, and covert action.

Johnson, Rob, Michael Whitby, and John France. *How to Win on the Battlefield*. London: Thames and Hudson, 2010. This superb compendium of military tactics offers case studies to illustrate 25 tactical variations used on modern and ancient battlefields.

Jomini, Antoine. *The Art of War*, in *Roots of Strategy*, Book 1, edited by T. R. Phillips. Harrisburg, PA: Stackpole Books, 1985. One of the two great strategists of the 19th century, Jomini is rivaled only by Clausewitz. Jomini is the vicarious architect of the strategy of the American Civil War, and it is said that Stonewall Jackson carried a copy of Jomini with him always.

Keegan, John. *Intelligence in War: Knowledge of the Enemy from Napoleon to Al-Qaeda*. New York: Alfred A. Knopf, 2003. This tour de force offers a view of war through the lens of intelligence, examining the contributions of intelligence collection, analysis, and action across a range of conflicts, from the Napoleonic Wars to the American Civil War and the wars of the 20th century.

Kiechel, Walter III. *The Lords of Strategy: The Secret Intellectual History of the New Corporate World.* Boston: Harvard Business School Press, 2010. The world of corporate strategy is a relatively young field, and it can seem byzantine to the outsider. But it encompasses a logic and a distinctive history that Kiechel shares with us in exciting and detailed fashion.

Kim, W. Chan, and Renée Mauborgne. *Blue Ocean Strategy: How to Create Uncontested Market Space and Make Competition Irrelevant.* Cambridge: Harvard Business Review Press, 2005. This powerful and influential volume introduced the term "blue ocean" into business discourse and guides us in our quest for creation of new market segments where we can excel.

Klein, Gary. *The Power of Intuition: How to Use Your Gut Feelings to Make Better Decisions at Work.* New York: Crown Business, 2007. Gary Klein presents the best of his cutting-edge research in this volume, based on 20 years of study of intuition. Klein's work is imminently applicable, with exercises and practical examples.

Kuhn, Thomas. *The Structure of Scientific Revolutions.* Chicago: University of Chicago Press, 1962. The origin of the term "paradigm shift" can be found in this incredibly important work that chronicles how leaps of intuition can propel science forward in a series of revolutions, destroying old paradigms and erecting new ones that inform our research programs.

Landes, David. *The Wealth and Poverty of Nations.* New York: W. W. Norton & Company, 1998. The author explores the sources of wealth and attempts to answer the question: Why are some nations wealthy and others poor? He examines alternative hypotheses and provides a rich narrative that traverses the causal impact of climate, natural resources, geography, and cultural characteristics.

Liddell Hart, B. H. *Great Captains Unveiled*. London: Greenhill Books, 1990, 1927. The author is acknowledged as one of the great strategic thinkers of the 20th century, which gives him a unique perspective in this excellent collection of essays on several of the lesser-known great captains of history, including Sabutai, Maréchal de Saxe, and Gustavus Adolphus.

————. *Strategy*, rev. ed. New York: Plume, 1991. The author is considered one of the finest military thinkers of the 20th century; his innovative theoretical notions in the interwar period revolutionized tank warfare and were responsible for the widespread adoption of the doctrine of the "indirect approach." The most successful application of this approach was in the technique of blitzkrieg warfare engineered by the Germans in World War II. Liddell Hart spans the centuries of strategic thought and practice leading up to the Great War, in which he fought; he demonstrates how a strategic imagination can actually discern and learn the patterns of history, while readying us to face an as yet unknowable future.

Luttwak, Edward N. *Strategy: The Logic of War and Peace*. Cambridge: Harvard University Press, 1987. Luttwak makes a powerful theoretical case for surprise as the "conscious use of paradox" to achieve decisive advantage in war.

Machiavelli, Niccolò. *The Art of War*. Mineola, NY: Dover Publications, 2006. More revered for his manual of political machination, Machiavelli also penned this powerful treatise on the conduct of war. He is considered a bridge figure between the ancients and the moderns.

McGraw, Phillip C. *Life Strategies: Doing What Works, Doing What Matters*. New York: Hyperion, 2000. Strategic thinking engages at multiple levels, and the most fundamental level is how we handle our own individual situations, how we interact successfully with the world around us, and how we build our custom strategies to deal with our own challenges. In this volume, the author offers multiple action steps to engage fruitfully in strategy building on a personal level, using powerful case studies to illustrate his points, including Oprah Winfrey's poignant battle with inner demons and outside attackers, which resulted in her ultimate triumph.

Mintzberg, Henry. *The Rise and Fall of Strategic Planning*. New York: Free Press, 1994. An influential volume that called into question the whole strategic-planning enterprise and called for reconceiving it as a kind of coupling of analysis and intuition.

Mintzberg, Henry, Bruce Ahlstrand, and Joseph Lampel. *Strategy Bites Back: It Is Far More, and Less, than You Ever Imagined*. Upper Saddle River, NJ: Pearson, 2005. Here, great and not-so-great minds of strategy appear in a cavalcade of strategic vignettes that illuminate the depth and sophistication of strategy. From the work of Rumelt, Porter, the duke of Wellington, and even Hans Christian Andersen, it becomes clear that good strategy is not easy, and bad strategy is quite common.

Paret, Peter, ed. *Makers of Modern Strategy*. Princeton, NJ: Princeton University Press, 1986. The revised edition of military strategy's ultimate handbook, this masterpiece takes us from the origins of strategic theorizing up to the modern nuclear strategists' contemplation of the complex modern chessboard of power politics.

Porter, Michael. *Competitive Strategy: Techniques for Analyzing Industries and Competitors*. New York: Free Press, 1980. This classic and seminal work by Harvard business professor and strategy practitioner Michael Porter launched a revolution in how we assess the competitive business environment and charted the way for strategic business practices for more than 30 years.

———. *On Competition*. Boston: Harvard Business School Press, 1998. This compendium of Michael Porter's work on strategy serves as a touchstone in the field of corporate strategy, its individual landmark articles charting the course of corporations and steering business schools worldwide for almost two decades.

———. "What Is Strategy?" *Harvard Business Review* (1996): 61–78. http://www.ipocongress.ru/download/guide/article/what_is_strategy.pdf. Porter's classic article on strategy is one of the most frequently cited articles from the *Harvard Business Review* and remains as perhaps the most concise explication of how strategy differs from mere managerial technique.

Rice, Bob. *Three Moves Ahead*. San Francisco: Jossey-Bass, 2008. The author, a businessman and excellent chess player, offers a scintillating exposition of how businesspeople can learn powerful lessons from chess strategy and tactics. The lesson writ large is, of course, that strategic principles can inform and enlighten enterprises as different and distant as a board game and business warfare. Rice's crisp style and his useful compendium of lessons at the end of each chapter make this a necessary read for anyone with serious interest in the broad scope and applicability of strategic ideas.

Ries, Al, and Jack Trout. *Marketing Warfare: 20th Anniversary Edition*. New York: McGraw-Hill, 2006. Two of the most famous marketing gurus working today have tied military tactics directly to the field of business marketing and make a strong case for the power of military thinking in the business realm.

Riggio, Ronald E. *The Charisma Quotient*. New York: Dodd, Mead, and Company, 1987. Charisma is an abstract term that can be reduced to individual behavior techniques learned by anyone, techniques that improve the odds of achieving strategic goals.

Rumelt, Richard P. *Good Strategy, Bad Strategy*. New York: Crown Business, 2011. This incredibly rich work by one of America's premier business strategists charts a compelling course for anyone in business, or in most any profession, to identify what strategy is and what it is not. Rumelt guides us in clear and persuasive language toward the holy grail of "good strategy."

Schafer, Mark, and Scott Crichlow. *Groupthink versus High-Quality Decision Making in International Relations*. New York: Columbia University Press, 2010. This study brings Irving Janis's *Groupthink* up to date with fresh U.S. foreign policy cases and substantiates many of Janis's initial contentions on the deleterious effects of groupthink.

Schelling, Thomas. *The Strategy of Conflict*. New York: Oxford University Press, 1963. Schelling applied game theory to arms control in this cutting-edge work that found a supremely useful metaphor for the nuclear arms race and an elegant way to capture its dynamic.

Schwartz, Peter. *The Art of the Long View*. New York: Doubleday, 1996. Scenario planning is essential for governments and businesses in the 21st century, a time when communication is almost instantaneous and the ability to react rapidly to changing circumstances can be the key to survival.

Sloan, Julia. *Learning to Think Strategically*. Oxford: Elsevier, 2006. A powerful volume that provides a brief history of strategic thought and suggests ways to develop the critical attributes of strategic thinking. The author's classical/historical approach bring us into the strategic mainstream, providing an essential didactic context, and then couples this historical background with an explanation of how we actually learn about strategic thinking, concluding with modern, practical techniques designed to improve any person's strategic thinking skill.

Spykman, Nicholas John. *America's Strategy in World Politics*. New York: Harcourt, Brace, 1942. This book, controversial and criticized when it was published, called for a postwar American strategic security policy that was based on cool calculation of national power afforded by geopolitical considerations. A theorist in the realist tradition, Professor Spykman, a professor of international politics at Yale University, was attacked as the "American Haushofer" for this and the publication of his subsequent work, *The Geography of the Peace*.

Stark, Rodney. *God's Battalions: The Case for the Crusades*. New York: HarperOne, 2009. A controversial history of the Crusades that focuses on the military, technological, and cultural differences between the antagonists.

Thucydides. *The Peloponnesian War*. New York: Penguin, 1954. Available in several editions, this ancient classic still serves as the archetype for the modern political theory of realism and, its proponents contend, evidence of the unchanging character of human nature.

Tracy, Brian. *Victory! Applying the Proven Principles of Military Strategy to Achieve Greater Success in Your Business*. New York: American Management Association, 2007. The author is one of the most successful self-help motivational leaders of the late 20th century, and his entry into the "military lessons" genre, brimming with examples from both ancient and modern battles, is worthy of review. Tracy's own life exemplifies the achievements open to a powerful strategic imagination, rigorously cultivated.

Trout, Jack. *Differentiate or Die: Survival in Our Era of Killer Competition.* 2nd ed. New York: John Wiley & Sons, 2008. The classic work on differentiation, by one of the most influential marketing practitioners of the 20th century. Trout zeros in on what it truly means to differentiate, and he explodes many of the misconceptions plaguing strategy.

Von Ghyczy, Tiha, Bolko von Oetinger, and Christopher Bassbord. *Clausewitz on Strategy.* New York: John Wiley & Sons, 2001. This book explicitly offers Clausewitz for the businessman. This abridged version of the classic *On War* was prepared by one of America's premier consulting companies and draws keen lessons from Clausewitz's deep insights with a mind to guiding modern business to successful outcomes.

Von Neumann, John, and Oskar Morgenstern. *Theory of Games and Economic Behavior.* Princeton, NJ: Princeton University Press, 1947. This seminal work on game theory, which propelled the authors to international acclaim, is dense throughout but worth a look as a primary source that launched a social science.

Weintraub, Stanley. *Silent Night: The Story of the World War I Christmas Truce.* New York: Free Press, 2001. A stunning example of cooperation in a conflict situation in the absence of communication and trust, the Christmas truce of 1914 demonstrates how undirected cooperation can evolve.

Whaley, Barton. *Stratagem.* Boston: Artech House, 1969, 2007. A key necessary element of surprise is strategic deception, and Whaley provides the most comprehensive historical resource on the use of stratagem, a powerful tool for use by the strategic thinker.

Bibliography

516

Web Sites:

Air & Space Power Journal, http://www.airpower.maxwell.af.mil. Interesting articles on the subject of strategy generally.

Bassford, Christopher, ed., Clausewitz Homepage, http://www.clausewitz. com/. A popular site and clearinghouse for all things Clausewitz.

Center for Strategic and International Studies, http://csis.org/. Features a library filled with downloads of the latest books on specific strategic issues.

Central Intelligence Agency, https://www.cia.gov/. The library section of the CIA site offers online versions of entire books on analysis and strategy.

Cohen, William A. Heroic Leadership: Leading Organizations with Honor, Integrity, and Valor, http://www.stuffofheroes.com/index.html. The site of one of America's most prolific authors on leadership.

U.S. Army War College, http://www.carlisle.army.mil/. This site has a large collection of downloadable publications and entire books on strategy.

Notes

Notes

Notes